W9-APS-626

3.95

X

Springer Series on Social Work

Albert R. Roberts, D.S.W., Series Editor

School of Social Work, Indiana University, Indianapolis

Advisory Board: Joseph D. Anderson, D.S.W., Barbara Berkman, D.S.W., Paul H. Ephross, Ph.D., Sheldon R. Gelman, Ph.D., Nancy A. Humphreys, D.S.W., Sheldon Siegel, Ph.D., and Julia Watkins, Ph.D.

Gary M. Gould, Ph.D., is the Head Coach of the Women's Basketball Team at Canadore College in North Bay, Ontario, Canada. Dr. Gould is also the Dean of Student Services and College Marketing at Canadore and a Social Welfare faculty member at Nipissing University College. He is a former Assistant Vice President and Director of the Industrial Social Work Program at the University of Southern California. He is currently serving as the Chairman of the National Association of Social Workers' Commission on Employment and Economic Support. Dr. Gould consults with organizations throughout the world on issues related to social work in the workplace.

Michael Lane Smith, M.S.W., M.S.P.A., Ph.D., is a tenured faculty member at Southwest Texas State University and a consultant on human services in the workplace. A former social work officer in the United States Air Force, he has practiced and taught in the areas of social work in the workplace, mental health, and substance abuse.

SOCIAL WORK
IN THE WORKPLACE
Practice and Principles

Gary M. Gould, Ph.D.
Michael Lane Smith, Ph.D.
Editors

Springer Publishing Company
New York

Copyright © 1988 by Springer Publishing Company, Inc.

All rights reserved

No part of this publication may be reproduced, stored in a retrieval system, or transmitted in any form or by any means, electronic, mechanical, photocopying, recording, or otherwise, without the prior permission of Springer Publishing Company, Inc.

Springer Publishing Company, Inc.
536 Broadway
New York, NY 10012

88 89 90 91 92 / 5 4 3 2 1

LIBRARY OF CONGRESS
Library of Congress Cataloging-in-Publication Data

Social work in the workplace : practice and principles / Gary M.
   Gould, Michael Lane Smith, editors.
       p.   cm.
   Bibliography: p.
   Includes index.
   ISBN 0-8261-5380-1
   1. Welfare work in industry.   2. Welfare work in industry—United
States.   3. Employee assistance programs.   4. Employee assistance
programs—United States.   I. Gould, Gary M.   II. Smith, Michael Lane.
HD7261.S63 1988   87-32246
658.3'82—dc19   CIP

Printed in the United States of America

This book is dedicated to
Kirby and Georgianna Smith
and
Wilf and Bea Gould

Contents

V The Role of Industry in the Community

VI Managing the Challenges of the Future

Foreword

Social Work in the Workplace provides the first authoritative overview of occupational and industrial social work. With chapters written especially for this book, it presents an objective and enlightening analysis of the emergence, important dimensions, and range of interventions practiced by occupational social workers. Gary M. Gould and Michael Lane Smith and their team of prominent contributors have made a major and original contribution to the social work and human service literature. They examine the challenges, principles, and practices involved in problem solving and improving the mental health of troubled employees. This volume is the first comprehensive introduction to the policies, programs, and human service intervention approaches for vulnerable workers, managers, and executives.

There are many different types of vulnerable and troubled individuals in the workplace, including substance abusers; victims of industrial accidents; single parents; terminated employees; transferred workers; and employees suffering from marital conflict, family violence, and/or depression. The central focus of this book is on what occupational social workers do and how they do it. The range of the varied functions of occupational social workers typically includes assessment and referral, crisis counseling, substance abuse treatment, education and training, and psychotherapy. Social workers in the workplace are also active in developing day care programs, preretirement workshops, wellness and health-enhancement programs, relocation counseling programs, outplacement services, and management consulting services.

This latest addition to the Springer Series on Social Work is a significant contribution to the principles and realities of an important field of practice—social work in the workplace. This outstanding text addresses all occupational social workers and students, social work educators, program supervisors, personnel directors, and administrators.

ALBERT R. ROBERTS, D.S.W.
Editor, Springer Series on Social Work

Introduction

This is a book about social work in the workplace—what it *is* and what it *can be*. It deals with a rapidly developing arena for human service, one with increasing popularity for a host of different human service professions and disciplines. Its subject matter continues to expand; the boundaries of its practice continue to evolve.

Social worker presence in industrial and business worksites is far from new. Even specific professional education for this arena of intervention has been tried before. What does seem to be different for social work in the workplace for the 1980s and 1990s is the scope, competition, intensity, and enthusiasm for human service interventions in industrial/occupational settings. As this book makes clear, social work in the workplace extends far beyond Employee Assistance Programs (EAPs) as those programs typically function. Social workers have found places in worksites for the practice of counseling and psychotherapy, assessment and referral, and education and training common to EAPs. However, they can also be found active in responding to complex human resource issues including those dealing with shift work, day care, terminations and retirement, affirmative action, and AIDS. In addition, social workers have found opportunities to enhance both individual and organizational functioning through organizational development (OD) and management consultation activities. Indeed, the practice influence of many social workers has been felt apart from the worksite as these individuals have focused on the interactions between organizations and external constituencies (for example, customers or nearby communities). Clearly, the breadth of social work in the workplace is staggering, and yet—for those familiar with the breadth of social work itself—entirely to be expected.

In addition to being broad, the occupational arena for human service practice is nontraditional. It is not regarded as an exclusive practice arena, reserved for professional social workers only. Psychologists, counselors, certified substance abuse counselors, recovering addicts, various human resource consultants, and others have recognized both the humanitarian and pecuniary opportunities for practice in the workplace. By virtue of differing theoretical orientations and differing practice roles and skills, representatives of these various professional and quasi-professional groups offer different visions of how workers and work organizations can profit from their contributions. The burden rests upon social work to make clear and make good the contributions its practitioners can offer.

This competition has contributed to the intensity that social work practitioners and educators bring to practice in the workplace. The challenge is more fundamental than establishing credibility in the face of other competing professions. Perhaps no other arena for social work practice accommodates such a broad array of professional knowledge and skill. The demands for broad and varied training have resulted in an expanding pool of educational opportunities for social work students and practitioners. This is especially noticeable in the number of graduate schools of social work that are currently advertising and marketing concentrations or specializations in industrial social work. These factors, too, contribute to the intensity of activity surrounding this field. From the perspective of the individual preparing for entry into practice in the workplace and from the standpoint of educational institutions hoping to promote such practice, the incentives to act and to act now are significant.

We hope that this book contributes to the success of our colleagues in preparing for effective and rewarding practice in the workplace. A few additional comments are in order. It is common for members of professions to quarrel over semantics and over the shades of meaning that different words for a concept convey. In the present case the terms *industrial social work* and *occupational social work* come to mind. Each label has its own history and advocates. Without denying the validity of the arguments presented by either side to this debate, we prefer to use the phrase *social work in the workplace* and to regard it as synonymous with both of the other terms. Consequently, all three labels for this type of practice are used throughout the book and are used to convey an identical meaning.

The content in this book is organized around six sections: Section I provides a conceptual, historical, and ethical orientation to this practice arena. Section II focuses on counseling programs in the workplace and deals with issues central to conventional employee assistance programs. It goes beyond the typical practice of such programs, however, in suggesting occupational social work responses to human problems frequently ignored in EAPs. Section III develops the role of social workers in mediating the relationship between people and their employing organizations, while Section IV emphasizes the opportunities to focus on the organization as a primary target system. The expansion potentials for social work in the workplace are the topics of Section V; these chapters address the opportunities to affect organizational impact on people outside the employing company. Finally, Section VI offers some observations on the changing world of work and the challenges likely to await social workers in the years to come.

It is our hope that this book will facilitate the search for knowledge and the mastery of skill that is required of those who hope to improve the lives of people through the practice of social work.

Contributors

Eleanor L. Brilliant, D.S.W., is an associate professor at the Rutgers University School of Social Work. She is a former professional staff member of a local United Way and consultant to numerous human service organizations.

Sam Brunstein, B.S.E.E., is an engineering manager and management consultant specializing in the effects of organizational culture on disaster survivors.

Edmund M. Burke, Ph.D., is the director of The Center for Corporate Community Relations at Boston College.

E. Gregory de Silva, Ph.D, is an associate professor at The University of Pittsburgh and is the director of the School of Social Work's curriculum on labor and industry, emphasizing the introduction of social work into utility companies and financial institutions.

Diana DiNitto, M.S.W., Ph.D., is an associate professor at The University of Texas at Austin. She has held administrative and direct service positions in community and statewide alcoholism and drug abuse programs in Florida and Texas.

Kathleen O. Ell, Ph.D., is an associate professor with the School of Social Work at The University of Southern California.

Vincent E. Faherty, D.S.W., M.B.A., is presently Head of the Social Work Department at the University of Northern Iowa.

Dorothy Fleisher, D.S.W., is a consultant for United Way, Inc. in Los Angeles County. Formerly an Associate Clinical Professor in Social Work at the University of Southern California, she was also a policy analyst with the National Policy Center on Employment and Retirement.

Wilbur A. Finch, Jr., D.S.W., is an associate professor with the School of Social Work at the University of Southern California.

MaryAnn Hosang, M.S.W., is a psychotherapist with emotionally disturbed youth and their families. In addition, she has worked and written in the areas of occupational social work, substance abuse, and domestic violence.

James L. Jenkins, M.S.W., Ph.D., is a colonel and Consultant for Social Work in the Office of the Air Force Surgeon General. A former faculty member in several schools of social work, he has written primarily in the areas of stress management and family violence.

Barbara Hade Kaplan, D.S.W., M.P.A., now retired, was director of the Staff/Faculty Counseling Service at the University of Southern California. She has also served as an Associate Clinical Professor for the Industrial Social Work Concentration in the School of Social Work there.

Margaret Ann Kilpatrick, M.S.W., is a Licensed Clinical Social Worker in private practice in La Canada Flintridge, California. As a consultant to NIMH, she has worked in responding to the socioemotional needs of victims of natural disasters, fires, and aircraft accidents.

Seth Koepler, M.S.W., is a clinical social worker with Jewish Family Services in West Los Angeles. He was formerly a staff associate for the Office of Employee Relations and Development at the University of Southern California.

Paul A. Kurzman, Ph.D., is a professor with the School of Social Work at Hunter College, The City University of New York. He has written extensively in the area of social work in the workplace.

Jacquelyn McCroskey, D.S.W., is an assistant professor and Chair, Industrial Social Work Concentration at the University of Southern California. She recently served as Researcher on the National Employer Supported Child Care project.

Diane Meadow, Ph.D., is Director of the Tri-County Campus of the School of Social Work at The University of Southern California. She has been a teacher, administrator, and clinical social worker for the past 18 years.

Henry Morgan, Sc.D., is Dean Emeritus, School of Management at Boston University. He is actively pursuing study of the profit-making workplace as a vehicle for producing social change.

Howard J. Parad, Ph.D., is a professor with the School of Social Work at the University of Southern California.

Kimberlee A. Rice, M.S.W., is a former planner for the United Way of Stamford, Connecticut and Manager of Corporate Contributions for MONY Financial Services. She is currently employed in the real estate business.

Robert B. Rowen, Ph.D., is an associate professor at the University of Tennessee College of Social Work–Memphis Branch.

David I. Siegel, D.S.W., is director of the Industrial Social Work Program at the University of Southern California.

Ruta J. Wilk, M.S.W., D.S.W., is an Associate Professor of Social Work at the University of South Florida. Her research interests include advocacy for disadvantaged populations and the interface of legal and social work issues.

Carl S. Wilks, Ph.D., A.C.S.W., is an associate professor at the University of Tennessee College of Social Work–Memphis Branch.

Judy Winkelpleck, Ph.D., is the director of the Employee Assistance Program at Iowa State University. She has served on the faculties of several universities and maintains her own management consulting firm.

Social Work in
the World of Work

1 Social Work in the Workplace: An Overview

Michael Lane Smith

Work is one of the most important dimensions in the life of the individual. To some extent, each individual defines *self* in terms of what that individual does in work. Along with marriage and parenthood, work marks one of the most significant transitions of the individual from childhood into adulthood. It provides the individual with a social identity—an anchor to the broader society and a medium through which a person's value and place in the society are made known to others (Perlman, 1968). Work provides opportunities and incentives to develop along various paths. The differing character of work among different people exposes them to dissimilar experiences, demands, and expectations. Differing work experiences and work contexts contribute to the development of all of us, both through our work and through those who influence us at our places of work.

Work and workplace are critically important factors in the person-in-situation equation that lies near the heart of social work. This approach to understanding human behavior (closely akin to the concept of *social functioning*) addresses the intimate interrelationships between the demands the individual places on others and the demands others simultaneously place on the individual. The psychological health, esteem for self and others, and accomplishment that adequate social functioning imply require that some reasonable, dynamic accommodation be maintained between the individual and her or his social environment. Because work and the workplace comprise such important elements in the identity and life experience of most individuals, the person-in-work equation becomes a particularly vital dimension of overall social functioning (Chestang, 1982). Consequently, the relationship of the individual as worker to the work itself and to fellow workers has become a critical concern to the profession of social work.

The field of practice within the profession most closely identified with the person-as-worker and person-in-work orientations is *occupational* or *in-*

dustrial social work. This label encompasses a very broad range of activities, roles, target systems ("clients"), and auspices. Occupational social work, in some respects, is an aspect of a broader, multidisciplinary development frequently referred to as *occupational mental health* that has as a primary goal the enhancement of quality of life at the worksite. Other professions contributing to study and practice in occupational mental health include psychology (in both its clinical and industrial traditions), psychiatry, and counseling. Within an occupational mental health context, industrial social workers are concerned with enhancing the social functioning of identified individual clients. They are also concerned with improving the social supports and opportunities available to whole groups of workers and their families through organizationally focused interventions.

Social workers in the workplace are also concerned with the relationship of employing organizations to their other major constituencies. In this respect, an organization's workforce is but one constituency. Consumers of the organization's products and people whose social–ecological niche is affected by the organization represent additional important constituencies. Occupational social workers are concerned with these people as well, at least to the extent that they are concerned with enhancing the social functioning of vulnerable populations.

PEOPLE AT RISK: THE NEED FOR WORKPLACE-BASED HUMAN SERVICES

This chapter includes references to vulnerable groups and at-risk individuals. The range of interventions described is suggestive of many of the types of people at risk for various human problems. Those who face the loss of work and the meanings work holds constitute a vulnerable population at the worksite. Indeed, the loss of one's employment can be a profoundly disturbing experience, both for the employee and for his or her family (Holmes & Rahe, 1967; Keefe, 1984; Madonia, 1983). Within this group, the characteristics of the people and nature of the job loss are quite variable. Some individuals facing unemployment are "new hires" still on their probationary periods. They may have little personal investment in the particular jobs they hold or in the organizations that employ them. Nevertheless, the loss of wages or salary through unemployment may be particularly disruptive. Others threatened with the loss of employment include people with serious alcohol or other drug problems. Many of these people occupy managerial or professional positions and have been with their employing organizations for years. Termination of employment for these people can carry with it the forced realization of inadequate coping skills, reevaluation of professional skills and identities, loss of companionship, and marked alterations in standards of living, to mention but a few consequences. Loss of employment through retirement can be either forced or voluntary. While the meaning of retirement varies depending on which type it is, it still represents a major life transition—one involving the loss of work and the experience of the stresses that this entails (Holmes & Rahe, 1967). Even voluntary retirement can elicit demands for major changes in the ways people view themselves, their lives, and others around them. Whenever events call for major alterations in the ways people view themselves or relate to people around them, crises exist.

Other workers (those not facing unemployment) are also at risk. Individuals whose jobs expose them to physically or psychologically harmful stimuli represent another vulnerable group. The experience of killing someone in the line of duty as either a law enforcement officer or soldier can be powerfully disturbing. Long-term work-related exposure to materials later found to be carcinogenic is both psychologically and physically damaging. Jobs associated with virtually unremitting pressures or boredom and few opportunities for relief or support endanger the health and welfare of the individuals occupying them (House, 1981; McLean, 1979). Within this context, the experiences of oppressed groups or individuals whose personal characteristics (such as race or gender) are new to a worksite frequently call for their inclusion into this at-risk population.

Transfer of workers and their families from one community to a different community or state entails the disruption of informal support groups, including friendship groups and extended family. Shift work frequently makes major demands on workers and families and tests their capacities to cope (see the discussion by Meadow in Chapter 10). Shift work can complicate the life of the single parent trying desperately to succeed in both work and in child rearing. Extended deployments and work-related travel can disrupt the relationships between family members, simultaneously eliciting stress and removing important sources of support to those affected.

Finally, there are people who, while not employed by an organization, find their lives affected by its operation. Many of these people are placed at risk by organizational decision makers whether anybody knows it or not. The decision to cut off electricity for nonpayment of bills to a low-income household may seem like a proper business decision. Unfortunately, such a decision can (and has) spelled death for elderly, isolated individuals who simply lack the resources to pay. Children playing in a creek are at risk when a company upstream dumps noxious wastes into its water, or otherwise inadequately addresses the ecological consequences of its operations.

This list of vulnerable individuals is suggestive of the range of persons and problems that warrant occupational social workers' attention. It is important to emphasize, however, that the notion of vulnerable groups extends beyond the employment boundaries of any particular organization. Family members of workers can find themselves at risk, as can the customers and neighbors of a company. Given this variety of vulnerable individuals, it is not surprising that occupational social work is an exciting, dynamic, and important field for practice. It is a field with a surprisingly rich past.

THE DEVELOPMENT OF SOCIAL WORK IN THE WORKPLACE

Many people look to the mid-1960s as the time when "modern" industrial social work emerged (Kurzman, 1983). Still, it is useful to look back further for a better appreciation of the history and appropriateness of social work in the work setting. Popple (1981) argues that occupational social work properly traces its roots back to the very formative stages of the social work profession itself.

As early as the 1880s, at least one pioneer social worker was employed by industry to provide services for its workforce. During the following several decades, more "friendly visitors" found employment in private sector companies. Here they were referred to as "welfare secretaries" and took as their professional goal the moral development and socialization of girls, women, and immigrant men, all relatively new to the American industrial workplace. Welfare secretaries adopted forms of casework and groupwork as their primary intervention methods, instructing their at-risk workers in hygiene and manners, literary appreciation, and constructive hobbies. At some worksites, these early social workers also supervised lunchrooms and other company benefits. By 1920 employment in industrial settings was a popular practice option for social workers, especially in the more heavily industrial East (Popple, 1981).

By 1920, however, the world had changed mightily from what it had been a scant 30 years before. Abraham Flexner's critique of social work in 1915 along with Freud's revolutionary notions of the dynamics of thought and feeling together rocked social work. World War I changed the face of Europe and the Middle East and produced millions of casualties, thousands of whom returned to the United States with severe mental illness or physical impairment. Schools of social work opened their doors; and with the convergence of theoretical advances, the establishment of academic centers, and the urgency of "professionalization," new opportunities for social workers developed. Meanwhile, labor unions rejected the welfare secretaries and the "welfare capitalism" they represented as paternalistic and as too closely aligned with the interests of management. The rise of scientific management and the development of the embryonic personnel management specialization presented business leaders with alternative approaches to dealing with workers. Both labor and management, then, were reluctant to support an expansion of the role and scope of the welfare secretary. Occupational social work entered the first of two dormant periods (Kurzman, 1983; Popple, 1981).

World War II created an entirely new set of problems for workers and entirely new opportunities for social workers in the workplace. In the United States, the U.S. Army began to utilize professionally trained social workers in its expanded medical corps (and in doing so established a social work presence in the armed forces that has continued to the present day). In response to the horrors and hardships of the Battle for the Atlantic, Bertha Reynolds, a well-known social worker, helped to shape a joint union–management industrial social work program on behalf of members of the National Maritime Union and their families. Elsewhere, the changing face of the American workforce—the increasing proportion of women and blacks in the industrial sector especially—gave rise to new needs and the recognition of old ones at the worksite. These landmarks in the development of occupational social work were followed by the end of war and demobilization, with returning veterans displacing thousands of women in the industrial workforce. Recognition of the need for industrial social work services again declined.

The 1960s and 1970s provided a renewed impetus for the development of social work in the workplace. Once again, large numbers of women began to seek work outside the home. Concern over the rights and welfare of employed persons found expression in important new laws. By the mid-1970s the Hughes Act, Vocational Rehabilitation Act, Occupational Safety and Health Act, Employee Retirement Income Security Act, Age Discrimination in Employment Act, and Title VII of the Civil Rights Act all affected the relationship of employer to employee by emphasizing the need to address problems facing workers (Kurzman, 1983).

THE RANGE OF SOCIAL SERVICES AT THE WORKPLACE

Alcoholism and Traditional Employee Assistance Programs

Critical to the development and acceptance of social workers in the world of work was the heightened recognition by business leaders that substance abuse—alcoholism especially—is both costly and widespread. The extent of this problem is staggering. The National Association of Social Workers (NASW) estimates that 10% of the workforce in the United States is affected by drug and alcohol problems with 95% of all alcoholics employed or employable. Forty-five percent of these working alcoholics occupy managerial or professional positions. The impact of alcoholism on organizational productivity and operating costs is dramatic. It is estimated that the average problem drinker functions at only two thirds of his or her potential while utilizing health care benefits three to four times more frequently than nontroubled employees. Incredibly, 50% of all production problems are traceable to persons with substance abuse or personal problems. Altogether, NASW estimates the annual loss from alcoholism and personal problems to American business and government organizations at a staggering $28 billion in lost production and an additional $18 billion in health and medical coverage costs (NASW, 1982).

Recognition within management circles of both (1) the tremendous costs of workforce alcoholism and (2) its intransigence in the face of conventional disciplinary methods has led to a greater receptiveness to provide qualified human services to workforce members (Donovan, 1984). The forms that worker-focused service programs take are varied. The most common general form is that of the *employee assistance program* (EAP) or *employee counseling program* (ECP). This form is defined by policies, procedures, and counseling-oriented services that identify or respond to employees having personal, emotional, or behavioral problems interfering with work performance. Programmatic response takes the form of confidential help or professional information, care, or referral to appropriate sources of assistance (Leavitt, 1983; Schmitz, 1982). In an EAP the primary target for professional services is the individual worker who is at some form of risk. Access to such a worker frequently requires considerable staff training and other supportive administrative activities. Management interest in EAPs is suggested by the estimated 8,000 employee assistance programs currently in operation, including programs in approximately 80% of the Fortune 500 companies (Maiden & Hardcastle, 1986).

Ozawa (1980) has argued that EAPs frequently conform to one of four possible (and frequently developmental) stages. The first stage (Stage I) is characterized by a narrow programmatic focus on one or a very few target problems, usually alcoholism. Intervention is frequently provided by a paraprofessional (generally someone with first-hand alcoholism experience), although professionally trained practitioners are also common. Service in these narrowly focused EAPs is generally limited to casefinding, assessment, referral, and follow-up in addition to staff training, employee education, and related ancillary tasks.

Stage II programs are characterized by an institutionalized recognition of the scope of human problems that impact a worker's performance and level of social functioning. Problems dealt with by EAP practitioners are much more varied and include emotional, financial, marital, legal, and familial problems. Services may include counseling or the provision of therapy, in addition to stress reduction and health promotion activities.

Stage III EAPs employ organizational interventions in addition to a concern for the individual worker. The practitioner in such an EAP is concerned with creating an organizational environment conducive to higher levels of employee social functioning. Dialogue with managers, process consulting, team building, and other forms of "organizational development" become critical new forms of intervention.

Finally, Ozawa argues that EAPs demonstrating Stage IV characteristics operate in organizational environments where traditional distinctions between management and labor are blurred. Such organizations exhibit a broad distribution of responsibilities and power. EAP practitioners, as participants in such dynamic arenas, have the opportunity to pursue interventions at individual, work group, organizational, or extraorganizational levels.

These various types of employee assistance programs suggest various practitioner roles for the social workers employed in them. Gould and McKenzie make this point quite clearly:

> While the counseling function is currently the most predominant, it is only one of many possible roles to be enacted by social workers. The potential roles can include referral agent, legislative analyst, researcher/evaluator, mediator, liaison, ombudsman, program development specialist, teacher/trainer, benefits administrator, and consultant. (1984, p. 3)

Organizational Interventions

Thus far, employee assistance programs have been considered primarily in terms of the *individual* as the prime target for social work intervention. While this is true for some forms of EAPs, it is an incomplete description of others. So-called broad-brush (or double-B) programs, in addition to responding to a wide variety of individual problems, also exhibit a wide variety of organizationally targeted efforts. EAPs characteristic of Ozawa's (1980) third stage are defined by the inclusion of the organization as a target for change. This involves the provision of

> micro and macro organizational diagnostic services, organizational development and effectiveness strategies, and consultation on such issues as performance appraisal and reward systems. While the specific objectives for these services vary with each task, the ultimate goal of management in sponsoring these endeavors is to maximize organizational effectiveness and efficiency. The primary goal of employee groups endorsing the programs as well as those directly involved is to promote the workplace well-being of employees. The challenge . . . is to identify the symbiotic interdependence of client constituencies and to develop services that satisfy their mutual goals. (Gould & McKenzie, 1984, p. 6)

Team building, process consultation, quality circles, leadership development, intergroup conflict resolution, and other forms of organizational development can be employed as organizationally focused interventions (Burke, 1982; Gould & McKenzie, 1984).

EAP Auspices and Structure

Ozawa's developmental scheme of EAP operation suggests that employee assistance programs can take many forms. Indeed, Fleisher and Kaplan (1984) point out:

> A company with 5,000 employees will not develop the same model as a company with 500. In fact, small companies, those with fewer than 1,000 employees, may be unable to support their own ECP and may come together to form consortia (Masi, 1982). Similarly, a company whose employees are concentrated in one site may opt for a different model than a company whose employees are dispersed over a wide geographical area. (pp. 39–40)

In Chapter 3 of this volume, Kaplan and Fleisher identify four models or forms that an EAP may take. They distinguish between the following forms:

• In-house staff providing a limited range of services.
• In-house staff providing a comprehensive range of services.
• External contractor providing a limited range of services.
• External contractor providing a comprehensive range of services.

Phillips and Older (1981) also distinguish among various EAP structures, suggesting a similar array. They point out, however, that *unions* can sponsor member assistance programs. Services within this type of program are provided at the union office or hiring hall, with heavy reliance on referral to community-based treatment facilities.

These alternative structures are not equivalent in their impact on client confidentiality, physical and psychological accessibility, staff expertise and availability, flexibility, accountability, or cost effectiveness (Fleisher & Kaplan, 1984; Minter, 1983; Phillips & Older, 1981). Indeed, very different employee assistance programs can result from the various choices for EAP structure that confront program planners. Nor are these various models equally expensive. Costs for program staffing and operation can vary markedly across the available models. Realistically, though, not all EAP models are equally viable for any particular organization. It is likely that whatever model emerges is the result of a dynamic combination of organizational size, complexity, and resources, as well as management philosophy, community resources, and organizational history (especially the extent and nature of "people problems" among the workforce and the legacy of particularly noteworthy responses to some of these problems).

In organizations that have unionized workforces, another critical factor must be considered. EAP utilization is vitally affected by the degree of compatibility between the perceptions of the program by management, on the one hand, and unionized labor, on the other. As suggested by the above models, both management and labor have the potential to develop EAP services independent of the other. Programs developed independently in a highly charged adversarial environment common to many organizations are likely to be regarded with suspicion by whichever group has been excluded from program development. Considerable attention must be paid to preventing the EAP from becoming involved in any contest between management and union. Communication between the two groups during EAP development is an important factor, as is the inclusion of representatives from both groups in whatever planning or policymaking committees are formed (Hudson, 1983). Joint union–management sponsorship of the employee assistance program is another option likely to forestall suspicion of the program and the consequent underutilization likely to flow from it.

In many respects the issues surrounding EAP development and utilization in unionized worksites highlight more general concerns equally applicable elsewhere. To the extent that management is involved in sponsoring an employee assistance effort, whatever EAP form emerges will be considered by workforce members in terms of both (1) individual and collective perceptions of what workforce members have to gain or lose from its utilization and (2) interpretations of management's intent in sponsoring the program in the first place. Organizational climates characterized by animosity and mistrust between labor and management will not be revolutionized by the mere creation and marketing of a new employee benefit, especially a benefit subject to real or imagined misuse by company leaders. EAP acceptance by a broad spectrum of the workforce is more likely to result when the total organizational climate is generally supportive of the organization's members and when those involved in planning the EAP have been open and sensitive to the concerns of all employee groups.

Expanding Workplace Services: Historical Factors

The broader professional concerns of social workers and others working within employee assistance contexts have contributed to a far more encompassing appreciation of the varieties of worker needs and problems requiring attention. This broadening of concern was facilitated by the confluence of changes in the meaning of work to maturing postwar baby-boomers, the increased importance of quality-of-life issues, and the impact of both the women's movement and the consumer advocacy movement. The rise of both female-headed households and women in the workplace encouraged the recognition that family problems (including child care and financial concerns) affect a worker's ability to perform on the job. The women's movement and the civil rights movement contributed to a new-found recognition of the human problems confronting minority members of an organizational workforce. The politicization of America's elderly (the "gray power" movement) and the maturing of the nation's populace as a whole have given rise to new concerns about the meanings of retirement and other major life transitions that involve work. All of these factors as well as others have contributed to the expansion of scope experienced by industrial social work. Willingness by management and others to provide services to the workforce means that an ever-larger segment of the 100 million Americans who work have available to them greater contact with social workers or other professional (or paraprofessional) service providers than before. Availability of human services at or near the workplace has helped to minimize the stigma frequently associated with their use. In addition, the sanction to practice at or near the worksite has facilitated the early identification, referral, and provision of helping services to hundreds of thousands of individuals. This is extremely important, since appropriate intervention early in the course of many human problems is more likely to result in successful outcomes than practice interventions that occur much later.

TWO OTHER MODELS FOR OCCUPATIONAL SOCIAL WORK PRACTICE

Without a doubt, employee assistance activities constitute the greatest proportion of effort expended by practitioners within the occupational social work arena. However, employee assistance programming embodies but one of three different forms of professional social work activity within the world of work.

Corporate Public Involvement

At the opposite pole of the practice continuum from EAPs is the *corporate public involvement* model (de Silva et al., 1982). Social work in this practice context "focuses on assisting corporations and businesses to make a commitment to the social and economic well-being of the communities in which they operate" (de Silva et al., 1982, p. 11). It entails a recognition that the people who live near organizational locations can have their lives significantly affected by the opportunities and problems the organization creates. Whole communities can be disrupted by the decision of organizational leaders to move their facilities to or from a particular location. Movement from a given community can rend families, force unemployment, diminish local tax revenues, and deplete the local economy generally. A decision to locate at a particular place can elicit different yet equally dramatic consequences. One need only consider the important social and health consequences of careless discharge or storage of noxious chemicals or radioactive wastes to appreciate how organizations affect the quality of life of those around them.

In other ways, organizations affect nearby communities. They draw labor from townspeople and pump money into local economies. Work organizations generally provide local leadership for United Way contribution drives and through this leadership influence the distribution of resources to a wide variety of social agencies serving an equally wide variety of people and interests. Even more directly, organizational leaders are commonly approached for major financial contributions to a seemingly neverending collection of charities, agencies, and causes. Their responses to these requests and the pattern of corporate giving that follows affect the manner in which organizations address their public responsibilities.

Social workers in the workplace can affect the way organizations meet these challenges. Few corporate leaders understand the dynamics of human service delivery at the community level as well as social workers do. Likewise, few organizational leaders have the time or training to identify and prioritize local social welfare needs. Occupational social workers have assisted organizational leaders in meeting public responsibilities by reviewing requests for corporate contributions and providing carefully considered recommendations for response. They have provided critically needed brokerage services between organizational leaders wishing to donate resources and human service actors seeking resource support. Social workers have contributed time and talent to specific community projects or trained and then evaluated organizational volunteers in the latters' attempts to improve the quality of life in their respective communities. In each of these ways, occupational social workers have contributed to the recognition that the people surrounding an organization—and, more generally, those whose lives are adversely affected by organizational operations—represent a constituency whose needs warrant attention.

Customer Service Model

Still another form of occupational social work practice (one that blends certain features of the other two) has been labeled the *customer service model* (de Silva et al., 1982). This form of social work in the workplace is particularly suited to those organizations whose clients, customers, or consumers include vulnerable or at-risk individuals. Occupational social workers have made important contributions in developing programs and procedures that assure the provision of gas, electric, and other utilities to low-income households. Bank trust departments offer a number of opportunities for professional social work practice. Examples of services offered by occupational social workers in such settings include:

- Identifying and providing community resources for trust customers
- Monitoring the care provided by community social agencies (including boarding homes and nursing homes) to trust customers

- Exploring additional resources for financial assistance when trust customers' funds approach exhaustion
- Providing budget counseling to trust customers
- Providing support and counseling to trust customers and their families involved in relocation or separation
- Providing ongoing consultation to trust officers regarding the psychosocial needs of trust customers (de Silva et al., 1982)

SUMMARY

Occupational social work is an exciting practice arena, one likely to witness marked growth in the years to come. It offers professional practitioners the opportunity to reach out to millions of people at or near their places of employment. The services offered in a well-conceived employee assistance program are likely to be more accessible and available to workers and their families than those provided elsewhere, and they are more likely to be stigma-free than services provided through conventional agency means. Heightened accessibility and proximity to the workplace combine to promote early identification, referral, and intervention in a large proportion of cases. In addition, familiarity with the workplace and with its key decision makers contributes to a practice environment conducive to primary prevention and organizational interventions, in addition to the more conventional responses to already existing personal problems (de Silva et al., 1982).

Beyond the employee assistance focus, social work in the workplace offers practitioners the opportunity to rationalize and humanize contemporary society. The social environment of the twentieth century is dominated by formal organizations (Hall, 1982). A key to shaping a society more sensitive to issues of equality, opportunity, and respect for people can be found in what we do to humanize the responsiveness of organizations to the individuals involved with them.

REFERENCES

Burke, W. W. (1982). *Organization development: Principles and practices*. Boston: Little, Brown.
Chestang, L. W. (1982). Work, personal change, and human development. In S. H. Akabas & P. A. Kurzman (Eds.), *Work, workers and work organizations: A view from social work*. Englewood Cliffs, NJ: Prentice-Hall.
de Silva, E. G., Biasucci, P. A., Keegan, M. & Wijnberg, D. (1982). Promoting the future of social work education through labor and industry: A three dimensional approach. Presented at Annual Program Meeting, Council on Social Work Education, New York.

Donovan, R. (1984). The dollars and "sense" of human services at the workplace—A review of cost effectiveness research. *Social Work Papers, 18,* 65–73. Los Angeles: School of Social Work, University of Southern California.

Fleisher, D., & Kaplan, B. (1984). Components and tradeoffs of four ECP models. *Social Work Papers, 18,* 39–46. Los Angeles: School of Social Work, University of Southern California.

Gould, G., & McKenzie, C. (1984). The expanding scope of industrial social work. *Social Work Papers, 18,* 1–9. Los Angeles: School of Social Work, University of Southern California.

Hall, R. H. (1982). *Organizations: Structure and process* (3rd ed.). Englewood Cliffs, NJ: Prentice-Hall.

Holmes, T. H., & Rahe, R. H. (1967). The social readjustment rating scale. *Journal of Psychosomatic Research, 11,* 213–218.

House, J. S. (1981). *Work stress and social support.* Reading, MA: Addison-Wesley.

Hudson, H. L. (1983). The function of neutrality in Employee Assistance Programs. *EAP Digest, September/October,* 32–38.

Keefe, T. (1984). The stresses of unemployment. *Social Work, May/June,* 264–267.

Kurzman, P. (1983). Industrial social work (occupational social work). *1983–84 Supplement to the Encyclopedia of Social Work* (17th ed.). Silver Spring, MD: National Association of Social Workers.

Leavitt, R. L. (1983). *Employee assistance & counseling programs.* New York: Community Council of Greater New York.

Madonia, J. F. (1983). The trauma of unemployment and its consequences. *Social Casework: The Journal of Contemporary Social Work,* October.

Maiden, R. P., & Hardcastle, D. A. (1986). Social work education: Professionalizing EAPs. *EAP Digest, 7*(1), 63–66.

Masi, D. (1982). *Human services in industry.* Lexington, MA: Heath.

McLean, A. A. (1979). *Work stress.* Reading, MA: Addison-Wesley.

Minter, J. (1983). A contracted or in-house EAP? *EAP Digest, May/June,* 20–23.

National Association of Social Workers. (1982). *Employee assistance program (EAP) fact sheet, Memo #10 6/82.* Silver Spring, MD: National Association of Social Workers.

Ozawa, M. N. (1980). Development of social services in industry: Why and how? *Social Work, 25,* 464–470.

Perlman, H. H. (1968). *Persona: Social role and personality.* Chicago: University of Chicago Press.

Phillips, D. A., & Older, H. J. (1981). Models of service delivery. *EAP Digest, May/June,* 12–15.

Popple, P. R. (1981). Social work practice in business and industry, 1875–1930. *Social Service Review, 55,* 259–270.

Schmitz, H. (1982). *The Handbook of Employee Counseling Programs.* New York: New York Business Group on Health.

2 The Ethical Base for Social Work in the Workplace*

Paul A. Kurzman

This chapter addresses the ethical issues that pertain to the growing field of the practice of *occupational social welfare*. Simply put, that term refers to professional social work practice under the auspices of organized labor or employing organizations (generally companies and trade unions, or in a formal contractual relationship with such institutions). This definition is explored in the introductory chapter of this volume and in some depth in other publications. What is important for the discussion here is that social work employment in this arena involves practice not merely in a host environment (such as in school, medical, and correctional social work practice) but practice as well in a nontraditional, non-human-service host setting. The somewhat alien nature of this host environment poses new issues for the social work profession. These issues pertain more to potential value dilemmas than to the adequacy of professional knowledge and skills.

Social work is a remarkably able profession, and non-social-work colleagues frequently are impressed with what we know and what we do. What often puzzles such colleagues are the stands we take on issues ranging from the rationale for our particular style of service to our pervasive commitment to social change. Without placing ourselves on a pedestal, or indirectly suggesting condescension toward others, we frequently find ourselves buffeted by contending forces when we take unpopular positions in the defense of principles of overarching significance from a valuational point of view. These dilemmas that we experience in human-service host settings become much more complicated in non-human-service or alien settings, such as those typical in the world of work.

This chapter is based in part on a paper presented at the Golden Jubilee Conference of the Wayne State University School of Social Work, Detroit, Michigan, March 1981, and on an article that appeared in *Social Casework*, February 1983.

*Adapted from "Ethical Issues in Social Work Practice," *Social Casework* 64 (1983): 105–111.
Copyright © 1983 Family Service America. Used with permission.

AN ETHICAL BASIS FOR SOCIAL WORK

Albert Jonsen and Andre Hellegers (1976), in their study of the ethics of medical care, note that ethics is more than a body of prescriptions and prohibitions; it is a comprehensive theory of human morality. In this respect, they note that an adequate study of ethics would consist of the exploration of at least three principal theories: the theory of virtue, the theory of duty, and the theory of the common good. At the risk of oversimplification, the theory of virtue refers to such traits as honesty, probity, and respect for others. Duty analyzes the relationship between intentions and consequences, between motivations and circumstances. A theory of duties, therefore, suggests prescriptions and prohibitions, contractual permissions and obligations. Social workers have a duty to refrain from prohibited interventions on the one hand, and, on the other, they have an obligation to engage in certain areas of prescribed activity that represent the social responsibility of the profession.

Jonsen and Hellegers suggest that the most complex and vexing dimension of professional ethics involves the theory of the common good. This theory is concerned with two essential questions: the definitional (that is, what the common good or goods might be) and the distributive (that is, how benefits and resources are allocated when the need or demand is greater than the supply). Simply put, the theory of the common good addresses the issue of social justice. John Rawls (1971) reminds us that institutions, not just individuals, are the vehicles for the distribution of the benefits and burdens of social life, and a theory of social justice therefore does not address merely the personal characteristics of individuals, but addresses the virtue of social insititutions as well. The fair and equitable assignment of rights and duties and the parallel distribution of benefits and burdens places the issue of social justice in an appropriately social and organizational context. While the individual practitioner is still bound by the concepts of virtue and duty, the theory of the common good, as a dimension of professional ethics, inevitably points toward the systemic dimension and the institutional context in which social workers practice.

There are, of course, many approaches toward the institutionally bound concept of the common good. Egalitarian philosophers, for example, would say that everyone should have equal access to resources—that the limited pool should be evenly divided. Proponents of a meritocracy view (such as veterans' organizations) would recommend that resources be distributed primarily to the most deserving—those who have merited the rewards. Advocates of a triage concept (frequently deployed in medical and rehabilitation settings) suggest that benefits should accrue first to those who can make best use of them. The utilitarians, such as John Stuart Mill (1975), advocate the distribution of scarce resources so that they do the greatest good for the greatest number.

Rawls (1971), however, proposes a theory of distributive justice. To achieve the common good, he suggests that the greatest resources should go to the most disadvantaged in the social system. In a compelling discourse, he offers a theory of equity rather than a theory of equality. In a society that places certain portions of the population at a competitive disadvantage for no reason or fault of their own, such a theory underscores the need to ensure fair and equitable distribution of scarce resources in the context of pervasive social inequality (see Bronfenbrenner, 1973; Vigilante, 1978). If we accept Rawls's proposition, we must look at social work in the workplace not only through the lens of its professional practitioners, but also in the context of the institutional arrangements in which they are employed. The virtue of organizations becomes as significant as the virtue of individuals, since people inevitably are agents of the institutions by which they are formally engaged.

Do labor and industrial organizations generally promote the common good in our society? In a relative framework, do they do so as frequently as primary and host human service organizations such as hospitals, schools, mental health clinics, family service and child welfare agencies, and correctional institutions? If a social worker is not a free agent (except perhaps to some extent in private practice), then is there a significant difference between the constraints and supports for practice in a human service setting from those in settings where the primary goals are different from the human service mission? To what extent can one meet the ethical obligation to pursue the common good, not merely to evidence duty and virtue, under the auspices of a company or trade union?

ISSUES OF PRACTITIONER RESPONSIBILITY

Rosalie Bakalinsky (1980) poses the question of the fundamental conflict between the profession's commitment to people's well-being and industry's dedication to profits. The firm thread binding the diverse settings in which social workers traditionally practice, she notes, is a humanistic philosophy that underlines the inherent dignity and worth of people. The common thread in a capitalistic economic system that binds industry, however, is the priority of production and profits. Individuals in industry—the workers— have an instrumental value in the context of a larger goal: They are a means toward an end or central purpose. How will social workers, philosophically and pragmatically, reconcile this apparent dichotomy between commitments when placed on the payroll of an industrial organization? Above all, how will they address the systemic issues inherent in the mandate to be humanistic agents of social change as well as instruments of human service? Lest these issues appear directed only toward the management side of the industrial social work equation, we are reminded of parallel dilemmas as an agent of organized labor. Leo Perlis (1978), who recently retired as long-time director of the Department of Community Services of the AFL-CIO, is an advocate of the concept of a *human contract* to build services at the workplace to meet the needs of labor force participants. Perlis further advocates that the service providers be "professionally trained in industrial social work." However, he also has written:

> The sole responsibility of the social worker is to help the client solve, in confidence, his personal and family problems. . . . It is pure fantasy to suggest at this stage of development that there is a role for social workers in union and corporation determination of the 4-day week, or flexitime . . . or affirmative action, or corporate and union community responsibility, or insurance coverage, or organizational change. (Perlis, 1978, p. 3)

In rebuttal, Theodore Walden (1978), a social work educator, argues that ignoring labor or industrial injustice—such as hazardous working conditions, worker dehumanization, and violations of affirmative action—will negate social work's contribution through a failure to fulfill its social change obligation. Even if social workers are dutiful, virtuous, knowledgeable, and skillful in meeting their ethical commitments to social service, would the ethical imperative to promote the common good in part be sacrificed by failing to be agents of change—by being careful not to "bite the hand that feeds them?"

The *Proceedings* of the First National Conference on Social Work Practice in Labor and Industrial Settings noted additional examples of this dilemma posed by its occupational social work participants (see Akabas, Kurzman, & Kolben, 1979). If an employing organization is about to lay off 500 workers, is it the social work function to defuse the situation? If the employer institutes a speed-up on the production line, does the practitioner treat workers who respond negatively to the stress as failures or as victims? If an approaching union election brings a flurry of directives to set aside program goals to assist in promoting the survival needs of the leadership (the practitioner's employers), how does one appropriately and ethically respond? And finally, as an employee assistance counselor in the corporation's personnel department, what does one do when a senior member of management requests confidential data (regarding an employee you are seeing) as a condition of future cooperation with and organizational support for your program?

There are few simple answers, yet we must be willing to wrestle with the issues. We should recognize, too, that these dilemmas are not uncommon in

most traditional agencies in which we work. Because social work is essentially an agency-sponsored profession, we all can recall constraints imposed by our employers—even when they were human service professionals
and colleagues. Such are the strains between organizational role and professional preference, and our knowledge of administrative theory reminds us
that these conflicts pervade all organizational life. The issue is in part one of
extent and degree, not of mere presence or absence of organizational demands by our employers.

In a corporate setting, especially in the "smokestack industries" of the
Midwest, large-scale layoffs, retrenchment, and plant closings are increasingly common. For the professional social worker who may be a staff
member of the company's Employee Assistance Program, Community
Affairs Division, or Human Resources Department, such an event may
trigger an understandable crisis regarding appropriate professional role and
function. Feeling helpless in reversing an economically based corporate
decision, and even guilty to be on board when others are facing employment
termination, social workers may wonder whether—by omission or commission—they themselves are agents of the event.

Ferman (1984, p. 122) notes that the principal ethical mandate in this
situation is for social workers to assume both a commitment to service
delivery *and* to an advocacy role on behalf of those displaced. In so doing,
they must follow William Ryan's (1976) admonition not to "blame the victim," but rather to serve and empower workers through individual and
family counseling, aid in the formation of self-help and mutual support
groups, and advocate collectively for and with these workers as a constituency in the community. This mandate would be supported by the
National Association of Social Workers' (NASW) *Code of Ethics* (1980, sec.
VI), which emphasizes that "the social worker should act to expand choice
and opportunity for all, with special regard for disadvantaged or oppressed
groups and persons," and "should act to ensure that all persons have access
to the resources, services and opportunities which they require" (p. 9). As
Briar (1983) observes, while few EAP staff are in positions to prevent
massive layoffs, corporate relocation, or capital flight, they generally can and
should mobilize community services, promote self-help groups, advocate for
entitlements, and initiate referrals to other employers in the community
who are hiring.

Briar and Vinet (1985, p. 346), moreover, suggest that it would be naive to
believe that such individual and collective (systemic) inequities are not also
present in traditional public and voluntary social work settings. However,
the profession's commitment to the concept of the common good highlights
the importance of the occupational social worker's deliberate use-of-self in
this instance to advocate above all for distributive justice.

Whose Agent Are We?

From an ethical perspective, the fundamental social work question here is: "Whose agent are we?" At times, organizational goals—in this situation productivity and profit maximization—are not entirely congruent with client needs. Yet neither can exist without the other: Clients need jobs and organizations need a workforce. The professional challenge is to recognize the symbiotic relationship and discover the equilibrium that optimizes the common interest of both parties (Akabas, Kurzman, & Kolben, 1979, pp. 17–18). External demands of the organization sometimes conflict with clients' best interests. When this occurs, following the theory of virtue, the dilemma must be shared openly so that clients may select the route or set of options they feel are in their best interests. Such situations are not frequent, but when they occur the social worker must advocate for the maximum options for clients and preserve their right to self-determination. Since the occupational social work mandate comes in part from the organizational subsystem (for example, personnel, medical, community affairs), which is the home base for the service, social workers often are protected within the organization in view of their special human service role within the larger institution. Finally, an additional point of reference is our profession. Social work's value system, formalized through commitment to the NASW *Code of Ethics*, not only gives occupational social workers a common external frame of reference, but constitutes clout within the organization in support of ethical positions (Akabas & Kurzman, 1982). Ultimately, as professionals, social workers must retain the right to leave, however personally difficult this might be, if they frequently are unable to resolve client and organizational interest (Benedict, 1973).

What becomes most important, from the outset, is the nature of the contract with the employer in labor and industrial settings. If occupational social workers suggest that they may bring greater productivity or profit to the company, for example, people (employees) will quickly become a means, not an end. If one defines the social work function, however, as helping the corporation fulfill its social obligations and its commitment to improving the quality of life for its workforce, the practitioner's role is more likely to become an ethical one. Occupational social work expertise is not in promoting profit maximization but in helping organizations meet the needs of individuals, groups, and communities in the world of work—and, reciprocally, in recognizing unions' and managements' obligation and vested interest in doing so. We are specialists in the human dimension of the workplace and in increasing our labor and industrial sponsors' commitment of both human and fiscal resources in this arena. Such clarity about our role and function is essential to ensure that people will be a central focus of our attention; that a goal will be to enhance the quality of life for workforce participants; and that our commitment will be both to the provision of social services and to the creation of humanistic forms of organizational change.

Confidentiality

The issue of confidentiality is frequently brought forward as a principal ethical dilemma in the area of the theory of virtues and duties. The concept is often bound by absolute and inviolable notions akin to protection of a military or diplomatic classification of "top secret." Helen Harris Perlman speaks to this issue:

> What exactly does the social caseworker promise when he [sic] promises confidentiality? Does he actually promise that what the client tells him will be known to no one but himself? If he does, it is unethical because it is not true. What the client tells him will be known to the typist who transcribes his record, to the supervisor who reads it, to the workers who follow after him. . . . All the caseworker can truthfully promise is that what the client tells him will be used responsibly and will be scrupulously guarded against misuses. (1951, p. 326)

Suanna J. Wilson (1978, Chapter 1), who has written a seminal study on the ethical issues pertaining to confidentiality in social work, makes the useful distinction between relative confidentiality and absolute confidentiality. She notes that the majority of social work practitioners in *all* settings function in terms of the former. Even in The Federal Privacy Act of 1974, which governs confidentiality practices in all federal programs, and in the state social work licensure laws in some 23 states that provide for privileged communication, the legal provisions for confidentialilty are always relative, not absolute. Further, most studies of the operational industrial social work programs show that maintaining confidentiality of client communication is not a major problem in actual practice, although special arrangements and cautions must be taken on a preventive basis (Erfurt & Foote, 1977; Kurzman & Akabas, 1981; Weiner, Akabas, & Sommer, 1973).

For example, in hospital-based employee assistance programs, social workers sometimes find themselves working with a medical staff person who is actively abusing drugs (e.g., heroin or cocaine) while on duty. Despite the fact that an emergency room nurse may be a voluntary client (e.g., self-referral), the EAP's policy of confidentiality must be weighed against the legitimate needs of the (hospital) organization and the patients it serves.

Leon Warshaw (1979, p. 41), a physician, states, "By design, [EAP] counselors serve as the agents of the employee even against the immediate interests of the organization," and that EAP staff therefore should reveal "no more than the employee wishes to have divulged." However, Akabas (1984,

p. 84) suggests that the issues here, when conceptualized in the ethical context of duties and virtues, are somewhat more complex than Warshaw might portray. There is a tension, she correctly notes, "between an individual's right to privacy and society's right to know so that it can protect its members and assure the accountability of its institutions." The concept of "relative confidentiality," as delineated by Perlman (1951) and Wilson (1978) above, governs in this situation, because the hospital (as the EAP's sponsoring institution) has rights and obligations too. One of a medical center's central commitments is to responsible patient care; and therefore knowledge it may have (even if voluntarily provided) that a staff nurse is seriously impaired and hence may place an emergency room patient's life at risk must take precedence over the general program policy of client confidentiality. Indeed, the NASW *Code of Ethics* (1980, Sec. II) provides for such a contingency when it states that "the social worker should share with others confidences revealed by clients, without their consent, only for compelling professional reasons." Briar and Vinet (1985) parenthetically note that such compelling situations are not limited to occupational social work practice, but are frequently encountered in traditional social work settings, in general, and in authoritarian host settings, in particular.

THE COMMON GOOD

The core ethical question returns to the theory of the common good. The issue is whether occupational social work practice offers opportunities for promoting distributive justice. Harold Lewis (1972) has proposed a set of principles to serve as guidelines for social workers that should promote distributive justice in the provision of services. Lewis suggests that there is a value base or a moral component to social work practice and to the specific practice principles he proposes.

If developing new social service delivery systems to meet the needs of currently underserviced portions of the population can be considered a proactive ethical mandate, then an example is in order. Working-class people are often caught in the well-known bind of not being eligible for publicly supported mental health services and unable to afford such services in the marketplace. Therefore, their mental health needs often go unmet. In addition, they frequently have no idea of where to go for such help because the agencies are usually not located where they live or work and are not open during the hours when they would be free. Social work in the workplace—free, on-site, available as needed, and responsive to working-class style and needs—frequently becomes an oasis in a desert, without which little professional intervention on behalf of this population ever would occur (see, for example, Filipowicz, 1979). Cavin P. Leeman (1974), for example, noted that 60% of the workers served in an on-site occupational social work program near Boston were unable to name one other source to which they might have gone for help with their problems.

Opportunities for creative program development that promote the principle of distributive justice also are available in labor and industrial organizations. For this reason, it is essential that social workers in these settings not see themselves merely as providers of service, but also as agents of program innovation. By documenting unmet needs in a direct practice unit, social workers in one trade union became the pivotal force in demonstrating the need for legal services. They translated this evidence into a preliminary program design and advocated for its approval by senior union officials. As a result, an innovative legal services program was implemented to fill a critical gap in services and now is available to more than 100,000 workers and their families (Akabas, Kurzman, & Kolben, 1979; Brill, 1979). Other occupational social workers, through their training and consultation function with line managers around the social and mental health needs of the workforce, have identified the necessity for job accommodation options, such as flexitime. As a result, opportunities have opened up for whole new sectors of the community, such as older workers, working mothers, and the mentally and physically disabled. Such innovations promote a more equitable distribution of opportunity to portions of the population who would not otherwise be able to compete for some of the tangible rewards of workforce participation.

In the occupational social work field of practice, moreover, a focus on advocacy is essential, as Theodore Walden (1978) has stresed. Charles Levy notes that within the framework of their employing agency's function, and in the context of their ethical obligations to society, social workers must impact on the institutional and social conditions that disadvantage portions of the client population: "The social worker's aim is in some way . . . to affect the society and its institutions so that . . . clients will be more equitably dealt with and receive a greater share of society's resources" (1976, p. 158). As stated in the new NASW *Code of Ethics*, "The social worker should advocate changes in policy and legislation to improve social conditions and to promote social justice" (1980, Sec. VI, p. 9). As the expert from within, one can identify what Lewis (1976) has termed *the cause in function, the ends in means*, and move with force and authenticity toward new and more equitable provisions. Not only is this mandate important in occupational social work practice, to mitigate against the counterpull of organizational co-optation; the opportunity to achieve these goals is unusually good because the practitioner is working under the auspices of exceptionally influential institutions in our society. "Social workers would do well to recognize and remember that the power of the industrial parties can be a vital ingredient *in making society responsive to people and their needs*" (Kurzman & Akabas, 1981, p. 59).

THE PROMISE OF REWARDS

Although there are risks for the social work profession through its engagement in the arena of industrial social welfare, there is the promise of rewards—such as promoting the common good—as well. At the same time, the need exists for a consciousness-raising of our profession in general, and for prospective occupational social work practitioners in particular, around the substantive ethical imperatives. Practitioners are venturing (perhaps to a somewhat greater degree in this than in other host settings) into alien terrain. Clearly, ethical quandaries are involved, but there are unique opportunities as well. The dangers are posed primarily by the potential for compromise of our virtues and, to a lesser extent, by the possibility of inattention to our duties. However, the NASW *Code of Ethics*, with its explicit delineation of our ethical responsibility to our clients, colleagues, and employers, as well as to society and the profession, should be extremely helpful to us in this regard.

The ethical challenge we feel is ultimately joined around the theory of the common good, as a critical component of an adequate ethics. We speak of the fair or equitable distribution of the benefits and burdens of social life in an institutional rather than individual context. Although the issue in occupational social work is never simple, the public and private institutions for which we as social workers traditionally work are not well positioned within our economic system to impact on issues of distributive justice. To the extent that we can maintain our sense of duty and virtue, and at the same time recommit ourselves to the social change component of professional practice, new opportunities may be envisioned. One therefore can recognize the enormous potential of this field, which must be weighed against the risks and the unknown. If labor and industrial organizations, for example, can be moved even modestly to accommodate to new populations and to new communal needs, the contribution of our profession in this arena will be warranted. It is the judgment of most participants and observers that in this context the risk is worth taking. In the end, what will be critical and essential will be our willingness as occupational social workers to bind ourselves to a normative discipline of morality that underscores the notions of advocacy and equity. Our conceptual clarity regarding these ethical issues, our professional readiness to discuss them, and our personal commitment to honor them in our practice will serve as the best protection—for our clients, ourselves, and the social work profession.

REFERENCES

Akabas, S. H. (1984). Confidentiality: Values and dilemmas. *Social Work Papers, 18*, 83–91.

Akabas, S. H., Kurzman, P. A., & Kolben, N. S. (Eds.). (1979). *Labor and industrial settings: Sites for social work practice.* New York: Columbia University, Hunter College, and Council on Social Work Education.

Akabas, S. H., & Kurzman, P. A. (Eds.). (1982). *Work, workers and work organizations: A view from social work* (Chapter 9). Englewood Cliffs, NJ: Prentice-Hall.

Bakalinsky, R. (1980). People vs. profits: Social work in industry. *Social Work, 25,* 471–475.

Benedict, D. S. (1973). A generalist counselor in industry. *Personnel and Guidance Journal, 51,* 717–722.

Briar, K. H. (1983). Layoffs and social work intervention. *Urban and Social Change Review, 16,* 9–14.

Briar, K. H., & Vinet, M. (1985). Ethical questions concerning an EAP: Who is the client? In Klarreich, S. H., Francek, J. L., & Moore, C. E. (Eds.), *The human resources management handbook.* New York: Praeger.

Brill, S. (1979, January 2). Lawyers for the workers. *Esquire Magazine,* pp. 9–14.

Bronfenbrenner, M. (1973). Equality or equity. *The Annals, 409,* 9–23.

Code of ethics of NASW: Professional standards pamphlet. (1980). Washington: National Association of Social Workers.

Erfurt, J. C., & Foote, A. (1977). *Occupational employee assistance programs for substance abuse and mental health problems.* Ann Arbor: Institute of Labor and Industrial Relations of the University of Michigan.

Ferman, L.A. (1984). Unemployment and personal distress: Ethical imperatives. In Dillick, S. (Ed.) *Value foundations of social work: Ethical basis for a human service profession.* Detroit: Wayne State University Press.

Filipowicz, C. A. (1979). The troubled employee: Whose responsibility? *The Personnel Administrator, 24,* 19.

Jonsen, A. R., & Hellegers, A. E. (1976). Conceptual foundations for an ethics of medical care. In R. M. Veatch & R. Branson (Eds.), *Ethics and health policy.* Cambridge, MA: Ballinger Publishers.

Kurzman, P. A. (1983). Ethical issues in industrial social work practice. *Social Casework, 64,* 105–111.

Kurzman, P. A. (1984). Ethical issues in industrial social work: Toward a framework for practice. In Dillick, S. (Ed.), *Value foundations of social work: Ethical basis for a human service profession.* Detroit: Wayne State University Press.

Kurzman, P. A., & Akabas, S. H. (1981). Industrial social work as an arena for practice. *Social Work, 26,* 52–60.

Leeman, C. P. (1974). Contracting for an employee counseling service. *Harvard Business Review, 52,* 24.

Levy, C. S. (1974). On the development of a code of ethics. *Social Work, 19,* 207–216.

Levy, C. S. (1976). *Social work ethics.* New York: Human Sciences Press.

Lewis, H. (1972). Morality and the politics of practice. *Social Casework, 53,* 404–417.

Lewis, H. (1976). The cause in function. *Journal of the Otto Rank Association, 2,* 24.

Meeting human service needs in the workplace: A role for social work. (1980). New York: Columbia University, Hunter College, and Council on Social Work Education.

Mill, J. S. (1975). *On liberty* (D. Spitz, Ed.). New York: Norton.

Perlis, L. (1978). Industrial social work: Problems and prospects. *NASW News, 23,* 3.

Perlman, H. H. (1951). The caseworker's use of collateral information. *Social Casework, 52,* 326.

Rawls, J. (1971). *A theory of justice.* Cambridge: Harvard University Press.

Ryan, W. (1976). *Blaming the victim* (rev. ed.). New York: Vintage.

Vigilante, F. W. (1978). Equity in admissions to a school of social work. *Social Casework, 59,* 83–88

Walden, T. (1978). Industrial social work: A conflict in definitions. *NASW News, 23,* 9.

Warshaw, L. J. (1979). *Stress management.* Reading, MA: Addison-Wesley.

Weiner, H. J., Akabas, S. H., & Sommer, J. J. (1973). *Mental health care in the world of work.* New York: Association Press.

Wilson, S. J. (1978). *Confidentiality in social work: Issues and principles.* New York: Free Press.

Yelaja, S. A. (Ed.). (1982). *Ethical issues in social work.* Springfield, IL: Charles C Thomas.

II Counseling Programs in the Workplace

3 Employee Assistance/Counseling Typologies

Dorothy Fleisher
Barbara Hade Kaplan

This chapter presents a conceptual framework for examining four models or "ideal types" of EAPs. Six criteria have been selected for assessing the advantages and disadvantages of each of these models and also for identifying the tradeoffs in selecting one or another of the ideal types. The framework enables executives and managers to explore the pros and cons of different models in order to decide which one would best suit their purpose. For researchers, the framework can aid in designing studies that produce empirical data to support or refute the premises upon which EAPs operate. For practitioners, the framework can help them anticipate issues in implementing and functioning within an EAP.

CONTEXTUAL CONSIDERATIONS

The size and distribution of a workforce, the mission of an organization, and its prevailing organization/culture climate, as well as the amount of resources allocated to the endeavor, will influence the model that is selected. It is within this context that the four major components—target population, range of services, program administration, and funding source—are designed and implemented. Decisions relative to these components acccount for the diversity of EAP models evidenced in the workplace.

Size

Organizations vary in the size of their workforce, regardless of whether they are in, for example, manufacturing, service, or finance. They may be local, regional, national, or international in scope. Companies with a workforce of fewer than 500 or 1,000 employees may be unable to support their own EAP and may come together to form a consortium (Masi, 1982).

Distribution of the Workforce

Variations in design result from the geographical distribution of the workforce (Erfurt & Foote, 1985). A company whose employees are concentrated in one location is likely to opt for a different model than a company whose employees are dispersed over a wide geographical area. What can be gleaned from the literature is that a variety of mixed models have been developed. For example, one company, CIGNA, has an internal EAP and also uses external contractors (Sapp, 1985). Another company, the Sheraton Corporation, implemented an in-house EAP across a worldwide network, which serves 100,000 employees in 500 different locations. An in-house EAP, within a large urban school district, provides services in a central location and also sends mobile workers to employees working in outlying communities. Airline companies also employ mobile workers to reach out to employees living in other cities. The variations are endless, but all stem from the distribution of the workforce unique to the organization.

Mission

The mission of an organization will also influence its choice of an EAP model. In contrast to other types of organizations, for security reasons a company doing sensitive government work may prefer an in-house model, located off of the premises but close by. This would enable family members desiring assistance the freedom to come and go without the necessity of a security clearance.

Cultural Climate of the Organization

The arena of corporate social responsibility has been broadened to include "equal opportunity, pollution control, poverty reduction, product safety and programs for the health and safety of employees. Corporate social responsibility has further expanded to include needed social services for employees, which has laid a solid foundation for the stabilization of EAPs in the workplace" (Scanlon, 1984, p. 3).

However, management's interpretation of what constitutes social responsibility differs. Unless the cultural climate of the organization is conducive, the realization that troubled employees cost millions of dollars in health care and lost productivity will not lead to implementation of an EAP. Executives and managers must be convinced that an EAP will have a decisive impact on work performance in their corporation. Only then are they likely to allocate the resources necessary to launch an employee assistance program with adequate staff.

Allocation of Resources

Going beyond the cost of hiring staff, the variation in EAPs is often directly related to the amount of additional resources allocated to the program. Some budgets earmark funds for the preparation and distribution of materials, training managers and supervisors in referral procedures, and upgrading the management skills of administrative personnel. Others invest in preventive programs such as wellness workshops and support groups. Still others include the indirect cost of allowing employees release time to encourage use of the EAP.

DESIGN COMPONENTS

In designing an EAP, management must make decisions about the structure of four components: the target population to be served, the range of services to be provided, the administrative structure, and the source of funding for the program. In examining each component, there are several alternatives that must be considered.

Target Population

In deciding who should be served, options include: providing assistance to employees only or extending it to include family members; serving only those with substance abuse problems and other work-related concerns, or extending help to those with problems that originate outside the workplace; limiting eligibility to full-time employees, or extending it to part-time, terminated, and retired employees.

Range of Services

Determination must be made of how narrow or broad-brush the program is to be. An EAP may provide only information and then refer the employee to a community resource. If counseling is offered it may be restricted to assistance with job-related problems. Services may be limited to rehabilitation and counseling or include preventive and educational programs. A broad-brush program can also include training for supervisors and managers, and consultation for departments in which systems problems are creating stress for employees.

Administrative Considerations

Decisions related to sponsorship, auspices, location, and staffing present many possibilities for potential combinations and also influence the utilization of the EAP services to be provided. The corporation, union, or association may sponsor the EAP individually or conjointly. Within the organization programs may be placed under the auspices of human resources, personnel, or medical departments. The EAP may be located on the premises within or adjacent to the department it reports to, or it may be located off-site in close geographical proximity. The EAP administrator and counselors may be hired directly by the organization, or contractual arrangements may be made with family service agencies, hospitals, community mental health centers, or private consultants, who will assign their staff members to the EAP.

Decisions must be made about the staff's availability, as to whether they are to be full-time, part-time, or only called in for crises and emergencies. The level of staff expertise required to carry out the designated functions of the EAP depends upon the range of services to be provided.

Funding Source

The alternatives include having the employer be the sole contributor, having only employees contribute, or adopting a formula for shared contributions. If the employer is the sole contributor, the source of funds may be third-party insurance payments, fringe benefits, or financial support from general operating expenses.

FOUR EAP MODELS: IDEAL TYPES

The structure of the models to be presented is based on four design components discussed in the previous section. The fourth component, funding source, although it involves essential decisions for implementing an EAP, does not lend itself to the identification of advantages and disadvantages based on the criteria selected. Rather, the nature of the funding source itself becomes a factor influencing both the utilization rate of the EAP and its stability. If employees are charged a fee for service it might negatively influence their decision to use the EAP. Were third-party payments to become the funding source, it might discourage utilization for two reasons. First, not all plans cover all employees equally, and second, the need for filing might be seen as violating confidentiality. The corporation's choice of funding the EAP out of the general operating budget or out of fringe benefits has ramifications for the stability and utilization of the program. If the EAP is funded out of the budget, it has the disadvantage of constantly competing with other operating expenses that may be seen as having a higher priority, whereas if it is funded out of fringe benefits it has two advantages. The first is stability of funding and the second is that employees' awareness that it is their contributions that are sustaining the program might encourage feelings of entitlement to services and thus increase utilization of the program.

The purpose of approaching the examination of EAPs from the perspective of models and ideal types is to enable comparison of programs that differ in the structure of their basic components. The bias underlying the construction of these four models is that they are conceptualized as originating from the workplace, whether or not they are sponsored solely by the corporation or jointly with labor. The limitation this imposes is that it omits examination of the advantages and disadvantages of employee assistance programs that are solely union- or association-sponsored.

All of the models described in Table 3-1 are projected as originating from the workplace. However, many labor unions have experimented with a variety of assistance models. The pioneers, The Amalgamated Clothing Workers in New York, enabled mental health workers, under its auspices, "to do outreach and, in some cases, even treatment, in the garment factories." They did this by adding a mental health unit to the industry's health center (Industrial Social Welfare Center, 1984, p. 14). Nationally, the AFL-CIO has developed a program under the auspices of its Community Services Organization. Union members are trained as peer counselors and provide information and referral services to their co-workers in the workplace. The advantage of this model is that it enables the identification of troubled employees at an early stage. "Moreover, since physical behavioral changes are an earlier indicator of chemical dependency than is deteriorating job performance, labor is in a unique position to intervene early in the disease, before it has taken a heavy toll on the victim and the family" (Tramm, 1985, p. 97). Peer intervention has also been used by the EAPs of both the Airline Pilots Association and the Association of Flight Attendants (Molloy, 1985). Other advantages of labor participation for providing employee assistance will be discussed under the evaluation criteria.

EVALUATION CRITERIA AND TRADEOFFS

To identify the most salient dimensions for comparative evaluation, six major criteria were selected: confidentiality, accessibility, staff expertise and availability, flexibility, accountability, and cost effectiveness. A review of the literature highlighted these criteria as most salient for pinpointing the advantages and disadvantages of different EAP models.

TABLE 3-1

In-House Models: 1 and 2

Model 1: Providing a limited range of services
Target population: Employees only
Range of services: Limited to diagnostic assessment and referral to community resources; special focus on substance abuse problems; and periodic training of supervisors in procedures for referring troubled and troubling employees.
Administrative considerations: Sponsored by the corporation, under the auspices of either the human resources, personnel, or medical departments. The EAP may be sponsored jointly by labor and management without requiring a change in the definition of any of the other components.

Model 2: Providing a comprehensive range of services
Target population: Extended to include family members
Range of services: Crisis intervention; short-term counseling; rehabilitation programs; special focus on substance-abuse problems; preventive interventions such as wellness workshops, support groups, and educational seminars; training of supervisors (and shop stewards) in referring employees; and consultation with management (and union and association representatives) concerning organizational stress factors.
Administrative considerations: Sponsorship and auspices may be the same as projected in Model 1.

External Contractor Models: 3 and 4

Model 3: Providing a limited range of services
Target population: Employees only, same as Model 1
Range of services: Diagnostic assessment and referral; focus on substance abuse; periodic training of supervisors, same as Model 1
Administrative considerations: Sponsorship by corporation only or jointly with labor. Under the auspices of external contractor (i.e., family service agency, hospital, community mental health center, or private consulting firm). Services are provided in-house and/or off-site, preferably close to the workplace. Joint sponsorship with labor does not require a change in the definition of any of the components.
Model 4: Providing a comprehensive range of services
Target population: Extended to include family members, same as Model 2
Range of services: Crisis intervention, short-term counseling, etc., same as Model 2
Administrative considerations: Sponsorship and auspices may be the same as projected in Model 3.

Confidentiality

Protection of confidentiality is the criterion that is basic to the success of the EAP regardless of which model is implemented. Unless confidentiality is assured, employees may choose not to contact the EAP. A letter from the executive officer of the organization to all employees, confirming confidentiality as company policy, and reference to this policy in materials issued by the EAP are the best means of making it known throughout the workplace.

Joint sponsorship with labor reinforces the employees' trust in the policy of confidentiality. Programs sponsored solely by a trade union or professional association, with services provided on their premises, greatly reduce concerns in this area.

Unwitting violation of this policy is most likely to occur at the supervisory and management levels. Seminars explaining the purpose and function of the EAP, training to demonstrate the use of work performance evaluations as a means of identifying troubled employees, and education in procedures for making referrals are essential to protection of confidentiality. Without this knowledge supervisory-level personnel mistakingly believe that not only must they confront troubled employees, but also that they must diagnose the problem and coerce them to seek help (Googins, 1975). Although Googins identified upper-level personnel's dilemma as early as 1975, the violations of confidentiality continue in those settings where management level personnel remain uninformed of the limitations of their responsibilities.

Policy also needs to be made explicit concerning access to client information by a nonclient. Without the client's signed informed consent, no access may be permitted, and in all circumstances the ramification of disclosure must be made clear to the client. Recordkeeping systems must be devised to protect the employee–client's identity (Masi, 1982). Code numbers must be used on all records relating to the employee's use of the EAP. Intake forms, which carry identifying data, must be kept separate from coded records. Only professional staff members whose code of ethics assures confidentiality and client protection should have access to all the records. Receptionists, typists, data collectors, and other nonprofessional staff members must be informed about the ethics of confidentiality and that any violation might jeopardize a client's employment. Some practitioners suggest installing a private telephone line that does not connect with the organization's switchboard. Providing access to services before and after working hours is also considered essential to preserving confidentiality (Thomlison, 1983). Rather than placing the program within the Personnel Department, placing the EAP under the auspices of the Human Resources or Medical Department is viewed as safeguarding confidentiality.

This issue of confidentiality is complex because it involves both ethical and legal considerations. Suanna J. Wilson (1978) has written an entire volume on this topic as it relates to social work. She clearly differentiates the moral code from the legal obligations involved: "The duty to keep matters confidential is governed by ethics. The right to refuse to disclose them is governed by laws" (Wilson, 1978, p. 97). Efforts continue to cover various professions with the right of privileged communication to avoid being forced to disclose confidential information. As a standard of conduct, social workers and other professionals, under their code of ethics, are morally bound to protect the client's confidentiality in all instances other than those when a client is a danger to self or others. Confidentiality explicitly stated as organizational policy supports the professional's protection of the employee.

In evaluating EAPs on this criterion, there is a debatable assumption that external contractors are less susceptible to pressure from the organization because they are not direct employees of the organization. The underlying issue not being addressed is: Are internal EAP employees and external EAP contractors bound by the same code of ethics? If they are, on what basis is it assumed that in-house employees are more likely to face a conflict of interest when confidentiality is involved? The real threat to confidentiality lies in the confusion and misunderstanding of the parameters of the legal obligation and the adherence by EAP personnel (internal and external) to a code of ethics. Another argument used to identify external contractors as better able to protect confidentiality is that employers are more likely to pressure internal mental health professionals for information about employees. A well-constructed policy of confidentiality will have foreseen this possibility and have provided for the protection of all employees. Once again, there is an unfounded assumption that external contractors would better resist such requests, as they have alternate contracts to turn to. The fact is that an external contractor is also obliged to make explicit the boundaries of confidentiality within which the EAP services will be provided. As professionals have become more experienced in providing services in the workplace, they have helped to formulate policies with precisely such protection.

Charles S. Sapp, Assistant Vice President of CIGNA's EAP, maintains that "in-house programs can be as confidential as any contracted program," and points out that "there has never been a suit filed at CIGNA regarding any EAP action . . . we go to great lengths to ensure . . . confidentiality" (1985, p. 9). In reviewing malpractice suits against physicians Wilson (1978) stated, "None of the suits revolved around violation of confidentiality or privilege." In discussing 13 cases directed against psychiatrists specifically, she pointed out that "all involved problems in treatment, commitment, suicide, or "miscellaneous." However, none of the "miscellaneous" included actions for violation of confidentiality or privilege" (pp. 143–144). "Social work has thus far escaped any significant volume of suits for breaches of confidentiality" (Wilson, p. 145).

Because Models 3 and 4 provide for employee records to be kept off-site and also insure added privacy by offering employees the option of being counseled off-site, these two models appear to provide the advantage of increased protection of confidentiality. However, it is important to base one's position on documentation of actual violations of confidentiality rather than on discomfort felt when policies are poorly constructed.

Accessibility

Program aspects that facilitate accessibility relate to employee awareness of the program, physical location of the EAP, and the referral process adopted. Employee awareness of the EAP can be achieved by adopting any number of strategies. In some organizations each employee is informed about the EAP and the services it provides at the time of orientation. Others periodically send out a communication in both English and Spanish (or whatever the alternative language of a large section of the workforce may be). Alternatively, the communication may be in the form of a card inserted in the pay envelope. In each text, whenever the word confidentiality appears, it is printed in bold type.

Accessibility is encouraged when services are provided in the employees' "natural life space and offers an opportunity to . . .[receive services]. . . unencumbered by elegibility and categorical requirements" (Kurzman & Akabas, 1981, p. 53). Services provided at the worksite help dispel the stereotype of mental health professionals as "charity workers." Blue collar and minority workers are more likely to use the EAP if the program is located in "their" environment (Kurzman & Akabus, 1981, p. 53). Results of a 3-year study of EAP operations in the federal and private sectors "suggest this may be the best way to reach underserved populations . . ." (Cahill, 1983, p. 32).

For some sections of the workforce, visibility contributes to employee awareness and encourages utilization. For others, privacy is a primary consideration and their preference is for locating the program in an inconspicuous area. Some employees will only avail themselves of services if they are provided off-site.

In addition to providing information about the EAP, additional referral strategies include conducting wellness workshops for employees and seminars to train management on how to refer troubled and troubling employees.

While on-site programs, as in Models 1 and 2, provide the convenience of physical location and familiarity of environment, off-site programs, as in Models 3 and 4, facilitate access for those concerned with privacy.

There are disadvantages inherent in Models 1 and 3 in terms of accessibility. Programs that provide a limited range of services will not implement all the strategies for creating employee awareness and thus will minimize accessibility. Another drawback of these two models is that employees requiring assistance beyond information must be referred to another resource. This two-step procedure often discourages use of needed services, regardless of ease of access.

In contrast, Models 2 and 4, which provide a comprehensive range of services, have the potential to implement all of the strategies for maximizing accessibility. An added advantage of Model 4 is that services are accessible both on- and off-site.

Staff Expertise and Availability

The expertise, visibility, and availability of staff affect the use of the EAP. To respond to employee needs, staff must be professionally educated and possess broad areas of expertise. In addition to substance abuse, which is often the tip of the iceberg, employees seek help with a variety of problems. Clients request help for coping with stress, marital as well as parent–child conflict, needs of elderly parents, counseling for financial and legal problems, and information about resources available in their community. In addition, staff need to have knowledge of the organization as a system: its communication channels, its personnel policies, and its informal structure. Staff who possess this added knowledge are able to facilitate resolution of workplace problems. Given the complexity of employees' problems, it is not surprising that Erfurt and Foote report that, "programs which rely on part-time, relatively untrained staff tend to show a lower level of penetration (i.e. see few clients) and make referral to more expensive types of treatment (inpatient rather than outpatient)" (Erfurt & Foote, 1985, p. 50). There is also some evidence that the training and background of program staff affect the type of clients identified. Counselors diagnose the types of problems with which they are most familiar. Therefore, in-service training of staff is essential to assure a breadth of expertise.

The visibility of the staff, as well as their availability in times of emergency, influence the effectiveness of the EAP. When staff members conduct seminars, serve as workshop leaders and trainers, and act as consultants, employees are able to personally evaluate their expertise. On-site staff are also able to engage employees in informal encounters during the workday (Masi, 1982). All of these activities reduce the anxiety of employees seeking assistance.

Some employees prefer being seen before or after working hours. Others, seeking help along with family members, can only use the EAP if services are available on the weekends. Although many organizations provide release time for employees using the EAP's services, many employees prefer to make appointments during their lunch hour to protect their privacy. Hours of availability must also be designed to accommodate employees who work on other than the traditional day shift. Immediate response in crisis situations (i.e., when an employee is a danger to self or to others and requires immdiate admission to a mental health facility) makes EAP staff availability a life-and-death matter.

The advantages of Models 1 and 2, which provide in-house staff, are that staff are more visible, readily available, and likely to be more knowledgeable about the organization and the special needs of the employees than are external staff, who rotate among many contractual organizations. The added advantage of Model 2 is that staff have more opportunities to interact with employees as they provide comprehensive services and are able to demonstrate their expertise in a variety of activities.

Flexibility

Economic conditions such as mergers, the search for new markets, and the development of new products all result in continuous reorganization and a shift in the employee population. The flexibility to respond to those whose lives have been impacted by these changes depends upon gaining the trust of both employees and managers. In-house staff have more potential for earlier identification of needs. They also may be more sensitive to the organization's culture and thus better able to select interventions to be implemented. In-house staff also have more opportunities to participate in joint planning and to serve as advocates to promote equal opportunity, occupational health and safety, and employee development.

Of the two in-house models, Model 2 has the greater advantage. Because it is comprehensive, it has the potential to implement new services as a response to needs as they arise. External staff, in Models 3 and 4, are more likely to restrict their contact with employees to those who apply for services. They have limited opportunities to meet employees informally and to interact with them on a basis that would enable them to identify emerging needs. Their knowledge of the organization's culture also occurs more slowly and incrementally, as they are not part of the daily routine of the workplace. Yet Model 4 does have one advantage where flexibility is involved. External staff, who are part of preferred provider organizations, can call upon other staff members who possess the specific skills and expertise required to respond to particular needs as they arise.

Accountability

When a new program is undertaken, especially one that extends the company's responsibility to uncharted waters, accountability in terms of the fiscal and programmatic use of resources is crucial. Through careful documentation, program decisions can be justified and a persuasive case for needed expansion can be presented. To monitor the EAP adequately, it is necessary that objectives be quantifiable. Data should be collected on characteristics of employees served, rate of utilization, type of referral (self, other employee user, supervisory), type of problems presented, services provided, hours of most frequent usage, employees' evaluation of services received, and cost per unit of service (Burggrabe & Swift, 1984; Hoffman, 1983).

In-house models are usually placed under the auspices of departments that have existing systems established for reporting to management. This carries a built-in assumption that the EAP will also periodically present data that will reflect its activities. In discussing service accountability, Klarreich (1985) maintains that, "This could be accomplished more readily and more regularly with an in-house program, simply because greater cooperation and closer supervision could take place, especially in the initial stages of the program" (p. 81).

Others maintain that external contractors, as a condition of their continued employment, are expected to present data reflecting their activities and therefore are more reliable in this regard. The incentive for internal EAP staff to monitor the EAP, through data collection and analysis, is to enable changes to be made to keep the program responsive to the needs of the workforce. In-house staff may also be less prone to conflict of interest, as they serve only one employer. In part, this may be reflected in a willingness to collect more comprehensive data and do long-term follow-up.

Of the two in-house models, Model 2 provides greater control. Staff doing the initial assessment continue their relationship with employees. Thus, counseling information is not lost; they can use their knowledge of the organization to facilitate the program, which does not occur when employees are referred elsewhere; and they are in a position to evaluate the program's effectiveness over a long period of time.

To assure that external contractors monitor the program regularly, the type and frequency of reports to be provided can be specified at the time the contract is negotiated. This would overcome this limitation in relation to external contractors.

Cost Effectiveness

The major goal of companies in starting an EAP is to increase their productivity. Alcoholism, drug abuse, family violence, divorce, economic problems, anxiety, and depression are recognized by top executives as contributing to tardiness, absenteeism, poor job performance, and an unstable workforce. Containing the costs of medical insurance premiums, as well as disability and workers' compensation claims, is another company goal. Overutilization of the health care system results from psychosomatic complaints, as well as from poor nutrition, hypertension, and smoking. The complexity of the work environment can cause stress, which can contribute to mental breakdowns and heart attacks, which are costly in terms of the loss of valued employees and added expenditures for disability and workers' compensation claims.

Documentation exists to illustrate that savings accrue as a result of investments in employee assistance programs. Ohio Bell reports that 60% of those treated through their alcoholism program recovered, saving the company four million dollars annually (Lanier, 1981). General Motors calculates that its alcoholism treatment program realized a return of three dollars for each one invested in terms of decreased absenteeism, accident payments, and hospitalization costs. GM also showed that it saved 37 million dollars in 1980, when 10,000 persons received services through its EAP (Lanier, 1981). PA International Management Consultants, in a 1979 study, found that weekly benefits paid to absent employees decreased by 52% as a result of EAPs (Lovenheim, 1979). A reduction in the use and cost of inpatient and outpatient medical services following psychotherapy was identified in another body of research (Roweton, 1983).

Model 3 may be the least expensive, in terms of direct costs, if charges are confined to the limited services to be provided. Models 2 and 4, which provide a comprehensive range of services, are more costly. Some of the operating costs of Model 2 may be offset, if third-party insurance payments revert to the EAP. The most cost effective, among external contractors, may be the nonprofit agencies who provide services at a lower rate than do private consulting firms (Harlin, 1983).

If problems become deeply entrenched, the time required for treatment is longer and costlier and the prognosis for improvement more limited (Comstock, 1983). Prevention and early identification of problems are the key to decreased health care costs. This would point to Models 2 and 4, with a comprehensive range of services, as the most cost effective. They can offer wellness workshops, as well as support groups for coping with problems of daily life, and thus provide new information and specific preventive techniques.

CONCLUSION

Employee assistance programs have the potential for increasing productivity, enhancing employee morale, and containing health care costs; as such they are an investment in human resources. The type of program a company will implement depends upon such contextual considerations as the size and distribution of its workforce, its mission and organizational climate, and the resources it has available. Regardless of what model is selected, there will be tradeoffs in terms of confidentiality, accessibility, staff expertise and availability, flexibility, accountability, and cost effectiveness. Sensitivity to these tradeoffs can assist those involved in planning, directing, and staffing EAPs to develop strategies for maximizing the advantages and minimizing the disadvantages.

REFERENCES

Burggrabe, J. L., & Swift, J. W. (1984). Evaluating your EAP: A practical approach. *EAP Digest, 4*(3), 12–17.

Cahill, M. H. (1983). Tailoring EAP service to organizational needs. *EAP Digest, 3*(4), 32–39.

Comstock, D. (1983). Employee assistance programs: Current dimensions. *EAP Digest, 3*(4), 46–47.

Erfurt, J. C., & Foote, A. (1985). Variations in EAP design. In S. H. Klarreich, C. E. Moore, & J. Francek (Eds.), *Human resources management handbook* (pp. 45–68). New York: Praeger

Googins, B. (1975). Employee assistance programs. *Social Work, 20*(6), 464–467.

Harlin, J. (1983). Evaluating EAP consultant services. *EAP Coordinator, 2* (Fall).

Hoffmann, J. J. (1983). Guide to evaluating an employee assistance program and staff. *EAP Digest, 3*(2), 36–38.

Industrial Social Welfare Center. (1984) *Human services at the workplace: Past experiences and future directions* [p. 10(1)]. New York: Columbia University School of Social Work.

Klarreich, S. H. (1985). Assessment/treatment model. In S. H. Klarreich, C. E. Moore, & J. Francek (Eds.), *Human resources management handbook.* New York: Praeger.

Kurzman, P. A. & Akabas, S. H. (1981). Industrial social work as an arena for practice. *Social Work, 26*(1), 52–60.

Lanier, D. (1981). Industrial social work: Into the computer age. *EAP Digest, 1*(2), 18–33.

Lovenheim, B. (1979, April 1). More care given employees' psyches. *New York Times,* Section 3, pp. 3–5.

Masi, D. A. (1982). *Human services in industry.* Lexington, MA: Lexington Books.

Molloy, D. J. (1985). Peer referral: A programmatic and administrative review. In S. H. Klarreich, C. E. Moore, & J. Francek (Eds.), *Human resources management handbook.* New York: Praeger.

Roweton, W. E. (1983). *Reducing medical utilization with psychotherapy.* Charlottesville, VA: Associated American, Ltd., Management Consultants.

Sapp, C. S. (1985). More on contractors. *The Almacan, 15* (December), 8–9.

Scanlon, W. (1984). Corporate cost benefit: Only one EAP factor among many. *The Almacan, 14* (June), 3.

Thomlison, R. J. (1983). *Perspectives on industrial social work practice.* Ottawa: Family Service Canada.

Tramm, M. L. (1985). Union-based programs. In S. H. Klarreich, C. E. Moore, & J. Francek (Eds.), *Human resources management handbook.* New York: Praeger.

Wilson, S. J. (1978). *Confidentiality in social work.* New York: Free Press.

4 Identifying and Referring Troubled Employees to Counseling

Judy Winkelpleck
Michael Lane Smith*

Pat has worked for you for 11 years. Her performance has always been exemplary and her relationships with co-workers have been excellent. In the last few weeks, however, she has made repeated accounting errors and has been late to work twice. Other employees report that Pat has been unnecessarily short with them and has spent an unusual amount of time on the phone, often talking with one of her children.

This is a hypothetical though common situation. How would you deal with Pat? In the past, supervisors, managers, and administrators at all organizational levels have had the options of talking directly to Pat, waiting to determine if her behavior changed, or providing discipline. Supervisors were frequently in a quandry. Discipline might not be appropriate at the present time but waiting might increase the problem—especially in the eyes of the other employees. Frequently the supervisor consulted other people in the work group, wondered what was wrong, and then finally spoke directly with Pat. If Pat indicated the nature of the problem and that it was personal, the supervisor was caught in the web of accommodation. In this situation the other employees often became increasingly intolerant of Pat and eventually complained about the lack of action on the part of the supervisor. The supervisor—with knowledge of Pat's personal life—often found it exceedingly difficult to focus on her job performance. In the worst of situations, Pat received little or no help for her personal problem, the entire office situation deteriorated, Pat was eventually terminated, and the supervisor's ability to supervise was seriously questioned.

Wrich (1980) indicates that 10% to 12% of the workforce has serious personal problems. Each person who has experienced a serious personal

*Authors contributed equally to this chapter.

problem knows the dramatic influence such problems can have on attitudes and behavior at work. Although exact rates of deterioration range dramatically, a 15% deterioration rate is commonly expected. Imagine that 10% of the people with whom you work today are only performing at 85% capacity. More painfully, imagine the emotional cost to these employees, to their co-workers, and to their families as the impaired job performance becomes more blatant.

The early signs of potential impaired job performance are subtle. Tension in the office or shop, poor morale, inefficiency of staff time, "on the job absenteeism," and excessive office visiting are difficult to measure but negatively affect the work environment. Frequently these early costs escalate into more easily measurable costs of impaired job performance. Accidents, decreased production, turnover, absenteeism, and elevated disability benefits and health insurance premiums are costs resulting, in part, from troubled workers. Are any of these possible outcomes preventable? Certainly. The concept of Employee Assistance Programs (EAPs) was developed to help supervisors and employees in just such situations.

THE SOCIAL WORKER AND REFERRAL TO THE EAP

Unfortunately, well-conceived policy and superior service providers are of little help in responding to human problems if the people who suffer never contact the employee assistance counselor. Social workers involved in employee assistance can promote and facilitate case-finding and referral. They can also use the supervisory consultation process frequently involved in employee referral as a vehicle for further promoting the EAP as an essential managerial resource.

The principles that underlie effective referral to EAPs are more extensive than might first be assumed. They involve the social worker in a variety of roles with a variety of audiences. Proper referral—appropriate to both the functioning of the EAP and the needs of workplace actors—requires that the social worker address referral issues as they arise in the following tasks:

1. Policymaking
2. Workforce education
3. Supervisory training
4. Supervisory consultation
5. Supervisory feedback
6. Evaluation

PLANNING AND POLICYMAKING FOR REFERRAL

Planning for effective referrals to the EAP really begins during the initial planning for the EAP itself. Who is to be covered by EAP services? What problems is the EAP to address? Will self-referrals be permissible? Will they be sought? Who will be given authority to make directive referrals to the EAP practitioner(s)? Will covered workers be permitted to bypass the EAP staff, yet claim company coverage for services received through a contracted agency provider? What rules are to be established about client confidentiality? The answers to these and other questions establish a framework within which the specific tasks associated with promoting effective referrals to the EAP are played out. Ideally, the occupational social worker has the opportunity to participate in making these decisions. In any event, decisions made here certainly shape the mechanics of referral for whatever type of EAP develops.

Four Approaches

One of the early decisions that must be made in planning for EAP operation is the choice of what type(s) of referral to the program will be permitted. Four major approaches exist for employee access to EAP services. First, program recipients can self-refer themselves for assistance. Second, supervisors can informally refer employees or, third, they can make formal referrals to the EAP. Finally, employees can contact service providers directly, claiming coverage under the EAP but bypassing the EAP counselor, a process labeled *indirect referral* (Thoreson, Roberts, & Pascoe, 1984, p. 184). In addition to these major forms of referral, peer and family referrals to EAP counselors are also common. It is important to note that each type of referral has its own unique dynamic as well as advantages and disadvantages with respect to work-related issues and types of employees.

Self-referral

Self-referral—the voluntary, self-initiated request for assistance by an individual eligible for EAP services—is an increasingly common utilization form. In fact, Wrich says self-referral is "a common characteristic of the more successful employee assistance programs" (1980, p. 62). Self-referral is an especially useful referral mechanism for EAP practitioners who wish to target executives, upper-level managers, professionals, and others in organizations who enjoy relatively high levels of job discretion and autonomy. It is also extremely useful for broad-brush EAPs—those programs that provide assessment and subsequent responses for a wide variety of human problems.

The frequency of self-referral is often a correlate of marketing. If the marketing approach emphasizes the EAP as an opportunity or benefit, users will likely see EAP staff as consultants whose job it is to serve the employee. This approach also increases the number of colleagues, friends, and family members who contact the EAP with concerns about an employee. The tone of self-referral is typically, "what resources exist that might help?" To emphasize this tone organizations frequently transmit EAP information directly to the employees. A letter from the company president mailed to each employee at home is a typical approach, as is including EAP information in the employees' pay envelopes. Employee information meetings, informational brochures in new employee packets, and educational articles in company newsletters are ways an organization encourages its people to consider the EAP as a source of assistance. The primary responsibility of the occupational social worker with regard to self-referral is that of accurately communicating the services and benefits available through the EAP, providing assurance of confidentiality, and becoming known and acceptable (i.e., psychologically accessible) to a broad spectrum of workers eligible for services. (See also the discussion below under the heading Workforce Education.)

Informal Supervisory Referral

Most EAPs provide for a supervisor's role in encouraging troubled workers to seek help. The supervisor's role can be either informal or formal. The tone of informal supervisory referrals is usually "It seems like something has been bothering you. Why don't you see if the EAP could help?" Informal supervisory referrals should be handled with caution, since work-performance deterioration (a foundation for formal supervisory referrals) may be lacking and the supervisor may be treading on sensitive ground. Nevertheless, Wrich argues that "referring employees for help with problems before job performance is affected is the hallmark of nearly every good EAP we have seen" (1985, p. 177). Typically, informal supervisory referrals are made by a supervisor who has a personal relationship with the employee being referred. For example, John's boss, Sue, with whom he has worked for 4 years, might well say, "John, going through the death of a child is tough. Why don't you go talk to the people at the EAP and see if they can help?"

Formal Supervisory Referral

In this type of referral, the supervisor formally responds to employee performance problems and the unassessed personal problems that may lie behind them. In this sense the referral is a management action and not the act of a lay counselor. It is important to emphasize that the supervisor is not expected to diagnose or assess personal or psychological problems. Indeed, this is inappropriate. However, supervisors need to be sensitive to patterns of behavior that suggest that standard company disciplinary action is insufficient and that referral to the EAP is necessary. Cohen describes the pattern of deteriorating work performance as typically progressing in the following manner:

1. Increased absenteeism
2. Unexpected vacation requests
3. Sporadic productivity and erratic performance
4. Missed deadlines
5. Increased tardiness
6. Increased strife with co-workers
7. Loss of enthusiasm for work
8. Unpredictable behavior
9. Increased conflicts with supervisors
10. Increased complaining and moodiness
11. An above-average rate of accidents at work
12. Costly errors
13. Difficulty remembering and following instructions
14. Outright defiance (1985, p. 184)

These behaviors suggest personal problems that lie behind impaired work performance, problems that generally lie outside the effectiveness of standard supervisory or disciplinary actions. Especially in the event of problems arising from employee alcoholism or substance abuse, conventional disciplinary action is ineffective in preventing continuing job performance deterioration. Likewise, the probability of the worker's self-referring himself or herself to the EAP counselor is slight. Supervisory referral of the employee to the EAP, carefully supported by documentation and constrained by the limits of proper supervisory authority, is called for. For example, a supervisor may suggest to an employee, "Your job performance is not going okay (as these reports clearly show) and you could use the EAP as one way to get help to improve." Dunkin's (1982, p. 82) comment that alcohol programs are "job performance action" programs also applies to EAPs. (See DiNitto's discussion of EAP responses to alcohol abuse in Chapter 6 of this volume.)

The roles and responsibilities of the social worker are many and varied with respect to both informal and formal supervisory referral of troubled workers. First, the social worker needs to promote the development of referral policies and procedures that are professionally ethical, organizationally appropriate, and workable. In order to do so, the social worker has to recognize EAP responsibilities to both the supervisor and the worker. In fact, there is frequently some overlap in the issues that need to be addressed, because troubled workers frequently elicit significant discomfort, anger, and self-doubt in their supervisors. Hence, the EAP practitioner needs to be sensitive to the feelings and problems of both the worker being referred and the supervisor doing the referral. Adequate attention to these matters during the policymaking phase of EAP planning can facilitate more effective referrals to the EAP later.

Indirect Referral

This mechanism eliminates the usual referral to the EAP counselor and the counselor's own responsibilities for problem assessment and subsequent counseling or referral for counseling. This indirect referral is described by Warshaw as "an arrangement whereby individuals may go to a . . . counseling service outside the company on their own volition, their own referral without fear of being identified. The . . . counseling service knows that the company will pick up the tab for a given number of visits on bills that are submitted anonymously" (1985, pp. 176–177). Obviously, the major advantage of indirect referral is the extraordinary protection of the worker's right to confidentiality. This referral mechanism should be considered during EAP policymaking for those organizations where worker concern over breach of confidentiality appears to present serious problems to EAP utilization. On the other hand, this form of referral to EAP services can present problems with respect to (1) the inability of EAP staff and key management personnel to carefully monitor employees involved in exceptionally sensitive work activities (for example, the maintenance of nuclear weapons systems), (2) the inability of EAP staff to engage in problem assessment and personalized referral to selected counseling services, and (3) concerns over unjustified funding of unscrupulous practitioners based on claims of service to anonymous employees. For organizations that choose to adopt this mechanism as one of their acceptable forms of referral, the social worker is responsible for educating eligible workers to the various service providers with whom indirect referral coverage has been negotiated, including the dissemination of service rates, types of services, and problems for which these services are appropriate. The social worker also needs to be especially careful when developing a network of community referral agencies and practitioners to minimize through this process the likelihood of even the suspicion of fraudulent claims in the future for services provided to anonymous workers.

Each of the referral mechanisms described has its own unique advantages and problems. During the policymaking phase of EAP planning, the social worker needs to clarify what these are and help all members of the planning body select those referral mechanisms that best address the problems and unique dynamics of the host organization and its workforce. In most cases the use of a variety of referral mechanisms is preferred over reliance on only one. A greater variety of problems and people from a greater variety of strata in the organization are more likely to receive EAP attention through the use of multiple entry channels into the EAP.

WORKFORCE EDUCATION

As we have suggested, employee utilization of EAP service is, to a great extent, a function of the success of ongoing workforce education and supervisory training. Both activities involve the active dissemination of information, although the specific purposes, audiences, and dynamics vary. Let us consider workforce education first.

The primary purpose of employee education is that of familiarizing all intended target groups of the existence and potential benefits of employee assistance program services. A closely related purpose is that of "selling" the EAP or otherwise developing support for it. Higher levels of workforce knowledge of and support for EAP services are likely to result in a greater number of referrals (especially self, peer, and family types).

Workforce education involves both formal and informal elements. Formally, the social worker is responsible for disseminating information about EAP purpose, policies, programming, and procedures. It is especially important that the social worker emphasize the different routes available to access the EAP, the kinds of human problems for which assistance can be given, the protection of client confidentiality, and the fundamental role of the EAP as a helping resource for workers and other covered groups.

Informally, the EAP counselor must sell herself or himself to organizational employees in addition to selling the concept of an EAP. No matter how attractive the services or how impaired the employee, EAP staff who are distant, unknown, or untrusted magnify the psychological barriers to all types of referral. Consequently, the occupational social worker needs to intentionally market himself or herself to employees at all levels of the organization. It is best that the social worker be viewed as approachable, professionally competent, and ethical, committed to the EAP and the workforce it serves, and neutral insofar as management–union struggles are concerned. Frequent visits to various worksites, "brown-bag" seminars, intentional use of the company cafeteria, newsletters and photographs on company bulletin boards, and a host of other techniques can be used to establish and maintain rapport with employees. The fundamental logic of these actions remains constant: Referrals to the EAP will be facilitated as the psychological and informational barriers to accessing it are reduced.

SUPERVISORY TRAINING

Supervisory Tool

Workplace supervisors occupy a key role in the operation and success of EAPs. Consequently, it is important that supervisors have a broad understanding of the EAP and become familiar with all the referral mechanisms the EAP employs. Supervisors can identify employees who they know are experiencing key changes in behavior. Also, supervisors need to be trained to alert the EAP staff when crises occur. Supervisors are often the pipeline through which EAP staff can monitor the organization's emotional stability (Hofmann, 1984).

Unfortunately, supervisors have often been left without resources to do their jobs. The engineer who is now head of the section may be a wonderful person who feels enormously helpless when dealing with employees' personal problems. An EAP is the supervisor's best friend in providing help with such situations. Previously, millions of company hours have been lost to production because supervisors were doing all they could to help employees. Well-developed EAPs free supervisors to do the jobs for which they are trained. In order to promote this outcome, more extensive training for EAP utilization—over and beyond workforce education—is vital.

Training Orientation

In spoken and written comments about supervisory training for EAP utilization, one needs to express a consistent orientation. This orientation should emphasize four guidelines.

1. Supervisors need to be encouraged to acknowledge the existence of employee problems so that appropriate managerial assistance can be employed (Foster, 1982). Supervisors need to understand that their job is to deal with job performance issues. If appropriate performance supervision and training have occurred and thus the probable reason for an employee's impaired job performance is personal, the supervisor's job is not identifying the personal causes. Such is the task of the EAP staff.

2. Supervisors need to be guided to see EAP as a resource to assist them with their human resource management tasks. Many supervisors are experts in their field but untrained in managing people. EAP staff are available as consultants to guide supervisors in dealing with troubled employees.

3. Supervisors need to know the manner in which all potentially involved parties will relate. In the most helpful EAPs, the outside referral is collaborative. The clear message to an employee is: "We all, including you, are

working together to help you." While this guideline represents an ideal philosophical orientation, it also discourages some of the dynamics that tend to occur with specific types of troubled employees, especially with those who are chemically dependent. Supervisors must be told of the limits of collaboration, such as specific organizational and legal limits to the sharing of information about employees (Wolfe & Beckworth, 1982). Supervisors also need to be afforded the option of discussing how to deal with other workers should the employee's use of a referral source result in an extended absence from work.

4. Supervisors need to be supported in dealing with all troubled employees in a manner that accords with organizational policy and good management but that expresses a human respect for each employee. This implies such behavior as talking with an employee in a private space. Frisch and Leepson (1984) provide an overview of the basic respect principle.

A TRAINING MODEL

What follows is a general description of one training model. The process is described as though the EAP staff trainer is conducting the training. In some companies, labor and management leaders might also be involved (Archambault, Doran, Matlas, Nadolski, & Sutton-Wright, 1982).

Introduction

Acquaint participants with the experiential workshop format. Supervisors should be reminded that each of them have had troubled employees who required great amounts of time and emotional energy. These troubled employees have the potential to create major problems for whole work groups. An EAP provides supervisors with an option to deal with such employees. The fact also is that employees, including the supervisors, can contact the EAP themselves.

Symptoms in Troubled Employees

Divide the supervisors into small groups and ask them to develop lists of the symptoms commonly occurring in troubled employees. These lists are later shared with other training participants. Typically, five categories of symptoms emerge. These categories and examples of specific symptoms, stated in acronym form (SPAAR) are:

1. Safety and security hazards: carelessness, accidents, disregard of safety and security consequences, ignoring safety warnings.

2. Performance quality: forgetfulness, ignoring details, sloppiness, inconsistent work quality, lowered productivity, waste of previous work, missed deadlines, mistakes, poor judgment, lack of initiative, obsession with working.
3. Attitude: don't care, lack of enthusiasm, overreact, wide mood swings, blame others, passive-aggressiveness, angry, depressed, lack of energy.
4. Attendance and participation: frequent absences (especially Mondays and Fridays), late to work, leave early, long lunches, disappear at work, misses meetings, not dependable, isolated, vague excuses for illnesses.
5. Relationships: avoid people, can't get along, not cooperative, changes friends, others complain about employee.

Supervisory Attitudes

The use of the SPAAR model as a basis for discussion encourages supervisors to identify personal attitudes. These attitudes usually encompass extremes from wanting to help to just getting the job done; from feeling like everything that goes on with each employee should be known by the supervisor to wanting to know nothing; from wanting to ignore problems to wanting to solve the problems immediately; from fearing talking to a troubled employee to wanting to "shape 'em up"; and from feeling responsible for any poor work performed by a subordinate to being totally removed from any responsibility for inadequate job performance. EAP staff who conduct training need to convey to supervisors that all these attitudes may exist. Even more importantly, some of these attitudes and the behaviors associated with them can actually contribute to prolonging and intensifying employee performance problems. In short, supervisors can assume the role of "enabler" for troubled employees. How can this happen?

Supervisors can easily be deferred from taking appropriate steps to confront troubled employees through a host of counterproductive self-statements. Examples of such denials, rationalizations, and misconceptions include the following:

- "My employee can't be alcoholic (or addicted or troubled, etc.)!"
- "It's probably better just to leave things alone."
- "It's too much hassle to try to refer him (or her)."
- "If I refer this person to the EAP, it'll hurt his (or her) career."
- "I'm a manager. I should be able to handle this myself!"
- "What if I'm wrong? What if this person doesn't have a personal problem?"

These self-statements can lead to a variety of supervisory behaviors that permit or even promote the continuation of employee problems. Supervisors can ignore the problem, or they may make excuses for troubled employees, even covering up their mistakes or deteriorating performance. They may withhold standard and expected disciplinary actions and neglect to document work-related problems. Some supervisors may transfer an impaired employee to an easier, less demanding job and may lessen their expectations for the employee's performance generally. On the other hand, some managers may actually promote the impaired worker into a new position—frequently one with even greater power and responsibility—and hope that the employee's problem will go away with time. Unfortunately, none of these actions is likely to promote an adequate and longlasting solution to the employee's problems, especially if the employee is experiencing substance abuse or serious interpersonal or intrapersonal problems. Unwittingly, supervisors who take these courses of action permit the employee to avoid the consequences of impaired performance, give greater time for personal problems to develop, and fail to use the leverage they have to encourage the employee to seek professional help.

EAP trainers need to address these issues and the supervisors' feelings that give rise to them. One needs to stress that these feelings are natural, as is the motive to help people who are in need. However, it is important to emphasize that these self-statements are based on inaccuracies or on incomplete knowledge, and the actions they suggest may well exacerbate, rather than resolve, employee problems.

At this point in the session the organization's commitment to an employee assistance program can be renewed. Reinforce the idea that supervisors are expected to deal with job impairment and that the EAP can be a real friend because the program is an option to suggest to troubled employees. Deal with each of the counterproductive self-statements so they no longer immobilize supervisors. For example, point out the realities of progressive illnesses such as alcoholism in confronting the notion that "it's better to leave things alone." Emphasize the importance and protection of confidentiality in responding to the fear that "referral will hurt the employee's career." This approach on the part of the trainer can encourage supervisors to hunger for the answer to the question, "What can I do?"

Supervisory Guidelines

Supervisors need to be instructed in the use of the various types of EAP referrals. In a formal referral, four elements should occur in the discussion between a supervisor and employee:

1. Focus on the facts: the when, where, and what of job impairment, together with the consequences of continued problematic work performance. Be sure to document the performance problems.
2. Be certain any needed but lacking performance supervision is identified. Establish steps and a timetable for job improvement.
3. Suggest use of the employee assistance program.
4. Conduct needed supervisory follow-up sessions.

Supervisors should be cautioned not to attempt to diagnose problems, nor should they accuse, threaten, or degrade employees during the interview. In addition, supervisors should become familiar with the major don't's when referring troubled workers to employee assistance programs. These prohibitions include:

- Don't attempt to solve the problem.
- Don't argue with the employee.
- Don't be taken in by sympathy-evoking tactics.
- Don't cover up for a friend.
- Don't moralize.
- Don't discuss the employee's problems with others, except for those with a strict "right to know" (these people should be identifiable through the company's EAP policy).

If a supervisor has identified a troubled employee, the supervisor should be encouraged to consult with EAP staff. This alerts EAP staff to the situation and the time sequencing that the supervisor will use. It also enables EAP staff to provide support and consultation to the supervisor during the confrontation and referral process.

A useful approch to trying to ensure that supervisors are well prepared for sessions with employees is to encourage them to write a letter. The letter is presented to the employee at the start of or at the end of the supervisory conference. In training, the use of this letter is easily described through the use of a sample case situation. The use of a letter, together with the verbal discussion, is the best attempt a supervisor can make at clear communication with an employee (Groeneveld & Shain, 1985).

Sample Employee Situation

Paul White had worked for his company for 9 years, gradually assuming more and more responsibility and receiving several promotions. All the other information pertinent to the supervisor is presented in a sample letter to Paul, a copy of which would ordinarily also go to the EAP staff.

June 10, 1985

Mr. Paul White
Stone, Iowa

Dear Paul:

As you know from the discussion you and I have had, I am concerned with your work performance. I am writing this letter to you because of my high regard for you and for your contribution to the company. In the last few months it seems that your performance has increasingly shown signs of impairment. A summary of specific reasons for my concern includes:

1. On two occasions I have been notified that you violated company policy on entering the building at night. On the nights of May 5 and 27, you did not enter through the main entrance and did not sign in with security.
2. Your work quality has changed substantially in the last two months. On our last three reports, major data omissions occurred.
3. Your work attitude has altered. On several occasions I have heard you say your work doesn't matter to anyone anyway.
4. Your attendance at departmental meetings has been irregular. In the last two months you have missed all Monday meetings and only attended two Friday meetings. Your absence meant input from your unit was not received.
5. Relationships with co-workers have deteriorated. Kay Silver has told me no one in her unit is willing to work directly with you on joint projects because of your outbursts of anger. One of the company pilots has reported you were two hours late for a flight and offered no explanation to her. These behaviors are unusual and atypical of the valued worker you have always been.

Because of your drastic changes, I feel there may be some personal issues you are currently facing. Our company provides a resource, the Employee Assistance Program (EAP), to help employees whose job performance in the past has been fine and then gradually deteriorates, possibly because of a personal issue. I strongly suggest that you consider contacting the EAP to help you resolve whatever issues may be causing you concern at this time. The coordinator, Mary Green, has the job of helping you understand what may be interfering with your ability to do your job and then helping you locate resources that might deal directly with the issue. The program provides referral; it does not provide counseling.

The program is confidential; that is, the coordinator cannot and will not tell me anything you say unless you decide you want her to. Because this is a formal referral to the program, she will give me a yes or no answer as to whether or not you went to the program. Again, I urge you to contact the EAP at 999-1111 so you might obtain help in returning to your previous level of performance. If you make an appointment during working hours, you will need to advise me of the appointment. You will be given release time from your work to meet with the EAP coordinator. My request is that you call by June 17 to make the appointment. Specific details of the EAP are presented in the attached brochure.

Again, Paul, we need your performance to return to normal and I very much hope using the Employee Assistance Program will be of benefit to you in your work and personally.

Sincerely,

S. Brown

Employee Reactions

Group discussion after this case presentation emphasizes the SPAAR model to identify job impairment. It should also be mentioned that employees, when confronted, can respond in many ways. Anger, negotiation, projection, defusion, compliance, and thankfulness are typical responses. Encourage supervisors to list likely employee reactions and then to consider appropriate personal responses to each of these possible reactions. Remind them, however, to contact EAP staff should an employee become very upset or emotional.

Demonstrations

At this point in the training EAP staff might demonstrate the supervisory conference through a role play. A second alternative is the use of an appropriate training film or videotape that captures the process of referral.

Practice Situations

Divide the training group into smaller groups and have them role play situations such as the following:

1. One of the people you supervise talks about her personal problems. Your office has always tended to be a friendly place, and discussing personal lives is part of the normal behavior. Lately, you have noticed this employee talking excessively about her personal life. Also, the employee tends to do a good job one day and a poor job the next day. Often when you go to discuss a work issue with the employee she cannot be found.
2. Careless or hazardous handling of equipment and an "I-don't-care attitude" characterize this employee, whom you supervise. In the last 7 years he has been hurt 10 times at work and has been hospitalized twice for ulcers. The employee appears to goof off and then work to exhaustion to compensate.

3. You supervise an employee who is one of the friendliest people you have ever met. He is the life of any party and always had a good joke. Often the employee talks about humorous incidents in which he was drinking. Sometimes his dress is immaculate and at other times it is sloppy. Job performance is very good and the employee was always the one person you really trusted. Lately, the employee seems to be lying to you.

The trainer may need to have participants reemphasize some of the previously covered material after the role plays are concluded.

Organization's EAP

Explain the specifics of the organization's EAP, with a brief history and data on the prevalence of EAPs in general. Supervisors should be informed of program policies and procedures (Dunkin, 1982). Supervisors are frequently interested in the outside referral sources. Also, trainers should cover the future involvement of the supervisor after a referral is made. In some organizations, attempts at referral continue until the employee appears at the EAP (Mojer & Gaylord, 1984). The role of the EAP staff, especially in regard to follow-up procedures with the supervisor and employee, should be discussed.

Evaluation

At the conclusion of training, participants should be provided with evaluation forms and asked to complete the form. In addition, regular follow-up by the trainees should occur in 3 or 6 months.

CONSULTATION AND FEEDBACK

Although supervisory training is essential for effective and timely referral to an EAP, it will hardly prove to be adequate when supervisors are finally confronted with the necessity to refer workers to the program. At such times, honest and supportive communication between the EAP counselor and the supervisor is called for. Both parties benefit from such exchanges. The EAP staff member can receive important information about the employee's work performance history and recent behavior. The nuts and bolts of the referral can be worked out and the supervisor instructed in the specific behaviors now expected of him or her. In addition, the EAP counselor can deal with the supervisor as a person and can support her or him during what may be a stressful experience for the supervisor. Remember, troubled employees can unwittingly test the patience, judgment, and confidence of their supervisors. The latter may feel anger, hurt, guilt, isolation, low self-esteem, or confusion. The consultation phase of referral enables the EAP counselor to discuss with the supervisor the appropriateness of the referral (and thereby diffuse some of the supervisor's anxiety) as well as to assist the supervisor in dealing with whatever other feelings he or she may have. The counselor can also at this time remind the supervisor of the nature of worker–counselor confidentiality and emphasize the limited forms of feedback permitted under EAP policy. This can also be a time for the social worker to coach the supervisor—through role playing, perhaps—in the behaviors conducive to effective referral to the EAP.

The social worker's responsibilities in facilitating referrals do not end here. A supervisor may still need to know, for instance, if the employee has, in fact, contacted the EAP staff member, what can be expected of the employee's work performance in the days or weeks to come, or what job or scheduling modifications are appropriate. During this period of postreferral feedback, the EAP counselor can reinforce the supervisor's decision to refer the employee to the program. In addition, the counselor can instruct the supervisor in what to look for in any future encounters with impaired employees having similar performance problems. Within the constraints of confidentiality, supervisors can be taught basic principles of early identification and appropriate confrontation and referral of troubled employees. As supervisors are kept informed of their responsibilities and their contributions to the EAP and as they experience the benefits of the EAP as a management option, the seeds are sown for effective future referrals to the EAP.

EVALUATION

EAP staff need to examine the referrals to their programs, for much can be learned about program strengths and weaknesses from their volume and nature. Referral patterns can be examined in terms of referral mechanism use (i.e., self-referral, informal referral, formal referral, etc.). What are the proportions of the various referral types and do these proportions correspond to what one should expect of a given workforce, of the EAP referral policies in effect, and of the major thrusts(s) of the program itself? Are certain categories of covered individuals relying on particular referral mechanisms? Are some categories of employees underrepresented in EAP utilization? Are all departments or divisions of the organization participating equally in the use of EAP services? What problems have arisen to necessitate changes in program policies or procedures? How can difficulties be addressed through changes in the training phase for referral or in subsequent follow-up sessions with supervisors? What modifications seem appropriate for workforce education efforts? Consideration of such questions can lead EAP staff to important improvements in program penetration rates, improved policies and procedures, and more responsive service to managers and impaired workers alike.

MANAGING THE RELUCTANT REFERRAL

Attention to the principles and tasks associated with employee referral to EAPs can do much to improve the effectiveness and support that EAP staff experience. Alas, it is no guarantee of success. EAP staff may continue to experience the frustration of limited penetration rates, uneven support from management or union officials, and suspicion from individuals or groups of workers. In such cases, it is wise to remember and reemphasize the purpose and role of the EAP and of one's own roles and responsibilities as a part of it. One can rarely please everybody. Fortunately, truly effective EAPs do not require everyone's wholehearted and enthusiastic support.

On the other hand, one need not give up or abandon troubled workers to their own misery. Aggressive and innovative workforce education efforts can stimulate self, peer, family, and indirect referrals. Formal and informal supervisory referrals involve the EAP counselor in responsibilities toward both the troubled worker and that worker's supervisor. Even if the worker refuses to comply with the supervisor's wishes and refrains from contacting EAP staff, all is not lost. The occupational social worker should use the consultation process to support the supervisor's decision to encourage referral. One still has a concerned supervisor to deal with, one who may need support, advice, or coaching. The counselor can encourage the supervisor to maintain appropriate expectations for the employee's work performance, remind the supervisor of the importance of performance documentation, and warn of the seductive dangers of enabling future impaired performance. In addition, the EAP practitioner can encourage additional referrals from the supervisor, either of other workers having significant work-related problems or of the original employee at some future date. Throughout this process, the EAP professional demonstrates in action one of the fundamental truths of the employee assistance program concept, namely that EAPs exist to support both troubled workers and the people who work with them. When supervisors learn this truth, serious reliance on the EAP begins.

CONCLUSION

Employee assistance programs exist as resources for all organizational employees. EAPs are particularly useful to supervisors by providing an option for assisting with troubled employees. For supervisors, the quality of the training often directly relates to the usefulness of the EAP. With strong organizational commitment to EAPs and with the increasing numbers of trained EAP professionals, the potential impact of employee assistance programs is greater than ever.

REFERENCES

Archambault, R., Doran, R., Matlas, T., Nadolski, J., & Sutton-Wright, D. (1982). *Reaching out: A guide to EAP casefinding*. Troy, MI: Performance Resources Press.

Cohen, M. (1985). EAP training to integrate performance appraisal, evaluation systems, and problem-solving skills. In S. H. Klarreich, J. L. Francek, & C. E. Moore (Eds.), *The human resources management handbook*. New York: Praeger.

Dunkin, W. S. (1982). *The EAP manual*. New York: National Council on Alcoholism.

Foster, W. O. (1982). The human manager. *EAP Digest, 2*, 20–23.

Frisch, M. H., & Leepson, R. E. (1984). Handling the troubled employee: The referral process in review. *EAP Digest, 4*, 48–52.

Groeneveld, J., & Shain, M. (1985). The effect of corrective interview with alcohol dependent employees: A study of 37 supervisor-subordinate dyads. *Employee Assistance Quarterly, 1*, 63–73.

Hofmann, J. J. (1984). EAPs: Corporate ombudsmen? *EAP Digest, 5*, 53–55.

Mojer, G., & Gaylord, M. (1984). Successful referral of resistant employees within a corporate EAP. *EAP Digest, 4*, 20–23, 54.

Thoreson, R. W., Roberts, K. S., & Pascoe, E. A. (1984). The University of Missouri—Columbia employee assistance program: A case study of implementation and change. In R. W. Thoreson & E. P. Hosokawa (Eds.), *Employee assistance programs in higher education*. Springfield, IL: Charles C Thomas.

Warshaw, L. J. (1985). Management's view of the problem. In P. A. Carone, S. F. Yolles, L. W. Krinsky, & S. N. Kieffer (Eds.), *Mental health problems of workers and their families*. New York: Human Sciences Press.

Wolfe, F. B., & Beckworth, M. J. (1982). Confidentiality of employee records in employee assistance programs. *EAP Digest, 3*, 34–35.

Wrich, J. T. (1980). *The employee assistance program: Updated for the 1980s*. Center City, MN: Hazelden.

Wrich, J. T. (1985). Management's role in EAPs. In S. H. Klarreich, J. L. Francek, & C. E. Moore (Eds.), *The human resources management handbook*. New York: Praeger.

5 Time-Limited Crisis Therapy in the Workplace: An Eclectic Perspective

Howard J. Parad

Because crisis intervention concepts are often so variously used and even misused, let's start with a brief definition. *Crisis intervention* is a method for actively influencing psychosocial functioning during a period of disequilibrium. Its general goals are, first, to reduce the immediate impact of disruptive stressful events and, second, to help mobilize the psychosocial capabilities and resources of those directly affected (and often of the key persons in the work or social environment) for coping adaptively rather than maladaptively with the effects of stress. Human service professionals have been attracted to crisis intervention as a promising and apparently effective method of delivering rapid services to large numbers of individuals under stress. Such services have been offered in a variety of primary social work agencies, as well as in many host or secondary agencies and most recently in many Employee Assistance Programs (EAPs). As an immediate treatment response to stress, crisis intervention attends to (1) the precipitating stressors; (2) the client's perception of stress as meaningful and threatening to such life goals as job security, health, and maintenance of self-esteem; (3) the client's response to stress, characterized by signs of tension and disequilibrium; and (4) the resolution of the cognitive (thinking), affective (feeling), and behavioral (doing) tasks imposed by the crisis (Parad, 1965).

Whatever definition may be favored, there is a consensus that crisis intervention deals with phenomena that affect the biopsychosocial functioning of the individual, family, or work group to create a state of disruptive disequilibrium or crisis. Included are problems stemming from disordered communication patterns, distressed role networks (especially relevant in the workplace), and incongruent value orientations. The causes of these dysfunc-

Reprinted from "Time-Limited Crisis Therapy in the Workplace: An Eclectic Perspective" by Howard J. Parad, 1984. *Social Work Papers, 18,* 20–30. Copyright © 1984 by the University of Southern California. Adapted by permission.

tional phenomena are as varied as the individuals and work groups experiencing them and may be as complex as the work organizations and larger social systems in which these individuals and work groups carry on their day-to-day roles.

Brief therapy in general, and crisis intervention in particular, by industrial social workers in unions, businesses, government, and corporate settings is drawing increasing attention. Masi (1983, p. 56) has pointed out that most EAP cases are likely to be "short term and crisis oriented in nature." According to both practice wisdom and systematic research, crisis-oriented and planned short-term, task-centered, problem-solving approaches represent the preferred clinical social work services in the workplace.

WORKPLACE STRESSORS

Especially relevant to crisis intervention in the workplace are the findings of Holmes and his associates, who developed the Social Readjustment Rating Scale (SRRS) to measure the crisis inducing impact of commonly encountered life change events from death of a spouse, which has a point value of 100, to minor violations of the law, given a value of 11 (Holmes & Rahe, 1967). Examination of the components of the SRRS reveals 8 work-related stressors, extracted from the 43 life events utilized in the scale:

Life Event	Mean Value
Fired at work	47
Retirement	45
Business readjustment	39
Change to different line of work	36
Change in responsibilities at work	29
Spouse begins or stops work	26
Trouble with boss	23
Change in work hours or conditions	20

Holmes and his colleagues state that when the total point value of changes experienced in a given year exceeds 300, a dangerous or crisis situation has been reached. In one group studied, 80% of those whose scores exceeded 300 exhibited serious signs of depression, had heart attacks, or suffered other serious illnesses.

If, in addition to Holmes' life-event SRRS items, we included other commonly encountered workplace problems that lead to demoralization, boredom, accelerated work pressure, tension with fellow employees, and fear of layoffs, we would gain an even more realistic understanding of the workplace as a source of personal and family crises. Such a view, of course, does not in any way diminish the positive importance of work as a source of social support and psychic input as well as financial security to workers (Akabas & Kurzman, 1982).

BRIEF THERAPY AND CRISIS THERAPY

An important question, often a source of confusion, concerns the relationship between brief and crisis therapy. Not all brief therapy is crisis-oriented, nor is all crisis therapy brief. In a nationwide study of brief crisis-oriented therapies, six was the modal number of interviews. This study also indicated that in family service and children's psychiatric services, from 80% to 90% of all planned short-term cases were seen for up to 12 interviews over a period of 3 months or less (Parad & Parad, 1968).

What, then, is brief crisis therapy? Brief crisis intervention involves a specific number or approximate range of goal-focused interviews as part of a predetermined treatment arrangement involving from 1 to 12 or more interviews. The approach I favor, combining crisis and planned short-term task-centered therapies (PSTT), includes three components:

1. Immediate or early accessibility at the time of the client's request (preferably within 24 to 72 hours of the "cry for help").
2. Utilization of time limits; that is, a specific number or approximate range of interviews or weeks of treatment, determined at intake.
3. Focused attention to the elements of the crisis configuration; that is, the nature of the precipitating event that disturbed the client's psychosocial equilibrium; the client's perception of that event as threatening to his life goals; the client's response to that event (characterized by the signs of crisis disequilibrium, namely, changes in cognitive, behavioral, and affective patterns); and the resolution of the crisis in the course of which the worker steers the client toward adaptive solutions. By definition, then, the approach avoids even short waiting lists, is premised on the early specification of realistic goals, and involves the worker in an active, outreaching, problem-solving, therapeutic stance.

Using an eclectic framework, this problem-solving action therapy provides a direct impact on the client's performance in the workplace as well as on his social functioning in other areas where there are focal problems. Because the counselor's basic task is to help the client change patterns that impede effective functioning on or off the job, he will find it helpful to develop a prudently eclectic approach that attends to the three domains of human functioning, namely, feeling, thinking, and doing. Thus, the counselor helps the client to mobilize the resources that will unblock and enhance his performance. While some authors may refer pejoratively to eclecticism, I believe that it is a fact of the therapist's daily professional life (Jayarante, 1978; Lazarus, 1976). Whatever theoretical persuasions they may espouse, in practice most brief-therapy and crisis-intervention workers are probably eclectic.

More specifically, theory, practice wisdom, and research point to eight familiar principles to guide the crisis counselor in doing brief therapy in the workplace:

1. It is important to select a focal problem on which to concentrate. Many authors have stressed that if the worker and client together cannot define a specific workable problem, it is highly unlikely that constructive help can be offered. The worker must differentiate a *general* task (for example, to improve communication between husband and wife) from an *operational* task (for example, an explicit contract between husband and wife specifying that they will talk with each other each evening for at least 15 minutes in order to maintain an open communicative relationship) (Reid & Epstein, 1972).

2. PSTT crisis intervention assumes that the core conditions originally postulated by Rogers and later investigated by Truax (namely, the worker's positive regard for the client, his nonpossessive warmth, his empathic response, and genuine congruence) are necessary but not sufficient conditions for the success of therapy (Truax & Carkhuff, 1967).

3. The worker emphasizes the client's need to experience the successful accomplishment of tasks in order to feel competent, thereby gaining mastery, and gradually increasing self-esteem and concurrently the ability to cope with future stress in an adaptive rather than a maladaptive manner.

4. PSTT in the workplace does not take place in a resource vacuum. Many social and health resources, including the availability of legal, medical, dental, day care, and housekeeping, are necessary to assist with task fulfillment. The worker is constantly attuned to the importance of support groups both in the workplace and in the community and should know the value of such self-help groups as Alcoholics Anonymous, Overeaters Anonymous, Parents Anonymous, and others in which clients help each other with problems of addictive behaviors and of daily living.

5. Among the specific techniques used are anticipatory guidance and role plays to help the client rehearse how he will cope with difficult situations. These may include talking with a supervisor, mediating conflict with a fellow worker, dealing with a personal or family problem that may impede work performance, and homework assignments to help the client complete specific tasks. Since there is a premium on the utilization of time, it makes sense

for the client to carry out such between-session assignments as investigating resources, conducting clarifying discussions with significant others, gathering information, inviting others to the interview situation, and taking training courses. Some clients are able to keep diaries in which they record critical incidents. Such report writing heightens the client's self-observation and self-awareness, thus accelerating his progress in treatment.

6. Session by session the worker monitors the outcome of the client's efforts at task fulfillment, reinforcing the client's positive achievements and exploring obstacles.

7. Throughout the treatment encounter, the worker must give systematic attention to the agreed-upon tasks in order to stay on course. The worker must also maintain an open, empathetic, and responsive stance toward the client, lest in zeal to be goal-focused the worker is overly rigid. Hence, the worker must give balanced attention to both the systematic and responsive elements of the communication process (Reid, 1972).

8. Preplanned follow-up interviews are fundamental to the responsible delivery of crisis-oriented PSST services in the workplace. Follow-up interviews, whether by phone or in person, should be planned during the initial structuring of the treatment contract in order that the worker may convey to the client a continuing interest in the client's well-being after sessions have terminated. Follow-up interviews provide an opportunity to give the client a "booster shot," thus encouraging the client's continued efforts at mastery. Increments in the client's self-esteem may explain the familiar observation that brief therapy often stimulates a growth process, the positive ripple effects of which may eddy out long after the last session has been completed. Follow-up interviews also provide valuable feedback information to the worker concerning the effectiveness of the service. Moreover, follow-up provides a professional ethical safeguard in the event that the worker, in choosing a more or less arbitrary number of interviews, may need to recontract with the client for another brief period of treatment if insufficient help had been offered. Experience shows that, while follow-up interviews are feared by some to encourage dependency and to encourage clients who might otherwise not return for treatment to return—thus increasing costs—these side effects are more feared than actually observed. Many clinicians plan their follow-up sessions in advance without experiencing any of the disastrous consequences predicted by Mann (1973).

ECLECTICISM

The following 5 steps provide guidelines for crisis counseling within a time-limited framework (Parad, Selby, & Quinlan, 1976). The eclectic approach outlined below is an amalgam of ego psychological, behavioral, task-centered, and problem-solving theories.

Step I: The search for the precipitating event and its meaning to the client.

1. When did the discomfort begin, or when did the client start feeling worse? Is the client self-referred or referred by a fellow worker or supervisor?
2. What recent change has occurred that represented a threat to instinctual needs or a threatened or actual loss of a significant role or relationship? How does the client interpret this event?
3. What reminders have there been of a previous situation that was upsetting?
4. Why is the client coming for help now? What is the presenting problem (preferably in the client's own words)?
5. What nonverbal cues as to affect and the impact of current distress does the client exhibit in discussion of recent and past events?

This line of inquiry provides clues for identifying the client's personal or social dilemma: the conflict situation with which he is struggling and that has thrown him into a crisis. Findings from this inquiry enable the counselor to formulate the dilemma for the client; that is, to make explicit the problem that is creating distress and confusion.

Step II: The search for coping means that are utilized by the client.

1. What did the client try to do to cope with the stress produced by the precipitating event?
2. What means of coping has the client used in the past in similar situations?
3. Where is the lack of "fit" between the particular dilemma (problem-to-be-solved) and the coping means the client has employed?

This line of inquiry helps the client and worker to identify what has been tried by way of resolving the problem and what has not worked.

Step III: The search for alternative ways of coping that might better fit the current situation.

1. What different approaches to modifying the problem might be feasible to try?
2. What outside resources might be needed and tapped for helping to resolve the dilemma?
3. What new plan for action can be tested now?
4. How can we help the client toward early termination?

This line of inquiry helps the client to mobilize new problem solving efforts and to take action on the basis of consideration of new alternatives.

Step IV: Review and support of client's efforts to cope in new ways: evaluation of results.

1. What worked, and what did not work, in the client's experimentation with new approaches to solving the problem?
2. What additional efforts might pay off?
3. When does the client begin to show signs of relief, improved ego functioning, and readiness to carry on alone?

Step V: Follow-up (prearranged prior to termination).

1. How is the client now coping with the original presenting problem?
2. Does the client recall what worked in previous coping strategies that may have been used in Steps III and IV above? Counselor offers "booster-shot" reinforcement.
3. What new coping efforts might a client use to supplement his familiar ways of problem solving? What EAP, self-help, family, and community resources might be used to help the client deal with her original presenting problem or new problems that may have arisen?
4. Is it appropriate to recontract with the client for another brief period of treatment?

As previously indicated, caring and systematic preplanned follow-up sessions in person or, if that is not feasible, by phone, serve four purposes: (1) they give the client assurance of the worker's continued interest in his well-being; (2) they provide information on the client's perceptions of the effectiveness of the service; (3) they afford an ethical safeguard against the possibility that the time limits used in therapy, more or less arbitrarily chosen, may be insufficient to help the client with his problem; (4) they give the counselor yet another opportunity to reinforce the client's ongoing efforts at adaptation, problem solving, and mastery through direct discussion or by making referrals to other community services. Such reinforcement and expression of the worker's encouragement and confidence may well avoid regression in the client's functioning at work or in the community.

Case Example I

Linda, a bright, slightly overweight, 29-year-old technician was referred to the EAP by a fellow employee who was concerned about her increasing lack of concentration on the job. Linda emphasized that her job was not in jeopardy, but she was worried that it might be if she continued to be as preoccupied as she had been the last week or so, ever since she and her fiance, Herb, had started to quarrel. In fact, she sobbed, their relationship was a "mess," and she and Herb might not go through with their plans to get married in 5 months.

A search for the precipitating event revealed that about 10 days earlier Linda had a "crazy fling" with another man while attending a weekend conference with fellow technicians from the plant. Her friend, Marian, who had also attended the conference, told Linda she was acting crazy. That's why Linda requested counseling. Further exploration indicated that a few weeks ago Linda had loaned almost $1,000 to Herb, ostensibly to help him buy a new car on the installment plan. Just before leaving for the conference, Linda learned that Herb had gone to Las Vegas, gambled, and lost her money as well as some of his own. Linda was furious. Herb, as usual, asked for another chance, stating that he had gambled because the money Linda loaned him was not enough for a down payment on the car he wanted.

With support and focused questions from the counselor, Linda tearfully said that her problem with Herb was similar to problems she had experienced with other men because of her tendency to rescue and mother them. She had to make a decision! Should she break off her engagement with Herb? She knew she could no longer avoid her problem with him. She hesitantly said that she was going to be 30 years old in 7 months; she feared she might be too old for marriage if she didn't get married soon—hence her sense of urgency.

Linda agreed to contract for eight sessions of therapy; they focused on helping Linda to come to a decision about Herb, as well as to explore why she had such a low opinion of herself even though her friends—as well as her supervisor and fellow workers—considered her personable, bright, and attractive, especially if she lost just a few pounds.

Linda was responsive in her noontime sessions. In her own insightful words, she was having a "crisis of self-esteem." Instead of "hiding" her problems with Herb (denial had been her customary coping device), she had several long talks with Herb about reasons for her dissatisfaction with their relationship. However, Herb continued to "tell stories and play games," so after her fourth session, Linda returned her engagement ring and "surprised" herself by feeling more relieved than sad. Herb did not want to undertake counseling for himself.

Anticipating that she would soon start dating other men, Linda agreed to join an EAP-sponsored weight-reduction group, although she struggled with her initial resistance to be weighed by the nurse.

With her counselor's active encouragement, Linda began to explore some of the reasons for her unrealistically low sense of self worth. When the counselor pointed out her tendency to identify with her mother's depressive tendencies, Linda was stunned. After absorbing the worker's comment, she laughingly stated she was having an "Aha!" response—the counselor was on target.

In the follow-up session, scheduled 1 month after the eighth session, Linda reported that she was "through with Herb," was "still relieved," had "slowly" begun to lose weight, and was occasionally dating other men. She had followed through on the suggestion that she talk more openly with her mother about the possibility of mother's getting therapy for her depression. Two months later, Linda called the counselor to share the news that she had just been promoted to the position of assistant supervisor in her department.

TOWARD AN INTERACTIONAL FRAMEWORK

The social worker in the workplace has unique opportunities for conjoint interviews with fellow workers, supervisors, selected family members, and significant others.

Case Example II

Pragmatically, it makes sense to try to include those who are involved in a work-related problem to contribute toward its solution. The importance of such an interactional crisis-oriented approach is illustrated in the case of the D family.

The D family consisted of Mr. D, a 31-year-old installation technician, Mrs. D, a 29-year-old homemaker, and their two children, Ralph, 7, and Mary, 4. An ongoing problem became dramatically aggravated when Ralph became terminally ill and Mr. D's work attendance became spotty. Indicating that his absenteeism was a serious problem and his job was at risk, Mr. D's supervisor referred him to the EAP counselor on an emergency basis.

In the initial interview with Mr. D, it became immediately clear that he was suffering tremendously. His grief and pain overwhelmed his personal, family, and work life. He needed a flexible work schedule to enable him to visit his son and to be with his family. He desperately needed to maintain his job for the money and a sense of belonging. Work was a place where he could escape from the imminent reality of his son's impending death. Because of heavy work pressures, his supervisor and unit manager were increasingly intolerant of his absences.

While the counselor deeply felt his pain, she also realized that he would have to make some tough decisions as to when to visit his son during the day at the hospital, when to be with his wife and daughter, and when to go to work. Moreover, he would obviously have to alert his supervisor in advance when he needed to be away—instead of just not showing up. As client and counselor talked, Mr. D began to see the company's perspective as well as his own. The counselor obtained a signed release to talk with Mr. D's supervisor and unit manager on his behalf and to invite them to a brief meeting to attempt to resolve the problem. At the meeting (attended by Mr. D, his supervisor, and unit manager, and the counselor) two related goals were achieved: First, the supervisor and manager were alerted to the actual situation facing Mr. D; they were sensitized to his anguish, isolation, and his feelings about his inability to relieve Ralph of his pain and prevent his death. Second, the counselor assured the supervisor and manager that she would be available to assist Mr. D in any further problems and that Mr. D would communicate with them openly in the future but that he would of course be with his son and family when the end came.

This meeting was successful in assisting management to become more sensitive to an employee's crisis while respecting the best interests of the company. The counselor's suggestion that Mr. D be temporarily assigned to another position because climbing in communication areas would be hazardous for him at this time was rejected by Mr. D because he wanted to be with his buddies at work, and a job transfer was more than he could bear at this difficult time. As it turned out, Mr. D's climbing partners took the situation in hand; they climbed while Mr. D did the ground work, a division of labor that seemed to satisfy all concerned. In addition, the counselor had two conjoint interviews with Mr. and Mrs. D, plus a visit to the hospital with Mrs. D to see Ralph. Mr. D's wish to have further interviews on an as-needed basis only was respected. The counselor maintained regular telephone contact with Mrs. D and helped answer her questions about her wish to help Mr. D and their daughter Mary deal with Ralph's illness and subsequent death. Feedback from management and the family indicated that the contacts were helpful in supporting Mr. and Mrs. D during the period following Ralph's death.

Still to be tested in the workplace are the exciting possibilities for group crisis counseling, which has been found to be an effective and economic medium for helping people experiencing similar life or work crises in a variety of mental health settings (Strickler & Allgeyer, 1967).

Increasing research evidence indicates that interactional therapies, including couple, family, and small-group approaches, are generally more effective in dealing with the client's problems in social living than are purely individual-centered approaches (Gurman & Kniskern, 1981).

EMERGING RATIONALES FOR CRISIS INTERVENTION IN THE WORKPLACE

Several interrelated professional developments have contributed to the growing interest in brief crisis intervention in industrial settings. These include research concerning stress reduction and coping behavior in the workplace; the short-term nature of most industrial counseling experiences; the fact that many persons seen in industrial settings are experiencing moderate or extreme stress and are therefore responsive to here-and-now interventions; the increasing use of time-limited task-oriented problem solving in the workplace (Taylor, 1977; Weissman, 1977); recurrent personnel and financial constraints, reflected in the current interest in health care cost containment; the reluctance of many insurance companies to reimburse industrial subscribers for long-term treatment; continued emphasis on accountability and related cost/benefit issues; the relevance of action-oriented crisis intervention services to certain ethnic groups; the contributions of the newer behavioral, humanistic, and other eclectic perspectives regarding problem solving and coping repertoires (Janis, 1983); and of course the accelerated increase in a variety of brief and emergency therapies (Bellak & Siegel, 1983; Budman, 1981).

It is clear, then, that social workers in industrial settings are increasingly turning to time-limited and crisis-oriented therapy as a means of helping to solve problems in psychosocial functioning. The frequency with which papers on brief therapy and stress-related phenomena are presented at meetings of personnel concerned with EAPs, the growing number of university and continuing education courses on brief therapy and crisis intervention, and the evident congeniality of both crisis-oriented and time-limited therapies with the principles associated with optimal prevention and remedial mental health care all combine to indicate that short-term crisis therapy is becoming firmly established. Also important to the brief crisis therapy approach is the burgeoning interest in interactional approaches, including work-related support networks and the possibilities of crisis group counseling in work settings. Thus, a rich variety of professional developments has begun to influence industrial social workers and to expand their thinking about the crisis experience and the use of short-term eclectic crisis therapy as a powerful therapeutic tool.

REFERENCES

Akabas, S., & Kurzman, P. (Eds.). (1982). *Work, workers, and work organizations.* Englewood Cliffs, NJ: Prentice-Hall.

Bellak, L., & Siegel, H. (1983). *Handbook of intensive brief and emergency psychotherapy.* Larchmont, NY: CPS.

Budman, S. (Ed.). (1981). *Forms of brief therapy.* New York: Guilford.

Gurman, A., & Kniskern, D. (Eds.). (1981). *Handbook of family therapy.* New York: Brunner/Mazel.

Holmes, T., & Rahe, R. (1967). The social readjustment rating scale. *Journal of Psychosomatic Research, 11.*

Janis, I. (1983). *Short-term counseling guidelines based on recent research.* New Haven: Yale University Press.

Jayarante, S. (1978). A study of clinical eclecticism. *Social Service Review, 52.*

Lazarus, A. (Ed.). (1976). *Multimodal behavior therapy.* New York: Springer Publishing Company.

Mann, J. (1973). *Time-limited psychotherapy.* Cambridge, MA: Harvard University Press.

Masi, D. (1983). *Human services in industry.* Lexington, MA: Heath.

Parad, H. (Ed.). (1965). *Crisis intervention: Selected readings.* New York: Family Service Association of America.

Parad, H., & Parad, L. (1968). A study of crisis-oriented planned short-term treatment. *Social Casework, 49.*

Parad, H., Selby, L., & Quinlan, J. (1976). Crisis intervention with families and groups. In R. Roberts & H. Northern (Eds.), *Theories of social work with groups.* New York: Columbia University Press.

Reid, W., & Epstein, L. (1972). *Task-centered casework.* New York: Columbia University Press.

Reid, W., & Epstein, L. (Eds.). (1977). *Task-centered practice*. New York: Columbia
    University Press.
Strickler, M., & Allgeyer, J. (1967). The crisis group: A new application of crisis
    theory. *Social Work, 12*.
Taylor, C. (1977). Counseling in a service industry. In W. Reid & L. Epstein (Eds.),
    Task-centered practice. New York: Columbia University Press.
Truax, C., & Carkhuff, R. (1967). *Toward effective counseling and psychotherapy*.
    Chicago: Aldine.
Weissman, A. (1977). In the steel industry. In W. Reid & L. Epstein (Eds.),
    Task-centered practice. New York: Columbia University Press.

6 Drunk, Drugged, and on the Job

Diana M. DiNitto

CHEMICAL DEPENDENCY

The most widely abused drug in the United States is alcohol. This chapter concerns alcohol abuse as well as the abuse of other psychoactive drugs, including illegal, prescription, and over-the-counter drugs. In the United States today, frequently abused illegal drugs include marijuana, cocaine, and heroin. New forms of illegal psychoactive drugs are reaching users with alarming frequency. "Crack" is a potent, highly addictive, but inexpensive form of cocaine that has recently caused the death of two prominent young athletes. Abused prescription drugs include minor tranquilizers such as diazepam (Valium) and chlordiazepoxide (Librium). Barbiturates are depressant drugs that are often prescribed as sleeping pills, and amphetamines are stimulants (often referred to as "speed") that can be obtained by prescription but are frequently obtained illegally. Among the most popular of the abused over-the-counter (OTC) drugs are cold remedies (including cough preparations), many of which contain alcohol. Others are those used to suppress appetite and those used to induce sleep. Dual addiction or polydrug abuse, in which an individual abuses more than one drug, is common today. The number of polydrug abusers is not known, but many people believe that such cases are more typical than atypical. Royce (1981) notes that "especially among women and youth, mixing alcohol with other drugs is most common" (p. 7).

In this chapter the term *chemical dependency* is used to mean the repeated use of one or more of the types of drugs mentioned above that results in

The author expresses thanks to Clayton Shorkey, Albert Mata, and Ann Starr for their comments on this manuscript and to the University Research Institute of the University of Texas at Austin for support in the development of this chapter.

serious life problems for the individual, including family, job, health, legal, and social problems.[1] Alcohol abusers are able to purchase their drug legally, while cocaine abusers are committing an illegal act in purchasing their drugs. However, in this chapter we assume that there is a good deal of similarity among chemically dependent individuals, regardless of their "drug of choice," and that many chemically dependent individuals respond to similar types of treatment (see Smith & Wesson, 1985).

CHEMICAL DEPENDENCY AND THE HELPING PROFESSIONS

Social workers have long recognized the role alcoholism plays in family disruption. During the late 1800s, the social work prototypes of the Charity Organization Society expressed concern about the problems posed by intemperance. But until recently, social workers and other helping professionals (e.g., physicians, nurses, and psychologists) were criticized for their lack of interest in chemical dependency treatment. Coursework on alcoholism and other drug abuse in professional education programs was noticeably lacking.

Beginning in the 1930s, many events occurred to change professional thinking about alcoholism. Alcoholics Anonymous (AA) was founded. The Yale Center, now the Rutgers Center on Alcohol Studies, was established. In the 1940s, the National Council on Alcoholism (NCA) was formed. The research of E. M. Jellinek contributed greatly to an understanding of the phenomenon of alcoholism. Social workers also contributed to the knowledge base needed to assist alcoholics and their families. Margaret Bailey studied case-finding of alcoholics through her work at the NCA, Margaret Cork began treating children of alcoholics through the Addiction Research Foundation in Toronto, and Gladys Price addressed the wives of alcoholics through the Washingtonian Center (Lewis, 1977). In the 1950s, the World Health Organization and the American Medical Association recognized the disease concept of alcoholism. In 1970 the federal government established the National Institute on Alcohol Abuse and Alcoholism, which has funded training, research, and treatment efforts that have prompted more helping professionals to work with alcoholic clients and their families. Concern about the abuse of other drugs resulted in the establishment of the National Institute on Drug Abuse. Self-help groups such as Narcotics Anonymous also developed to help addicts remain drug-free.

In this chapter we focus on the types of individuals affected by chemical

[1]For further elaboration on definitions of problem drinking and alcoholism see Plaut (1967, pp. 37–41) and Davies (1976). See Tarter and Sugerman (1976) and Estes and Heinemann (1982) for introductory texts on alcoholism and Ray (1973) for an introductory text on a variety of abused drugs.

dependency in the workplace, the role of occupational social workers in identification and referral, and the types of treatment resources available to aid chemically dependent individuals and their families in recovery.

CHEMICAL DEPENDENCY AT THE WORKPLACE

Chemical dependency manifests itself in the workplace in four ways. First, employees may themselves be chemically dependent. Second, an employee may be affected by a significant other (spouse, child, parent, or other loved one) who is chemically dependent. Third, an employee may be an adult child of a chemically dependent parent(s). Fourth, employees may be selling and using drugs at the worksite.

Chemically Dependent Employees

The characteristics exhibited by troubled employees on the job are presented in Figure 6-1, which relates job performance problems to the four stages of alcoholism.[2] Similar work-related problems develop with the abuse of other drugs. In the early phase, the alcoholic drinks to relieve tension. Tolerance to alcohol builds and the alcoholic must drink more to obtain the same effect. Employees frequently come in late and leave early. Lying is not uncommon, and the employee becomes increasingly sensitive to criticism. Job performance begins to deteriorate through missed deadlines and mistakes. In the middle stage the alcoholic does more drinking in private. Guilt about excessive drinking mounts. Absenteeism increases, job performance deteriorates further, and inability to get along with co-workers is evident. In the late-middle and late phases, job peformance is incompetent; financial and medical problems mount; absences increase due to prolonged drinking bouts and hospitalizations.

Significant Others

The employee involved with a chemically dependent loved one may also show signs of impaired job performance. Family members often act as enablers and co-dependents. Enablers unwittingly help the chemically dependent individual to continue abusing drugs by covering up. They call in to the office saying their spouse is sick. They make the abuser promise he or she will never get drunk or high again. But all their efforts fail. As a result of enabling, the employee becomes a co-dependent. Co-dependents may not

[2]These four phases are generally thought of as comprising the disease model of alcoholism. For more information on the disease concept see Jellinek (1960) and Johnson (1980). For a discussion of some challenges to the traditional disease model see Pattison, Sobell, and Sobell (1977).

HOW A CHEMICALLY DEPENDENT EMPLOYEE BEHAVES

BEHAVIOR	EFFICIENCY	CRISIS POINTS DURING DETERIORATION	VISIBLE SIGNS
EARLY PHASE Drinks to relieve tension. Alcohol tolerance increases. Blackouts (memory blanks). Lies about drinking habits.	90%		Late (after lunch). Leaves job early. Absent from office. Fellow workers complain. Overreacts to real or imagined criticism. Complains of not feeling well. Lies. Misses deadlines. Mistakes through inattention or poor judgment. Decreased efficiency.
MIDDLE PHASE Surreptitious drinks. Guilt about drinking. Tremors during hangovers. Loss of interest.	75%	CRITICISM FROM BOSS FAMILY PROBLEMS LOSS OF JOB ADVANCEMENT FINANCIAL PROBLEMS, e.g. WAGE GARNISHMENT WARNING FROM BOSS	Frequent days off for vague ailments or implausible reasons. Statements become undependable. Begins to avoid associates. Borrows money from co-workers. Exaggerates work accomplishments. Hospitalized more than average. Repeated minor injuries on and off job. Unreasonable resentment. General deterioration. Spasmodic work pace. Attention wanders, lack of concentration.

SUPERVISOR'S EVALUATION

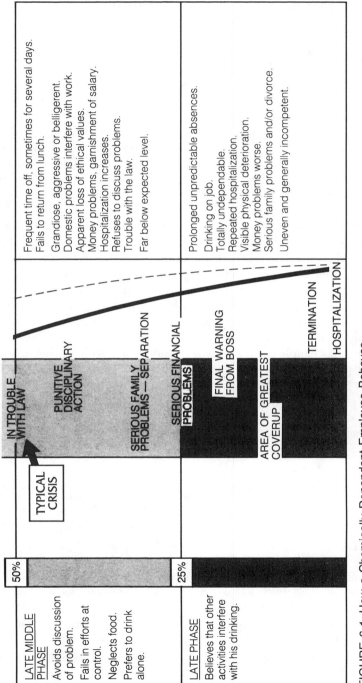

FIGURE 6-1 How a Chemically Dependent Employee Behaves

Reprinted from *Counseling on Alcoholism and Related Disorders* by Doyle Lindley, p. 59. Copyright © 1967 by Doyle Lindley. Adapted by permission.

abuse drugs themselves, but at home and at work they behave in ways very similar to the chemically dependent individual. They may become depressed and fail to show up for work or fail to produce as much on the job. They may utilize all their sick and vacation leave staying at home nursing a sick partner, parent, or child.

Adult Children

Adult children of chemically dependent parents can pose a problem in the workplace. The source of their difficulties is often overlooked. They may have no contact with their parents, but they can still be affected. Many of these adult children continue to harbor poor self-concepts and hidden feelings of guilt and resentment. Growing up, children of alcoholics take on certain roles: hero, lost child, scapegoat, mascot (Wegschieder, 1976, 1981). The family hero is the child who excelled but was never able to change the chemically dependent parent no matter how well the child did. As an adult, this child is likely to become a workaholic, always striving for perfection. The lost child is often withdrawn, receives little attention, and may become an adult with little excitement for life. The scapegoat receives the blame for family problems, gets in trouble outside of the home, and may grow up to be the office troublemaker. Mascots are cute children who take the heat off emotionally trying situations and provide comic relief for the family. As adults, they may handle stress poorly. Inability to deal with conflict, inability to discuss problems, lack of trust, and other problems that develop in a chemically dependent home can spill over into the workplace. Although these issues are not likely to be identified as chemical dependency problems in employment settings, a careful assessment by the occupational social worker can help lead the troubled employee to the right source of assistance.

Dealers and Users

The sale and use of illegal drugs at work is a mounting problem. General Dynamics has fired 52 workers, stating that "the sale of drugs and use of drugs on company property is an offense that results in termination" ("Company Fires 52," 1985). And in a survey of calls to a toll-free national cocaine hotline, "seventy five percent of callers said they used cocaine on the job and were late or had missed work because of cocaine use; half said they sold the drug there; one-fourth said they had lost a job because of cocaine use" (DeQuine, 1985). Although this chapter is primarily concerned with the first three types of chemical dependency problems discussed here, drug use and sale at the worksite have obvious implications for the health and safety of workers and the quality and quantity of work produced. Drug abuse can add to other workplace problems such as fraud and embezzlement, which can result when an employee is attempting to maintain a high-cost drug habit like that of cocaine (DeQuine, 1985). In the wake of growing concern about drugs at work, some companies are making serious attempts to ferret out the problem, including the use of employee urinalysis and drug-sniffing dogs (Castro, 1986).

WOMEN AND CHEMICAL DEPENDENCY IN THE WORKPLACE

Of the 10 million adult alcoholics and alcohol abusers in the United States, National Institute on Alcohol Abuse and Alcoholism (NIAAA) (1978), estimates indicate that at least one fourth are women (see Gomberg, 1976, 1982). There is conflicting information on the chemical dependency problems of women in the workplace. P. B. Johnson (1982) reported that among women who drink, those who were both employed and married were more likely to experience alcohol-related problems than were married women who did not work outside the home and single women who worked outside the home. However, Wilsnack, Wilsnack, and Klassen (1984/1985) found no significant differences in heavy drinking between married women who did and did not work outside the home, but they did find that never-married women who worked full-time were especially likely to be moderate or heavy drinkers. A Johns Hopkins study (Trost, 1984) indicated that female executives were less likely to be heavy drinkers than were their male counterparts, but younger women were conspicuous among the heavy drinkers.

Evidence indicates that women are quite susceptible to the effects of alcohol (see Shaw, 1980). Since women's body weights are generally lower than men's, and since women have less water content in their bodies, their blood alcohol levels are usually higher than men's after consuming the same amount of alcohol. Women may also find it difficult to predict the extent to which alcohol will effect them at any given time because their reaction to alcohol appears to be dependent on the phases of the menstrual cycle (Jones & Jones, 1976). In the days just prior to menstruation, effects from alcohol seem to be greatest. Women also appear to be more susceptible to liver disease than are men (Spain, 1945). The quantity of alcohol consumed may, therefore, not be a good indication of the extent of a woman's drinking problem. Women may consume less alcohol than men but still experience serious alcohol-related problems.

There are many similarities between the drinking problems of men and women, but researchers have identified some differences in the patterns of drinking between male and female alcoholics. For example, female alcoholics may do less bender drinking and have fewer blackouts (periods during which they were conscious but were later unable to recall events), but they make more suicide attempts than men (Rimmer, Pitts, Reich, & Winokur,

1971). Female alcoholics drink alone more often than do men (see Vourakis, 1983, for a discussion of this issue), and they are more likely than are men to associate the onset of heavy drinking with a traumatic life event such as the death of a loved one or a divorce (see Curlee, 1970; Gomberg, 1976; Wilsnack, 1982). Women may also have a tendency called the "telescoping effect" to develop a drinking problem in a shorter period of time than do men (see Beckman, 1976; Gomberg, 1982).

Absenteeism, low productivity, and inability to get along with co-workers are recognized indicators of impaired job performance, but according to Kurtz, Googins, and Williams (1980), supervisors often fail to use these indicators to identify troubled employees, and employees often manage to hold on to jobs in spite of alcohol abuse. For example, in a study of a small sample of first- and second-level female managers recovering from alcohol abuse, Kleeman and Googins (1983) note that although these women believed they were not working up to par, they considered their work "acceptable" and most received satisfactory performance evaluations for "several years" while their drinking was a problem. To the extent that women occupy jobs where tasks are repetitive and have already been sufficiently mastered, the effects of chemical dependency might be even easier to mask.

Although women comprise 43.5% of the workforce ("Blue Collars are Turning Pink," 1984), they are underrepresented as referrals in employee assistance programs (Roy, 1983). In an effort to determine why, the NIAAA funded three research studies (Solomon, 1983). Each revealed that supervisors were reluctant to confront chemically dependent women. Supervisors and co-workers can easily fall into the role of enablers. They are frequently better at covering up than confronting. In an effort to increase self-initiated and supervisor-initiated referrals of chemically dependent women to EAPs, the researchers tried a number of techniques. These included voluntary women's occupational groups in which problems associated with alcoholism were discussed (Reichman, 1983); publicity, audiovisual presentations, brief educational presentations, and a resource directory for employees (Schuft, 1983); and employee orientation (Cahill, 1983). All included supervisory training. Although none of the methods produced significant increases in referrals (Roy, 1983), additional effort is needed to promote intervention at the workplace. "Many women are single parents supporting families in whole or in part; many are economically disadvantaged and cannot afford to lose even a minimum wage job, and others are so personally invested in their work that the loss of a job is a very serious consequence" (DiNitto, Starr & Smith, 1986, p. 59).

Some believe that female alcoholics exhibit more psychological pathology and are more difficult to treat than their male counterparts (see Curlee, 1970 for a consideration of this issue). This belief may be due in part to traditional beliefs that women are more emotionally unstable than men. It may also be due to the double stigma associated with being a female alcoholic, which may cause women to make more efforts to hide their drinking and to delay treatment. But the number of women in treatment has increased as treatment programs have offered more services sensitive to female alcoholics. Child care, assertiveness training, and women's groups are examples of these services. Although more men than women receive treatment in public programs, it is not uncommon for private programs to report that half of their clients are women. Given treatment options that meet their needs, there is every reason to believe that women have a good prognosis for recovery. The number of specialized services for gay and lesbian alcoholics has only begun to grow, even though the incidence of alcoholism among this group is considered to be higher than in the general population (Brandsma & Pattison, 1982; see also Vourakis, 1983, for a discussion of the treatment of homosexual substance abusers).

SOCIAL WORKERS AND SUPERVISORS' ROLES

A key function of occupational social workers is to train supervisors in the recognition of job performance problems. The literature on employee assistance programs emphasizes the need for supervisory training as an essential ingredient of successful EAPs (Masi, 1982; Trice & Beyer, 1982). According to the SPAAR model, identified in Chapter 4 of this volume, when sufficient job performance problems have been identified by the supervisor, a meeting with the employee is arranged and job problems are discussed. Considerable coaching and consultation by the occupational social worker is often needed prior to the meeting because of supervisors' hesitancy to directly confront troubled employees. The employee may become defensive and deny that there is a problem, or the employee may agree that there has been a problem but assures the supervisor that the situation will improve.

When the problem is chemical dependency, it is sometimes resolved temporarily. Many alcoholics and drug abusers have proven to themselves or others that they are not hooked by "going on the wagon." Many are successful at staying "dry" or "clean" for a period of weeks or even months. These are periods when work productivity increases and the abuser may seem like a better employee than ever. In fact, the supervisor may begin to question whether there was a problem in the first place! Without treatment, however, the abuser will likely return to alcohol or other drugs, and job performance will again be adversely affected.

A widespread belief in the treatment of chemical dependency is that unless there is a reason to change, the drug-taking behavior will continue. A crisis generally occurs that motivates the abuser to seek help. Common crises are a spouse's threat of separation or divorce, an arrest, a health problem, and, of most concern here, the threat of job loss. When employees fail to seek help at the repeated suggestions of their supervisor or an occupational social worker and job performance continues to deteriorate, there is one more strategy to be tried before employment is terminated. In the field of chemical dependency it has been called "intervention" (Johnson, 1980), "constructive confrontation," "caring coercion," and even "tough love." More recently the terminology has been softened to include "the invitation" to treatment and recovery (Gustafson, 1985, 1986). As applied in the workplace, the supervisor calls another meeting with the employee. Again, job performance problems are discussed, and the supervisor does not attempt to diagnose the problem. The confrontation basically leaves the employee with two options: seek help or be terminated. The constructive part is that the meeting is conducted with concern for the well-being of the employee. The employee is assured of confidentiality in pursuing EAP services and continuing employment if job performance improves satisfactorily (Trice & Sonnenstuhl, 1985).

The weight of the evidence is that constructive confrontation in the workplace is a useful tool in getting the chemically dependent employee into treatment and promoting recovery (Royce, 1981; Schramm & DeFillippi, 1975). Chopra, Preston, and Gerson (1979) studied alcoholic men who were referred to treatment by employers and those who were referred by other sources and found that those referred by employers entered treatment earlier, had experienced fewer alcohol-related problems, were more likely to report abstinence after treatment, and were more likely to participate in follow-up. Smart (1974) was unable to confirm that coerced employees improved more than voluntary clients, but Trice and Beyer (1982) call the success of constructive confrontation "proven and remarkable" (p. 969). Evidence from a recent study indicates that "75 percent of problem drinkers and 55 percent of other problem employees showed a marked improvement in performance as a result of having experienced constructive confrontation" (Trice & Sonnenstuhl, 1985, p. 35).

SELECTING APPROPRIATE TREATMENT

In addition to providing training, consultation, and coaching to supervisors, the occupational social worker assesses the troubled employee's situation and recommends appropriate treatment. Chemically dependent employees generally require a combination of treatment options along a continuum of care. The options selected are based on the severity of the chemical dependency, the characteristics of the employee, the availability of treatment resources, and the employee benefit package. Insurance coverage and health maintenance organization benefits may restrict the types of chemical dependency treatment that are reimbursable and the types of professionals who may provide the treatment. If the services needed are not covered under employee benefits, the employee's ability to pay for treatment is considered. Most communities offer some services on a sliding-scale basis. Below is an overview of the most frequently utilized treatment resources.

Detoxification

Detoxification programs are used when an individual is physically addicted to alcohol and/or other drugs. Detoxification may take place in a hospital, especially when the most severe types of alcohol and other drug withdrawal occur. Many communities operate primary-care centers to assist individuals with less severe problems in safely withdrawing from alcohol, but many of these centers are not equipped to assist patients in withdrawal from other drugs. Polydrug abusers may go through withdrawal from one drug, followed by withdrawal from another drug. Physically addicted individuals experience certain symptoms when they stop using drugs. For example, the alcoholic may experience mild, moderate, or severe withdrawal symptoms ranging from sweats, nausea, and tremors to hallucinations, seizures, and delerium tremens. Unfortunately, many lay people underestimate the serious risks associated with alcohol withdrawal. Medical management is necessary to prevent severe medical problems. Death can occur when alcohol withdrawal is not properly managed. Some patients require medication for withdrawal on a short-term basis. Milder forms of alcohol withdrawal may not require drug treatment, but careful monitoring and emotional support are important. Detoxification and abstinence from alcohol and other drugs are the first steps in recovery.

Inpatient Treatment

The number of inpatient facilities for the treatment of chemical dependency has grown rapidly in the last decade. Some have a detoxification component, while others require that the client be past the acute withdrawal stage before admission. Although treatment regimens vary, many inpatient programs use a similar approach. Education is considered critical, since abusers frequently harbor many misconceptions and misunderstandings about chemical dependency. They often blame themselves and feel that they should be able to quit on their own, or they continue to deny the problem and project blame onto others. The educational phase of the program provides accurate information about chemical dependency that forms a basis for the treatment that follows. Although individual therapy is utilized, group therapy is emphasized. Interaction with other group members and the therapist are important tools in the progress of clients. Although Alcoholics Anonymous and Narcotics Anonymous (NA) operate independently from inpatient treatment programs, most inpatient programs are strong advocates of these self-help groups. Patients are often expected to participate in AA or NA while in residence. It is also common for inpatient programs to incorporate family education and treatment. Inpatient treatment is recommended when chemical dependency is severe. At this stage, the employee may need a leave of absence from work. Inpatient treatment programs last about 4 to 6 weeks. However, some treatment programs are experimenting with new formats including evening and weekend residence, which allow the employee to remain on the job. Employees frequently balk at the thought of a leave of absence. A decision about the need for leave time often requires the consultation of the occupational social worker.

Halfway Houses

Most communities have at least one halfway house for alcoholics and/or other drug abusers. Although a major purpose of a halfway house is to provide a supportive living environment for those in recovery, this alternative seems to be chosen only when the employee has no other viable living arrangements. Halfway house residents are usually those with limited financial resources and unstable home environments. Halfway houses vary widely, ranging from structured treatment programs to those resembling a boarding house with residents encouraged to attend AA.

Outpatient Treatment

Outpatient treatment may follow inpatient treatment or it may be the first type of treatment recommended for the employee; this generally depends on the severity of the problem. Outpatient chemical dependency treatment is provided through a number of different types of programs. Most communities have mental health centers that provide some type of outpatient chemical dependency treatment (some also provide detoxification, inpatient, and halfway house services). Other communities operate alcoholism and drug abuse programs separate from the community mental health center. Hospitals offering inpatient chemical dependency programs may also operate outpatient services. A number of private practitioners offer outpatient treatment. Some private practices specialize in chemical dependency treatment, while others offer this as one of several services. Some practitioners offer expertise in treating chemically dependent women, some may cater to younger or older abusers, and others may reach out to gay and lesbian clients. Urban communities often have a number of programs; rural communities usually have limited options. Education and individual, group, family, and marital counseling are among the services offered.

Outpatient services are utilized when it is codependents or adult children who are seen by the occupational social worker. A number of therapists view co-dependency as a primary problem, requiring independent treatment. Co-dependency treatment is directed at helping family members live more productive lives whether or not the chemically dependent individual recovers and whether or not the co-dependent remains in the relationship. Professional treatment for the adult children of alcoholics has also received much more attention in the past few years.

Aftercare and Follow-up

The treatment methods described above are important in the recovery of chemically dependent individuals and their loved ones, but equally important is a program of aftercare or follow-up. Recovering alcoholics and addicts find that it is easier to remain free of chemicals and to enhance their everyday lives with these services. Some treatment programs operate aftercare and follow-up programs for "graduates" or "alumni" of their programs through periodic meetings. Some offer booster sessions when clients relapse or experience difficult periods during which they fear they may drink or use drugs. Many people utilize AA and NA as frameworks for organizing their lives and finding the support necessary to remain sober and "clean." Some people are surprised that recovering individuals are involved in support groups throughout their lives, but recovering alcoholics and addicts have long known that this is an important contributor to long-term sobriety.

Adjunct Services

When an individual's primary problem is chemical dependency, it is important to treat this problem first. Too many times, chemically dependent clients have been misdiagnosed based on their denial of an alcohol or other drug-abuse problem or the failure of therapists to recognize that chemical dependency was the basis for depression, anxiety, marital or family problems, or other complaints. However, it is also true that once a client is chemical-free, other problems frequently need to be addressed. Chemical-dependency treatment does not automatically repair a bad marriage. Financial problems do not disappear overnight. Occupational social workers frequently make referrals for these types of problems.

Services to Families

The clientele of occupational social workers are generally employees of the company or organization, but these social workers may also provide some assistance directly to employees' families. Occupational social workers usually do this following a self-initiated or supervisor-initiated referral; they may recommend a joint meeting with the employee's family in which the problem and service options are discussed. Occasionally a family member might initiate a call to the occupational social worker with or without the employee's knowledge. When a family member calls without the employee's knowledge and participation, the social worker is careful to maintain the employee's confidentiality, but the social worker may respond to family members' needs and desires for assistance by providing information about chemical dependency. The social worker may also mention intervention and treatment options and refer the family to appropriate resources. The inpatient, outpatient, and adjunct treatment services described above usually serve family members as well as chemically dependent individuals and welcome contacts by concerned families.

Twelve-Step Programs

Since its inception in 1935, the fellowship of Alcoholics Anonymous has helped countless alcoholics recover. AA is a 12-step program. The first of the 12 steps is, "We admitted we were powerless over alcohol—that our lives had become unmanageable," and the twelfth step is, "Having had a spiritual awakening as the result of these steps, we tried to carry this message to alcoholics, and to practice these principles in all our affairs" (Alcoholics Anonymous World Services, 1955, pp. 59–60). AA is not a religious program, but the importance of the spiritual component of recovery should not be underestimated. Spirituality is a personal concept defined only by the individual. It means many different things to many different people. Some agnostics and atheists as well as individuals from many religious persuasions have successfully recovered through the AA program (Alcoholics Anonymous World Services, 1952).

Although AA operates with little formal structure, there are groups all over the United States, as well as in many other countries. Directories of groups in the United States and abroad are available, and most telephone directories have an AA listing. Recovering employees who travel can usually find a meeting to attend. This is especially important in the early stages of recovery. It is also an excellent alternative to a lonely motel room. The only requirement for AA membership is a desire to stay sober. There are no fees for membership or participation. Members who wish and are able to do so make contributions that help the groups carry out their functions. Through AA World Services and local groups, concerned individuals can obtain literature about alcoholism and the AA program.

Everyone working in employee assistance programs should be familiar with the AA program and with other self-help groups such as Narcotics Anonymous, Cocaine Anonymous (Ehrlich & McGeehan, 1985), and Women for Sobriety.[3] Although "closed" meetings may be attended only by

---

[3]For information on Women for Sobriety, write to P.O. Box 618, Quakertown, PA 18951. Most communities have listings for Narcotics Anonymous in the telehone directory.

persons concerned about their own drinking or other drug use, "open" meetings may be attended by anyone interested in chemical dependency. Other support groups include Alanon, for the family and friends of alcoholics. Alateen and Alatot are specifically designed for teenagers and younger children of alcoholics, respectively. Self-help groups for adult children of alcoholics are also springing up in many communities. Naranon offers support to the family and friends of narcotics abusers.

Chemically dependent individuals and their loved ones are usually reluctant to attend their first meeting because they do not know what to expect. Frequently, someone simply suggests or tells an alcoholic, addict, or codependent to attend, but there are more effective ways to make a referral. AA members often accompany newcomers to their first meetings. Professionals who are not members need contacts in 12-step programs. The chances of clients' attending a meeting are greater if they have an opportunity to meet a member who can accompany them to a meeting, introduce them to other members, and explain what goes on in meetings. Like any other referral resources used by professionals, it is important to have some information about local groups. Location and group composition are considerations when recommending self-help groups to employees. Groups may be found in all types of communities: upper, middle, and lower socioeconomic status; white, black, and Hispanic. Some groups are especially interested in attracting women, others in young people, and some are especially sensitive to gays and lesbians.

There are many reasons for the success of AA. The alcoholic has an opportunity to meet other individuals who have successfully recovered. Members frequently "tell their stories," and newcomers are able to see the similarity between their situations and that of others. More important, they see that recovery is possible. The AA program encourages a lifestyle that is conducive to maintaining sobriety.

Social workers should not be surprised when employees return after their first meeting and say "the program is not for me," "the members were too old," "the members had much more serious problems than me," or that something else was wrong. No one learns the program in a single meeting. Although attendance at AA meetings is voluntary, social workers frequently recommend that clients attend a series of meetings before deciding whether the program is right for them. Most professionals in the field of chemical dependency treatment agree that 12-step programs are perfectly compatible with the goals of professional treatment. Many recovering individuals are introduced to AA and NA through inpatient and outpatient treatment programs. On the other hand, many recovering alcoholics have utilized the AA program and have not sought professional help. Occupational social workers generally recommend both types of assistance to the employees they see.

IMPAIRED PROFESSIONALS

Chemical dependency can strike anyone—men and women, people of all ages, ethnic, cultural and racial backgrounds and religious persuasions. No professional group is immune either. Physicians, nurses, and pharmacists who have considerable knowledge of drugs and access to them can fall prey to the insidiousness of chemical dependency. Psychologists, the clergy, social workers, and other helping professionals are not immune either. Many professional groups—physicians, pharmacists, nurses, and attorneys— are realizing the importance of confronting chemically dependent colleagues. Some have developed intervention programs for impaired members of their own ranks (those with chemical dependency or other problems that adversely effect job performance). At its 1984 Delegate Assembly, the National Association of Social Workers adopted Resolution 21, which recognized the importance of identifying and assisting impaired social workers. How can social workers help colleagues suffering from chemical dependency? Let's look at a fictitious but perhaps not uncommon example.

John H is a social worker in a child welfare agency. He has held this position for about 2 years and his work consists of investigating complaints of child abuse and neglect. This work keeps John out of the office much of the day. John is in his thirties. He has been divorced about four years. There are three other social workers in John's unit. On many Friday afternoons John and his co-workers go to a nearby bar for happy hour. In the past 6 months, John's alcohol consumption has increased, but no one thought much of it until about 2 months ago when John drank more than usual on Friday afternoon and did not appear capable of driving. He let another co-worker give him a lift home. John also became intoxicated at the office picnic last month.

John has been away from the office more often than usual, but he has mentioned that several of his cases have required lengthy investigations in the field. John's co-workers had no reason to doubt him until a few social workers from other agencies and staff from the juvenile court called complaining that he had not been returning their calls. John's absence from court one morning resulted in the postponement of an especially sensitive case. This behavior is not like John, and his co-workers begin to wonder if something might be wrong, but they also want to help. They begin by taking John's calls. Bill, John's closest colleague on the unit, also decides to talk with John and ask if anything is wrong. John complains about his health and says he has seen several doctors recently, who agree that he is suffering from fatigue. He thanks Bill for his concern and for helping him out, but denies that anything else is wrong. John's behavior at work improves during the next few weeks, but eventually the same problems reccur. Two of the workers on the unit, Martha and Ann, have smelled alcohol on his breath during working hours. At other times he seemed high but no one smelled alcohol.

John's supervisor, Susan, has just returned from a 2-week vacation. This morning she is looking for John. There is a new development on one of his cases, and she is quite perturbed when she cannot find him. The other workers on the unit do not know where he is. John's co-workers go to lunch together; their conversation turns to John. They are concerned that he is experiencing more difficulty at work and they are concerned about his drinking. They decide that they should do something, but what? Bill brings up the possibility of an intervention. He has read about the process in the professional literature but no one in the group has been involved in one. They have heard that the social worker in their department's EAP office has conducted some programs for staff on chemical dependency and other problems that can impair job performance. The three make an appointment to see her. They do not mention John's name but they describe his behavior. The social worker talks with them about chemical dependency and discusses the intervention process. She gives them some literature and suggests that they return if they wish to pursue an intervention. The social worker also assures them that she will keep their visit confidential.

The next day the three decide to follow through. The EAP social worker meets with them over the next 2 weeks to educate them and take them through the steps of the intervention. They role play the intervention; the social worker plays John and the others practice what they will say to John when the moment arrives. In order to arrange the actual intervention, they tell John that an important 10:00 staff meeting has been called for the following day. When John arrives at the meeting, Bill tells him that they have all been concerned about him and they hope he will sit and listen to them. Martha begins by telling John about a specific incident in which she covered for him last Wednesday when the juvenile court officer called about a particular case. Ann also relates a specific incident about smelling alcohol on John's breath one morning when he was particularly late for work. Although they do not label or diagnose John's problem, they recount several other incidents in which they have covered for John or were concerned about his drinking. Throughout the intervention they emphasize their concern for John. They also tell him that they can no longer cover for him with their supervisor or other agencies' staff, and they hope he will see the social worker in the EAP office.

John is obviously surprised by the intervention. At first, he shows some defensiveness, claiming they have exaggerated the incidents and denying a drinking problem, but as the intervention progresses, John becomes less defensive. He agrees to see the social worker in the EAP office.

Even if the intervention had not ended this successfully, John's colleagues took an important step that many others might have chosen to ignore. This description has been brief and there are additional details to consider in conducting an intervention (see Johnson, 1980). Readers are cautioned not to attempt an intervention before seeking the assistance of a qualified professional who can prepare them for the experience.

THE ROAD TO RECOVERY

Chemical dependency is a major cause of problems at work, and employment settings are primary sites for early intervention. Occupational social workers and other employee assistance professionals have a responsibility to be well-versed on the subject of chemical dependency. This chapter has identified the major categories of abused drugs, and alcohol has been identified as the most frequently abused drug. Alcohol abuse has long been a concern of employers in the United States; as a result, the first employee assistance programs were industrial alcoholism programs. But it is not only the abuser who is identified as having performance problems in the workplace. Family members also suffer the effects of chemical dependency, and this is frequently reflected in a deterioration in their performance at work.

Although the numbers of women in the workforce continue to swell, there is concern that the numbers of women referred by supervisors for chemical dependency problems is lower than expected. EAP professionals are considering special strategies to encourage supervisory and self-referrals of chemically dependent women.

Since there are frequently a range of treatment options available for chemically dependent individuals, each employee assistance professional must evaluate which programs in the community are particularly committed to helping chemcially addicted individuals through the recovery process. Of special concern is the reality that most chemically dependent people relapse at least once during their recovery. Relapse should not be considered a failure; instead, information about the relapse can be used to assist the employee in preventing future relapses (see Gorski, 1986). The occupational social worker often has contact with the employee during these periods and encourages the client to seek the assistance necessary to return to sobriety. EAP professionals are also wise to recommend that employees see them should they feel particularly vulnerable to relapse.

Professionals in the employee assistance field are the link between chemically dependent employees and an early chance at recovery. As more organizations adopt EAPs, the opportunities for early intervention, treatment, and recovery will continue to increase. Involvement of EAP professionals in conducting research and evaluation of their programs is critical for the indentification of new and better models for prevention and intervention that will continue to enhance the already positive outcomes of EAPs around the country.

REFERENCES

Alcoholics Anonymous World Services. (1952). *44 questions and answers about the A.A. program of recovery from alcoholism.* New York: Author.

Alcoholics Anonymous World Services. (1955). *Alcoholics Anonymous*. New York: Author.

Beckman, L. (1976). Alcoholism problems and women: An overview. In M. Greenblatt & M. Schuckit (Eds.), *Alcoholism problems in women and children* (pp. 65–96). New York: Grune & Stratton.

Blue collars are turning pink. (1984, August 12). *Time*, p. 82.

Brandsma, J. M., & Pattison, E. M. (1982). Homosexuality and alcoholism. In E. M. Pattison, & E. Kaufman (Eds.), *Encyclopedic handbook of alcoholism* (pp. 736–741). New York: Gardner.

Cahill, M. H. (1983). Training employees and supervisors to increase use of EAP's by women. *Alcohol Health & Research World, 7*, Spring, 18–22.

Castro, J. (1986, January 27). Battling drugs on the job. *Time*, p. 43.

Chopra, K. S., Preston, D. A., & Gerson, L. W. (1979). The effect of constructive coercion on the rehabilitative process. *Journal of Occupational Medicine, 21*, 749–752.

Company fires 52 in drug inquiry. (1985, November 23). *Austin American-Statesman*, p. A9.

Curlee, J. (1970). A comparison of male and female patients at an alcoholism treatment center. *Journal of Psychology, 74*, 239–247.

Davies, D. L. (1976). Definitional issues in alcoholism. In R. E. Tarter & A. A. Sugerman, *Alcoholism, interdisciplinary approaches to an enduring problem* (pp. 53–73). Reading, MA: Addison-Wesley.

DeQuine, J. (1985, November 28). Officials taking a second look at addictiveness of cocaine. *Austin American-Statesman*, p. E23.

DiNitto, D. M., Starr, A., & Smith, S. (1986). Doing better but feeling worse. Women and substance abuse in the workplace. In M. C. Barrett, S. K. Collins, & L. D. Knezek (Eds.), *Women and work, selected papers, 1985 symposium*. Arlington, Texas: The University of Texas at Arlington.

Ehrlich, P., & McGeehan, M. (1985). Cocaine recovery support groups: The language of recovery. In D. E. Smith & D. R. Wesson (Eds.), *Treating the cocaine abuser* (pp. 73–90). Center City, MN: Hazelden.

Estes, N. J., & Heinemann, M. E. (1982). *Alcoholism: Development, consequences and intervention*. St. Louis: Mosby.

Gomberg, E. S. (1976). The female alcoholic. In R. E. Tarter & A. A. Sugerman (Eds.), *Alcoholism: Interdisciplinary approaches to an enduring problem* (pp. 603–636). Reading, MA: Addison-Wesley.

Gomberg, E.S.L. (1982). Women with alcohol problems. In N. J. Estes & M. E. Heinemann, *Alcoholism: Development, consequences, and interventions* (pp.217–230). St. Louis: Mosby.

Gorski, T. T., & Miller, M. (1986). *Staying sober: A guide for relapse prevention*. Independence, MO: Independence Press.

Gustafson, L. (1985). The Minnesota model. *Austinet News, 10*, 1–2. Austin, TX: The Greater Austin Council on Alcoholism and Drug Abuse.

Gustafson, L. (1986). Intervention—Then and now. *Austinet News, 1*, 3. Austin, TX: The Greater Austin Council on Alcoholism and Drug Abuse.

Jellinek, E. M. (1960). *The disease concept of alcoholism*. New Haven: Hillhouse.

Johnson, V. E. (1980). *I'll quit tomorrow* (rev. ed.). San Francisco: Harper & Row.

Johnson, P. B. (1982). Sex differences, women's roles, and alcohol use: Preliminary national data. *Journal of Social Issues, 38:* 93–116.

Jones, B. M., & Jones, M. K. (1976). Women and alcohol: Intoxication, metabolism and the menstrual cycle. In M. Greenblatt & M. A. Schuckit (Eds.), *Alcoholism problems in women and children* (pp. 103–136). New York: Grune & Stratton.

Kleeman, B., & Googins, B. (1983). Women alcoholics in management: Issues in identification. *Alcohol Health & Research World, 7,* (Spring), 23–28.

Kurtz, N. R., Googins, B., & Williams, C. (1980). Clients' views of an occupational alcoholism program. *Labor Management Alcoholism Journal, X,* (November), 102–113.

Lewis, D. C. (1977). Addiction. In J. B. Turner (Ed.). *Encyclopedia of social work* (pp. 13–22). Washington, DC: National Association of Social Workers.

Masi, D. (1982). *Human services in industry.* Lexington, MA: Heath.

National Institute on Alcohol Abuse and Alcoholism. (1978). Third special report to the U.S. congress on alcohol and health. Washington, DC: Author.

Pattison, E. M., Sobell, M. B., & Sobell, L. C. (1977). *Emerging concepts of alcohol dependence.* New York: Springer Publishing Company.

Plaut, T.F.A. (1967). *Alcohol problems: A report to the nation by the Cooperative Commission on the Study of Alcoholism.* New York: Oxford University Press.

Ray, O. (1983). *Drugs, society, and human behavior.* St. Louis: Mosby.

Reichman, W. (1983). Affecting attitudes and assumptions about women and alcohol problems. *Alcohol Health & Research World, 7* (Spring), 6–10.

Rimmer, J., Pitts, F. N. Jr., Reich, T., & Winokur, G. (1971). Alcoholism. II. Sex, socioeconomic status and race in two hospitalized samples. *Quarterly Journal of Studies on Alcohol, 32,* 942–952.

Roy, S. A. (1983). From the editor. *Alcohol Health and Research World, 7* (Spring), 2.

Royce, J. E. (1981). *Alcohol problems and alcoholism, a comprehensive survey.* New York: Free Press.

Schramm, C. J., & DeFillippi, R. J. (1975). Characteristics of successful alcoholism treatment programs for American workers. *British Journal of Addiction, 70,* 271–275.

Schuft, C. C. (1983). Reaching women problem drinkers through a multimedia information campaign. *Alcohol Health & Research World, 7* (Spring), 11–17.

Shaw, S. (1980). The causes of increasing drinking problems amongst women. In Camberwell Council on Alcoholism, *Women and Alcohol.* London: Tavistock.

Smart, R. G. (1974). Employed alcoholics treated voluntarily and under constructive coercion, a follow-up study. *Quarterly Journal of Studies on Alcohol, 35,* 196–209.

Smith, D. E., & Wesson, D. R. (Eds.). 1985. *Treating the cocaine abuser.* Center City, MN: Hazelden.

Solomon, S. D. (1983). Women in the workplace. An overview of NIAAA's Occupational Alcoholism Demonstration Project. *Alcohol Health & Research World, 7* (Spring), 3–5.

Spain, D. M. (1945). Portal cirrhosis of the liver. A review of two hundred fifty necropsies with references to sex differences. *American Journal of Clinical Pathology, 15,* 215–218.

Tarter, R. E., & Sugerman, A. A. (1976). *Alcoholism, interdisciplinary approaches to an enduring problem*. Reading, MA: Addison-Wesley.

Trice, H. M., & Beyer, J. M. (1982). Job-based alcoholism programs: Motivating problem drinkers to rehabilitation. In E. M. Pattison & E. Kaufman (Eds.), *Encyclopedic handbook of alcoholism* (pp. 954–978). New York: Gardner.

Trice, H. M., & Sonnenstuhl, W. J. (1985). Constructive confrontation and counseling. *EAP Digest, March/April*, 31–36.

Trost, C. (1984, December 18). *Wall Street Journal*, p. 1.

Vourakis, C. (1983). Homosexuals in substance abuse treatment. In G. Bennett, C. Vourakis, & D. S. Woolf (Eds.), *Substance abuse: Pharmacologic, developmental, & clinical perspectives* (pp. 400–419). New York: Wiley.

Wegscheider, S. (1976). The family trap . . . no one escapes from a chemically dependent family. Crystal, MN: Nurturing Networks.

Wegscheider, S. (1981). *Another chance: Hope and health for the alcoholic family*. Palo Alto, CA: Science and Behavior Books.

Wilsnack, S. C. (1982). Alcohol abuse and alcoholism in women. In E. M. Pattison & E. Kaufman (Eds.), *Encyclopedic handbook of alcoholism* (pp. 718–735). New York: Gardner.

Wilsnack, S. C., Wilsnack, R. W., & Klassen, A. D. (1984/1985). Drinking and drinking problems among women in a U.S. national survey. *Alcohol Health & Research World, 9 (Winter)*, 3–13.

7 Counseling Survivors of Workplace Accidents and Disasters

Sam Brunstein
Margaret Ann Kilpatrick

A disaster begins with a believable warning and ends when the physical and emotional damage is repaired. This may take years. Untreated, the trauma of disaster can cause profound behavioral changes in people and organizations alike. Stress reactions may severely reduce life quality for an individual and significantly impair the effectiveness of an organization.

Social workers have multilevel disaster responsibilities. The organization and its people must be made aware of potential consequences before a disaster occurs. Appropriate training must be designed and implemented despite company tendencies to ignore psychological planning for emergencies. During and immediately following a crisis, social workers must provide psychological first aid, provide guidance for emergency notifications, help maintain a stable decision-making process, and watch for burnout in others and self. Later, social workers must lobby for benefits for personnel, make provisions for therapy for individuals and organizational elements, educate managers and significant others on expected behavior from survivors, and stave off efforts to ignore long-term psychological effects. All in all, it is a difficult job.[1]

DISASTERS

Stages

The literature on natural disasters names seven physical phases (Dynes, 1974) and four emotional phases (Farberow & Frederick, 1978a) that also apply to man-made disasters. Not all phases occur in every disaster.

[1]Cohen and Ahern (1980) have information useful (though intended for community disasters) for program design. So do Dynes (1974), and Parad, Resnick, and Parad (1976).

For example, a tornado alert is the *warning*, the first of the physical phases. Sightings begin the *threat*. A tornado strike is the *impact*. Then, people take *inventory*—am I injured? is there water? and so forth. Next comes *rescue*. Police, firefighters, paramedics begin work. During *remedy*, the injured are moved to hospitals, and shelter is found for the needy. Finally comes *recovery*, with long-term solutions (e.g., rebuilding homes and streets).

The first of the emotional phases, the *heroic*, occurs just before, during, and after the impact when altruism and heroism are common. During the *honeymoon* (rescue, remedy, and part of recovery) civic and government groups work well together to assist survivors. But, somewhere in recovery, turf battles start, regulations are discovered, promises are withdrawn, and the spirit of community dissolves. Thus begins *disillusionment*. Finally, realistically, the survivors enter the *reconstruction* phase. Survivors have often reported that disillusionment was worse than the impact. It is important to consider the effects of each phase whether treating survivors or organizations.

Similarities among Disasters

Workplace disasters typically involve people in a familiar environment that they perceive as safe and under their control, but over which most have little actual control. Suddenly, the environment turns unsafe, and the lack of control becomes clear. There is fear, uncertainty, danger, and often injury and death. During and after the impact, escape or rescue may be difficult because the familiar has become grossly unfamiliar.

Survivors of group disasters have reported that they felt alone, angry, powerless, vulnerable, afraid, violated, bewildered, and globally lacking in trust. Survivors of rape, muggings, auto accidents, and other single-victim incidents have reported similar feelings. In addition, survivors can exhibit a temporarily diminished cognitive function (Kilpatrick & Brunstein, 1983; see also Cohen & Ahern, 1980).

Thus appears a common thread among disasters: an intense, life-threatening, environment-scrambling crisis over which individuals have little control and that causes them to feel alone, angry, powerless, afraid, violated, and vulnerable, with probable temporary impairment of the cognitive process. The intensity of the resultant stress can cause severe emotional trauma, whatever the disaster.

PSYCHOLOGICAL TRAUMA

Clinical Implications

The clinical reactions of an individual to disaster stressors will depend heavily on the life experience of the survivor. However, we believe that two effects are almost universal, in varying degrees. These are: (1) loss, with resultant mourning and grief; and (2) regression, with resultant loss of initiative, autonomy, and trust.

While mourning and grief are usually associated with the loss of a person, people are often also object-bonded and may be strongly affected by the loss of a work station, a familiar environment, a machine, or even documents that contain important and personally meaningful work. Individuals with a high perceived sense of loss and strong object-bonds may need a lengthy and complete mourning process to work through the loss.

The term *regression* is used in the context of Erikson's (1950, 1968) developmental stages and tasks: early infancy—trust versus doubt; later infancy—autonomy versus mistrust; preschool—initiative versus guilt; school—industry versus inferiority; adolescence—identity versus role diffusion; young adult—intimacy versus isolation; middle adult—generativity versus stagnation; maturity—integrity versus despair. It appears that the disorientation, demonstrated powerlessness, and other consequences of the disaster can temporarily undo part or all of this maturation process. This regression may be gradually repaired by the individuals themselves, but it can require brief to extensive psychotherapy for complete regrowth.

To demonstrate the point, consider the impact of a disaster on three ego models. The examples are simplistic, but illustrative of regression, modified by life experience. The disaster itself occurs without warning, and from a cause that is completely beyond the control of any of the survivors. Some survivors will have developed a low self-esteem and a belief that the locus of control of their lives is completely outside of self. These survivors will have their mistrust, dependency, and passivity reinforced, thus hampering their ability to cope. Some survivors will have an unrealistically high self-assessment, with the belief that their lives are totally within their own control. These survivors will have their belief system shattered, with a regressive impairment of the ability to cope. Other survivors will have healthy self-esteem, tempered by the understanding that many life events are outside their direct control, but that the locus of control of self-response and successful coping is within themselves. These survivors will have their developmental system substantiated positively and will cope productively.

A crisis is not necessarily negative. When dealing with survivors, teaching others, or referring survivors for therapy, remember that a crisis presents an opportunity for productive growth because the defense mechanisms are stressed and capable of being remolded.

Symptomatology

Typically, those affected are reacting normally to the impact of the disaster. People are generally not made mentally ill by disaster. Any severe emotional consequences are probably exacerbations of preexisting psychiatric conditions.

Reactions may appear in any of five groups: somatic, cognitive, emotional, behavioral, and interactive (social behavior) (Brunstein & Kilpatrick, 1984). Symptoms may appear in minutes or be delayed for years. Reactions can appear from any category, with any order, intensity, or timing.

Common *somatic reactions* include colds and flu, low energy, gastrointestinal distress, skin eruptions, chest pain, back pain, hyperventilation, hypertension, sleep disorders, headache, muscle spasm, allergies, grinding of teeth, and clenched jaws. Physical symptoms should be checked by a physician, as a temporary community-wide deterioration in general health has been noted following a major disaster (Melick, Logue, & Frederick, 1982).

Cognitive reactions may appear as confusion, impaired memory and thought processes, inability to prioritize, reduced trust in one's judgment and decision-making ability, short attention span, limited creativity, repetitious thoughts, speech difficulty, stuttering, and difficulty in choosing words.

Emotional reactions may take the form of emotional numbing, disbelief, and bewilderment; survivor's guilt; feelings of fear, vulnerability, and powerlessness; profound global distrust; phobias; extreme mood swings; irritability and anger; rage; global anxiety; grief; sadness; and depression and loneliness. Initially, "numbing" may predominate, but not necessarily.

Behavioral reactions may be productive or nonproductive. Some productive behaviors are self-care, adequate rest, good nutrition; comfort with expressed feelings of self and others; gathering or avoiding information about the disaster, depending on personal need; spending time alone or with others, or mixing the two, depending on personal need; and self-honesty. Some nonproductive behaviors are refusing to cooperate with medical/psychological treatment, excessive activity to escape thoughts and feelings, displaced anger, self-neglect, becoming accident-prone, and refusing normal social interactions. Note that some reactions can be productive or nonproductive, depending on personality and the intensity of the reaction. Judgment should be cautious.

Interactive reactions may appear as disregard for social norms; anger and irritability, vented in the workplace, with significant others, or globally; frequent arguments; fighting; and generalized antisocial behavior.

The Impact of Untreated Trauma on People and Organizations

When people and organizations are not given appropriate posttrauma treatment, the quality of life may suffer for the employees, and effectiveness may suffer for the organization. Employees exhibiting the effects of suppressed or repressed emotional damage (e.g., absenteeism, reduced decision-making ability, alcoholism) will not be effective employees. Organizations whose employees have lost faith in their ability to cope, or whose employees have become alienated because of perceived mistreatment, will not be effective organizations. Organizations where internal managerial recovery roles are inadequately or inappropriately defined may have difficulty remaining viable. Social workers must be thoroughly familiar with the culture of the organization in order to treat the person–organization system. Just as a disaster can amplify a preexisting emotional condition in a person, so can it exacerbate a preexisting organizational schism. An excellent discussion of counterproductive organizational cultures can be found in *The Neurotic Organization* (de Vries & Miller, 1985). The discussion of family stress found in Smith (1983) is also useful because of the similarities between the adaptive mechanisms of a family and those of an organization.

Some Factors Affecting Traumatization and Recovery

The severity and nature of the disaster: Psychoemotional trauma is affected by free exit versus entrapment, how long one is aware of approaching danger, preparation time, the nature and extent of injuries and deaths, and the speed with which aid arrives.

Assigned/assumed responsibility for others: Those who feel responsible for the safety of others may place unachievable expectations on themselves. A sense of guilt or failure can complicate recovery.

Physical and emotional proximity: The degree of impact to an individual is related to the amount of physical involvement. However, even people who are *physically* distant can be *emotionally* close to the event through feelings of "family" and closeness in the organization, group, or industry involved.

Previous experience in crises: If earlier crises were successfully resolved, learned coping skills are available for the newest trauma. If not, then the new event can reactivate old issues, which may add to the impact of the new disaster.

Stress status at the time of the disaster: The energy available for coping is related to other stresses already using one's emotional, physical, and cognitive resources.

Interpersonal interactions: Survivors interact with others. Each interaction affects the trauma, or the recovery process, or both. Trained personnel can desensitize the impact for many survivors. Insensitive personnel can "set" or intensify the trauma.

Survivors may interact with co-involvees, rescue workers, mental health workers, significant others, friends, co-workers, company officials, benefits personnel, union officials, media personnel, accident investigators, coroners, and morticians. Significant others also may interact with any of these.

Clearly, the various interactions to be considered are many and complex.

The immediacy of psychological support and treatment: It is intuitively obvious that psychological support and treatment can be most effective in the hours, days, and early weeks following the incident, before negative effects are fully set.

Consider these factors when assessing the degree of trauma and deciding on appropriate treatment (Cohen & Ahern, 1980; Kilpatrick, 1981). Note that social workers can influence the last two factors by training and consciousness-raising in the organization.

TREATMENT

Counseling the Disaster Survivor

Both individuals and organizations can be considered to be survivors. The organizational culture will be jarred by the event that traumatized the employees. Of course, counseling means working with people, singly and in groups, but the thrust of the counseling may be toward reduction of individual trauma or reestablishing an effective organizational system. Whether individual or organizational, disaster counseling has a short-term element (crisis intervention) and a longer-term element—grief counseling, regrowth (trust, etc.), psychotherapy for intensified preexisting trauma, organizational development intervention, and so forth. Individuals or organizations may require referral to an outside professional if internal resources are not sufficient for long-term counseling.

Crisis intervention will reestablish some feelings of compentency in most survivors. The major crisis intervention steps are: establishing rapport; identifying, defining, and focusing on the problems; evaluating the problems; evaluating available resources; and developing and implementing plans for problem solutions (Farberow & Frederick, 1978a).[2]

Considerable stress reduction can be accomplished in individuals and organizations by holding group debriefings within a few hours to a few weeks after the impact. We have developed and used this methodology for groups ranging in size from 3 to 300. Typically, about half a day is required per group. The group debriefing consists of five steps, beginning with an introductory explanation of the purposes, steps, and expectations of the meeting. The last step is the integration of the information and feelings from the meeting. The other three steps are: (1) ventilation of feelings; (2) information about the disaster, the steps being taken to recover, and expected behavior and stress-reaction symptoms; and (3) establishment of feelings of normalcy

---

[2]Further discussion of crisis intervention is found in Brunstein and Kilpatrick (1984), Cohen and Ahern (1980), Hafen and Peterson (1982), Hafen and Brog (1983), Parad, Resnick, and Parad (1976), and Resnick and Ruben (1975).

about emotional reactions and feelings of support and community in the group. The order of these middle three steps is dictated by group culture and dynamics. Choreography of all five steps is a delicate and artistic process requiring careful monitoring of group behavior. Interweaving the middle three steps is an especially delicate process requiring diligent attention to subtle cues from the group concerning members' needs. Mitchell (1982, 1983) has developed a similar method for rescue workers.

It is also important for social workers, peer counselors, managers, and so forth to understand the grief process to appropriately counsel, refer, and manage those individuals requiring a lengthy mourning process. According to Simos (1979, p.8), "the therapeutic task in regard to loss is threefold: to help the bereaved know that they have experienced a loss, to facilitate the expression of normal and appropriate grief, and to find healthy restitution for that which has been lost."[3]

Long-term Eriksonian regrowth will be necessary for some survivors. Psychodynamic or other insight-oriented therapies are often the modality of choice. Progressive desensitization can sometimes be useful in reestablishing feelings of trust and autonomy. This can be likened to the process that children go through as they grow, the process of exploring and learning to trust and control the environment. Reparenting may be necessary in extremely severe cases. In some cases, gentle touch (e.g., massage, physical therapy, etc.) has been useful in rebuilding trust in self and in others. Therapy for exacerbated preexisting conditions is highly individualized and beyond the scope of this chapter.

Guidelines for Triage

Immediately postdisaster, triage may be necessary to match available resources. The National Institute for Mental Health (NIMH) has developed guidelines for estimating two degrees of trauma (Farberow & Frederick, 1978a). These have been modified into three categories: mild, moderate, and severe (Brunstein & Kilpatrick, 1984). Persons in the mild category probably do not need immediate help. People in the moderate category will likely benefit from immediate intervention. Victims in the severe category probably cannot be helped on-site and need long-term professional therapy.

Individuals experiencing severe trauma will be either *inappropriately or not at all interactive*. They will probably show serious disorientation, short attention span, irrational or no response to conversation, inability to fully care for themselves, and a general demeanor of not being "there" (nonclinical, but well understood). People moderately traumatized will be dazed and

[3]Additional valuable information on grief can be found in Crosby and Jose (1983), Tatelbaum (1980), and Worden (1982).

disoriented, but *appropriately interactive*. They will be capable of sensible conversation with possible mild cognitive dysfunction, be able to care for themselves, and seem somewhat disconnected, but "there." Those with mild trauma will be cognitively functional. They will know who and where they are, and the day, date, and approximate time (person, place, and time criteria).

Gauging emotional trauma is a process of forming an overall impression, so proceed cautiously. More leisurely off-site professional evaluation should always be a consideration.

Providing Guidelines for Lay Persons

The disaster survivor resumes contact with the ordinary world while still having out-of-the-ordinary needs. Social workers should alert others to these needs, especially significant others. Survivors can be hurt by husbands, wives, friends, co-workers, and others when the significant other lacks understanding of the survivors' needs to ventilate. The expectation seems to be that, once physical injuries are healed, the incident is over. People do not expect the survivor to continue to have special needs many months after the disaster.

Social workers must provide information on the effects of disaster trauma, at least to significant others and to co-workers of survivors. Brochures and orientations can be prepared in advance and used postdisaster.[4]

Nor can the organization be ignored. Social workers must provide information to management about the expected extent and length of diminished organizational capacity and decision-making ability. Physical repair does not necessarily make the organization completely functional, any more than it does the person.

MINIMIZING THE EFFECTS OF DISASTER-INDUCED STRESS

Decision-Making in an Emergency

In crisis, effective decision-making practices are often abandoned in the name of time and emergency. However, poor decisions can be harmful now or expensive later. Poor decisions can exacerbate disaster trauma. Social workers must encourage an environment for effective decisions.

Good decisions require careful identification of the problem, a thorough study of alternatives, a thorough survey of objectives, the careful evaluation

---

[4]For examples of informative brochures about disaster trauma, see Farberow and Frederick (1978b, c) and Kilpatrick (1981).

of consequences, a thorough search for relevant and reliable information, and unbiased assimilation of new data, the careful reexamination of consequences, and thorough planning for implementation and contingencies (Janis & Mann, 1977). Effective problem solving is iterative (De Greene, 1982): problem—information—alternatives—solution—action—feedback—new data—repeat, as necessary.

In an emergency, this process must be swift even while managers' analytical abilities are reduced by emotional loading. Social workers can assist key personnel in venting their emotions, then use crisis intervention techniques to promote effective problem solving. They can encourage managers to gather data and opinions from subordinates, superiors, and peers before making serious decisions. The training of managers in decision making under stress will prove invaluable in any kind of emergency.

Selection and Training of Emergency Personnel

The basic task of emergency personnel (whether professional or volunteer) is to deal with the physical aspects of the disaster—to save lives and property. However, emergency workers can use techniques that begin the psychological care of the victims and that help to protect their own psychological health (Brunstein & Kilpatrick, 1984). Social workers can select appropriate professional personnel and train them in these techniques. Where volunteers are selected from among nonprofessionals, it is appropriate for social workers to lend their expertise in the selection process.

Good candidates for training are natural caregivers who adjust rapidly to change. The disaster environment will be extraordinary, and the workers must respond accordingly. An appropriate criterion is a history of effectively solving work and personal problems.

Social workers can train the emergency workers to "humanize" their work and to treat victims with courtesy and consideration. Emergency workers should introduce themselves to survivors; establish and maintain eye contact; team-build by asking for cooperation; use eye contact, smiles, gentle touch, and comforting words; project confidence; keep the victim informed; allow expression of emotion; and transfer the victim with a new introduction and a warm goodbye (D. Kilpatrick, 1982).

When victims are seen as human, emergency workers become emotionally involved. Caring involves risk. However, open, honest emotion, and open, honest expression are both caring and self-protective. Deep suppression or repression is harmful (Brunstein & Kilpatrick, 1984). Social workers must teach the emergency workers to humanize their task while dealing with their own emotions and must also provide debriefing opportunities, during and after the disaster, to help them work through their feelings.

Selection, Training, and Use of Peer Counselors

A disaster can overwhelm the personal resources of a social worker. Peer counselors (psychological paramedics), pretrained from within the organization, can be invaluable during and after the disaster. Coming from within the ranks, they are viewed by employees as "understanding" better than anyone else.

Peer counselors should come from the ranks of natural caregivers. They should be self-aware, trustworthy, empathic, realistic, nonjudgmental, and other-centered. They should be skilled in interviewing, unraveling complexity, identifying problems, setting priorities, identifying options, formulating action plans, and balancing helper/helpee responsibilities. Then they should be trained[5] in listening, empathy, crisis intervention, grief counseling, emergency notification, stress management, suicide prevention, and company resources and benefits.

In a disaster, peer counselors can be used as the first line of treatment for the moderate trauma group. They can caretake the severe trauma group until transported and give first aid where required. Postdisaster, the peer counselors should serve as the initial screen and as the first advocate for survivor problems. The personal resources of the social workers should be saved for problems that no one else can handle. There will be enough of these.

Emergency Notification of Death or Injury

The notifier virtually controls how others are given the news of death or injury, and the immediate support that they receive. At the instant of conveyance, the recipient has only the notifier for support. The information must be given sensitively, and support must be provided for the initial shock.

Guidelines are available (Brunstein & Kilpatrick, 1984). Notifiers should begin by identifying themselves and confirming that they are talking to the appropriate person to receive the notification. They should increase the level of distressing news slowly, using personal perceptions of the recipient's tolerance. The gauge is what is asked. Nonessential information should not be volunteered, but an attempt should be made to answer every question. Facts should be made clear, using sensitive and accurate words. If data are not available, that should be said and an offer made to provide it later, if possible. Some people will become angry or show other strong emotions.

[5]Farberow and Frederick (1978a) have outlined a training program intended for use in major natural disasters. It is adaptable to peer counselor training. For information useful in training, see Farberow and Frederick (1978c), Hafen and Peterson (1982), Hafen and Brog (1983), Resnick and Ruben (1975), Simos (1979), Tatelbaum (1980), and Worden (1982).

Notifiers should not personalize this reaction. Notifiers must sensitively and quietly provide people with time and freedom for emotional release. They should allow for silence—time to integrate the information. The recipient of the news must be helped to gather support or decide where support can be found. Notifiers can begin to close the conversation by helping the person establish a plan for the next few hours. Finally, they can ask if there are any more questions, answer them, and then close. The notifier should then take a break and express personal feelings. If the last step is overlooked, the notifier is in serious danger of personal emotional overload.

The Survivor's Bill of Rights

If the survivors are ineptly treated by their organizational management, their emotional trauma will often be aggravated. Social workers should be advocates for the survivors. Emotional injuries must be taken as seriously as physical injuries. No one would think to say, "It's all in your arm," to a person with a broken arm, but it's easy to say, "It's all in your head," to a person with a broken emotion. If applied unthinkingly, simple administrative procedures can intensify an emotional injury. Helping people with emotional injuries requires special skills.

Survivors need their injuries acknowledged, respected, and treated, whether the injuries are physical or emotional. A poorly set bone will mend crookedly. So will an improperly set emotion. Treatment for psychological trauma should be as readily available as for physical trauma, and so should the means of payment. Also, salary continuation, sick pay, disability benefits, and so forth should make specific provisions for psychological trauma as a reason for benefit eligibility.

Burnout

Burnout is the inability to perform at one's usual competency because of too much stress for too long. Symptoms may appear in any of the categories mentioned previously: somatic, cognitive, emotional, behavioral, and interactive. However, the most probable indicators of approaching burnout are excessive fatigue, irritability, anxiety, and impatience.

Social workers should be aware that they also will be affected by the disaster. Each practitioner must be responsible for personal awareness and self-care. Helpers must have internal and external resources for support as they deliver services to others. It is strongly recommended that the social workers have peer support and consultation, as well as a therapy relationship with a professional outside of the organization. Failure to provide self-care may result in loss of perspective, emotional depletion, and burnout to the detriment of both oneself and those being helped. Disaster intervention places one at high risk because of the intensity and magnitude of the workload.

How to prevent burnout? Rest. Eat well. Conduct briefings and debriefings with peers. Enter or continue a therapy relationship. Use humor. Finally, take good care of yourself.[6]

CONCLUSION

Social workers planning for, working during, and cleaning up after a disaster have a difficult, multilevel task. Organizational management seldom sees a need for disaster planning. Even when the need is recognized, there often is not the recognition of a requirement for a mental health element in the plan. During the disaster and the immediate aftermath, the emphasis is on physical recovery. Months after the event, everyone is expected to have recovered without aftereffects. Within the bounds of this environment the social worker must strive for effective planning and intervention.

REFERENCES

Brunstein, S., & Kilpatrick, M. (1984). Earthquake: The first 72 hours—The survival of workforce and physical plant. La Canada-Flintridge, CA: Author.

Cohen, R., & Ahern, F. (1980). Handbook for mental health care of disaster victims. Baltimore: Johns Hopkins University Press.

Crosby, J., & Jose, N. (1983). Death: Family adjustment to loss. In C. Figley & H. McCubbin (Eds.), Stress and the family, Vol. II, Coping with catastrophe. New York: Brunner/Mazel.

De Greene, K. (1982). The adaptive organization: Anticipation and management of crisis. New York: Wiley.

de Vries, M., & Miller, D. (1985). The neurotic organization. San Francisco: Jossey-Bass.

Dynes, R. (1974). Organized behavior in disaster. Newark, DE: Disaster Research Center, University of Delaware.

Erikson, E. (1950). Childhood and society. New York: Norton.

Erikson, E. (1968). Identity, youth, and crisis. New York: Norton.

Farberow, N., & Frederick, C. (1978a). Training manual for human service workers in major disasters (NIMH, DHEW Publication No. ADM 777-538). Washington, DC: U.S. Government Printing Office.

Farberow, N., & Frederick, C. (1978b). Human problems in disasters: A pamphlet for government emergency disaster services personnel (NIMH, DHEW Publication No. ADM 78-539). Washington, DC: U.S. Government Printing Office.

[6]For more on burnout see Cohen and Ahern (1980), Farberow and Frederick (1978b), Hafen and Peterson (1982), and Mitchell (1982, 1983).

Farberow, N., & Frederick, C. (1978c). Field manual for human service workers in major disasters (NIMH, DHEW Publication No. ADM 78-737). Washington, DC: U.S. Government Printing Office.

Fink, S. (1986). *Crisis management*. New York: Amacom.

Hafen, B., & Brog, M. (1983). *Emotional survival*. Englewood Cliffs, NJ: Prentice-Hall.

Hafen, B., & Peterson, B. (1982). *The crisis intervention handbook*. Englewood Cliffs, NJ: Prentice-Hall.

Janis, I., & Mann, L. (1977). *Decision making*. New York: Free Press

Kilpatrick, D. (1982). Los Angeles City Paramedic, personal communication.

Kilpatrick, M. (1981). Coping with survival. La Canada-Flintridge, CA: Author.

Kilpatrick, M., & Brunstein, S. (1983). The invisible injury. La Canada-Flintridge, CA: Author.

Melick, M., Logue, J., & Frederick, C. (1982). Stress and disaster. In L. Goldberger & S. Breznitz (Eds.), *Handbook of stress*. New York: Free Press.

Mitchell, J. (1982). The psychological impact of the Air Florida 90 disaster on fire-rescue, paramedic, and police officer personnel. *Proceedings of the First International Assembly on Emergency Medical Services,* Baltimore, MD, June 13–17. National Highway Traffic Safety Administration, U.S. Department of Transportation, 239–244.

Mitchell, J. (1983, January). When disaster strikes—the critical incident stress debriefing process. *Journal of Emergency Medical Services,* pp. 36–39.

Parad, H., Resnick, H., & Parad, L. (Eds.). (1976). *Emergency and disaster management: A mental health sourcebook*. Bowie, MD: Charles Press.

Resnick, H., & Ruben H. (Eds.). (1975). *Emergency psychiatric care: The management of mental health crises*. Bowie, MD: Charles Press.

Simos, B. (1979). *A time to grieve: Loss as a universal human experience*. New York: Family Service Association of America.

Smith, S. (1983). Disaster: Family disruption in the wake of natural disaster. In C. Figley & H. McCubbin (Eds.), *Stress and the family. Vol. II. Coping with catastrophe*. New York: Brunner/Mazel.

Tatelbaum, J. (1980). *The courage to grieve*. New York: Harper & Row.

Worden, J. (1982). *Grief counseling and grief therapy: A handbook for the mental health practitioner*. New York: Springer Publishing Company.

8 Relocation Counseling and Services

David I. Siegel

Relocation of corporate managers and employees to various sections of this country and abroad has been a traditional management development tool (Moore, 1982). The inward flow of new talent provided by relocation is vital to many a company's well-being (Mangum, 1982). A survey of Fortune 1000 executives conducted by Opinion Research Corporation found that "two out of three respondents believed that varied functional and geographical experience was significant in grooming senior management talent" (Magnus & Dodd, 1981, p. 539).

John M. Moore (1982) summarizes the role of relocation for management planning: "As a management development tool, relocation serves two purposes: growing (developing) management talent internally to meet executive staffing needs as often as possible, and broadening the experience of high potential managers" (p. 31). He further states:

> Effective human resource planning, including the creation of a strategic relocation policy to place employees where they are needed and/or can best be developed, benefits both company and employees. It increases morale; broadens developmental experience; places key people in strategically important positions and improves productivity. (p. 31)

Other reasons for relocation include:

1. Most managers believe hiring from inside rather than outside decreases the risk of performance failure.
2. More sophisticated and automated work processes require more competent and better trained people (Moore, 1982).

Relocations peaked during the 1970s when there was a 5% to 8% increase in their number each year (Haight, 1983, p. 21). However, Catalyst's latest survey indicates that "the number of relocations is likely to plateau, or even increase" in the years to come (Sekas, 1984, p. 38). Currently, approximately 300,000 employees are transferred each year (Guillet, 1980; Haight, 1983; Minor, 1984).

This chapter reviews various issues surrounding relocation that are particularly relevant to social workers in the workplace. These include (1) the various problems and concerns that confront workers and families facing relocation, as well as (2) the financial, personnel, and employee assistance programming available to help them. An underlying theme of this chapter is that social workers have the knowledge and opportunity to greatly expand their efforts in helping people respond to the stresses of relocation.

RESISTANCE TO RELOCATION

Despite the benefits claimed for it, the 1980s have seen a growing resistance to relocation by corporate managers and their families. The sources of this resistance include (1) its increasing financial costs, (2) changing values and lifestyles, (3) family disruption and psychological stress caused by relocation, and (4) the growth of dual-career couples.

Financial Costs and Incentives

From the standpoint of the family, increasing costs associated with a changing economy have been a strong source of resistance to relocation. Potentially high mortgage interest rates in the new area, a potentially higher cost of living, and transfer to high-housing-cost areas are major concerns of potential transferees (Milbrandt, 1981). To these can be added other costs of relocation such as (1) the potential loss or reduction of a spouse's income, (2) spouse's expense in looking for a new job, (3) the cost of moving family and belongings, (4) the costs of selling one's old residence and looking for a new one, and (5) the cost of making trips to scout the new location.

Industry has had to develop components of relocation benefit packages to respond to the financial concerns of potential transferees and thus provide financial incentives to relocate. These components include:

1. Mortgage Interest Differentials: Companies make a payment to relocating employees based on the difference between their mortgage interest rate on their old home and that on their residence in their new job location (Magnus & Dodd, 1981; Milbrandt, 1981).
2. Cost-of-Living Differentials: A payment is made to employees based on the difference in cost between their new location and the old on all major cost-of-living components (Magnus & Dodd, 1981).

3. Relocation Taxation Policies: Some companies provide compensation for increased tax burdens in a new location or for taxes on the reimbursement of moving costs (Milbrandt, 1981).

4. Zero-Based Relocation Policies: In accord with these policies, each planned relocation is examined by the company to determine if it is cost effective and appropriate for the employee's career path (Milbrandt, 1981). If the magnitude of the difference in living costs between the old and new locations is too great, or if the career ramifications of the move are not in the interest of the employee, the transfer may not be approved.

5. Home-sale Assistance.

Other financial benefits include:

6. Shipment of Household Goods to the New Location.
7. Transportation of the Family to the New Location.
8. Temporary Living Expenses at the New Location.
9. House-hunting Trips to the New Location.
10. Closing Costs on the New Home.
11. Miscellaneous Expenses (such as allowances for utilities hookups, draperies, etc.).
12. Term Loans: A low-interest or interest-free loan is provided to help transferees buy a more expensive residence in a new area.
13. Rental Assistance: A payment is paid to compensate employees for higher rental payments in a new area.
14. Equity Advance: This enables the transferee to buy in the new area before the sale of the former home is completed (Magnus & Dodd, 1981, pp. 542–543).

Changing Values and Lifestyles

As a result of changing values and lifestyles, many managers are not as wedded to their corporate careers as in the past and therefore may be reluctant to relocate. Quality of life and leisure interests are more important now (Guillet, 1980), while today's managers, more independent than their predecessors, are more likely to resist the hardships involved in a move (Moore, 1982). Gaylord (1979) believes resistance to relocation is partly the result of the youth movement, "with its accent on personal values, self fulfilling lifestyles, and questioning of the 'establishment's' way of doing things" and the women's movement, as women now are not as willing to follow their husbands. They have "become more conscious of the importance for them personally of exercising their own choices regarding their destiny" (p. 186).

Psychological Stress and Family Disruption

Corporate executives who are offered the choice to relocate often experience a dualism of thought and feeling. They may initially experience feelings of excitement and anticipation, as the offer may mean promotions, greater responsibility, and increased career opportunities (Gullotta & Donohue, 1982, p. 37). Relocation may mean recognition of their skills and increased respect in the eyes of fellow workers.

However, these initial optimistic feelings are often replaced by symptoms of stress associated with relocation. These include anxious anticipation, anxiety, sleepless nights, short attention span, lack of productivity, short temper, headache, and gastrointestinal disturbances (Gullotta & Donohue, 1982; Johnson, 1984). Studies of lifestyles of persons with high rates of job turnover indicate that these people frequently experience a mobility syndrome. Symptoms here include depression, deterioration in health, increased risk for alcoholism, little community involvement, pervasive feelings of social anonymity, diffusion of individual responsibility for social acts resulting in lack of involvement, destructive aggression, strong dependency on the marital relationship for emotional satisfaction, marital discord, and increased risk of divorce (Anderson & Stark, 1985/1986). Arlene Johnson (1984) states that "relocation is stressful because it involves change—changing homes, school and community, leaving old friends, changing job and job responsibilities, and perhaps even changing wardrobes, social expectations and eating habits. So much is new and, therefore, unknown and unfamiliar" (p. 30).

Employers may be insensitive to the stress caused by relocation, may provide inadequate information regarding the living style and housing situation of the new site, and may require relocation in a short period of time, all of which add to the stress of the situation. Furthermore, prospective transferees may be increasing their levels of responsibility and stress each time they relocate.

Despite the considerable stress that the relocating workers face, they may in fact experience less disruption in their lives than do other family members. For example, relocation may be particularly difficult for the corporate wife (Foster & Liebrenz, 1977; Gaylord, 1979; Gullotta & Donohue, 1982). While she may initially experience the joy of her husband's job advancement, she may do so at great price. She may have to give up close friends, contact with community, group memberships, and other support systems, while in many cases her career may be sidetracked. The move is usually made for the benefit of the husband's career, and he maintains most of his important social contacts at the office, while his wife may feel like a helpless victim (Gaylord, 1979).

The traditional role of corporate wife and her presumed appropriate behavior may contribute to negative adjustments to the move. She is encouraged to preserve acceptance and harmony with an attitude of sportsmanship. The corporate wife is expected to let her husband know she is happy and willing to be his partner in this new test. Characteristically, the wife will not blame the move for her stress, but she internalizes and blames herself with consequent loss of self-esteem (Gaylord, 1979). "It is therefore hardly surprising that many corporate wives are seen clinically during their third and fourth decades of life as chronically depressed, lacking in hope or desire, and frequently addicted to alcohol, tranquilizers, and barbiturates" (Gaylord, 1979, p. 188).

In many cases the marriage contract has been defined so that the wife carries primary responsibility for the domestic front. When relocation is imminent, the husband may provide clues to his wife to lessen home responsibilities on him. These may include comments such as "pressures are building" or requests that she "understand." "The less willing and more resentful she is of this role expectation, the greater the likelihood that she will experience feelings of anger and depression" (Gullotta & Donohue, 1982, p. 37).

Relocation also has important effects upon children. Young teenagers are particularly affected since they are at an age when change is all about them. They are moving from a child-focused system of education to one that is subject-focused. They are experiencing hormonal changes that will turn them from children into young adults. They are at a stage of social–emotional growth that finds them using peers as their reference groups (Gullotta & Donohue, 1982). Doubt and uncertainty about the self are already problems, and their adaptive energies are overloaded (Gaylord, 1979). At this stage of life, a stable home environment is particularly important and relocation may be difficult. According to Anderson and Stark (1985/1986), relocating teenagers "are at high risk for impaired social relationships and acting out through violently destructive behaviors and substance abuse" (p. 40).

Children in general may be severely affected by loss of friends and community life just when there is a need for a stable and supportive environment (Gaylord, 1979). Children who move often may not be able to form close ties because they do not want to go through feelings of loss again and again (Magnus & Dodd, 1981, p. 544).

During any move it is easy for children to feel ignored (Gaylord, 1979). They can feel pushed aside with resultant feelings of isolation. The loss of friends and suddenness of the decision to move (particularly if the young person is uninformed until the move occurs) can produce strong feelings of abandonment, helplessness, and isolation. Emotional problems, weight loss, nightmares, and bedwetting often result. Difficulties occur most often for those who have problems making friends and whose mothers are not satisfied with the move (Gullotta & Donohue, 1982).

Gaylord (1979) points out that "a small child's fears and suffering when moving are caused by misinformation and misinterpretation arising from the fantasy world in which he or she is occupied." Following an analytical interpretation she argues:

> Small children frequently interpret a move as punishment and as an act of hostility on the part of powerful parents and often incorporate the move itself into their primitive theories of existence, with at times frightening results. (p. 188)

Fortunately, moves are not always traumatic for children, since the family's reaction to and coping with the move affect them in very important ways. A 2-year study conducted by Brett and Werbel categorized family patterns of coping with relocation. According to this study, "active coping is typified by exerting extra effort to deal with an unfamiliar situation: passive coping is exemplified by increased smoking, drinking more than usual, irregular eating, and actively seeking social and emotional support from relatives and friends" (Magnus & Dodd, 1981, p. 543).

Another consideration of the effects of relocation is whether the family is already experiencing difficulties. Anderson and Stark (1985/1986) wonder about the effect on the "blended" family and the noncustodial parent and the child, as well as the family that requires special services for a developmentally disabled child or for an aged parent. They also mention research that shows that different types of people react differently to moves. Indications are that "Happy Homebuilding" wives, "open" laissez-faire families, and couples with complementary work/home involvements are less likely to develop move-associated problems.

Dual-Career Couples

Dual-career families and the changing role of women are important to consider when understanding resistance to relocation (Driessnack, 1982; Foster & Liebrenz, 1977; Magnus & Dodd, 1981; Mathews, 1984; Sekas, 1984). The number of women in the labor force grew from 33.5 million in 1972 to 48 million in 1982, an increase of 43%. Almost 60% of employment gains made by women occurred in male-dominated occupations, and "women now account for over 27% of the managers and administrators in the American workforce" (Mathews, 1984, p. 55).

The changing role of women, their enhanced career opportunities, greater economic independence, greater proportion in administrative and management positions, and their greater participation in family decision making have created resistance to relocating corporate executives and have increased the need for further types of relocation benefits (Foster & Liebrenz, 1977; Mathews, 1984; Sekas, 1984). Women are now more likely to consider their jobs to be careers, and they are less willing to disrupt their own careers for their spouses' careers. In addition to the disruption of their careers caused by relocation, spouses may face changes in job status, changes in family status, and loss of workforce credibility (Mathews, 1984, p. 58).

In addition to the variety of stresses experienced by relocating families in general, there are other ingredients for dual-career couples. A potential move and the potential financial benefits of a promotion and relocation benefits must be balanced by the effect on a spouse's income. The spouse may be forced to take a lower-paying job in the new location, may experience a loss of salary and benefits while looking for a job, and may experience the high costs of a job search. A serious reduction in the couple's combined earning power can sometimes be the result (Mathews, 1984).

RELOCATION SERVICES AND OCCUPATIONAL SOCIAL WORK

As a result of the various resistances to relocation, corporations have had to develop relocation counseling and services in addition to the financial incentives already mentioned. These services are usually provided by the human resources or personnel departments of corporations, by relocation consulting firms, or by relocation service centers developed by the real estate industry. To this point, social workers have not been as active in this area as they can be in light of the appropriateness of their generalist and systems orientation. Successful relocation involves the application of macro-organizational policies, mezzotraining, education and stress management, and micropersonal, family, and psychosocial interventions—all of which can easily be incorporated within a social worker's professional repertoire.

Maxine Gaylord (1979) indicates the possibilities for social work intervention by stating, "A staff person outside the department of the employee, who is knowledgeable about the problems of a move, has a helping attitude, and knows the community and its resources, could provide effective, supportive intervention before any problems in adjustment arise" (p. 190). Other alternatives are for companies to hire social work consultants on a part-time basis or for many corporations with similar relocation problems to avail themselves of the services of a social work agency specializing in relocation (Gaylord, 1979).

It would seem that a corporate Employee Assistance Program (EAP) should be a prime mechanism for addressing personal relocation issues. However, "in industries where job relocation is prevalent, few have an Employee Assistance Program," and "it is rare to find an industry that has a well-established system of Employee Assistance Program Services which addresses the needs of relocating employees and their families" (Anderson & Stark, 1985/1986, p. 47). Those that do have employee assistance programs still tend to define relocation as a personnel or human resource issue and refer it to those departments.

Employee assistance programs, as they respond to the needs of management and the increases in health benefit costs, should increasingly emphasize prevention and health promotion and may become part of corporate management development policies (see Chapter 9 of this volume). As these trends become evident, social workers employed in EAPs would seem most appropriate to provide counseling at the various levels of relocation assistance, so relocation can be recognized as relevant to all aspects of life functioning. These include (1) interpreting corporate relocation benefits and policy to employees and enabling them to best utilize benefits; (2) providing information as to the stresses involved in a move and the planning and decision making needed; (3) providing information about the new community including areas such as housing costs and practices, climate, people, schools, services, and cost of living; (4) arranging helping networks in the new location of company employees and those previously relocated; and (5) providing personal counseling to address particular adjustment problems of relocation and problems of family disruption.

Career Assistance for Spouses

In light of the growth of the dual-career family, some companies have begun to offer career and employment assistance to the spouses of relocating executives. The similarities between these services and those provided to terminated workers through outplacement counseling are obvious (see Chapter 12 of this volume). The following types of career services—at least some of which could be provided by social workers—include:

1. Counseling: There may be a great deal of resentment and hostility, which must be dealt with before a spouse can mobilize for a job search (Magnus & Dodd, 1981).
2. Assessment: Assessment may include a full review of the spouse's background experience, education, and skills, and discussion to outline career objectives and possibilities (Driessnack, 1982; Magnus & Dodd, 1981).
3. Field Analysis and Investigation: An analysis can be made of the spouse's field of interest and the jobs available throughout the country and in the specific city of relocation (Magnus & Dodd, 1981).
4. Developing a Marketing Plan: Spouses are counseled on resume preparation, interviewing techniques, writing effective letters, developing contacts, using recruiters and employment agencies, and general skills of job finding (Driessnack, 1982; "Have Spouse," 1982; Magnus & Dodd, 1981).

5. Follow-up and Support: Throughout the job-hunting process, spouses are provided with support and backup and a review of interviewing skills.

Other important career assistance for spouses includes:

1. Job Referral: Corporate personnel officers can use their own informal networks for referring spouses to appropriate people or may send resumes to local search firms. To find career opportunities for relocating spouses of employees, the mechanism of career-continuation networks has been developed. In these networks, resumes of high-calibre spouses can be shared among groups of organizations and given preference in hiring. In addition to addressing spousal resistance to relocation, these networks benefit the corporations by providing the availability of high-calibre personnel, increasing the bases of technical and managerial talent in a community, and enabling them to share relocation costs through the advantages of large scale (Mathews, 1984; Sekas, 1984). It is important to point out, however, that possible conflicts with the organization's commitment to Equal Employment Opportunity and Affirmative Action policies and practices must be resolved (see Chapter 14 of this volume for a discussion of these issues).
2. Hiring the Spouse: In order to overcome resistance to relocation, many companies have eliminated rules prohibiting the hiring of a spouse.
3. Flexible Relocation Plans: In addition to a basic plan of relocation benefits, additional benefits can be offered on an optional basis, permitting relocating employees to select one or two additional benefits of greatest importance to them (Mathews, 1984).

Overcoming Stress through Education

The provision of information, through any number of vehicles, can ease the stresses of relocation. One principle involved is the need to establish communication between the corporation and its executives and the relocating family (Foster & Liebrenz, 1977; Johnson, 1984; Magnus & Dodd, 1981; Moore, 1981). Making the employee and family part of the decision to relocate and providing information at crucial points of the process helps to alleviate resistance and overcome anxiety.

Foster and Liebrenz (1977) recommend that an important part of the premove stage should involve a process of bridge-building. They argue, "An effort by the corporation to share the reasons for the proposed transfer and the role of the individual executive in the firm with the spouse can go far in reducing the psychic costs of relocating" (p. 73). Face-to-face meetings are needed in order to provide a triangular linkage between corporation, executive, and family.

Another important principle is for the corporation to communicate relocation policy in a manner that is clearly understood by the employee. Beginning in the premove stage, the personnel department can be helpful in interpreting and helping families use relocation policies (which can be quite complicated).

A number of logistical concerns can be addressed, such as the best use of time frames provided, which documents should be readily available, details of the company's plan to dispose of the family residence, instructions on completing and coordinating the paperwork involved, and what approval channels are necessary (Moore, 1981).

Johnson (1984) recommends providing information on the new location, including information about affordable neighborhoods, lifestyles, schools, housing, and athletic and cultural facilities. However, she further suggests that information about the moving process itself is also crucial. Transferees need to know that exhilaration, ambivalence, loneliness, excitement, and anger are normal feelings associated with relocation.

Education through television and newspapers can be effective in "forewarning and fore-arming the moving family" (Gullotta & Donahue, 1982, p. 42). A newsletter giving practical advice on the nature of relocation, managing family stress, finding time for family, and meeting the family's emotional needs can be useful.

Relieving Stress through Counseling and Support

Corporations have begun to provide various types of personal counseling to relieve the psychological stress and family disruption involved in relocation. For example, in the premove phase, group seminars and workshops can be valuable. These can help the employee evaluate the relocation decision, anticipate problems, and formulate responses that will ease adjustment into the new job and location (Johnson, 1984). It is important in these premove seminars that families express their feelings, particularly regarding the reasons the move is being made and the tradeoffs involved. This helps alleviate any guilt the employee may be feeling concerning the move and helps the family resolve important issues (Magnus & Dodd, 1981). In addition to personal counseling regarding these issues, pretransition counseling can include special methods, such as family or group role plays of special issues and personal growth groups that focus on coping mechanisms and adaptation (Anderson & Stark, 1985/1986). Counseling may also help the family develop reality-based expectations about special needs that family members may have and may stimulate their adaptive planning about these needs (Anderson & Stark, 1985/1986).

Once the premove phase is over and employees have chosen a community, transferees enter what Foster and Liebrenz (1977) call "the integrating stage." They recommend that the family be allowed to visit the prospective community before making the move so that they can correct unexamined prejudices against a city or area. The toughest time for the new family may be right after the move is made, as they must become oriented to the community. Moore (1981) comments on this time: "The family needs time to become established, learn local back roads, make friends, meet neighbors, resume favorite interests, and find comfortable and convenient daily routines" (p. 68).

Anderson and Stark (1985/1986) recommend telephone or face-to-face contact by a transfer counselor upon arrival "to monitor progress, review expectations, reassure and to discern problems that have emerged requiring special assistance" (p. 51).

To help people adjust during the integrating stage, other company families and earlier transferees can be encouraged to take an interest in the newly arrived family (Anderson & Stark, 1985/1986; Foster & Liebrenz, 1977; Johnson, 1984; Magnus & Dodd, 1981; Moore, 1981). They can share information about the community and can help alleviate the newcomers' anxiety through personal contact and support. As an example, in their Families in Transition Project, Gullotta and Donohue (1982) encouraged two parents to begin a welcoming group for newly arrived families. When a new child was enrolled in school, arrangements were made for a "friendly visitor" to call at the home of the newcomer and provide information on stores, eating establishments, clubs, and town events.

Gullotta and Donohue (1982) point out that by enabling expression of sadness, loneliness, identity loss, and anger, small groups provide ideal vehicles for the development of a sense of universality and cohesiveness. Consequently, they suggest the use of natural caregivers and self-help to ease relocation stress.

Anderson and Stark (1985/1986) suggest that the stresses of relocation may be eased if the corporation is engaged in a process of affiliation. They suggest the development of company groups and activities to provide potential sources of support for relocation. These include programs such as a Youth Services Club, a Cultural Arts Fair, a Family Newsletter, and a Babysitter's Exchange Cooperative.

A program of community education and linkage is important and should include the mobilization of a variety of community resources and people representing organizations from different community systems (Gullotta & Donohue, 1982). The connection of families to needed resources is particularly important for those with special needs such as special education, psychiatric treatment, or services for an elderly parent (Anderson & Stark, 1985/1986).

Several corporations and employee assistance firms offer course seminars and workshops to provide support during the adjustment period. For example, the Plastics Business Group of General Electric sponsors a workshop tailored to participant interests but one that generally begins with a discussion of the "highs" and "lows" of relocation. Participants become familiar with the new area through activities as disparate as treasure hunts and listening to guest speakers (Johnson, 1984).

CASE EXAMPLE

The experience of the author, recently relocated from New York to Los Angeles and single at the time, illustrates some of the major themes of this chapter.

Dualism of Thought and Feeling

Dualism of thought and feeling was a major theme of my relocation. It was an opportunity for a new beginning and a first step toward eventual career advancement. This opportunity to wipe the slate clean was quite exhilarating and provided the energy to juggle the various tasks and emotional pressures of a sudden move.

On the other hand, relocation meant leaving my closest relatives and friends behind, and this loss of intimacy, and regaining intimate relationships, remained the one truly difficult task of relocation. While there were many supportive efforts provided by colleagues and other helpful people, I felt the lack of people to trust and confide in. This dualism of thought and feeling can be quite disorienting, as one's mood and perspective change quickly.

Family Disruption and Stress

As many others, I experienced the stress of family disruption. As the eldest of three sons in a family whose father had recently died, my relocation had a significant effect on my role in the family, as well as on my mother and two brothers. I had both emotional and task-oriented responsibilities toward the family that were part of my identity. Changing this responsibility contributed to some feeling of loss of self while at the same time creating freedom and independence. It also meant my two brothers had to shoulder more family responsibility with consequences to their own senses of self.

As a result of my need for family, upon coming to Los Angeles I almost immediately developed a relationship with a proverbial lost relative (a first cousin) and his wife. We became confidants. In addition, my stress in relocating was eased by the relationship with my present wife. This began a few months after the move. Without these relationships, the lack of family and friends would have been quite difficult. Relocation does increase the significance of the nuclear family or lack of it.

Cultural Differences

While New York and Los Angeles are both big cities with high levels of excitement and many diverse ethnic and cultural groups, there are several cultural differences that contribute to stress. For example, in Los Angeles there is a law against jaywalking, and one must walk to the corner and wait for the light in order to cross. This can be disconcerting to one who is used to running madly through crowded New York City streets. My dress seemed a little off, because in Los Angeles people dress in a very relaxed style, appropriate for the outdoors or the beach, while I was addicted to my comfortable blue blazer. While looking for an apartment, I discovered that in contrast to New York, where leases are mandatory, in Los Angeles landlords pride themselves on renting month-to-month. In Los Angeles, the automobile is extolled and people drive everywhere, and initially I seemed to be the only one walking around my neighborhood. These small cultural differences, while destabilizing only for a month or two, contributed to my sense of disorientation. I would have benefited greatly from information packets describing life in Los Angeles, as well as from the informational counseling suggested in this chapter.

Denial

As a result of the various stresses involved in relocation, I found that initially I was tending to deny the importance of the move. I felt as though I was preparing for a long trip rather than for a permanent reorganization of my life. I was able to control the deeper emotional concomitants of the move by engaging in the more concrete tasks of relocation. It was not until the cross-country trip through places like Effingham, Illinois, and Laredo, Texas, that reality set in and I began the adjustment process.

SUMMARY

Social workers, whose training emphasizes systems concepts and a generalist approach to practice, are ideal for assuming roles as relocation counselors. Interventions can include (1) helping to develop corporate relocation policies and interpreting them to employees, (2) providing information and workshops regarding the stresses involved in moving and the planning and decision making needed to carry it out, (3) providing information about new communities, (4) arranging helping networks and mobilizing community resources in new locations, and (5) providing personal counseling to address particular adjustment problems of relocating families.

REFERENCES

Anderson, C., & Stark, C. (1985/1986). Emerging issues from job relocation in the high tech field: Implications for Employee Assistance Programs. *Employee Assistance Quarterly, 1,* 37–54.

Driessnack, C. H. (1982). Spouse relocation: A creative approach to recuitment and employee transfer. *Personnel Administrator, 27,* 59–65.

Edwards, L. (1978). Present shock and how to avoid it abroad. *Across the Board, 15,* 36–43.

Foster, L. W., & Liebrenz, M. L. (1977). Corporate moves—Who pays the psychic costs? *Personnel, 54,* 67–75.

Gavin, J. (1983, September 5). On the move: Working couples put to test by career moves. *Las Vegas Review-Journal,* p. 7c.

Gaylord, M. (1979). Relocation and the corporate family: Unexplored issues. *Social Work, 24,* 186–191.

Groh, K. F. (1984). Relocation-counseling centers ease adjustment to a new city. *Personnel Journal, 63,* 88, 90, 92. (Adapted with permission from *Runzheimers Reports on Relocation,* (1984), 2)

Guillet, D. R. (1980). Getting employees to relocate . . . when they won't. *Administrative Management, 41,* 43, 75+.

Gullotta, T. P., & Donohue, K. C. (1982). Preventing family distress during relocation: Initiatives for human resource managers. *Personnel Administrator, 27,* 37–40, 42–43.

Haight, G. G. (1983). Job transfer survivors. *Across the Board, 20,* 20–26.

Have spouse will travel: If you find us both a job. (1982). *International Management, 37,* 21–22.

Johnson, A. A. (1984). Relocation: Getting more for the dollars you spend. *Personnel Administrator, 29,* 29–32, 35, 136.

Magnus, M., & Dodd, J. (1981). Relocation: Changing attitudes and company policies. *Personnel Journal, 60,* 538–548.

Mangum, W. T. (1982). What mortgage rates are doing to executive mobility. *Administrative Management, 43,* 59–60, 86–87.

Mathews, P. A. (1984). The changing work force: Dual-career couples and relocation. *Personnel Administrator, 29,* 55–56, 58–59, 61–62.

Milbrandt, G. F. (1981). Relocation strategies: Part 1. *Personnel Journal, 60,* 551–554.

Minor, A. (1984). An overview of relocation services: How is the industry responding to new financial, social and technological forces? *Personnel Administrator, 29,* 64–66.

Moore, J. M. (1981). Employee relocation: Expanded responsibilities for the personnel department. *Personnel, 58,* 62–69.

Moore, J. M. (1982). The role relocation plays in management planning: A vital tool for developing talents. *Personnel Adminstrator, 27,* 31–34.

Sekas, M. H. (1984). Dual-career couples—A corporate challenge: An overview of how various companies are handling the relocation of dual career couples. *Personnel Adminstrator, 29,* 37–38, 40+.

Upson, N. (1974). *How to survive as a corporate wife* (pp. 77–78, 82). Garden City, NY: Doubleday.

Human Resource Management Programs

9 Health Enhancement Programs: Balanced Lifestyles, Physical Fitness, Smoking Cessation, Stress Management, and Weight Control

James L. Jenkins

The recent formation of the Association for Fitness in Business is an indicator of the significance of health enhancement programs in the workplace today. Fitness and physical activity have opened the door for other health enhancement programs. Today a more generic meaning is applied to the term *fitness* by the Association for Fitness in Business, a meaning that encompasses total physical, mental, and social well-being.

How does the workplace-based social worker become involved with fitness and health enhancement programs? Isn't that the turf of the exercise physiologist and the health educator? This chapter addresses these and other questions relating to the role of the occupational social worker in health enhancement programs. The underlying theoretical and conceptual frameworks and practice guidelines utilized in the design of health enhancement programs are discussed. The development and implementation of company-specific programs are outlined and two case examples are presented. The introduction of social workers into the workplace has expanded the field of practice into a variety of health enhancement programs designed to upgrade the quality of life of employees and their families.

HISTORICAL BACKGROUND

Historically, the workplace has been a major factor in compromising the health of workers in America. Poor working conditions, long hours, and little regard for the human factor all took their toll on the health status of the workforce. Early work reforms focused on children at work, the physical plant, and the length of the workday. Later, health and safety improvements were imposed on employers (White, 1983). Business and industry apparently viewed the worker as a static commodity and had little appreciation for the relationship between the health status of employees and productivity and profit.

Today the worker with compromised health represents a serious threat to our national economy. Employers have become increasingly sensitive to the health status of workers as they have gained a greater investment in the cost of health care. American businesses currently pay approximately one half of the nation's health care bills (Cohen, 1985). It is cost effective to help impaired employees due to the high cost of replacing them. Unhealthy people are less productive, have higher rates of absenteeism, and make greater use of medical benefits. Consequently, there has been a clear shift toward disease prevention and health promotion in the workplace, with an underlying belief that "people maintenance" is good business. Employee health enhancement programs have been shown to improve health, reduce absenteeism and turnover, and increase worker productivity.

Initially, employee assistance programs focused on the alcohol-impaired worker. In recent years there has been a shift in focus toward prevention and health enhancement through health promotion and wellness programs. These programs have expanded the range of services beyond safety and periodic health screenings to include proper nutrition and exercise, stress reduction, and the reduction of health-compromising lifestyles such as smoking, substance abuse, overeating, and insufficient physical activity. The workplace is an excellent setting in which to enhance and monitor the health of employees and their families, in the sense that extended periods of observation facilitate early detection and intervention.

Social workers have moved quickly to assume an active role in employee assistance and health enhancement programs in the corporate setting. This was highlighted by the overwhelming success of the first Conference on Occupational Social Work sponsored by the National Association of Social Workers in May 1985. The list of presenters reads like a who's who in occupational social work and includes social workers employed in such organizations as AT&T Technologies, Boston College, the Chicago Police Department, Digital Equipment Corporation, Hazelden Foundation, Polaroid Inc., Time Inc., United Airlines, the United States Air Force, and Westinghouse Corporation. The experience of these and other companies has provided an opportunity to conduct evaluation and research, which can serve as a baseline for the development of a theoretical framework for health enhancement programs in the workplace.

THEORETICAL FRAMEWORK

A sound theoretical framework provides the foundation upon which health enhancement programs are built. The primary theoretical issues underlying these services include the relationship between health and work, personal health practices, and the health enhancement process. A discussion of these issues is provided to assist social workers involved in such programs.

Work and Health

The environment in which an individual works has a significant effect upon that person's health. Physical agents (such as chemicals and other pollutants) and psychological stress compromise the health of employees. On the other hand, worksites that control occupational health hazards and adapt work to human goals and needs are health-enhancing. Physical work in a proper environment can improve physical capacity, while psychologically pleasing work can enhance self-esteem and provide a sense of self-actualization. An understanding of the relationship between work and health is only beginning to be appreciated in American business and industry. As recently as 1978 there were more than four billion person-days in which workers reduced their usual activities for the day due to illness or injury (White, 1983).

Occupational Safety and Health

The Williams Steiger Occupational Safety and Health Act of 1970 was enacted to ensure safe and healthful working conditions. This act requires that employers conduct programs that protect workers from occupational illness, injuries, and death. It requires that employers provide workers with a safe and healthful work environment in which recognized hazards have been eliminated or controlled. It also authorizes workers to decline to perform assigned tasks because of a reasonable belief that the task poses an imminent risk of serious bodily harm or death.

Work-related Health Problems

In addition to occupational safety and health problems, there are a number of work-related health problems associated with exposure to such factors as work overload, a lack of sufficient attention to ergonomics in the design of equipment and work stations, and psychosocial factors such as interpersonal conflicts and production pressures. An individual's susceptibility to work-related health problems is further influenced by personal health practices, work habits, and lifestyle.

The quality of work, organizational roles, shift work, and migration have been associated with work-related health problems. The quality of work includes both (1) work overload, too much work or work that is too difficult, and (2) work underload, work that is repetitive, routine, and insufficiently stimulating. The role of an employee within an organization can be health-compromising when role conflict or role ambiguity occur. There is a strong correlation between role conflict, ambiguity, and job satisfaction (Kasl, 1978). Shift workers present common complaints of sleep disturbances, disturbances of appetite, and disruption of social contacts (see Chapter 10 of this volume). Frequent relocations associated with job transfers result in significant physical and psychological problems among workers and their families (see Chapter 8). In addition, locomotor and psychogenic disorders such as low-back pain, hypertension, headache, and persistent general fatigue are common work-related health problems. Low-back pain is a significant work-related disorder and one of the major causes of lost time from work. It is estimated that 2% to 5% of industrial workers in Western countries experience low-back pain (Snook, 1983), and over 19% of employed white males have definite hypertension.

Health Practices in America

The major causes of death among Americans aged 25 to 64 are (in descending order) heart disease, cancer, stroke, and cirrhosis of the liver. Major contributing factors to these conditions include obesity, smoking, consumption of alcohol, stress, lack of exercise, and a high-fat diet. These factors are highly correlated with individual health practices. This suggests that the primary health risks that eliminate employees from the workforce, or that reduce their productivity, are directly related to their lifestyle behaviors.

In 1983, Louis Harris and Associates interviewed by telephone 1,254 randomly selected members of the adult public across the country. This initiative was part of a larger project to measure where America stands when it comes to preventing disease and promoting good health and longevity. At a time when evidence from many sources shows that the health consciousness of Americans has reached an all-time high, this national survey of health behaviors revealed that Americans get poor marks in a number of key health and safety habits. Harris and Associates found that:

1. Only one fifth say they wear seatbelts all the time when in the front seat of a car. A majority say that they never wear seatbelts at all.
2. Three in 10 drivers say they drive after drinking at least part of the time.
3. Less than a quarter of adults are within the weight range recommended for their height, build, and sex; 47% are overweight.
4. Only one in three adults gets strenuous exercise 3 or more days a week; 24% never get strenuous exercise at all.
5. Less than 50% of the adult population say they "try a lot" to avoid high-cholesterol foods, and barely more than half make such claims with respect to fat consumption and control of salt and sugar intake (Irving, 1983).

Health Enhancement

The Individual's Role

The determination of each individual's health status is a personal responsibility. Each day people make health decisions about whether to smoke, how much they exercise, how much they weigh, what they drink, and what drugs they take. They decide when to seek health care, what to tell doctors, and whether to follow medical advice. There is strong evidence that a person's health status is a product of lifestyle choices. In a study of lifestyle and life expectancy, researchers found that adults who ate three meals a day, avoided snacks, had daily breakfast, exercised moderately two or three times a week, slept 7 or 8 hours a night, did not smoke, were not overweight, and drank little or no alcohol had a life expectancy more than 11 years longer than those who did not (Combs, Hales, & Williams, 1981).

The Company's Role

The workplace provides an ideal setting in which to provide employees with the resources and psychological support that promote health enhancing lifestyle choices. The workplace facilitates regular participation, social support from co-workers, environmental supports such as healthy food in the cafeteria, protective smoking policies, lower costs, and accessibility (Cohen, 1985).

Cost versus Benefit

The quantification of the benefits of health enhancement programs in the workplace is difficult at best. The beneficial claims of such programs include increased productivity, reduced absenteeism, reduced worker turnover and training costs, reduced costs attributed to work-related health problems, and the prevention, early detection, and effective treatment of selected diseases (Hanley, 1982). A study of one company reported annual savings of nearly $14,000 associated with reduced replacement requirements and decreased payments for sick time and time off. Another study reported a 52% improvement in work attendance among troubled employees as well as a 74.6% reduction in worker-compensation costs (Witte & Cannon, 1979). However, little information is yet available on the evaluation and cost effectiveness of health enhancement programs. Because these programs are often non-revenue-producing, in times of economic restraint it is often difficult to make a case for the indirect savings of reduced turnover, lower absenteeism, and higher productivity (Steinberg, 1981). There is a need for further research to quantify the cost effectiveness of these programs. In the final analysis, it is the bottom line of the profit margin that compels employers to address employee health issues in the workplace.

The theoretical framework supporting health enhancement programs in the workplace is based on the direct relationship between an individual's lifestyle and health practices, and one's health status and capacity to be a productive worker. Employers who appreciate these relationships and understand the implications for the economic success of their company will have increased motivation to incorporate health enhancement programs in their company. In an effort to encourage such programs, Senator Cohen (R-Maine) introduced legislation in the Preventive Health Care Incentive Act (S. 1618, 1983) to provide tax credit to employers who provide preventive health programs for their employees (Cohen, 1985).

This theoretical framework that follows suggests key concepts that have been used to formulate a conceptual framework for health enhancement programs.

CONCEPTUAL FRAMEWORK

Health enhancement programs reflect the use of a number of key concepts in their design, development, and implementation. The primary concepts discussed here include prevention, systems theory, consultation, self-determination, the intervention pyramid, and organizational assessment.

Prevention

The literature on prevention describes a prevention continuum incorporating three areas of prevention: tertiary, secondary, and primary (Caplan & Grunebaum, 1972). The health care system in the United States places most resources in the area of tertiary prevention, with an emphasis on treating individuals who have existing health problems. Primary prevention, efforts directed at keeping communities, groups, and individuals healthy, has received little emphasis. In fact, less than 2% of the total amount spent for health care has been devoted to keeping people well (Cohen, 1985).

America's health care strategy needs an increased emphasis on health promotion and disease prevention. The objective of health enhancement is to place the primary amount of resources on primary prevention in order to keep people healthy. Such programs should be designed to reduce work-related health problems and diminish those conditions known to cause them (Gilbert, 1982).

Systems Theory

A solid understanding of systems theory is essential for social workers. Health enhancement programs in the workplace must encompass all structural levels within the company and address the relationship between the company and the individual employee. A failure to employ this concept will result in a narrow scope of services that could sabotage the program goals.

Consultation

Many social workers have a clinical perspective and are oriented toward treating individuals, families, and groups. The development and implementation of health enhancement programs requires a shift in orientation from the individual to the company, from a clinical to a consultation perspective. As a consultant, the social worker becomes actively involved with members of the organization in identifying work-related health problems and designing programs that will reduce them.

Self-determination

Self-determination is a basic social work concept that is often disregarded when major programs are developed and implemented within large organizations. The primary goal of health-enhancement programs, the prevention of illness and injury and the enhancement of health, can only be accomplished if the program participants achieve self-determined lifestyle objectives.

The Intervention Pyramid

The intervention pyramid represents the levels of intervention that facilitate the desired outcome of health enhancement programs: the achievement and maintenance of peak performance among the employees of the sponsoring company. The intervention pyramid illustrated in Figure 9-1 involves sequential steps based on knowledge, attitudes, behaviors, health, and performance.

Knowledge

Information provides the foundation for peak performance. It is important that people understand the relationship between health status and performance capacity. They must also understand that lifestyle choices have a significant effect on health status. Information about specific skills that are required to practice a healthy lifestyle must be provided. However, many health enhancement programs fall short of their objectives because they stop with information and fail to provide the remaining components.

FIGURE 9-1 The intervention pyramid.

Attitudes

An acceptance of one's personal responsibility for health enhancement should follow an understanding of the relationship between lifestyle and health status. People will not be motivated to modify their behavior if they do not accept responsibility for their health and believe that their lifestyle influences their health status. In addition, awareness of such psychological factors as resistance to change, secondary gain, and maintaining realistic expectations will influence success. Finally, program participants need to make a personal commitment to act. These attitudinal factors greatly increase the probability of successful behavior modification.

Behaviors

The application of information and the influence of attitudes on desired behavior can be facilitated by behavior modification techniques, support systems, and resource utilization. Behavior modification techniques and support groups can be designed as part of the program to reinforce desired behaviors and provide encouragement. Programs that are accessible and responsive to individual needs will experience higher rates of participation and retention. Many people approach lifestyle changes with enthusiasm and determination, only to revert to former patterns of behavior within a few months. Maintaining desired health-enhancing behaviors requires skilled program directors who can provide incentives for maintaining involvement in the program.

Health

The relationship between lifestyle and health has been clearly established. Consequently, it is important for individuals who want to enhance their health to understand the concept of wellness. The traditional concept of health maintains that people are healthy unless they are diagnosed with an illness. The wellness concept, on the other hand, is based on enhanced levels of health. A person can be "not sick" and yet not have the strength and endurance to perform daily tasks for extended periods of time without fatigue. An understanding of enhanced health and the associated benefits for a higher quality of life helps motivate people to practice healthy lifestyles.

Performance

The desired outcome of health enhancement programs is increased performance capability. The benefits of programs that provide a knowledge base, positive attitudes, behavior change, and enhanced health result in increased performance capability. The rewards to workers and employers include increased availability at work, decreased absenteeism and health care utilization, and increased energy, strength, stamina, concentration, emotional stability, and self-confidence. All of these benefits to individual employees are likely to generate increased productivity for the company.

Organizational Assessment

The social worker should conduct an assessment of the structure, function, and process of the organization in order to gain a clear understanding of where employees fit into the organizational structure, their assigned job responsibilities, and how they carry them out.

Structure

The initial phase of an organizational assessment employs systems theory to identify each subsystem within the organizational structure of the company. In most organizations there are three distinct structural levels: workers, supervisors, and managers. Agencies within the community that have an active relationship with the client organization and influence the health status of employees should be considered as an additional structural level or subsystem, as well as family members. Figure 9-2 illustrates how the organizational structure can be conceptualized with each level constituting a subsystem within the total system. Defining the structure in this manner enables the health enhancement program staff to take each subsystem into account during the program-design phase.

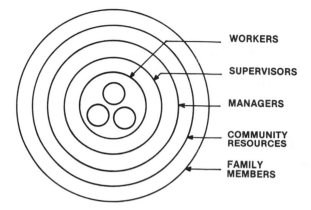

FIGURE 9-2 Organizational structure: subsystems of the client company.

Function

The duties performed by employees within each subsystem of the company should be evaluated to identify specific work-related health problems associated with those duties. This provides a baseline from which to determine the types of programs that should be included in the health enhancement initiative.

Process

In addition to understanding who does what work, it is important to understand how the work is done. Psychosocial factors address the human element of work and are an essential component of process. How people feel about their work, opportunities for decisional participation, and the level of job satisfaction experienced by workers should be understood. Studies on the nature of work reveal that there is a direct correlation among the degree of participation in decisions about one's work, job satisfaction, and productivity (Jenkins, 1974).

These key concepts have provided a conceptual framework that can be applied along with the theoretical framework to construct practice guidelines for health enhancement programs.

PRACTICE GUIDELINES

Practice guidelines for health enhancement programs are the product of theoretical and conceptual frameworks because they are operationally applied to the requirements of a specific organization. This involves the design of a comprehensive health enhancement program that takes into account

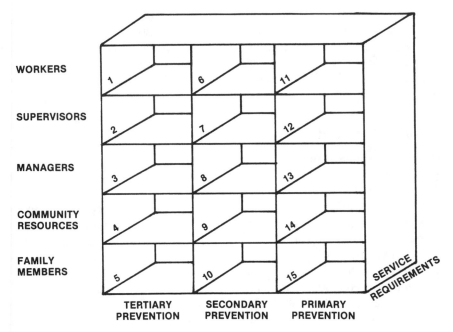

FIGURE 9-3 The intervention matrix.

each axis of the intervention matrix illustrated in Figure 9-3. Practice guidelines must also consider practitioner roles and responsibilities during program design. Each of these dimensions of the guidelines are discussed below.

Intervention Matrix

A useful three-dimensional model for designing health enhancement programs is illustrated in Figure 9-3. The horizontal axis consists of the three elements of the prevention continuum: tertiary, secondary, and primary prevention. The vertical axis consists of the five subsystems of the organizational structure: workers, supervisors, managers, community resources, and family members. The third dimensional axis consists of service requirements.

The Prevention Continuum

Traditionally, the prevention axis of the intervention matrix in employee assistance programs has focused almost exclusively on tertiary prevention, with services being provided primarily to impaired employees. An impaired employee is defined as one whose work performance, though at one time satisfactory, is now impaired by personal problems. These can include conflicts with supervisors or peers, absenteeism, substance abuse, family or marital discord, financial difficulties, and legal problems (Brill, Herzberg, & Speller, 1985). This is a critical issue for occupational social workers who must be effective at shifting the focus of health enhancement programs to primary prevention with a goal of maintaining the health of all employees and enhancing the company's productivity.

Organizational Structure

The organizational structure axis of the intervention matrix should identify each subsystem within the client company. The worker is at the base level of the organization's structure. Traditionally, it has been the impaired worker who has been the identified client of employee assistance programs. Business and industry responded to the impaired worker by having supervisors diagnose the problem and counsel the worker. Supervisors have often ignored the problem, hoping it will go away, or have simply fired workers without trying to salvage them for the company (White, 1983).

Supervisors constitute another important level in the organization's structure and play a critical role in linking health enhancement and employee assistance programs. An important aspect of occupational social work services involves training supervisors to identify and refer impaired employees for help. Social workers can provide ongoing consultation to supervisors and help them maintain an appropriate relationship with workers that is based on job performance. Support groups can provide supervisors an opportunity to share common frustrations and gain insight into fulfilling their role with the impaired worker without attempting to treat personal problems (Good, 1984; Hawthorne & Davidson, 1983; White, 1983). (See Chapter 4 of this volume for further discussion about referring the impaired worker to employee assistance.)

Management, the third level in the organizational structure, holds the keys to resources and sanction within the company. Consequently, the support and commitment of the chief executive officer and other managers is critical to gaining acceptance for health enhancement programs throughout the company. An excellent strategy to achieve management support is to help the management acquire psychological ownership of the program by involving them in program planning and implementation. In addition, the social worker can assume an advisory role to management by assisting in understanding the psychosocial impact of policies and procedures. Participation in staff meetings and conferences is helpful to both management and the program.

Community resources are another important level in the company system and should be carefully evaluated in terms of their potential contribution in the design of health enhancement services. Health enhancement programs can range from in-house programs with company staff and resources to those that rely upon community resources exclusively. Some mix between the two is also possible. In addition, if a single organization cannot support a program on its own, several companies may set up a central unit for conjoint utilization (Steinberg, 1981).

The final subsystem in the organizational structure consists of the family members of employees. This level in the company system is often neglected in health enhancement programs, yet it is probably the most significant level for achieving the long-term goals of enhanced employee health and increased productivity. The involvement of family members is consistent with current theories and research on motivation, compliance, and behavior change. The support of significant others is crucial in achieving and maintaining changes in health behavior. Those employees who participate with family members experience a higher rate of participation and maintain the desired behavior longer.

Initially, the introduction of social workers and other human service professionals into the workplace was based on services targeted at the first grid of the intervention matrix, workers with identified problems. The current scope of service delivery has broadened to cover the entire spectrum of the matrix, with health enhancement programs being targeted primarily at grids 11 through 15, where primary preventive measures are employed (Brill, Herzberg, & Speller, 1985).

Service Requirements

Service requirements constitute the third axis of the intervention matrix. In addition to determining the tertiary, secondary, and primary prevention program requirements for each subsystem within the organization, health enhancement programs must address program requirements within each grid of the intervention matrix. Health enhancement service requirements should be directly correlated to work-related health problems. An assessment of these problems throughout the organizational structure can provide a baseline for determining service requirements.

There are a number of variables that can be used to obtain a health-problem profile of a company: medical diagnosis, lost time from work, hospitalizations, health care costs, and employee terminations. The specific variables selected will be influenced by the data that are available in company records. Data analysis should identify high-impact work-related problems that are lifestyle-related and have a high potential for risk reduction through health enhancement programs. Emphasis should then be placed on developing primary prevention programs that focus on those high-impact, work-related health problems that can be reduced through health enhancing lifestyle behaviors (Green et al., 1980).

Practitioner Roles and Responsibilities

An effective health enhancement program requires clearly defined roles and responsibilities for a carefully selected multidisciplinary staff. In addition to a social worker, other disciplines that should be available, either as staff members or consultants, include a nutritionist, an exercise physiologist, a physician, an occupational and a physical therapist, and a health psychologist. Factors that should be considered when determining the composition and responsibilities of the health enhancement staff include personal characteristics, accountability, quality assurance, accessibility, assessment, marketing, consultation, referring, and program compliance.

Personal Characteristics

Health enhancement practitioners must have a broad base of professional skills and experience. Occupational social workers require a background that includes clinical services to individuals and groups, consultation, program development, community organization, and administration. Interpersonal and communication skills, flexibility and creativity, sound judgment, and decisiveness are desired character traits. They should be comfortable with themselves, effective at doing business with a broad range of people, and maintain a personal lifestyle that provides a role model for program participants. In addition, they should have the necessary credentials, certification, or license to provide their specific professional services.

Accountability

The location of the health enhancement program within the structure of the organization is very important. It is strongly recommended that the program director report to an administrative head, such as the director of human resources. In addition, close liaison with the personnel department is imperative due to the intimate relationship between employees and the health enhancement staff (Steinberg, 1981). The organizational structure should also reinforce the necessary linkage between health enhancement and employee assistance programs.

Quality Assurance

The provision of professional services in the workplace requires uncompromised confidentiality with secured and discreetly maintained records. The release of information about participants to supervisory or management staff should be limited to "a need to know" and with the knowledge and consent of the employee. Failure to maintain high standards in this area will compromise the credibility of the program.

Accessibility

Health enhancement services should be easily accessible to employees. Both the physical location and timing of services are important. The convenience of worksite programs enhances participation. The timing of services is also an important consideration. For example, maintaining a quick response at the time of a referral increases worker acceptance and involvement. Programs that minimize worker participation during duty hours will receive more support from supervisory personnel. The program staff should avoid being office-bound and move throughout the work environment of the company.

Cost

The fee for services rendered should be carefully considered. The psychology of fees influences participant commitment to compliance. A variety of alternatives can be considered: total company support, user fees, incentives, or employee payments with a single fee for all participants or a prorated fee based on income. Regardless of the fee policy, one should be carefully developed with an understanding of its meaning to the company and the program.

Health Assessment

The health enhancement staff should participate in an assessment of the health status of both applicants for employment and current employees. Applicants for employment should be screened for potential health risks and projected health care costs to the company. When employees are referred for marginal performance, it is essential to differentiate performance problems attributable to lack of skills and disciplinary issues from those generated by an identifiable impairment (Barr & Lerner, 1984). This is a controversial issue and raises both ethical and legal questions. Nevertheless, each company should assess both current and potential employees and establish a clear health assessment policy.

Marketing

Gaining and maintaining employees to participate in health enhancement programs is a crucial task of program staff. A number of authors have provided information on the use of incentives to enhance program participation (Chapman & Gertz, 1985). While voluntary participation is preferred, "job jeopardy" is sometimes used to motivate employees to participate. Employees are told to either participate in the program and improve job performance or lose their jobs. Orientation programs can be presented in staff meetings to market the program and reduce misinformation and negative perceptions.

Consultation

The social worker based in a health enhancement program has an extensive consultation role. Supervisors and managers can be assisted in understanding the impairment and needs of troubled employees. Other professional staff, both company- and community-based, can be assisted in understanding the relationship between lifestyle, health, and performance.

Community Organization

Facilitating the coordination of community agencies providing services to the company is an important role of the program staff. Community agencies can be identified to provide services in response to unmet needs of the company, its employees, and family members.

Referrals

The health enhancement staff is in an excellent position to identify a broad range of service requirements of employees, many of which are beyond the designated roles and responsibilities of the health enhancement program. Some social workers find it difficult to refer clients to another agency for services that they are qualified to provide. The health enhancement staff must set clear parameters around their appropriate responsibilities and become skilled at referring employees to other agencies.

Maintaining Compliance

A critical role of health enhancement staff members is maintaining involvement and compliance on the part of program participants. The goals of enhancing health and upgrading performance capability will only be achieved through a lifetime of compliance with health enhancing behaviors. To have employees begin a program and make positive lifestyle changes for a few months, only to return to health-compromising habits, is of little value to individuals or the company. The involvement of family members has been demonstrated to increase long-term compliance.

PROGRAM DEVELOPMENT AND IMPLEMENTATION

The theoretical and conceptual frameworks, coupled with practice guidelines, provide an essential foundation for the development and implementation of programs that meet the specific needs of the client company and its employees. These programs need to be responsive to the specific workplace situation, work-related health problems, individual health practices, and the lifestyles of employees. Resources need to be allocated for the development and implementation of programs that address work-related health problems that are reducing the performance capability of employees. Without health enhancement programs, employee assistance initiatives are likely to assume a posture of responding to impaired employees. Viable health enhancement programs provide proactive primary prevention programs that enhance the health of employees and increase the productivity of the company.

Healthy Lifestyles

Personal health practices and lifestyle choices are the essence of health enhancement programs. The health status of each employee is directly related to daily lifestyle behaviors. Health enhancement program elements are designed to assist employees in reducing health compromising behaviors. Examples of such program elements include increased physical activity, responsible food choices and weight control, smoking cessation, and stress management. These program elements are interdependent, and their application involves a balanced lifestyle.

Lifestyle Assessment and Awareness

A lifestyle assessment that provides program participants with reliable information and increases their awareness regarding their own lifestyle behaviors should constitute the initial phase of a health enhancement program. This provides the participant with a required knowledge base and facilitates attitudes essential for achieving program goals. People need to understand the relationship between lifestyle and health and to assume a sense of personal responsibility and commitment for modifying health compromising behaviors. A personal lifestyle assessment should include a review of the lifestyle components illustrated in Figure 9-4 and provide participants with a report card on their health practices.

Environmental Safety

Environmental safety incorporates self-protection and risk reduction. The use of protective equipment, driving practices, accident prevention, and fire protection are some of the lifestyle behaviors to consider. Additional factors include the control of pollution and noise, and providing adequate lighting.

Physical Fitness

Physical fitness involves regular physical activity that provides flexibility, increases cardiorespiratory capacity, and develops strength. People who are physically fit tend to experience less illness and increased productivity.

FIGURE 9-4 Balanced lifestyle components.

Historically, physical fitness has been viewed as the foundation of a healthy lifestyle and is often the lifestyle component that receives the most attention.

Social Skills

Social skills involve meaningful interpersonal relationships, communication skills, and the ability to share affection. People who maintain intimate relationships experience less illness, have shorter convalescence periods, and tend to live longer. The relationship between people and animals has received considerable attention in the literature, with a clear positive correlation being established between pet ownership and enhanced health (McCarthy, 1987). Play and humor are also important factors in the area of social skills.

Personal Affairs

Having one's personal affairs in order and maintaining financial independence and security are important health practices. This involves the ability to maintain employment, to budget one's income and live within one's means, and to keep legal documents current. Problems with personal affairs are a major cause of emotional disturbances.

Nutrition, Weight Control, and Substance Use

The types and amounts of food and chemicals we introduce into our bodies are directly correlated with our body weight and our health status. The practice of responsible food selection requires basic nutrition awareness.

Responsible eating habits that regulate both what and how people eat are important for proper weight control. The responsible use of alcohol and drugs influences our health and work performance. Alcoholic employees experience approximately twice the average rate of absenteeism. The use of tobacco is the single greatest health risk behavior (Cohen, 1985).

Self-awareness

Self-awareness involves one's emotional status, belief systems, and self-esteem. An objective self-concept and emotional stability are key elements for enhanced health.

Coping Skills

Coping skills involve the ability to manage the external stimuli in one's life through such practices as problem solving, decision making, conflict resolution, and stress management. Stress management is a comprehensive process that incorporates many additional coping skills and is discussed in more detail later in this chapter.

Health Care

Health care involves effective self-care practices and responsible utilization of the health care system. Effective self-care practices include adequate protection against "the elements" and timely and appropriate care of minor injuries and illness. Responsible health care utilization includes avoiding abuse of services through unnecessary utilization of medical resources as well as seeking health care when it is required. Noncompliance with prescribed treatment programs and medication usage is a major problem in this area.

A Balanced Lifestyle

A balanced lifestyle is one in which moderation and common sense dictate a reasonable degree of compliance with the principles of each component of one's total lifestyle. Neglecting or emphasizing any component can result in some degree of imbalance. For example, a person who devotes excessive amounts of time and energy to physical fitness at the expense of spending time with his or her family is practicing an imbalanced lifestyle.

Physical Fitness

Historically, a physical fitness program was generally the first, and often the only, element of a corporate health enhancement program. Corporations have invested extensive resources for gymnasiums, weights, exercise equipment, and staff in order to provide employees with facilities to develop and maintain a high level of physical fitness. There seems to be a greater acceptance of the relationship between exercise and health than other life-style behaviors. Yet relatively few people seem to understand proper physical fitness behaviors. In fact, while almost 8 out of 10 adult Americans say they get "regular exercise," only one third of adults exercise strenuously three or more times a week and 24% say they never "exercise strenuously" (Irving, 1983). A physical fitness program should include 20 to 30 minutes of aerobic activity such as walking, running, or swimming at least three times a week. Individuals who exercise regularly feel better, have more energy, and often require less sleep. Regular exercisers report both physical and mental benefits, including weight loss, improved muscular strength and flexibility, enhanced self-esteem, greater self-reliance, and relief from mild depression. A successful physical fitness program can help decrease absenteeism, hospital utilization, and the incidence of heart attacks.

Weight Control

There is a clear relationship between body weight and health and performance. Being overweight increases health risks and introduces medical problems including diabetes, high blood pressure, and joint problems. People who are overweight have more difficulty performing physical tasks due to decreased flexibility, mobility, and endurance.

Weight control is a very complex issue that requires psychological and behavioral changes. Both eating behavior and physical activity are involved in weight control. Weight control programs should place responsibility for outcome on the individual and provide information, adjust attitudes, and modify behavior. Encouragement and support from family, co-workers, and self-help groups such as Overeaters Anonymous are essential for the desired long-term results. Without an ongoing support system, most people regain the lost weight and add still more weight within a year. Information about food choices, food selection, and food preparation can be provided by a nutritionist. Behavior modification techniques such as reducing portion sizes, recording caloric intake, and exploring alternative responses to the urge to eat can be provided by a psychologist or social worker. A nurse or physician can address the medical aspects of obesity, while a physical therapist or occupational therapist can design exercise and physical fitness activities. The workplace cafeteria can provide special "lite" menu items and fresh fruits for employees.

Smoking Cessation

Cigarette smoking is the single lifestyle behavior that causes the greatest risk to health and is the most preventable cause of illness and premature death.

It has a significant negative impact on productivity in that persons who smoke one or more packs of cigarettes a day have a 50% greater risk of hospitalization and absenteeism (White, 1983). Cigarette smoking has been shown to increase the user's risk of lung cancer, bronchitis, emphysema, coronary heart disease, and a number of other chronic illnesses. Between 8% and 10% of all health care costs have been attributed to smoking (White, 1983).

Smoking cessation has been a primary area of successful health enhancement among American adults. While over 50% of American adults smoked as little as 10 years ago, today 7 out of 10 adults say they do not smoke cigarettes (Irving, 1983). Passive or sidestream smoking has also been shown to be a health risk to nonsmokers.

There are a number of commercially produced smoking cessation programs available that can be provided for employees at the worksite. These programs vary in their specific structure and content but generally have a cognitive/behavioral approach and emphasize lifestyle elements including physical activity and proper nutrition. They address handling urges, developing negative associations to smoking, and breaking the association between routine daily tasks and smoking. It has been found that 33% to 80% of participants in smoking-cessation programs are able to stop smoking with intensive clinical and educational assistance, but far fewer stop when provided only with information, brief instructions, and encouragement. Of those who stop smoking, the majority tend to relapse and resume smoking within 6 to 12 months (Kasl, 1978).

Smoking cessation has been shown to have dramatic positive consequences for the health of former smokers. For the average smoker, cessation reduces coronary heart disease mortality risk from 200% to 150% of that of nonsmokers within 1 year, and within 5 to 10 years the mortality rate for ex-smokers is virtually equivalent to that of nonsmokers. Lung cancer risks also decline after smoking cessation, although at a slower pace. Risk is reduced by approximately two thirds after about the first 5 years and approaches that of a nonsmoker by 10 to 15 years after cessation (Kasl, 1978).

Stress Management

The workplace is a major source of stress for employees. Studies on occupational stress reveal that serious stress-related problems are found among 10% of the working population. Job stress has been labeled as one of the major health problems in the United States today, with costs to American industry estimated at $75 billion to $100 billion a year. Expenses come from absenteeism, diminished productivity, increased health insurance charges, and direct health-related expenses (Cohen, 1985). Social workers providing health enhancement services can make a major contribution to the health of employees through the development and implementation of effective stress-reduction services. Stress management programs should incorporate the four phases of the stress process: increased stressor awareness, increased sensitivity to personal stress responses, aquiring stress management skills, and developing a personal stress management plan.

Stressor Identification

The stress process is initiated by events or situations that require adaptation. If the event or situation is perceived as positive or negative and requires considerable adaptation, then it may become a stressor. A stressor is defined as a positive or negative event or situation that requires a significant degree of adaptation. An event may be a stressor for one person but not another, depending on the perception, assigned meaning, and adaptability of the individual (Jenkins, 1985).

Stress management participants should identify the specific stressors that affect their work performance. While occupational stress is the primary focus, stressor identification should not be limited to job-related stress, in that family and social stressors can carry over to the workplace and affect job performance. Common occupational stressors include loss of control, unpredictability, work overload, task ambiguity, role conflict, extreme amounts of responsibility, constant change, job transfers, and performance appraisals (White, 1983). Employees should develop a comprehensive list of their own stressors. Group discussions are an excellent vehicle for facilitating this process.

Personal Stress Response

Once a list of stressors has been developed, participants should determine their personal response patterns to each of the stressors they have identified. This can be accomplished by exploring each of four stress response categories: cognitive, affective, physiological, and behavioral. This approach provides a structured framework that many people find useful.

The ability to make an accurate appraisal of an event or situation provides the basis for effective stress management. The principles of cognitive therapy can assist people to think rationally and to make a more objective appraisal of a potential stressor (Ellis, 1979; Ellis & Harper, 1975; Maultsby, 1975). The emotional component of the stress response is highly correlated with the cognitive component. Irrational thinking can aggravate stress-related emotional dysfunction, while rational thinking increases emotional stability.

The physiology of the stress response is also regulated by the mind. Once the brain determines that an event requires an adaptive response, it activates a complex series of neurochemical activities that cause multiple physical reactions known as the "fight or flight response" (Selye, 1956). This response causes increased heart rate, elevated blood pressure, rapid respiration, dilated pupils, increased strength of the large skeletal muscles, and many other actions that prepare the body to protect itself against the perceived threat. This process increases the ability to function by enhancing the energy level and motivating people to act. However, if the neurochemical activity becomes excessive or prolonged, it can have a detrimental effect and result in decreased functioning. A stress response that enhances our functioning is known as *eustress,* while one that decreases our level of functioning is known as *distress* (Selye, 1956). People who are in an extended state of distress with ongoing neurochemical responses are at risk for health-compromising psychosomatic illness. The formula for stress management that provides enhanced health and peak performances is to regulate one's stress exposure so that there is sufficient stress to motivate and energize while avoiding excessive stress that compromises performance.

Stress Management Skills

The third phase of the stress process involves the development of coping skills that enhance one's ability to regulate mental, emotional, physiological, and behavioral stress responses. By effectively employing these stress management skills, a person can learn to maximize the benefits and minimize the costs of stress. Stress management programs that are sustained over a period of several weeks, require home practice, and provide follow-up services are more likely to result in enduring behavior change (Manuso, 1983).

Stress management skills can be classified as preventive, preparatory, and responsive. Preventive strategies focus on the stressor and are designed to eliminate or minimize their impact. Program participants should review their lists of stressors and identify those they can do something about. For example, if driving in congested traffic is a stressor, preventive strategies might include driving alternate routes or times, using public transportation, or car pooling. When people accept that there are some stressors over which they have no control, they can then focus their efforts on regulating their stress response to those stressors.

Preparatory coping strategies are those that prepare us to respond to stressors more effectively. A healthy lifestyle that incorporates regular exercise, good nutrition, maintenance of ideal body weight, avoidance of tobacco, moderate use of alcohol and caffeine, and obtaining adequate sleep is an effective preparatory coping strategy. A healthy lifestyle builds physical and mental stamina and provides strength, endurance, and determination to respond when stressors do occur (Jenkins, 1985). Finally, responsive coping strategies involve skills that are learned ahead of time and then implemented after the onset of a stressor. The acquisition of stress management skills constitutes the primary component of stress management programs and is designed to develop rational thinking, emotional self-regulation, assertiveness, communication, time management, problem solving, social skills, and the relaxation response (Goldberger & Breznitz, 1982). Individuals in supervisory and management positions should be exposed to effective decision making, planning, and delegation skills.

A Stress Management Plan

After identifying their stressors, becoming more sensitive to their stress responses, and understanding the coping skills for stress management, program participants should then develop a personal stress management plan. A list of personal stressors should be developed and reviewed. Those that can be regulated should be prioritized and placed in rank order on a stressor management list. Specific alternatives for minimizing the impact of each stressor should be listed. Participants should select a few of their most significant stressors and write down their stress response patterns for each. Appropriate coping skills that will reduce the amount of distress experienced should then be identified. Training and follow-up with support and reinforcement help develop a high level of competency at employing the skill during periods of intense stress. An effective stress management program will incorporate all phases of the stress process and facilitate the skillful application of stress management skills.

CASE EXAMPLES

There are many case examples of health enhancement programs in the workplace. Most of these programs have a physical fitness emphasis and are directed by exercise physiologists. The Association for Fitness in Business is developing credentialing and quality assurance standards for such programs. There has been a recent shift in the focus of health enhancement programs from exclusive physical fitness programs toward the psychosocial elements of health promotion and wellness. This has rapidly increased the requirement for professional employees such as social workers, who have begun to develop a role in both the public and private sectors. An overview of two programs, one private and one public, is presented.

The Xerox Corporation

The health enhancement program of the Xerox Corporation provides a model of a large international corporation with a corporate headquarters and multiple decentralized offices. This program provides a wide range of health enhancement services. The physical fitness component operates 10 physical fitness centers within the United States, which provide physiological evaluations and aerobic exercise regimens. An exercise module pamphlet is provided to interested employees. A health education component provides a copy of *Take Care of Yourself,* which is mailed to the residence of every Xerox employee. In addition, a quarterly health education publication is provided to each employee. This program component also sponsors a "Courtesy in Smoking" campaign.

An employee assistance component provides confidential professional services through a contract with the Family Service Association of America. A health appraisal component provides physician-administered examinations to identify health problems so that early detection can reduce health care costs and prevent decreased production. Finally, a recreational component provides recreational facilities and facilitates social activities for employees and their families. The Xerox Corporation conducted an evaluation of its health enhancement program and found that there is widespread consensus among employees that these services have contributed significantly to the avoidance of costs (Wright, 1982).

The United States Air Force

The United States Air Force established a comprehensive health promotion program in 1985 to develop and implement health enhancement services. The Air Force has had many health enhancement programs without centralized management for many years. There are extensive physical fitness facilities, occupational safety and health programs, drug- and alcohol-abuse programs, consumer health education, smoking cessation, hypertension screening, and stress management services.

In 1985 the theoretical and conceptual frameworks and practice guidelines described in this chapter were employed to implement the Air Force Health Promotion Program. An organizational structure was established that provided centralized management. Health care utilization data were analyzed to identify lifestyle behaviors associated with high-impact medical conditions. These findings were utilized to develop specific programs to enhance the health of all Air Force personnel and their families. Lifestyle behaviors that have been targeted include physical fitness, nutrition and weight control, drug and alcohol abuse, hypertension screening, smoking cessation, and stress management. In addition, an awareness campaign has been implemented to provide information and teach coping skills in the eight lifestyle categories of a balanced lifestyle. One category is featured during each quarter over a 2-year period. The objective of this program is to maintain a high level of wellness and performance capability among Air Force personnel and their families.

SUMMARY

This chapter has presented an overview of health enhancement programs in the workplace and identified the requirement for occupational social workers to assume an active role in providing these services. The underlying theoretical and conceptual frameworks and practice guidelines utilized in program design were discussed along with their application in program development and implementation. Two case examples were presented to assist the reader in understanding alternative applications in both the private and public sector. The involvement of social workers in the workplace provides an opportunity to make a significant contribution to the health status of workers and their families.

REFERENCES

Barr, M., & Lerner, W. (1984). The impaired nurse: A management issue. *Nursing Economics, 2*, 106–201.

Brill, P., Herzberg, J., & Speller, J. L. (1985). Employee assistance programs: An overview and suggested roles for psychiatrist. *Hospital and Community Psychiatry, 36*, 727–732.

Caplan, G., & Grunebaum, H. (1972). Perspectives on primary prevention: A review. In H. Gottesfeld (Ed.), *The critical issues of community mental health*. New York: Behavioral Publications.

Chapman, L. S., & Gertz, N. E. (1985). A prescription for lower health care costs. *Personnel Journal, 64*, 48–52.

Cohen, W. (1985). Health promotion in the workplace: A prescription for good health. *American Psychologist, 40*, 213–216.

Combs, B. J., Hales, D. R., & Willams, B. K. (1981). *An invitation to health: Your personal responsibility*. Menlo Park, CA: Benjamin/Commings.

Ellis, A. (1979). *Reason and emotion in psychotherapy*. Secaucus, NJ: Citadel.

Ellis, A., & Harper, R. A. (1975). *A new guide to rational living*. North Hollywood, CA: Wilshire.

Gilbert, N. (1982). Policy issues in primary prevention. *Social Work, 27*, 293–297.

Goldberger, L., & Breznitz, S. (Eds.). (1982). *Handbook of stress: Theoretical and clinical*. New York: Free Press.

Good, R. (1984). What Bechtel learned creating an employee assistance program. *Personnel Journal, 63*, 80–86.

Green, L. W., Kreuter, M. W., Deeds, S. G., & Partridge, K. B. (1980). *Health education planning: A diagnostic approach*. Palo Alto, CA: Mayfield.

Hanley, M. J. (1982). Preventive medicine: Health promotion and screening by the occupational physician and staff. In H. M. Alderman & M. J. Hanley (Eds.), *Clinical medicine for the occupational physician*. New York: Dekker.

Hawthorne, W., & Davidson, B. N. (1983). The alcoholic's supervisor: Another victim in need. *Occupational Health and Safety, 52*(10), 28–29, 40.

Irving, S. (1983). *The prevention index: A report card on the nation's health*. Emmaus, PA: Rodale.

Jenkins, J. L. (1974). The effects of decisional participation upon organizational effectiveness: A study of social work officers in the United States Air Force. Unpublished doctoral dissertation, University of Denver.

Jenkins, J. L. (1985). The stress of leadership. In *Dimensions of leadership*. Maxwell AFB, Alabama: Air University.

Kasl, S. V. (1978). Epidemiological contributions to the study of work stress. In C. L. Cooper & R. Payne (Eds.), *Stress at work*. London: Wiley.

Manuso, J. (1983). The Equitable Life Assurance Society program. *Preventive Medicine, 12*, 658–662.

Maultsby, M. C. (1975). *Helping yourself to happiness through rational self-counseling*. New York: Institute for Rational Living.

McCarthy, P. (1987, March). Take Valium or get a pet. *American Health*, 126.

Selye, H. (1956). *The stress of life*. New York: McGraw-Hill.

Snook, S. H. (1983). Back and other musculoskeletal disorders. In B. S. Levy & D. H. Wegman (Eds.), *Occupational Health*. Boston: Little, Brown.

Steinberg, S. L. (1981). Employee assistance program conserves human resources. *Hospital Progress, 62*(2), 50–51.

White, S. (1983). Recent trends in occupational mental health: An overview. In S. L. White (Ed.), *New advances for mental health services*. San Francisco: Jossey-Bass.

Witte, R., & Cannon, M. (1979). Employee assistance programs: Getting top management's support. *Personnel Administrator, 24*, 23–27.

Wright, C. C. (1982). Cost containment through health promotion programs. *Journal of Occupational Medicine, 24*, 965–968.

10 Managing Shift Work Problems

Diane Meadow

One aspect of occupational health that has received little attention in the literature is the impact of night shift work on employees and their families. The need to examine this relationship is critical, especially when one considers that as of 1981 there were at least 10 million Americans regularly engaged in some type of shift work, with 2.1 million employed on a night work schedule (Finn, 1981). Social work practice has the potential for offering professional services in this arena of the workplace because of our systemic understanding of human behavior and our commitment to addressing the transactional needs of person-in-environment.

This chapter begins with an overview of shift work development in the United States and follows with a discussion of the major issues confronting the employer, employee, and the family as they struggle to meet the multiple demands of life in the 20th century. It concludes with a strategy that can be implemented in the workplace to help lessen the stressors facing this sector of the workforce.

HISTORICAL DEVELOPMENT

With the advent of the Industrial Revolution, the factory system, and the technological advances of the 19th and 20th centuries, shift work has become an increasingly acceptable part of the American work scene. In 1972 the Director General of the United Nations International Labour Organization issued a call for the reevaluation of shift scheduling. He wrote that: (1) mechanization and automation in many industries have led to round-the-clock operation; (2) expensive data-processing equipment has extended shift work to many nonmanual occupations; and (3) as shift work increases, the social problems it presents for both management and society need to be addressed (Tasto & Colligan, 1977).

There are two types of industries in which shift work scheduling has become the way of life (Tasto & Colligan, 1977):

1. *Continuous process industries* such as steel mills and oil refineries. Here goods are manufactured by equipment that cannot be started and stopped within the duration of a single shift because the process is long-cycle.
2. *Continuous operations or round-the-clock industries* such as law enforcement, fire protection, and health care facilities. In these industries, services rendered are on demand 24 hours a day.

As the nature of work-related tasks changed, society recognized the economic benefits of continuous utilization of production systems along with the idea that shift schedules enable industry to maximize the use of capital equipment for stepping up output to meet increasing demand. By the 1960s an increase of electronic data-processing equipment into offices led to shift work scheduling. This was a potent forerunner to widespread use of round-the-clock information processing. By early 1970, previously enacted laws that prohibited women from working night shifts were declared unenforceable or were repealed. Since 1973 the number of shift workers has increased at the same ratio as has daytime workers (Hedges & Sekschenski, 1979). With this increase a continuing concern has developed in the United States about the quality of working life, which could eventually lead us to reconsider the social costs of shift schedules. As early as 1970 the National Board for Price and Income Control issued a report that stressed the need to balance the enonomic gains of shift scheduling against any identifiable human and social costs. However, identifying such costs and benefits seems to present a major challenge. What are the stressors that workers experience, and in what ways have the technological changes of today moved ahead of our ability to adapt effectively with them? Folkard and Monk (1979) identified three factors that influence the level of performance efficiency: (1) the demands of the task; (2) the type of shift system that impacts upon the potential for both short- and long-term adjustment; and (3) the individual differences between workers in the degree to which their circadian rhythms adjust to night work.

RESEARCH FINDINGS

Job Performance

It is important to understand performance efficiency because it has a direct effect upon one's work life and an indirect effect on one's social and psychological functioning. The circadian rhythm of the sleep cycle is one influence on job performance. Most rhythms within human systems approximate a 24-hour pattern referred to as circadian rhythms. These are synchronized with factors in the environment called *zeitgebers* (Aschoff, 1971; Wingate, Hughes, & La Dou, 1978). When a phase of a zeitgeber is shifted (e.g., when the light/dark cycle is shifted as it is during night work) the physiological rhythms either shift with the zeitgeber or become desynchronized. When this occurs, internal rhythms and external environment become desynchronous with each other.

Several research studies report that when the sleep/work cycle is desynchronized from the light/dark cycle, the result is extreme fatigue, leading to difficulties at work and in family life. Folkard and Monk (1979) showed that the time of day one works has an effect on performance efficiency in a variety of perceptual-motor tasks and in the circadian rhythms of the body temperature. Because night workers, in general, go to sleep immediately after work and take leisure hours before going to work, there is a lack of synchronicity between workers and their environment. Workers tend to adapt to the unusual schedule, often unaware of the impact on their physical health or of family problems and unmet social needs that may result from this lack of synchronicity. In response to these concerns, some organizations have implemented a variety of rotating-shift schedules, but the research findings in this area have been contradictory, with the common theme being that night shift work is unnatural, unhealthy, and in the long run not as cost effective for industry as earlier assumed. However, the realities of the workplace dictate the need for some industries to function round-the-clock. How to best meet the needs of the workplace and the workers in the most efficient manner is still open for consideration. First we must take a good look at this sector of the workforce. Who are the people employed on shift work schedules? What are their needs, concerns, and hopes for the future?

Worker Characteristics

According to Hedges and Sekscenski (1979) married men and women comprise three fifths of all full-time shift workers, as compared to two thirds of day workers. People working late shifts are usually younger, with a median age of 31.5 years. Blacks appear to be overrepresented on late shift schedules and whites underrepresented, with the percentage of Hispanics about the same as those on day shifts. Workers tend to have more long-term financial commitments than do day employees, and they are more likely to have both dependent and independent children. Financial need appears to be a critical factor in determining whether people enter shift work, but with the acquisition of new skills many can escape this work schedule and still make adequate wages (De la Mare & Walker, 1968).

Frost and Jamal (1979) looked at shift workers' attitudes associated with their work schedule. They found significant differences between day shift and other shifts in that day workers experienced more fulfillment of their work needs and had a positive sense of emotional well-being. Furthermore, day workers expected to stay longer with their present companies and had more social opportunities outside work.

What appears to emerge here is a picture of the shift worker as one who has entered a distinct phase of the life cycle associated with heavy expenditures that cannot be met as an unskilled or semiskilled employee working at day rates. Thus this stage of the life cycle, according to Brown (1975), ensures a maximum level of potential role conflict for an individual. Young and Wilmott's (1973) research findings support this picture and conclude that shift work provides the working-class family with an opportunity to avoid the normal drop in standard of living associated with the years when children are born and raised.

Social Relationships

Keeping the general picture of the shift worker in mind, it is important to identify more specifically their unmet "felt needs." Furthermore, employer concerns regarding shift workers must also be taken into consideration. Once these areas have been defined, professional interventions aimed at facilitating a more nurturing fit between the worker, the worker's social network, and the employer can be undertaken.

There is consensus in the literature that in a shift work family, familial and social life are disturbed even when the worker responds positively to working a shift schedule. To understand the relationship between shift work and family life, David Brown (1975) uses the concepts of *role* and *role expectations*. He argues that there is a culturally sanctioned time schedule for social activities through which social integration occurs. Social integration is the network of relationships in which an individual has meaningful participation and thus serves as the time that binds together the elements of life in modern industrial society. Therefore, a common work schedule helps people in differentiated sets of roles to be available when a particular role task is required. Shift work threatens this time synchronization and makes social integration problematic by reducing the possibilities for certain forms of social interaction. Night workers sleep when the rest of the community is awake, and they eat and play when most of society is working. They are forced to adapt to family and community schedules if they wish to spend time with spouses and children. These social pressures create dissatisfaction in the worker and restrict the ability to adapt to an abnormal work schedule.

Employer Issues

In examining the issue of adaptation and shift work schedules, Zedeck, Jackson, and Summers (1983) raised the question of whether perceptions of poor performance-reward relationships influence satisfaction with one's shift, or if satisfaction with one's work schedule influences perceptions of performance-reward transactions. In attempting to understand this relationship, Gannon, Norland, and Robeson (1983) found four major explanations for the observed relationship between shift work, absenteeism, and productivity: (1) conflict that people experience when they attempt to exercise their various roles; (2) the integration of shift workers into the community; (3) the personal characteristics of each worker; (4) the specific manner in which the shifts are constructed. In support of this last point, the 1977 National Institute for Occupational Safety and Health (NIOSH) Report (Tasto & Colligan, 1977) concluded that particular shift workers and the order of shift rotation are important factors in determining work performance. Other significant areas to consider when trying to understand the impact of work schedules are work pace, environmental conditions, and the physical demands of the job. Flexibility in work scheduling can provide management with a chance to optimize productivity and job performance. Wedderburn (1967) and Walker (1966) both investigated the consequences of rapidly rotating shift schedules and concluded that the flexibility in scheduling helped offset boredom and helped workers' social life by providing some evenings every week when the worker was free to socialize with spouse and friends.

Community involvement is another area of concern for the shift worker. Chadwick-Jones (cited in Brown, 1975) found that for steelworkers the community's expectations for leisure group activities on the weekend either prevented or delayed their acceptance of continuous-shift schedules. Lipset, Colman and Trow (cited in Brown, 1975) reached a similar conclusion. They found that printers on night shifts felt a positive integration to their work environment, which became a substitute for unavailable alternative community social groups. If a worker has no family responsibilities, this type of substitution is fine. However, when there are others to think about, this substitution can lead to all types of additional stresses for the worker.

A final employer issue centers around the efficiency of shift work schedules. Wyatt and Marriott's (1953) research demonstrated that output of night work was slightly less than day work, with about one third of the workers being equally productive. These findings are supported by Bjerner and Swennsson's (1953) investigation, which found that the quality and quantity of production appeared to be negatively related to shift work. McDonald's (cited in Brown, 1975) findings add further support for the inefficiency of shift work by concluding that the level of effort needed to sustain this type of work schedule indefinitely is not possible because there are absolute disadvantages in terms of health, domestic happiness, and the overall enjoyment of life that are beyond monetary compensation. Furthermore, Maurice's (1975) investigation found that accidents are more frequent but less serious among day workers than night workers, and that there are no significant differences in absenteeism rates between the two groups. Workers at some point will become dissatisfied with the wage-effort bargain and, if feasible, leave the shift work position.

Thus it appears that in many instances shift work is neither socially desirable nor, over the long run, economically desirable. For some jobs, like police work, shift work is essential, but there are other jobs where it is required for limited economic advantages to the employer but at a great cost to the worker, family, and community. What this means for management is that there is a need to understand the impact of night shift work on the functioning of the organization, production of goods, and the long-term impact on the worker—which in turn will influence the efficiency and effectiveness of the organization. Shipley (1980) calls for enlightened management to provide sleeping and recreational facilities to combat individual ill-health effects and to maintain systems efficiency. Peter Finn (1981) believes that there are benefits for the employees and that it is advantageous for industry to become familiar with the major effects that working nights has on all concerned. With this knowledge, it will be possible to develop ways to modify the features that are hazardous while retaining or strengthening the benefits of the shift work experience.

Employee Issues

Many workers dislike shift work. Yet it seems to be on the increase, and workers have a less gloomy view than previously thought to be the case. Sergean (cited in Brown, 1975) surveyed British steel workers and found that 46% of his sample disliked shift work because of (1) the effects on their social life, (2) irregular sleeping times and working at night, (3) irregular meal times, (4) early rising, and (5) effects on their health. However, these same people favored shift work because of (1) additional pay, and (2) access to higher-paying and more responsible jobs that carried high status in the local community.

In the study by Zedeck et al. (1983), the same ambivalences regarding work schedules appeared. He found that although the older and more satisfied shift workers perceived themselves to be in poorer health, they were unwilling to change work schedules. This probably relates in part to adaptation and acceptance of what is familiar in their work and social environment.

Community life also poses concerns for shift workers. Gannon et al. (1983) found that workers seem to resent night shift less when there are other people in the community with similar schedules; thus they have more companions during their leisure time, and recreational facilities tend to be open hours when they can make use of them. If shift workers are not integrated into the community they frequently form an occupational community among themselves, such as the firefighters and many groups of police officers. However, this can lead to additional problems if there are families involved because social supports are work-related and thus do not include family members. On the other hand, McDonald (cited in Brown, 1975) found that shift workers had low prestige in the community he studied; the way the workers handled this was to turn inward to their work environment. Thus it appears that even when shift workers receive a salary that enables them to develop middle-class consumption patterns, they may not get the prestige usually associated with these patterns.

From these studies it is clear that shift work schedules raise issues that can have both negative and positive impact upon the worker. For example, the positive experience of a supportive family-like work environment can have a resulting harmful impact upon the worker's family because of the kind of conflicting social alliances the worker experiences.

Peter Finn's (1981) findings give a good overview of these conflicting alliances. In this study, workers reported reduced satisfaction with jobs and problems with their health, their family life, social activity, and safety on the job. His sample identified as the benefits of shift work: (1) more jobs available and a wage differential averaging about 13 cents per hour; (2) time to increase income by moonlighting with daytime jobs; (3) more opportunities for young people to work while pursuing their educations; (4) more free time during the day; (5) for some, the removal of unwanted family responsibilities while the camaraderie of certain night jobs becomes a substitute for normal family and social life; (6) some workers feel more relaxed on the job because of less supervision and fewer interruptions from other personnel; and (7) shift work accommodates people who function poorly in the morning and best during evening or night hours.

This same sample identified as the drawbacks of shift work: (1) workers are out of rhythm in their minds and bodies; (2) family and social life and the routine of the community are on a different schedule; (3) by disturbing the circadian rhythm cycle, additional physical and emotional problems may surface; (4) fatigue is a chronic problem and can lead to physical disorders and problems in mental and psychomotor performance, which may then increase on-the-job accidents.

All of these issues are critical to keep in mind when developing any type of seminar designed for the shift worker. The quality of life for these workers and their families can be strengthened if support and resources are made available to them within the reality constraints that affect their lives.

Marital and Community Issues

The impact of work schedule on family life is also important to understand. Pleck, Staines, and Lang (1980) surveyed day workers and found a direct relationship between excessive time at work, fatigue and irritability, and the degree of conflict within the family. These findings are important because if you add the additional stressors faced by night workers, the strains are likely to increase. For night workers family problems may be due, in part, to the lack of synchrony between hours on the job and the family's daily routines (Finn, 1981). There is less time with children and less time to spend with mates (who many times would alter their own sleep, mealtime, and recreational patterns to accommodate the shift worker's schedule). Furthermore, the time spent with family is usually less satisfying due to fatigue. Shift workers frequently experience difficulty when trying to perform duties attached to marital roles, including sexual activity.

Spouses' attitudes are also critical to the workers' adjustment to shift schedule. Banks (1956) found the attitudes of steel workers' wives to be quite negative, especially with regard to weekends, because of the work schedules' interference with family activities along with the low status attached to this type of work. But other studies, such as the one by Young and Wilmott (1973), found that shift work varied in its impact on family life, and some families were able to exploit the advantages inherent in a different pattern of leisure. In their London sample, the major stress focused upon the strain experienced by spouses in coping with the children. All studies seem to emphasize role competition as a major contributing factor to family stress. Recognizing and identifying these problems and helping find new solutions are other goals for seminars developed to help workers manage life in a shift work family. In his study, Zaluskey (1978) found that the effect of irregular hours on home life tended to be cumulative, resulting in a general reduction in marital happiness.

A THEORETICAL FRAMEWORK

As one takes into account the range of factors that can interact to impact the physical and emotional health of the shift worker and her or his family, it is clear that some sort of organizing framework is needed in order to understand the transactions between worker and environment. The ecological approach or "life model" of Carel Germain (1981) provides such a framework for assessing the person/environment fit. Using this perspective we can think about the shift worker as a system in interaction with work, home, and community as the environments. Our goal in understanding the interrelatedness of these components is to help develop a more adaptive interplay between the parts. We must keep in mind that work is an integral aspect of the life space of individuals, and its impact needs to be considered when trying to understand the concerns of shift workers. This idea is supported in the organizational literature. For example, Shipley (1980) calls for a model of organization that emphasizes job/person fit: a dynamic accommodation to the interchange and interactive effects of changing environments and changing people. He discusses such environmental aspects as office equipment and building design, which can be adjusted by individual users to meet their own needs. The research findings of Frost and Jamal (1979) also support the assumption of a fit between work and nonwork hours. They found that the attitudes and behavior at and away from work have a positive correlation with one another.

Germain (1985) defines adaptation as a transactional process in which people shape their physical and social environments and in turn are shaped by them. Stress occurs when there are upsets in the relationships between person and environment that damage either or both. This is certainly true when one thinks about the effects of fatigue resulting from night shift work as it impacts the worker's health, social functioning, and job performance. Germain looks at adaptation and stress in relation to three factors: demand, capability, and the discrepancy between them. One needs to identify the *demands* on the person, family, or community that are generated by environmental events or by their internal psychological and biological needs. *Capabilities* are the abilities, capacities, and resources at hand for meeting the demand. *Discrepancy* between these—that is, the perceived demand and the perceived capability—is the transactional space that must be understood and made more adaptive. The aim here is to facilitate successful coping by helping shift workers secure adequate information about both their personal needs and the resources available to them, while simultaneously developing and maintaining satisfactory internal conditions and keeping up a degree of autonomy. Shift workers need to experience a sense of self-worth that facilitates their problem-solving abilities through the empowerment that comes with knowledge and emotional support from others.

There are two other ecological concepts that are useful in understanding shift work/environment interaction: the concepts of *habitat* and of *niche*. *Habitat* refers to the place where the organism is found, the physical and social settings within a cultural context. Physical settings (e.g., work environment) must support the social settings of family and social life in ways that fit with a person's lifestyle, age, and gender. Germain (1985) says that social workers need to pool their knowledge and use their skills to work in new ways to improve the habitat of the client system. One way to do this in the workplace is to develop mutual-aid systems, such as support groups, for exchange of information and other resources. Here the employee can be helped to review his or her needs and the family's needs in relation to the use of time by monitoring, priority setting, and coordinating activities within the limitations and context of work responsibilities.

The concept of *niche* is equally important. Here we refer to the status occupied in the social structure by a particular group, especially in relation to issues of power and oppression. Niche is shaped by rights as perceived by individuals in their transactions with others. Shift workers must first understand their own needs and then consider these within an organizational context. They should know what their employer is committed to, the priorities of these commitments, and the role of the worker within the organization from the employer's perspective. This can then set the tone for a partnership to be built that is mutually enabling for both workers and management.

Keeping in mind the transactional nature of person/environment and the concepts outlined here, we will now turn our attention to the development and implementation of a program for managing shift work problems in the workplace.

A PRACTICE FRAMEWORK

Using an ecological perspective, a program for support groups in the workplace geared to the needs of night shift workers will be discussed. These groups can help ameliorate some of the stressors experienced by workers while simultaneously sensitizing management to the impact of work scheduling on employee functioning. This program will provide workers with a structured forum within which to mobilize their internal resources through self-understanding. This can then improve the quality of exchanges with their environment while also increasing the responsiveness of the workplace to their needs. Within the goals and objectives of the organization, the social worker can focus group discussion on the obstacles that prevent reduction of job-related stressors. In ecological terms, the aim is to improve the transactions between work, home, and community by first acknowledging some common themes facing all shift workers and then looking at the different ways they can be dealt with. For example, night workers experience chronic fatigue resulting from a problematic work/sleep cycle, which then influences their efficiency at work and their personal lives. In a group setting, the universality of this issue can be emphasized along with discussions of options and new resources that can help employees feel more empowered. This empowerment can lessen feelings of helplessness, incompetence, and depression by identifying new problem-solving skills, managing negative feelings, and at the same time requiring environmental resources and a supportive community structure. But this requires motivation, incentives, and rewards from the workplace for sustaining individual motivation and coping efforts.

The seminar is divided into three phases (Apgar et al., 1982; Fallon, 1982):

Phase I: Sensitization

This includes sensitizing employers and employees to the impact of shift schedules on the workplace, on the worker, and on the worker's network of social relations, along with the transactional impact of these issues on one another. Suggestions will then be made to management that illustrate how group services might help improve these transactions. This will be followed by outreach efforts aimed at recruiting employees to participate in the seminar.

Sensitizing Employers

First the proposed program idea is discussed with management. This includes a discussion of why the seminar is needed and what it can do for the worker and for the workplace. To support your ideas, refer to the literature on such work-related issues as research on fatigue for shift workers and its cumulative impact upon functioning in the workplace, absenteeism, and job-related accidents. Inquire into what management's experiences have been with shift scheduling and how they believe this program can best be of service.

This sharing is then followed by a suggestion for holding an Outreach Meeting to outline the seminar to the workers. Content for this meeting will include the purpose and goals of the seminar as well as a reaching out for the workers' ideas and integrating them into the planning process.

The presentation to management should conclude with some understanding of the type of commitment the employer is willing to make regarding resources: time for meetings, place, and fees. Also, a determination is made as to whether management is committed to the Outreach Meeting only, followed by further discussion with them, or to a total program.

Sensitizing Employees

This phase should begin with an informal meeting with supervisory and senior shift work personnel. The purpose is to get suggestions for most effectively publicizing the Outreach Meeting. The meeting should be set for an hour during the most convenient time for workers and held at a convenient place at work. Plan to provide some type of refreshment and to leave some time at the end for a brief period of informal socializing.

At the Outreach Meeting the following format is suggested:

1. Welcome people and share the purpose of today's meeting, including what you are interested in developing with them and why. Indicate that you have management's support and, if appropriate, share what-

ever guidelines you and management have agreed upon, such as the resources they are willing to provide.

2. Introduce yourself, and present your personal and professional background that illustrates your interest in shift work problems. The purpose here is to let workers get to know you and to give you credibility as a professional, and not as someone sent by management to "help" them.

3. Share general observations about problems confronting many shift workers throughout the world and how these may be impacting on their own lives in and outside the workplace. The purpose is to universalize problems and demonstrate that you have some knowledge of what they might be experiencing.

4. If time permits, you could ask them to take 5 minutes to complete an Eco Map (Hartman, 1978), which would help them think about their social networks and how supportive and/or stressful interactions with these may be. Explain the purpose of the Eco Map and how it can serve as a reference point in defining potential and present problem areas. This then leads into a discussion of the purpose of the seminar, which is to identify stressors in their lives, how these are coped with now, and to learn new ways of problem solving.

5. Outline the structure of the proposed seminar, including the number of meetings you will have, where these will be held, and at what times.

6. Get the employees' reactions and open up the discussion concerning the seminar idea, any specific suggestions they have as to topics to cover, and any concerns or reservations they might have. Be very clear about the issue of confidentiality. Have a sign-up sheet ready for people to complete when the meeting is over.

7. At the conclusion of the meeting, let people know when and how you will get in touch with those interested in attending the seminar. Also, have some notification procedure ready for those who decide later that they want to participate in the program.

If, after the Outreach Meeting, it is clear that few people are interested in the seminar, you should have a meeting with management. Suggest that you develop and mail out a brief questionnaire to be completed by the workers, which can help identify specifically what they did not like about the proposed seminar and what changes would be needed for them to reconsider attending. A summary of this data is forwarded to management and a revised program is developed, if appropriate. This procedure can also give you feedback that can be useful in planning other seminars.

Phase II: Formal Groups

This phase begins before the first group meeting. Here you develop a conceptual framework of the group that takes into account the information gathered at the Outreach Meeting along with what you know about shift work issues. Roselle Kurland (1980) developed a model for planning group services that can be modified to help you in this activity. The model consists of seven interrelated components (Figure 10-1). Each part should be considered separately as well as transactionally in relation to its impact upon the other components of the model.

Agency/Organization Context

Here you need to consider the supports and constraints that the organization will place upon the seminar. Ask yourself: What are the conditions that exist in this organization that will have an impact upon this seminar? What kinds of arrangements do I have to make for intraorganizational coordination or collaboration? What are the resources the organization is willing to commit, including space, time off for workers, and funds? Does the organization view us as having a working partnership? What organizational policies, both written and unwritten, should I be familiar with? Is the basis for the program clear to management? How do I involve the supervisors without interfering with the working alliance that needs to be developed with the shift workers?

Within this context the following areas interact:

1. *Composition:* Includes those people interested in attending the seminar following the outreach meeting. Some of the issues to consider here are the number of potential members and their descriptive and behavioral characteristics, which help determine how homogeneous or heterogeneous the group will be. Keep in mind that a certain amount of homogeneity is important because it facilitates the rapport needed for trust and cohesion to develop. However, heterogeneity in such areas as ethnic background, religion, and interactional style are also important for enabling the group to broaden discussion and identify alternative solutions for problem solving.

2. *Need:* What are the workers' needs for the seminar? Ask yourself what you perceived from the outreach meeting, discussions with management, and your own knowledge about shift work that can be addressed through seminar participation.

3. *Purpose:* Here you think about the ends and objectives that the seminar will pursue as a collective (e.g., group purpose) and what you think might be some of the expectations of prospective participants. For example, keeping in mind that an ecological approach supports an understanding of shift work issues as a biopsychosocial phenomenon, this seminar will:

a. Provide a support group wherein members and leader can meet together and become resources for one another

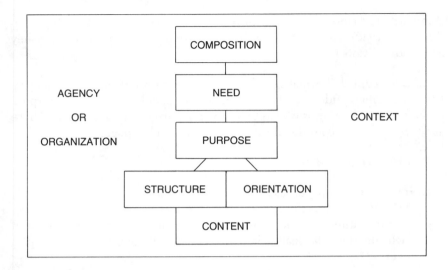

FIGURE 10-1 Components of planning group services.

  b. Help members learn different coping and problem-solving skills
  c. Develop cognitive understanding of the relationship between work-related problems and problems in living as a transactional process
  d. Provide mutual help in the belief that sharing concerns with others in a similar situation relieves anxiety; here the members can use their collective experiences, abilities, and knowledge to develop understanding toward one another

    4. *Content:* What might be the overall framework and some specific topics to be covered during the seminar? This will provide a beginning overview, since content will probably be redefined once the group begins to meet. Keep in mind that in addition to content, group purpose will also help you determine the structure of the group and any orientation that seems appropriate in facilitating members' involvement. Ask yourself how you conceptualize the content of meetings; for example, discussion, didactic material? What is to be done in the group? How will it be done? Why will it be done?

    5. *Structure:* This includes the concrete arrangements such as meeting place, time, size of room needed, provisions for refreshments if wanted, number of meetings, length of each session, and, of critical importance, how to handle the issue of confidentiality.

    6. *Orientation:* This will occur at the beginning of the first meeting as you clarify purpose, goals, and needs of members. What are members' concerns, expectations, and reasons for joining the seminar? What do they wish to achieve, and how realistic are these expectations given the structure of the

seminar? Try to lessen any initial anxiety through exercises and/or discussion (Meadow, 1982). Explain that they do not have to share problems until they are ready to do so.

As you begin the formal group session, keep in mind that each meeting has a beginning, middle, and ending phase that should relate to the purpose of the specific meeting as well as to the overall purpose of the seminar. There are three areas to consider during this formal group stage:

1. *Structure and Methods:*

a. Introduce group purpose
b. Answer questions/clarify concerns
c. Agenda-gathering to identify areas for discussion at the beginning of each meeting; the leader links up issues with those covered in past meeting

Remember that the seminar model is an educative, preventive, growth-oriented group approach to problem solving. The emphasis is cognitive and "here-and-now" focused. The goals are to impart knowledge, to develop skills, and to modify attitudes to deal with present and future issues. The leader's primary purpose is to interpret behavior as interpersonal and universal.

2. *Potential Agenda Items:*

a. Job satisfaction/understanding limitations of shift work by looking at work schedule in relation to its impact on the many aspects of workers' lives, taking into account the worker's skill, age, and financial responsibilities
b. Life satisfactions
c. Physical and psychological health
d. Marital and/or family situation
e. Community involvement/social networks
f. Skills and techniques in working with management around shift work issues

3. *Role of Group Leader:* Keep in mind that you provide the background information and act as facilitator for both employees and for management. Use your knowledge of the commonalities among shift workers to universalize issues and thus give others permission to acknowledge how they feel. Other leader responsibilities include:

a. Creating an atmosphere for learning and self-exploration

   b. Keeping discussion focused and relevant; clarify the normal range of
      reactions and behaviors as they develop through group discussion and
      help link connections between work schedule, fatigue, and resulting
      impact on health, job functioning, and marital and family issues
   c. Be active and flexible; model good communication and introduce prob-
      lem-solving techniques
   d. Be supportive; help members to develop group norms and values that
      facilitate a growth-oriented group culture; protect members from in-
      appropriate or hostile members
   e. Help members look realistically at their work environment, what can
      be changed and what must they learn to adapt to

Phase II: Evaluation

   1. Evaluate the group experience with members at the last session.
   2. Develop recommendations for further action, if appropriate.
   3. Identify resources, both within the organization and those that could
      be developed or used outside.
   4. Discuss with management the impact of the seminar for the workers
      and how some of the issues covered could be integrated into the
      workplace.

FUTURE DIRECTIONS

This chapter has outlined the development and impact of shift work over
time in relation to the organization, the worker, and the worker's social
networks. A seminar has been proposed for use in the workplace as a tool for
addressing the stressors this type of work schedule appears to produce.
However, it is clear that additional research and understanding are needed if
we are to effectively facilitate a more adaptive fit between the worker and his
or her environment. Shipley (1980) calls for the need to look at our approach
to work design. Work environment should, as realistically as possible, be
tailored to meet individual needs, allowing people to pace themselves and
have a say in their own job design. We all have a need for stability and
predictability, which many times can come into conflict with the commercial
goals of the organization at which we are employed. Both Dunham (1977)
and Zedeck et al. (1983) support this idea and also the need to promote
flexible recreational activities in the community where workers live. Brown
(1975) calls for more research to identify the ways in which shift work
interferes with role performance. There is agreement that shift work alters
the character of the roles that an individual can offer and results in declining
feelings of social solidarity with the broader community. Taking these con-

cerns into account as we develop and evaluate programs offered to shift
workers in the workplace can help us to better provide for the needs of this
vulnerable population.

REFERENCES

Apgar, K., Riley, D., Eaton, J., & Diskin, S. (1982). *Life education in the workplace*.
New York: Family Service Association of America.

Aschoff, J. (1971). Human circadian rhythms in continuous darkness: Entrainment by
social clues. *Science, 171*, 213–215.

Banks, O. (1956). Continuous shift work: The attitudes of wives. *Journal of Occupational Psychology, 30*, 69–84.

Bjerner, B., & Swennsson, A. (1953). Shiftwork and rhythm. *Acta Medica Scandana-
vica Supplement, 178*, 102–107.

Brown, D. (1975). Shiftwork: A survey of the sociological implications of studies of
male shiftworkers. *Journal of Occupational Psychology, 48*, 231–240.

Chadwick-Jones, J. K. (1969). *Automation and behavior: A social psychological
study*. London: Wiley Interscience.

De La Mare, G., & Walker, J. (1968). Factors influencing the choice of shift rotation.
Journal of Occupational Psychology, 42.

Dunham, R. (1977). Shift work: A review and theoretical analysis. *Academy of
Management Review, 2*, 624–634.

Fallon, B. C. (Ed.). (1982). *Training leaders for family life education*. New York:
Family Service Association of America.

Finn, P. (1981, October). The effects of shift work on the lives of employees. *Monthly
Labor Review*, 31–35.

Folkard, S., & Monk, T. (1979, August). Shift work and performance. *Human
Factors, 21*, 483–492.

Frost, P., & Jamal, M. (1979). Shift work, attitudes and reported behavior: Some
associations between individual characteristics and hours of work and leisure.
Journal of Applied Psychology, 64(1), 77–81.

Gannon, M., Norland, D., & Robeson, F. (1983, May). Shift work has complex
effects on lifestyles and work habits. *Personnel Administration*, 93–97.

Germain, C. (1981). The ecological approach to person–environment transactions.
Social Casework, 62(6), 323–331.

Germain, C. (1985). The place of community work within an ecological approach to
social work practice. In R. Roberts & S. Taylor (Eds.), *Theory and practice of
community social work*. New York: Columbia University Press.

Hartman, A. (1978). Diagnostic assessment of family relationships. *Social Casework,
59*, 465–476.

Hedges, J., & Sekschenski, E. (1979, September). Workers on late shifts in a
changing economy. *Monthly Labor Review*, 14–22.

Kurland, R. (1980). A model for planning for social work with groups. D.S.W.
dissertation, University of Southern California, Los Angeles.

Lipset, S., Coleman, J., & Trow, M. (1956). *Union Democracy*. New York: Free
Press.

Maurice, M. (1975). *Shiftwork, economic advantages and social costs*. Geneva: International Labor Office.

McDonald, J. D. (1958). The social and psychological aspects of night shift work. Doctoral dissertation, University of Birmingham, England.

Meadow, D. (1982). The effects of a client-focused pregroup preparation interview on the formation of group cohesion and members' interactional behaviors. Ph.D. dissertation, University of Southern California.

Pleck, J., Staines, G., & Lang, L. (1980). Conflicts between work and family life. *Monthly Labor Review, 103*.

Sergean, R. (1971). *Managing shiftwork*. London: Gower.

Shipley, P. (1980). Technological change, working hours, and individual well being. In E. Duncan (Ed.), *Changes In Working Life*. New York: Wiley.

Tasto, D., & Colligan, M. (1977). *Shiftwork practices in the United States*. Washington, DC: National Institute for Occupational Safety and Health.

Walker, J. (1966). Frequent alteration of shifts on continuous work. *Journal of Occupational Psychology, 40*, 215–225.

Wedderburn, A. A. (1967). Social factors in satisfaction with swiftly rotating shifts. *Occupational Psychology, 41*, 85–107.

Wingate, C., Hughes, L., & La Dou, J. (1978). Physiological shifting: A review. *Journal of Occupational Medicine, 20*(3), 204–210.

Wyatt, S., & Marriott, R. (1953). Night work and night shift changes. *British Journal of Industrial Medicine, 10*, 164–172.

Young, M., & Willmott, P. (1973). *The symmetrical family*. London: Routledge and Kegan Paul.

Zaluskey, J. (1978, May). Shiftwork—A complex of problems. *The AFL-CIO American Federation*, 1–6.

Zedeck, S., Jackson, S., & Summers, E. (1983). Shift work schedules and their relationship to health, adaptation, satisfaction and turnover intention. *Academy of Management Journal, 26*(2), 297–310.

11 Employer-Supported Child Care

Jacquelyn McCroskey

SOCIAL WORK INVOLVEMENT IN CHILD CARE

For many years social work involvement with child care has been limited to providing remedial services for families identified as being at-risk-of or exhibiting some kind of pathology (e.g., child care for victims of abuse or neglect or for "special-needs" children). Although social workers in settlement houses were among the early sponsors of high-quality educational programs for immigrant children, latter-day social workers, by and large, have not defined this kind of child care as part of their professional territory. For most of this century, child care ("day care") was not even listed in standard texts or reference books as one of the possible services provided by child welfare agencies. Only during the past 10 years has some of the professional literature referred to child care or day care as one of a number of services provided by social workers for families and children.

The change in terminology is telling: In the social work literature *child care* refers to the care of children in group homes and residential institutions, while *day care* is provided for children or the elderly in day care centers. Other professionals in the child care field (education, child development, developmental psychology) stopped using the term *day care* long ago because of its pejorative connotations (in many people's minds, day care centers were only for families that had somehow failed—which was, indeed, the primary thrust of most social work day care programs) and use the term *child care* to refer to a much broader range of services. Child care services include a range of formal and informal arrangements for children of all ages from infancy through school age. Care may be provided in the child's own home by relatives, friends, or paid babysitters, in family day care homes (in which providers care for small groups of children in their homes), or in child care centers, nursery schools, and preschools. Programs that care for school-age children during nonschool hours include before-school and after-school programs, holiday and summer camps, and many less structured arrangements that cover the times until parents return from work.

This chapter provides a brief background of the history of child care service provision, a discussion of the need for child care services in the workplace, an orientation to the child care market, a review of the major research to date, a framework for social work practice in different kinds of workplace child care programs, and some program examples that illustrate the wide variety of approaches taken by employers to help employees maintain the delicate balance between work and family responsibilities.

THE HISTORICAL TRADITIONS OF CHILD CARE

There have been two parallel traditions of child care in this country. One has been a "custodial" child welfare tradition originating in the day nursery programs of the large Eastern cities in the first half of the 19th century. These programs were designed to provide for the safety and custody of children of immigrant and poor working parents. The other tradition originated with the kindergartens, developed at the turn of the 20th century, based on the ideas of the German educator Friedrich Froebel. These provided the basis for "educational" programs, often half-day, to enrich the learning of children of nonworking mothers (Fein & Clarke-Stewart, 1973; Joffe, 1977). Until recently, many people still made a similar distinction between day care centers (which provided full-day care for the children of working parents) and nursery schools (where parents were expected to be available to participate and to pick up their children after a few hours of intellectual stimulation). With escalating demands from middle-class parents for full-day care and for a balance of cognitive stimulation, nurturance, and socialization from parents with children in all kinds of programs, these distinctions have begun to disappear—nursery schools stay open all day, day care centers provide high-quality educational programs, and individual program names are more likely to be a product of history and circumstance than an indicator of program distinctions.

However, there is another child care tradition that has not changed—child care remains primarily an economic issue. Public support for child care as a service has been historically tied directly to the economics of manpower needs such as in the WPA nurseries, the wartime Lanham Act Centers, the 1962 public welfare amendments, the Work Incentive Program (WIN), the Comprehensive Employment Training Act (CETA), the Job Training Partnership Act (JTPA), and many national and state efforts at welfare reform. Whether the goal was to get women to work in the war industries or to get them off welfare rolls, decisions about child care have not been based only on what is best for children, but on bread-and-butter issues of productivity and the drain on public resources. The point is best illustrated by numbers—in 1945, when Rosie the Riveter was needed for wartime production, 1,600,000 children were in federally financed full-day care, but by 1971, when the federal perception was that women were not really needed in industry, there were only a little more than a quarter of that number of children (440,000) in federally financed full-day care.

Clearly, employer-supported child care is also closely tied to economics. Employers worried about the recruitment, retention, and productivity of workers because of their child care problems have been those most likely to consider the possibility of supporting child care programs. Although employers are very concerned about the quality of the programs they support (businesses want their names associated with model programs, not with run-of-the-mill or mediocre programs), child care is primarily a bottom-line issue. Corporations, unions, industries, and small businesses support child care services because they believe that these services will increase employment, improve productivity, cut costs, increase profits, and improve business. They are absolutely right.

THE NEED FOR CHILD CARE SERVICES

The recent resurgence of professional social work interest in child care comes in the wake of a "subtle revolution," a gradual but constant increase in female labor force participation (Smith, 1979). Radical change in family life brought about by employment of both parents of even very young children, rising numbers of single-parent families, and lack of extended family or community resources for young families compel both public and professional attention.

There have also been important professional advances in three areas:

1. Two decades of research on the effects of child care on children and their families culminating in several controlled longitudinal studies document the long-term benefits of early childhood intervention programs (Belsky & Steinberg, 1978; Berrueta-Clement, Schweinhart, Barnett, Epstein, & Weikhart 1984; Ramey, Yeates, & Shorte, 1984).
2. Highly organized and effective advocacy efforts have brought child care policy and funding issues to public attention (Steiner, 1976; Zigler & Gordon, 1982).
3. Many social work writers and educators have adopted the ecological model as a conceptual framework. This involves a broader conception

of family needs, accompanied by increased attention to supportive, preventive, and early intervention services (Germain & Gitterman, 1980; Meyer, 1983).

Child care is an extremely complex field, combining as it does the perspectives of different disciplines, the needs of vastly different families, varieties of services, often-conflicting policies, and intricate funding arrangements. It is also a greatly needed service for families and, for that reason, all social workers should have a much better understanding of the difficulties families face in finding adequate care and of the issues involved in service provision.

For social workers in work settings, this knowledge is essential. A brief review of recent changes in female labor force participation makes a clear and compelling case for employer concern about child care (Children's Defense Fund, 1982):

- By 1990, about 45% of the labor force will be parents of children under 18 (in two thirds of these families, both parents will be employed).
- Single-parent families will increase to include about 1 in 10 of these parent workers.
- About 80% of female employees will become pregnant during their working years (there will be about 4 million babies born per year, almost as many as during the 1950s baby boom).
- 57% of school-age children and 44% of preschool children had mothers in the labor force in 1982. Children from families with higher incomes were even more likely to have had working mothers; almost 60% of all children with family incomes over $25,000 and more than two thirds of all black children with family incomes over $15,000 had working mothers.
- The proportion of children with working mothers increased 36% over the decade of the 1970s, from 38.8% in 1970 to 52.8% in 1980; continued increases in subsequent decades are forecast.

Employers are providing a range of services to help their employees resolve child care problems. A 1984 assessment of existing services estimated that about 1,850 employers were involved in child care: the programs included 550 on-site or near-site child care centers (400 associated with hospitals), 30 family day care programs, 30 school-age child care programs, 20 initiatives to serve sick children, 300 information-and-referral programs, and 825 financial assistance programs. An additional 500 to 1,000 employers were estimated to be giving charitable contributions to community-based child care, and another 500 to 1,000 were estimated to be providing educational programs for parents (Friedman & Burud, 1984).

THE SCOPE AND STRUCTURE
OF CURRENT SERVICE PROVISION

Before reviewing the results of research on employer-supported child care, it is important to understand some of the variables that determine the structure of the child care market. Some child care is subsidized by federal, state, or local funds, or by private nonprofit agencies, but the great majority of parents who use child care pay for the full cost of care themselves.

Public funds also help provide some regulation of the service system through state or county licensing programs; however, only a portion of the available care in any community is regulated. The child care that is not regulated includes the babysitters, relatives, friends, and neighbors who help out with child care, as well as small family day care homes exempt from licensing based on size, and those that just do not bother with licensing. We have no way of knowing what proportion of the service system is un-regulated, because this kind of care is more or less invisible; however, it is likely that it is as large as the regulated system.

Regulated or licensed child care (in some states family day care is reg-istered rather than licensed, a distinction that may imply lower standards and less intensive monitoring) includes programs financed under public, nonprofit, or proprietary (profit-intended) auspices. In each community, public child care funding may include federal funding of programs such as those mentioned earlier (WIN, JTPA, etc.); state funds used to augment federal programs, and state-originated programs (some examples would be children's centers attached to some elementary schools, and subsidy pro-grams for eligible high-risk parents such as protective service cases); county funds; or city funds used, for example, to support child care at recreation sites or as subsidies for center buildings. Each community is unique in its array of child care services and resources. In most states or counties there is no single office in charge of coordinating all of these funds, though typically there is a committee on child care composed of representatives of many different interests. This lack of coordination makes it very difficult to track and organize all of a community's child care efforts.

Some nonprofit agencies also run child care programs. Groups such as the YWCAs and Girls Club have expanded their services to include infant and preschool care and, of course, many run programs for school-age children. In some areas United Way has also recognized the increasing need for child care and taken leadership in encouraging member agencies to provide needed services. Proprietary companies have recognized the need for child care and established chains such as Kindercare and Children's World (fran-chise efforts such as these were immortalized in a popular press phrase, "Kentucky Fried Children"). There are also a large number of preschools and nursery schools run by individual proprietors on a profit-making basis.

The Difficulties of Finding Adequate Child Care

It is extraordinarily difficult for parents to locate available child care, to understand the distinctions between all of these arrangements, or to know how to select the best possible care for their children. Uncertainty only increases parents' natural anxiety about leaving their children for a large part of the day. For this reason, many communities have established specialized child care resource-and-referral agencies (R&Rs), which keep up-to-date listings of child care resources to help parents locate care, help them learn to look for high-quality care, and give technical assistance to child care providers. These R&Rs are another way in which public or charitable funds are used to help regulate the child care system by linking the potential user to the market (most such agencies can provide services without cost to parents or providers because they are supported by public and private sector funds).

Even with the information of a child care R&R to help in negotiating the shoals of the child care system, parents face agonizing choices. The truth is that, in most communities, there simply is not enough child care to go around, especially for very young or school-age children. With so much competition for the available spaces, parents do not feel that they really have a choice. They are often forced to settle for a program that is open the right hours and that they can afford, rather than one they feel is of high quality or best matches their family's needs (in terms of program philosophy, child-rearing values, religious orientation, culture, or personality of the provider). Having reliable child care is essential to enable parents to work, yet most parents are unprepared and are on their own when it comes to the frustrating business of finding, choosing, and keeping adequate child care arrangements.

RESEARCH ON CHILD CARE

Effects on Children

Since the mid-1960s a very active child care research community has turned out a series of important studies centered around some basic questions about the effects of child care. In summary, the findings are that:

1. A child's attendance at care does not seem to disrupt the emotional bond of attachment between child and parent.
2. It seems that attendance at child care is not associated with long-term cognitive gains *except* in the cases of disadvantaged children, for whom high-quality child care seems to attenuate declines usually seen in cognitive functioning.
3. For disadvantaged children, early-childhood education seems to im-

prove school readiness and to be associated with significant long-term advantages in almost all areas—less need for special education, higher achievement, reduced juvenile delinquency, less welfare dependence, fewer adolescent pregnancies (Berrueta-Clement et al., 1984).

4. High-quality child care does not seem to have negative effects for children, but findings on exactly what positive effects are found are mixed and may depend on the design of the specific program.

5. Finally, it seems that maternal employment is not associated with negative effects on children and may have some personal as well as financial benefits (improved self-images of daughters, for instance) (Belsky & Steinberg, 1978; Ziegler & Gordon, 1982).

Benefits to Employers

There has not been a great deal of research on employer-supported child care; however, the few studies that have been done in the area have documented the bottom-line benefits to employers for such programs. A 1971–1973 study of the Northside Child Development Center in Minneapolis showed significantly lower turnover and absenteeism among center parents than among controls (parents not using the center and other employees) (Milkovich & Gomez, 1976). A 1978 survey of civilian and military centers found that more than half of the employers reported benefits in job turnover, absenteeism, morale, recruitment, and publicity (Perry, 1978). A 1978 survey of 204 corporations with child care programs reported that almost all employers felt the program's benefits outweighed the costs (Magid, 1983). The two most important benefits cited by these employers were an advantage in recruiting new employees and improved morale; other benefits were lower absenteeism, reduced turnover, and attraction back to work of employees on leave.

The National Employer Supported Child Care Project reported numerous benefits based on its survey of 415 companies. Companies reported significant benefits from the child care program in terms of decreased turnover (65%), recruitment (85%), morale (90%), public image (85%), productivity (49%), absenteeism (53%), scheduling flexibility (50%), equal employment opportunity (40%), decreased tardiness (39%), improved quality of products or services (37%), and quality of the workforce (42%) (Burud, Aschbacher, & McCroskey, 1984). A few studies have looked at the specific effects on productivity, and others are currently under way (Bureau of National Affairs, 1984; Dawson et al., 1984; Miller, 1984). Related studies have described the strategies used to develop employer support for working parents in five cities (Friedman, 1983), how corporate executives view workplace and family issues (Axel, 1982), and how parents currently arrange their child care (Emlen, 1982).

There is also some indication that parents feel positively about employer-supported child care programs. As a small part of the National Employer Supported Child Care Project, this author surveyed 691 parents using 19 employer-supported centers and compared their expressed satisfaction with responses of a group of parents using non-employer-related child care services: Parents using employer services expressed significantly higher satisfaction with all aspects of care. In addition, the parents said that child care affected their job performance positively in terms of recruitment (38%), less turnover (69%), better performance (41%), positive morale (63%), reduced absenteeism (47%), and recommending their employer to potential employees because of the child care program (53%) (Burud, Aschbacher, & McCroskey, 1984).

FRAMEWORK FOR PRACTICE

Practice in this arena is interdisciplinary. Social workers bring valuable assessment, process, and intervention skills, but they need to collaborate with management and employees who will be affected by the program as well as with technical experts including community-based child care professionals (on local resources), attorneys (on tax and liability matters), and child care program designers (on space usage, curricula, and playgrounds). The keys to working effectively are an understanding of the many kinds of expertise required for a successful project, willingness to work through a process that helps people become involved and invested in the project as it develops, and a systematic approach to analyzing the child care needs and best program options for the company.

Analysis of a company's child care needs begins with understanding the framework within which the program will operate. The social worker should be familiar with the company's philosophy, goals, and culture and understand how these are reflected in both formal and informal systems. A company may have an explicit framework within which all of its benefits and services are developed. This framework includes the employer's philosophy or policies about benefits and services, how family-oriented benefits fit into the company's future, and perhaps an overall plan for action (McCroskey, 1982). However, it is more likely that social workers will have to piece this information together from existing policies and discussions with company personnel. Once the worker has a sense of the overall framework, the worker can assess the applicability of different kinds of child care program options.

Child Care Options

The child care program options used by companies fall into four major categories:

1. *Flexible personnel policies* help to reduce the need for out-of-home child care by freeing parents at more convenient hours. These include flexible hours, part-time work, and job-sharing plans.
2. *Informational programs* help employees locate child care. Program options include child care resource and referral, whether under contract with an existing community-based child care R&R or through an in-house company program (in areas where there is no such service or the information does not meet the specific needs of employees), or on-site parent education and training programs such as brown-bag seminars and group discussions.
3. *Financial assistance programs* lower the cost of child care for eligible parents. Programs designed to partially reimburse parents for their child care expenditures work best, of course, in communities where there is enough child care available. Another approach is through contributions to community child care programs, either earmarked for employees or as a traditional charitable contribution.
4. *Direct service programs,* including on-site or near-site centers or family day care programs, are the most familiar form of employer-supported child care. Each program is unique because there are so many possible ways of setting up a direct service program. Companies may decide to allow some community children to enroll, rather than limiting enrollment to the children of employees. They may set the program up as a separate nonprofit agency qualifying for IRS Code Sec. 501 (c) (3) (in which case it could not be limited to company employees), as a voluntary employees' beneficiary association [IRS Code Sec. 501 (c) (9)], or as a department of the company. They may serve infants, toddlers, and school-age children as well as preschoolers. (For detailed information on how to set up each of these kinds of child care programs, see Burud, Aschbacher, & McCroskey, 1984.)

In order to make appropriate decisions about program options, child care needs and resources should be considered from three perspectives—the company's, the community's, and the parents'. Companies consider child care for many reasons—some companies are concerned about recruitment, some about turnover, some about PR or community image, and some about productivity. Clearly, programs should be designed to maximize results in the areas of major company concern. If a company is concerned about its community image, it may want to set aside some child care spaces for children from community families, whereas one that primarily needs a recruitment advantage may want to restrict enrollment to the children of employees. Both the amount and form of support the company is able to give may modify plans—a company with extra space may be interested in an on-site center, and one that can only donate time and services may be able to make arrangements with a local child care center to serve children of employees.

The supply of child care in the community will also directly impact program design: Employers will want to augment and support rather than duplicate existing services. Coordinating with existing providers will help ensure maximum return on the employer's investment.

Another way to maximize the investment is to be sure that the program is designed to meet the particular needs of parent employees. Child care needs generally fall into five categories:

1. The need for an adequate supply of child care services, particularly for young and older children.
2. The need for care at a reasonable cost.
3. The need for information on available care.
4. The need for convenient and accessible child care, especially for parents working unusual hours or shifts.
5. The need for child care programs that fit parents' standards of high quality.

Although recognizing that the specific needs of parents will change as children grow and family arrangements shift, it is nonetheless important to have as clear an understanding as possible of how parents define their problems.

Problems and Issues in Implementation

There are a few key issues that come up consistently in discussions with employers. Although these are complex issues that require systematic analysis and discussion, they are briefly noted here so that workers can be prepared. The first issue is liability—companies ask, "Are we liable if something happens to a child in child care?" The response to this question is that child care programs carry their own liability insurance in addition to standard company insurance coverage. However, the possibility of sexual and physical abuse by child care providers has received such widespread attention recently that insurance rates for child care providers have increased astronomically. Although providers still carry insurance, changes in rates and mechanisms will continue to be an issue of major concern to the child care community. (By the way, very few children are abused in child care programs; the great majority of abused children are abused by relatives and friends, not by child care providers).

Another liability issue has been raised in relation to child care R&Rs. Child care R&Rs do not tell parents which program is "best" for their child: They give a list of possibilities and information on what kinds of questions to ask, but they do not make judgments. The best advice of attorneys in the field is that *all* listings should meet specific criteria (for instance, licensed care), but referrers should refrain from evaluating which of the list is "best," both because they cannot know which will best meet the needs of an individual child without a great deal of information (and that is really a matter of parental choice) and because lawsuits have been brought on the basis of such discrimination.

Another major issue is the question of equity. Companies may ask, "How can we set up a benefit or service that is only needed by a few of our employees? Isn't it inequitable?" There are several answers to this concern. First, many benefits are not equitable, either in design or in use—disability is only for those who need it, dental care is used more by some than others, maternity leave is only for those who are pregnant, and so forth. And child care is one of the few benefits that help keep people on the job rather than supporting time away from the job. The second part of the answer is that children are not only a resource to their parents but to all of us. Companies that demonstrate their concern not only for the work role of employees but for their family lives as well by supporting child care programs report that employees (whether they may have a child someday, have grown children, or do not plan any at all) feel good about working for a company that demonstrates its concern for families and children.

The third major issue that is raised has to do with the tax advantages of support for child care programs. In general, changes in the Economic Tax Recovery Act (1981) brought the tax deductions for child care programs into line with all other business deductions. Companies should set up formal Dependent Care Assistance Plans (DCAPs) outlining their program to qualify for tax advantages. One of the financing mechanisms used by some companies is to allow employees to reserve part of their pretax salaries to be administered by the company as a reimbursement plan for child care expenditures (salary reduction plans). Experts in the field believe that federal tax legislation will not change employer-supported child care in regard to tax deductability for employers, child care tax credits for employees, salary-reduction plans, or DCAPs. There may be changes in deductions for charitable contributions to community child care programs. It is important to work with a knowledgeable tax attorney to determine the specific rulings that may affect an individual company's program.

PROGRAM EXAMPLES

The following examples illustrate the range of child care options and the ways these have been tailored to meet the specific needs of companies in communities with very different child care resources. The descriptions are based on data collected by the author and colleagues for the National Employer Supported Child Care Project.

A Resource-and-Referral Program: MASCO, Boston, Massachusetts. A consortium of health care agencies and schools contributed to start an R&R geared to the needs of medical personnel. MASCO is a service for hospitals that brought the Harvard Community Health Plan, Joslin Diabetes Clinic, Children's Hospital Medical Center, New England Deaconess Hospital, Harvard Medical School, Harvard School of Public Health, Sydney Farber Cancer Institute, and Beth Israel Hospital together for child care resource-and-referral services.

An Educational Program for Parents: Steelcase, Inc., Grand Rapids, Michigan. Parent education is provided by child care coordinators through individual discussions, workshops, distribution of written materials, information and referral, technical assistance to existing providers, and child care advocacy.

A Reimbursement Program: Title Data, Denver, Colorado. On presentation of a monthly bill for child care expenditures, the company reimburses 50% of the cost of any kind of child care. The program is tracked by the office manager, who is also responsible for other employee benefits. Since the company has fewer than 25 employees at their Denver office, they wanted a program that was as direct and simple as possible. There are no restrictions on the type of care that may be used. Employees present child care bills and are reimbursed for the cost of care during days worked (days off are pro-rated and deducted from the bill). The office manager reports that the program is very popular, easy to administer, and a help in retaining skilled employers.

An On-site Child Care Center: Official Airline Guides, Oakbrook, Illinois. OAG employs about 700 people on the outskirts of Chicago. The center opened in January 1981, and is licensed to serve 66 children between 6 weeks and 5 years old. The company contributes remodeled space, start-up capital, janitorial services, nursing, and food. Approximately 10% of the parents have been men and about 10% single parents. The company projects a formal evaluation at the end of 3 years of full operation, but preliminary reports indicated that the program had been highly successful and very good for business.

A Family Day Care Program: Illinois Masonic Hospital, Chicago, Illinois. The hospital sponsored a network of seven homes in addition to its child care center. Children from 3 months to 30 months are cared for in these satellite family day care homes (satellite homes are used as adjuncts to center programs).

A School-age Child Care Program: Fel-Pro Industries, Skokie, Illinois. The company developed a rural recreational property 40 miles from the factory as a summer camp for children from age 6 to age 15. Buses provide transportation from the factory to the camp daily. In operation since 1973, the camp serves about 300 children each summer.

A Union Program: The Hyman Blumberg Child Day Care Center, Baltimore, Maryland. Start-up funds were donated by local textile companies giving 1% of the gross hourly payroll for several years before opening. The Health and Welfare Fund of Amalgamated Clothing and Textile Workers' Joint Board oversees the program, which opened in 1969 for preschoolers whose parents are union members. Ongoing funds are also contributed by the companies, which give 2% of gross hourly payroll to the union's Health and Welfare Fund (the Fund also sponsors other services). Licensed for 300 children, the program is open from 6 A.M. to 6 P.M., providing two meals and medical and dental screening in addition to child care at a very reduced cost.

Corporate Support of Child Care: The San Juan Bautista Child Development Center, San Jose, California. The program received start-up funds from the Levi-Strauss and Hewlett-Packard Foundations for a program for sick children. The City of San Jose also gave a block grant to support the program, which offers a "sick bay" or "get-well room" in a large child care center staffed by trained assistants and supervised by registered nurses and public health nurses.

A Multiservice Parent Support Program: Transamerica Life Companies, Los Angeles, California. A child care task force, composed of representatives from many departments of the company, assessed employee needs, considered options, and recommended establishing a child care referral service as a first step in meeting the needs of employees. Since employees commute from all parts of the county to downtown, there was some question about what kinds of services would be most effective. The EAP counselor given charge of developing the child care referral service contacted the child care R&Rs in the county to try to coordinate service. It soon became evident that the referral approach was too limited and that child care needed its own identity separate from the EAP. A child care coordinator (with a nursing background) was hired to set up a highly visible office in the building's lobby. The service includes parent support groups, educational seminars on child development and other issues, individualized referrals and support for specific parent problems (for example, handicapped children), referrals to the child care R&Rs, and help for breast-feeding mothers. The coordinator takes an active interest in the concerns of all employee parents and develops new services as needed. The company also contributes to a program recently established in a nearby hospital to care for sick children while their parents work. This multiservice approach has been extremely effective and company managers report improved productivity and morale as a result of the program.

SUMMARY

Employer-supported child care is a very exciting field—the number of companies with child care programs is increasing rapidly and most major companies have expressed an interest in investigating the topic. During the last 5 years the idea has become widely accepted with support from national organizations such as the President's Council on Private Sector Initiatives, the Junior League, the American Association of University Women, and the Conference Board, in addition to child care advocates and professionals.

Every social worker should have a basic understanding of child care because the problems and benefits of child care are with us to stay. Because child care is primarily an economic work-related issue, it is even more crucial that occupational social workers understand the dynamics of supply and demand and the structure of the child care market. Even if the social worker is never formally asked to assess the need for child care or to develop an employer-supported child care program, the worker will undoubtedly hear about child care problems simply by talking to people at work. Child care is a critical social issue—we have come a long way and, perhaps with the help of employers, we can take some useful steps down the long road that remains.

REFERENCES

Axel, H. (1982). *Workplace issues and the family: How the corporation responds*. New York: Conference Board.

Belsky, J., & Steinberg, L. (1978). The effects of day care: A critical review. *Child Development, 49*, 929–949.

Berrueta-Clement, J. R., Schweinhart, L. J., Barnett, S. W., Epstein, A. S., & Weikart, D. P. (1984). *Changed lives, the effects of the Perry Preschool Program on youths through age 19*. Ypsilanti, MI: High/Scope.

Bureau of National Affairs. (1984). *Employers and child care: Development of a new employee benefit*. Washington, DC: Bureau of National Affairs.

Burud, S., Aschbacher, P., & McCroskey, J. (1984). *Employer supported child care: Investing in human resources*. Boston: Auburn House.

Children's Defense Fund. (1982). *Employed parents and their children: A data book*. Washington: Children's Defense Fund.

Dawson A. G., Mikel, C. S., Lorenz, C. S., & King, J. (1984). *An experimental study of the effects of employer-supported child care services on selected employee behaviors*. Washington, DC: Department of Health and Human Services.

Emlen, A. C. (1982). *When parents are at work: A three company survey of how employed parents arrange child care*. Washington, DC: Greater Washington Research Center.

Fein, G. G., & Clarke-Stewart, A. C. (1973). *Day care in context*. New York: Wiley.

Friedman, D. E. (1983). *Encouraging employer support to working parents: Community strategies for change*. New York: Carnegie Corporation of New York.

Friedman, D., & Burud, S. (1984). Update on employer supported child care initiatives. Workshop presentation, Los Angeles, National Association for the Education of Young Children.

Germain, C. B., & Gitterman, A. (1980) *The life model of social work practice*. New York: Columbia University Press.

Joffe, C. E. (1977). *Friendly intruders: Childcare professionals and family life*. Berkeley, CA: University of California Press.

Magid, R. Y. (1983). *Child care initiatives for working parents: Why employers get involved*. New York: American Management Association.

McCroskey, J. (1982). Work and families: What is the employer's responsibility? *Personnel Journal, 61*(1), 31–38.

Meyer, C. H. (Ed.). (1983). *Clinical social work in ecosystems perspective*. New York: Columbia University Press.

Milkovich, G. T., & Gomez, L. R. (1976, March). Day Care and Selected Employee Work Behaviors. *Academy of Management Journal*, 111–115.

Miller T. I. (1984). The effects of employer-sponsored child care on employee absenteeism, turnover, productivity, recruitment on job satisfaction: What is claimed and what is known. *Personal Psychology, 37*.

Perry, K. S. (1978). *Survey and analysis of employer day care in the United States*. Doctoral dissertation, University of Wisconsin at Milwaukee.

Ramey, C. T., Yeates, K., & Shorte, E. (1984). The plasticity of intellectual development: Insights from preventive intervention. *Child Development, 55*, 1913–1925.

Smith, R. E. (Ed.). (1979). *The subtle revolution: Women at work*. Washington, DC: Urban Institute.

Steiner, G. Y. (1976). *The children's cause*. Washington, DC: Brookings Institute.

Zigler, E. F., & Gordon, E. W., (Eds.). (1982). *Day care: Scientific and social policy issues*. Boston: Auburn House.

12 The Outplacement Process

Michael Lane Smith
Gary M. Gould
MaryAnn Hosang

Carl was flooded with emotions. Waves of panic alternated with unspeakable rage. This couldn't be happening—it must all be some terrible dream, some foolish mistake. Just moments before, Carl's boss informed him that he was being "released," that his job was being eliminated. This was the job that Carl had been doing for 15 years. It was the foundation of his life, the bedrock of his identity and security. And now it was about to be taken from him. Behind the denial and anger, Carl became aware of the quiet, growing feeling of shame. He had been fired! Just like that! What could he possibly tell his wife? How could he look his son in the face?

Losing a job can be a devastating experience. It can mean loss of the ability to function as an independent, instrumentally effective adult. It can involve the disruption of one's social identity and the loss of important peer relationships. It can trigger profound stress while simultaneously removing from the individual important forms of psychosocial support (Keefe, 1984). It can do and mean all of these things, but it does not have to have these consequences. Both the process and meanings of losing one's job can be shaped to provide the victim of job loss with hope, social support, and specific knowledge and skills to move beyond the experience of termination as a tragic event. One family of interventions employed for the purpose of minimizing the trauma of job loss and maximizing the effectiveness of personal responses to it is referred to as *outplacement counseling* (OPC).

Outplacement counseling involves both management consultation and planning and job search skills development provided to either groups or individuals victimized by job loss. It involves personal counseling, career and interest assessment, strategy development for the job search itself, and skill development and encouragement until a new position is found or until the period of coverage is exhausted (Monaco, 1983). These services are provided by or through the employing organization at no cost to the people who are facing job loss. OPC is not a job search itself. Instead, it is service designed to aid job-loss victims in developing and mobilizing their resources for the purpose of individually ferreting out attractive and rewarding employment.

Outplacement counseling has two basic, yet related, purposes. On the one hand, its purpose is to limit for both job loss victims and others still employed the emotional and financial costs involved in termination. These purposes reflect a number of reasons why OPC is being recognized as an important tool for management, a vital resource for job loss victims, and an attractive facet of occupational social work.

WHY OFFER OUTPLACEMENT COUNSELING?

Businesses that operate in competitive economic environments are understandably concerned with the number of employees they pay for the services or products they sell. Many companies have recently been experiencing particularly intense pressure to reduce their labor costs as a result of foreign competition or corporate mergers. The president of one executive search-and-consulting firm has estimated that as many as 600,000 middle-management jobs alone are being eliminated each year as companies seek leaner, more efficient workforces (Goldman, 1986). Despite the economic logic of such actions, job loss frequently impacts the lives of its victims in profound ways.

For many people the outstanding characteristic of outplacement counseling is its humane expression of caring for individuals in crisis. Job loss is frequently traumatic. It can call for serious intrapersonal and interpersonal adjustment to conditions beyond the control of the affected individual. The specific skill and knowledge development promoted through OPC and the emotional support provided through it may be valued as important psychosocial resources available to individuals in need, and vital to promoting effective levels of social functioning. Because job loss frequently results from technological change, reorganization, or vague interpersonal discomfort between boss and subordinate ("bad chemistry"), the loss of one's job is frequently beyond one's own control. In these situations, especially, the provision of OPC services represents an important expression of "corporate social responsibility" (Adams, 1980).

The reputation that an organization can earn as a "good corporate citizen" can have a positive impact on the organization itself. Vigorous outplacement efforts—especially if available to both classified and unclassified employees—can contribute to a very favorable public relations profile. OPC can enhance the reputation of an organization as a progressive, yet humane arena for work. This can be a distinct advantage in the competitive process of recruiting talented new workers. Within the organization itself, outplacement counseling programs can promote higher levels of employee morale. This may be especially true over a period of several years as the number of people availing themselves of OPC services grows and as continuing employees of the organization encounter first-hand former colleagues who have profited from outplacement assistance.

One of the more quantifiable benefits of outplacement programs is the cost savings that frequently accrue to sponsoring organizations. On the one hand, effective OPC services offer the manager a psychologically acceptable alternative to retaining marginally productive employees. All too often, poor performers in organizations are not fired but are simply shunted to "safe" and unchallenging positions and permitted to stagnate. This practice offers little benefit to organizations or employee; and while it does save the manager from the discomfort of terminating a marginal worker, the consequences of diminished morale, inadequate performance, and worker discontent are likely to create even greater (and more longlasting) problems. By providing both the supervisor and employee important forms of assistance, OPC can promote the exercise of termination whenever it is truly appropriate. This can promote an organizational workforce that is both leaner and more vigorous (Morin & Yorks, 1982).

In addition to cost savings resulting from the separation of marginal performers, OPC can contribute to maximizing the bottom line by reducing the total amount of severance pay organizations expend. Outplacement counseling typically enables job-loss victims to secure attractive positions in less time (and with more fortunate results) than the time required for reemployment by people who do not, or cannot, participate in OPC programs. The more quickly severed workers find employment, the less severance pay the former employer may be obligated to spend (Adams, 1980; Driessnack, 1980; Morin & Yorks, 1982).

Finally, employers may find that OPC interventions help to reduce the number and intensity of vindictive acts possible (and frequently considered) when employees face the loss of their jobs. Workplace sabotage is frequently an expresssion of the frustration and anger experienced by people without a sense of potency and without hope for the future. Outplacement counseling is designed to help people channel their feelings into socially appropriate and personally rewarding channels. It is designed to help people recapture hope and grasp success. Outplacement counseling is believed to have prevented long-term vindictiveness and other problems that can result when former employees eventually find positions with suppliers or competitors (Driessnack, 1980).

THE PHASES OF OUTPLACEMENT COUNSELING

Comprehensive outplacement counseling programs offer at least four different, yet related, types of services. These differing forms of activity can also
be conceptualized as phases of a comprehensive outplacement process,
because they define a temporal sequence of intervention. The phases are (1)
systemwide intervention, (2) pretermination coaching, (3) crisis intervention, and (4) posttermination counseling and coaching.

Systemwide Interventions

The first of these forms of intervention focuses not on a specific employee
but on the host organization itself. Here the outplacement counselor con-
centrates on identifying and bringing to management's attention workplace
procedures or policies that inhibit the ability of employees to pursue higher
levels of social functioning. Inadequate or unavailable day care services for
working parents, inflexible work schedules, discriminatory promotion or
retention practices, and other types of work-related barriers to effective
social functioning can all impact in important ways on members of the
organizational workforce. In the broad context of occupational social work,
these barriers are implicated in a host of problems related to impaired social
functioning. In the narrower context of outplacement counseling, they are
frequently associated with (and frequently precipitate) job loss itself. Consequently, preventive intervention systemwide can reduce the need to rely
upon other more traditional forms of OPC. Social worker advocacy for
organizationally sponsored day care, flexitime, job sharing, and early retirement programs are just some of the options that can promote higher levels of
employee social functioning. With respect to organizational termination
policies, the outplacement counselor can advocate for sensitive and rational
job-performance appraisal systems as well as coherent and routine access to
OPC services and reasonable benefit packages for victims of job loss.

Pretermination Coaching of Supervisors and Managers

The termination process can be a painful, stressful experience for the person
who fires an employee. Indeed, many workers are "carried" by their employing organizations because continued inadequate performance is less costly
psychologically to their supervisors than is the termination interview. For
the job-loss victim, as well, the termination interview can be a confusing or
excruciating experience. Fortunately, enough is known about this process to
be able to educate supervisors and personnel specialists in the skills of
releasing employees with consideration and clarity.

    As with many unpleasant things, a common human desire is to delay or minimize bad news as much as possible. It is not uncommon for supervisors to delay termination interviews until late in the day, late in the week. A weekend away from the office can be useful therapy for the unpleasant experience of firing an employee. When finally confronting workers, managers may attempt to minimize the import of the "bad news." Managers may offer hints or suggestions about problems in employees' work performance or may encourage workers to consider attractive career options in other organizations or in new lines of work. However, many people leave termination interviews still not knowing that they have, in fact, been "terminated!" The reward for managers is that job-loss victims are still emotionally intact (and so are the managers, for that matter). Unfortunately, in their confusion, such workers are unlikely to proceed to appropriate disengagement and job search actions, and a subsequent, far more confrontive and abrupt termination interview is likely to occur in the near future.

Social workers can help managers conduct these painful but necessary encounters in ways that limit the pain and confusion to both subordinate and supervisor alike. If properly conducted, these interviews can also stimulate job-loss victims to take steps crucial to emotionally managing job loss and successfully orchestrating job searches. This assistance takes the form of coaching supervisors in the skills of an acceptable termination interview.

Proper timing of the interview is an important factor. Termination interviews held late in the day or late in the week can contribute to a sense of defeatism and isolation for the job-loss victim. Interviews conducted late in the work week also interrrupt the outplacement process itself and can constitute a barrier to the worker's need for counsel in the critical period immediately following the news of job loss.

The supervisor's role in the termination/outplacement experience needs to be clarified. Supervisors are not counselors and their role is not that of providing primary emotional support for terminated workers. The supervisor is responsible for communicating to the worker clearly and un-ambiguously that the individual is being fired. It is important that this message be communicated to the worker within the first few minutes of the interview so as not to lull the employee into a false sense of security. Clarity and honesty are important elements to this aspect of the termination interview.

It will be easier for most supervisors to conduct themselves accordingly when they are confident that they can manage their own feelings in response to the job-loss victim. This involves knowing one's self and one's own values and patterns of relating to others, as well as one's own feelings about work and its meanings. Social workers can help supervisors examine these aspects of their personalities and can suggest ways of managing their emotions in the interest of facilitating the total outplacement process. Knowledge of typical worker reactions when they are confronted with the reality of termination as well as knowledge of methods of responding to them is also important to supervisors. Persons conducting termination interviews need to learn to avoid arguments or debates with persons losing their jobs, while simultaneously acknowledging workers' feelings of anger, loss, and fear. Likewise, they need to understand how important it is that they recognize workers' strengths and express gratitude for worker contributions or efforts. Discussion, demonstration, and role playing are typical methods useful for developing this knowledge and skill.

Finally, supervisors involved in the termination interview need to be aware of the severance benefits available to workers. Job-loss victims need to know whether their offices are still available for use and whether secretarial support is still available. Workers need to know for how long they will be paid and at what level. Likewise, workers need to understand what fringe benefits are still available to them and for how long. This information should be summarized in writing and presented to them during the termination interview.

In this context, outplacement counseling represents an important fringe benefit, and one that may be immediately useful. Supervisors must understand the importance of referring job-loss victims to the outplacement counselor and must develop the skill to do so in a way that communicates optimism to people who may otherwise be stunned or sullen. In this regard, the social worker should educate supervisors as to the behavioral portraits of individuals most especially in need of prompt and immediate counseling and should emphasize the importance of making prior arrangements with the outplacement counselor for immediate client referral whenever individuals are to be confronted with job loss.

Crisis Intervention

For many people, the reality of job loss constitutes a crisis of the first order. Job loss necessarily involves some reorganization of interpersonal relationships and for many people intrapersonal readjustment as well. Emotions of the job-loss victim are likely to be fluid and intense. Confusion, anger, fear, and shame are common reactions to the news of job loss. Working with the client to overcome or avoid feelings of desperation or hopelessness is vitally important. Toward this end, the occupational social worker in outplacement counseling needs to be available to the job-loss victim immediately upon closure of the termination interview.

This period of crisis intervention bears some resemblance to crisis intervention in traditional mental health settings (see also Chapter 5 of this volume). The situation confronting the client is immediate and of central importance. The relationship between the social worker and the client is well focused and (with respect to this phase of the outplacement process) time-limited. The social worker attempts to help the client ventilate feelings, explore the client's own interpretation of the crisis situation, and examine resources and options available to the client for responding to the problem. In this context, OPC services represent an important resource available to the job-loss victim—but these are services that the client must value in order to be useful. Consequently, crisis counseling in an OPC context also includes an attempt to help the client reframe the job-loss experience as a beginning as well as an ending. The social worker needs to describe the outplacement process, its intent, and the skills it helps to develop as a continuing service that the organization makes available. Although the past employer no longer needs the services of the job-loss victim, the latter is not being abandoned. Crisis counseling in OPC is directed to helping the client deal with feelings in the present while also engaging the client's hope for the future.

It is important for the social worker to address with the client several immediate issues that can exacerbate the latter's sense of crisis and impair an otherwise successful OPC experience. One of these concerns has to do with how the client is going to inform her or his spouse of the termination. For many people the crisis of job loss becomes fixed on the dilemma of how and when to inform other family members. Practitioner reassurance and counsel can help clients deal with this issue, thereby freeing them to continue with the outplacement experience unencumbered by deception.

Another concern of immediate importance is the client's financial status. Here the social worker can help the client take stock of assets and financial obligations, offer assistance in money management, and help the client frame realistic plans for managing the next several months on what is likely to be a reduced income.

During this period of crisis management, the client needs to be made aware of the dangers of precipitate action. On the one hand, the job-loss victim should be encouraged not to exhaust his or her best job contacts within the next few days. The outplacement process is not geared to helping the individual find just any job, but rather a position that is both financially and personally rewarding. This involves time and reflection and may well lead to a more fruitful use of these known contacts.

On the other hand, precipitate action can take much more drastic forms. Homicide and suicide are not unknown reactions of people experiencing job loss. Crises can elicit heightened emotions and extraordinary reactions. The social worker involved in OPC needs to make a critical assessment: Is the client dangerous to self or others? Where, specifically, is the client going upon leaving the social worker's office? What does the client intend to do for the rest of the day? Who does the client plan to see? Practitioner response to apparently dangerous or suicidal clients must take into account both the ethics and technologies of social work intervention and the unique legal framework within each state pertaining to liability for failure to notify appropriate persons whenever a client threatens harm to another.

The crisis intervention phase of outplacement counseling is necessarily time-limited. In addition to emotional support, assistance is given the client in solving immediate problems, especially those involving family members and finances. A crucial component of the support offered the client is specific knowledge detailing the process and likely usefulness of the last phase of the outplacement process. In short, the practitioner needs to address the emotional and instrumental concerns of the job-loss victim, but the practitioner also needs to communicate the advantages of outplacement services to the client as well.

Posttermination Counseling and Coaching

Being terminated is only the beginning of trauma for the dismissed employee. Searching for a new job is a long, grueling process, generously peppered with rejection, discouragement, and frustration. Compounding the stress of looking for a job are the feelings of self-doubt, ego deflation, and low self-esteem that result from the recent termination. If the person lacks job search skills, the ordeal is intensified. Educating terminated persons in the techniques of self-appraisal and securing new employment appropriate to their needs and talents becomes the task of the outplacement counselor in the fourth stage of outplacement counseling (Morin & Yorks, 1982).

Before beginning the job search, it is important for the terminee to first engage in self-assessment and career assessment. The terminee should be encouraged to make an inventory of all skills, talents, assets, and accomplishments he or she can legitimately claim, both on and off the job, and prioritize them in order of importance and/or level of enjoyment. Stating skills in the language of the past career should be avoided, because it may not truly represent the specific talents involved (Bolles, 1985). For example, "campaigning for political candidates" does not really give a clear picture of the skills involved, such as organizing, persuading, and motivating. The social worker should not be surprised to find that some terminees will be reluctant to take the time to do an in-depth self-assessment. Many people fear the process of self-investigation, and others, even though they are willing to self-examine, will get caught up in the "yes, but . . ." game, thereby discounting skills or rejecting a career option they have always desired (Morin & Cabrera, 1982). It becomes the job of the social worker to encourage that self-assessment and help the terminee see the worth and validity of her or his skills and goals.

The next step should be for the terminee to determine possible careeer paths best suited to his or her talents. Bolles (1985) suggests determining answers to the following questions:

1. What basic materials or kinds of people or forms of data/information do you want your skills to serve?
2. What kinds of values or goals do you want your skills to serve?
3. What sort of work environment, physical, emotional, and spiritual, do you need for the most effective employment of your skills?
4. What level do you want to be working at—supervisory, or as a member of a team, or as an individual working by yourself?
5. Do you want to work for another, or work in your own enterprise?

Another task of the outplacement counselor may be to provide management-style consultation, when the management style of the terminee has been a factor in the termination.

Morin & Yorks (1982) suggest a three-step process:

1. Create an awareness of the problem.
2. Focus on a few critical behaviors.
3. Help the person understand the types of environments in which she or he is most likely to succeed or fail.

The outplacement counselor should also be prepared to provide training in job search skills. The job hunter will need help in mapping out job-search strategies. Which companies to contact, how to find out who has the power to hire in each company, how to introduce yourself (phone calls, letters of introduction, etc.), and when to use business contacts are all important questions to be answered. The job search should not be conducted in a haphazard, panic-stricken fashion; every detail should be carefully planned out.

The client will also need guidance in preparing a concise resume that presents him or her in the most positive possible light. Occupational social workers should become familiar with the different kinds of resumes and what employers look for in a resume. To this end, there is a plethora of manuals and guides concerning resumes: *What Color Is Your Parachute* (Bolles, 1985) is one such source.

Job hunters may also need some help with interviewing skills: Perfectly planned campaigns and beautiful resumes will not mean a thing if interviewees can't present themselves well. Videotaping role-played interviews is a very effective way of providing feedback concerning self-presentation and personal communication style. The counselor should be aware that practice interviewing can be very anxiety-producing for some clients, and support and encouragement, as well as some positive feedback, are necessary.

Personal counseling should be interwoven throughout the job-search process, from termination to ensconcement in a new job. Being unemployed for an extended period of time has pronounced effects on the unemployed person. Self-esteem is likely to be adversely affected, along with self-identity. Some experts contend that the self-esteem is permanently affected (Kaufman, cited in Madonia, 1983). The primary role of the social worker during ongoing counseling is to offer encouragement, moral support, and direction throughout the job-search process. In addition, there will be times when the client will need to ventilate pent-up emotions, and at these times the most helpful thing the counselor can do is to engage in active listening, employing open-ended questions, restatement, expanders, and silence to encourage ventilation of feelings (Morin & Yorks, 1982). It should be stressed that active listening and offering moral support are *not* the same as offering sympathy. The fired worker should not be coddled, because this would encourage the person to become immobilized while wallowing in self-pity. The social worker must keep the terminee oriented toward action.

Finally, the counselor has the responsibility to avoid getting involved in areas beyond her or his expertise (Morin & Yorks, 1982). In a situation as emotionally charged as unemployment, it would be easy to do more harm than good. The social worker should be aware of resources elsewhere in the community and refer clients to those sources if it becomes necessary.

CONSIDERATIONS WHEN IMPLEMENTING AN OPC PROGRAM

OPC programs exist in a variety of modes and in varying degrees of quality. The major decisions to be made when implementing an OPC program involve whether to provide in-house or out-of-house services, whether services will be provided on an individual or group basis, and how to choose an OPC counselor.

In-house versus Out-of-house

Outplacement services can be provided either in-house or externally, and there are advantages and disadvantages to both. The most obvious advantage of an internal program is that it is more economical then hiring an outside consultant. Considering that most outplacement consulting firms charge from 15% to 25% of each terminated person's compensation level (Morin & Yorks, 1982), it becomes obvious that, over time, an outplacement service contained within the company becomes considerably more cost effective.

A second advantage of an internal program is the accessibility of the expertise of the outplacement specialist. Not only can the counselor be readily available to meet with the ex-employee immediately following the termination interview, this specialist is also in a position to spot potential problems in the company's termination policies.

Many experts feel that using an outside consultant is preferable to an internal program (e.g., Dreissmack, 1980). One argument for hiring an outside consultant is that an in-house program requires the terminated employee to make frequent visits back to the worksite, which can be potentially problematic. For instance, a terminated employee may not be comfortable facing former colleagues and for that reason decide not to participate in the program at all. Conversely, colleagues who remain employed may not be comfortable seeing the terminated employee because it reminds them of their own career mortality. Another potential problem associated with an on-site outplacement facility is that returning to the worksite may serve as a catalyst, keeping wounds open and fueling hostility. An extremely hostile former employee may even act out anger on the organization by being destructive. Also, frequent visits back to the organization may make the separation issue psychologically unclear. An ex-employee who is having difficulty detaching from the organization is not helped by coming back and being reminded of former bonds.

Another problem with an in-house program is that the need for outplacement services is often intermittent (Dreissmack, 1980). Once the program is developed and termination policy firmly established, there may be not be a full-time need for outplacement services.

A third advantage of using an off-site consultant is that the terminated employee may more easily trust a counselor who is not perceived as part of the organization and, therefore, as an adversary (Morin & Yorks, 1982). Trust is crucial if the ex-employee is to feel free to ventilate feelings.

Group versus Individual Services

OPC services can be provided either on an individual or a group basis, and there are advantages and disadvantages to both. Individual services are commonly provided for management-level employees. In a one-to-one counseling relationship, the opportunity exists for tailoring the program to fit each client's needs. There is also more personalized contact between the client and the counselor, which provides more opportunity for insight into intrapersonal and interpersonal problems, which may have been a factor in on-the-job problems. Further, there are more opportunities for the counselor to aid terminated employees to get in touch with their feelings about being out of work. The disadvantages of individual services are that they are expensive and may be impractical if not impossible during a layoff or plant closure when services are needed simultaneously for a large number of workers, especially lower-level employees.

Group OPC programs are generally advantageous when large numbers of employees are let go at once. A typical group program would involve the same basic process as an individual program, presented as a 3- to 4-day workshop with between 7 and 16 participants (Broussard & DeLargey,

1979). An obvious advantage of providing OPC services to lower-level employees in a group setting is the cost efficiency: One estimate places the
savings at $14.50 in unemployment expense for every dollar invested in the
group OPC program (Bailey, 1980). Another advantage of a group program is
the mutual support network that can develop among the participants. A
productive group can reassure members that others share the same fears,
anxieties, and doubts; and they are less likely to feel alienated from the
world. The closeness and interdependency fostered in the group can continue after the completion of the OPC program.

The major disadvantage of group OPC programs is the lack of one-to-one
counseling sessions, from which some terminees really benefit (Barkhaus &
Meek, 1982). Another possible disadvantage of group programs is the concern some participants generally have prior to beginning the program about
conducting such a personal and emotional activity in a group setting.
However, Barkhaus and Meek (1982) found that over 85% of the participants
in their workshop were "very positive about conducting outplacement
counseling in a group setting" (p. 78), although many had grave reservations
prior to attending the workshop.

OPC Staff Qualifications

It is essential that an OPC program be staffed with competent, qualified
people. Unfortunately, at this time there exists no certification, licensing, or
accreditation process for outplacement counselors, so it is impossible to tell a
competent OPC counselor from an incompetent one just by the credentials
presented. It will be necessary to ask around, to find out which programs are
qualified. When choosing an OPC counselor, look for the following qualifications:

1. Ability to interview skillfully and establish effective positive relationships.
2. Familiarity with executive, managerial, and technically professional
   positions and career paths.
3. Sensitivity to organizational ("political") dynamics.
4. Astuteness in job-hunting procedures.
5. Ability to counsel people who are under pressure.
6. Ability to motivate, support, and rebuild confidence in others.
7. Assertiveness and ability to follow through on details.
8. Possession of a broad range of business and industry experience.
9. Familiarity with the managerial labor market.
10. Possession of career and personal counseling experience (Monaco,
    1983).

SPECIAL CONSIDERATION: THE OLDER WORKER

Terminating a long-term older employee is a very difficult task for the supervisor, whatever the reason for the termination. Traditionally, in an effort to avoid the unpleasantness of terminating long-term employees, the older worker whose performance had deteriorated or whose skills were obsolete was either forced into involuntary early retirement or stuck on a shelf within the company until retirement age. Recently, however, federal legislation has eliminated many forms of involuntary retirement, and because it is not feasible to keep an ineffective employee on the payroll until age 70, more and more older workers are being terminated.

Older workers in the job market are at a distinct disadvantage, and it generally takes them twice as long to find a job as the younger worker. American industry routinely discriminates against older applicants, albeit unconsciously. Curiously, most discrimination against older workers is perpetuated by other older workers who are in management positions, and who do the actual hiring (Knowles, 1984)! Myths, such as those proclaiming higher absenteeism among older workers and older workers' inability to adapt to change, run rampant and contribute heavily to the bias of management against hiring them. A further concern is that the older worker will use company-sponsored health insurance more than younger workers and therefore cost the company more.

On a brighter note, attitudes toward aging workers do seem to be improving. In these times of economic instability, some companies are beginning to recognize the advantages older employees can provide. They are seasoned and experienced; they bring to the job an expertise and wisdom that younger workers cannot offer. Older workers also bring to the job hunt itself the experience to plan and execute a balanced, more efficient job search, along with a much broader network of contacts in the business world (Dunn, 1984). The point to be stressed here is that social workers providing outplacement services need not view the terminated older worker as a hopeless case: With guidance and encouragement, the older worker can find another good job at a comparable or better salary.

The Outplacement Counselor's Role with the Older Worker

The OPC specialist's responsibilities with regard to the older employee are twofold. First, the social worker will need to do pretermination counseling, both at the corporate level and at the supervisory level. Pretermination counseling at the corporate level is necessary for two reasons. First, the Age Discrimination Employment Act and other antidiscrimination legislation protect workers over 40 years old. Companies need to promulgate policy concerning proper documentation of reasons for terminating long-term employees, along with fair termination packages that recognize the years given in service to the company by the employee. At the supervisory level, the social worker should do extensive pretermination counseling with the supervisor of the employee. As previously stated, firing a long-term employee is a very stressful task for the supervisor. The supervisor may need extensive coaching about how to approach the termination interview, as well as some guidance about how to handle the possible feelings of guilt. Also, the supervisor will need guidance concerning how to handle co-workers who may be upset about the company's treatment of a long-term employee and who view it as a statement of the company's lack of loyalty toward them. The workers will need to be reassured that the termination was, in fact, necessary. Actually, provision of OPC services in itself goes a long way toward reassuring co-workers that the company does feel a sense of responsibility concerning the displaced workers.

Immediately following the termination interview, the social worker's focus shifts to the newly unemployed worker. The counselor should proceed as with any other terminated worker but keep in mind the unique concerns of the older worker. The first issue faced by the older worker may be as basic as making a decision to either find a new job or to retire early. A client wrestling with this decision needs to evaluate both his or her financial state (to see if retiring is even feasible) and the possible ramifications to one's self-esteem of losing her or his identity as a worker. It may even be helpful to counsel with the spouse, who would also be profoundly affected by a decision to retire.

Assuming that the unemployed worker does decide to stay in the workforce, long-term support and guidance are essential. The long-term employee has probably been out of the job market for many years, and interview skills and such may be rusty. It is the responsibility of the counselor to help hone such skills. Also, the worker must make a decision whether or not to relocate, and if so, where. Often, it is prudent to consider relocating in an area where the worker would like to retire later, possibly avoiding moving expenses upon retirement.

SUMMARY

Crises require significant intrapersonal or interpersonal adjustment. Job loss can represent one of the most painful crises that people experience in their lifetimes. Social workers can provide sensitive and timely assistance at such times, and organizations can fulfill their broader responsibilities to employees through the provision of outplacement counseling services. These services can minimize the disruption of job loss for both continuing and terminated employees. They can help individuals recapture hope. They can also save companies a good deal of money. Outplacement services represent an important component to a comprehensive social work presence in the workplace.

REFERENCES

Adams, D. N., Jr. (1980). When laying off employees, the word is "out-training." *Personnel Journal*, September.

Bailey, T. (1980). Industrial outplacement at Goodyear, Part 1: The company's position. *Personnel Administrator*, March.

Barkhaus, R. S., & Meek, C. L. (1982). A practical view of outplacement counseling. *Personnel Administrator*, March.

Bolles, R. N. (1985). *What color is your parachute?: A practical manual for job-hunters and career changers*. Berkeley, CA: Ten Speed Press.

Broussard, W. J., & Delargey, R. J. (1979). The dynamics of the group outplacement workshop. *Personnel Journal*, December.

Driessmack, C. H. (1980). Outplacement—The new personnel practice. *Personnel Administrator*, October.

Dunn, A. F. (1984). Outplacement. *California Business*, January.

Goldman, E. (1986, September 15) Stepping down in size but up in rewards. *Wall Street Journal*.

Keefe, T. (1984). The stresses of unemployment. *Social Work, 29*, May/June.

Knowles, D. E. (1984). Middle aged and older workers—An industry perspective. In S. F. Yolles, L. W. Krinsky, S. N. Kieffer, & P. A. Carone (Eds.), *The aging employee*. New York: Human Sciences Press.

Madonia, J. F. (1983). The trauma of unemployment and its consequences. *Social Casework: The Journal of Contemporary Social Work, 64*(8).

Monaco, D. A. (1983). Outplacement counseling: Business and profession. In Manuso, J. S. J. (Ed.). *Occupational clinical psychology*. New York: Praeger.

Morin, W. J. & Cabrera, J. C. (1982). *Parting company: How to survive the loss of a job and find another successfully*. New York: Harcourt Brace Jovanovich.

Morin, W. J., & Yorks, L. (1982). *Outplacement techniques: A positive approach to terminating employees*. New York: Drake Beam Morin.

13 Human Resource Issues and Aging

Carl S. Wilks
Robert B. Rowen
MaryAnn Hosang
Seth Knoepler

Older or aging employees merit special consideration by occupational social workers due to the exceptional problems they face on the job. Employers have traditionally been biased against older workers for several reasons:

1. Older workers have had more time to acquire skills, credentials, and experience that can be used to negotiate higher wages and salaries than are typically paid to younger, less experienced workers (Suzuki, 1976).
2. There is a tendency for aging employees to utilize certain fringe benefits, such as employer-sponsored health insurance (Rosen, 1985), which makes them more "expensive" than younger workers (Craft et al., 1979; Sheppard & Rix, 1977).
3. The stereotype of the older worker as a less productive and adaptable employee is well-established (Mercer, 1981), although the research on this has been contradictory (see Cleveland & Landy, 1981; Meier & Kerr, 1976; Panek et al., 1979; Price et al., 1975).
4. The bias against older workers is being perpetuated by managers and supervisors, who are likely to be older workers themselves (Stagner, 1985).
5. As workers age, supervisors' expectations for performance tend to decline, which in turn causes the workers to lose confidence in their own ability, which negatively affects their level of performance—thus setting up a vicious cycle (Yolles et al., 1984). Further, as workers get older, retirement looms ever closer on the horizon and is often anticipated with dread.

Occupational social workers are in a position to respond to the special needs of the older worker on several levels. At one level, they can inform and educate supervisors about the special considerations and benefits of managing an older employee. Administratively, they can assist in the development of corporate policy that affects older workers. They can design and implement preretirement programs to educate and prepare the older employees for retirement. And they can provide counseling for troubled older workers. In order to effectively meet the needs of these workers, it is imperative that the social worker be well aware of the unique challenges facing older employees.

THE ROLE OF THE OLDER WORKER

Older, more experienced workers frequently have a unique role to play at the workplace. On-the-job training and learning through experience are processes in which older, more experienced workers play a critical role and thus continue to make important contributions to helping newer workers learn about what is expected of them. When supervisors understand the way experienced workers can help instruct their younger colleagues about a variety of work-related subjects, from the idiosyncrasies of certain machines to where to go for a good sandwich, the older worker can be an essential component of efforts designed to lessen anxiety and alienation among junior employees and to help integrate younger workers into the prevailing "organizational culture" of the company (Deal & Kennedy, 1982).

Technological Change and the Older Worker

The implications of the ever-increasing rate of technological change in modern societies have for some time been a subject of intense, often heated debate. There seems to be some agreement that aging workers are less likely than their younger colleagues to benefit from and are more likely to suffer from technology-driven changes in the way that work is done and organized (McAuley, 1977; Rosen & Jerdee, 1976). Older, more experienced workers are less likely to have received campus-based instruction in the latest technological innovations. Thus, at least in the short run, employers often have a built-in incentive to hire and promote younger, recently educated workers who can go "on-line" with the latest technologies immediately, without any further training.

However, the very same technological forces that tend to put older, experienced workers at a disadvantage can, in the long run, actually serve to enhance their prospects for employment and promotion. The furious pace of technological change, at least in some industries, can quickly render obsolete the skills of even the most recently trained employee, perhaps in as little as 5 or 10 years (Dubin, 1972). Under such circumstances, a manager hoping to retain an employee's services for a longer period of time must anticipate the necessity of retraining the worker at some point during the person's tenure with the company. The relative advantage to such an organization of hiring someone fresh out of school, while in some respects real, appears less significant, since it may not be very long before even the newest employee becomes an old hand whose skills are outdated. Rather than taking a chance on a new, untested worker, whose technical abilities are only currently state-of-the-art, prudent managers and personnel specialists may decide instead to accept the costs of retraining a trusted, experienced member of the organization's current staff.

There is one other way the increasingly rapid pace of technological change may eventually prove to be beneficial for many older workers. Though allegations of performance deficits among older workers continue to be a source of controversy among researchers and managers alike, such deficits are more likely to emerge in tasks where sheer physical capacities play the predominant role in determining a worker's performance (Dirken, 1972; Noble et al., 1964; Panek et al., 1979). However, new industrial technologies are rapidly redefining the nature of work in such a way as to reduce the proportion of jobs in which purely physical abilities are most important (consider, for example, the burgeoning robotics industry and other forms of automation). In this respect, technological change may reduce some of the disadvantages that aging workers face.

Adapting to a Changing Work Environment

Closely related to the common stereotype of the aging worker as a slower, less productive employee is the belief, also widespread, that younger workers are more adaptable to changes in the way that goods are produced and services provided than are their older counterparts. The available research suggests that, while there is some factual basis to depictions of aging workers as more resistant to innovations in the way that work tasks are accomplished, it is a serious mistake to attribute to most older workers a stubborn unwillingness or inability to "learn new tricks." Thus, both Chown (1972) and Stagner (1985) found evidence that older workers tend to experience more problems as a result of management-imposed changes in the intrinsic aspects of their jobs. However, Haberlandt (1973) found a *negative* correlation between a worker's age and the amount of time and money that were needed to retrain the person, and both Chown (1972) and Cobb (1974) have reported that the rigidity or flexibility of an employee's personality plays a larger role than does age in determining how a worker adapts to job changes.

Notably, older employees consistently report both more overall job satisfaction than younger workers (Weaver, 1980; Hunt & Saul, 1975; Smith et al., 1969) and a greater concern with the intrinsic aspects of their work (Andrisani & Miljus, 1977; Murchinsky, 1978). Thus, greater reluctance on the part of some older workers to embrace changing work circumstances may be an unavoidable concomitant of the fact that these workers are, on the average, more oriented toward such intrinsic considerations and more content with the status quo. When faced with management-imposed programs of job redesign, older employees who have subjectively more to lose may be basing their reactions on realistic assessments of the situation as it appears to them.

Retraining the Older Worker

Unfortunately, even the the most eager and willing older employee may have considerable difficulty obtaining the necessary training or retraining when managers implement changes in the worker's job or in the way that a section or department is organized. Even more unfortunate is the fact that these difficulties may be a consequence of the managers' perception of aging workers as less flexible and adaptable, a perception that has a limited basis in fact.

In view of the unprecedented speed with which many industrial technologies are changing, many managers and personnel administrators are coming to appreciate the futility of simply trying to replace all those employees whose skills have become obsolete with new recruits freshly trained in the now-latest technologies. However, this does not mean that organizations are turning to the oldest, most experienced segments of their workforces when it becomes necessary to retrain current staff. In fact, there are indications that managers often prefer not to retrain their most experienced employees but will instead offer retraining opportunities to somewhat younger, less experienced workers (McAuley, 1977; Mercer, 1981). This appears to be a result of a tendency to stereotype older workers as being set in their ways and hence more difficult to retrain (Rosen & Jerdee, 1976; Stagner, 1985). Additionally, many managers who prefer to retrain younger workers base their decisions, at least partly, on the implicit assumption that it makes better economic sense to retrain an employee who can spend an additional 15 or 20 years with the organization than it does to update the skills of someone who is relatively close to retirement age.

Social workers need to alert managers and personnel administrators to the fact that retraining older workers is considerably more complex than either of these generalizations suggests. For one thing, stereotypes to the effect that older workers are unretrainable are, as we have seen, largely inaccurate, and such stereotypes obscure substantial individual differences in this area among younger and older workers alike.

Secondly, it may be that traditional assumptions about people's work histories and career trajectories are in the process of themselves becoming obsolete (Bolles, 1985; Morin & Yorks, 1982). This calls into question retraining decisions that assume that a younger or middle-aged employee is more likely than an older one to remain with the company long enough to justify the expense of retraining. Older workers could become increasingly attractive candidates for retraining in the eyes of managers who fear that a younger, more occupationally mobile worker might use newly acquired skills to obtain a more lucrative position elsewhere, perhaps with one of the company's competitors.

In many cases, educating managers about the advantages of hiring, promoting, and retraining older workers and the competitive disadvantages associated with underutilizing them will be sufficient to significantly affect an organization's personnel policies as they pertain to older employees. However, it seems inevitable that some managers will continue to allow their decisions to be influenced by inaccurate stereotypes that assume that older workers are less efficient and adaptable than younger ones. Consequently, it is essential that antidiscrimination laws like the Federal Age Discrimination in Employment Act or ADEA (1967, amended in 1977 to cover workers between the ages of 65 and 70) be enacted and vigorously enforced.

Unfortunately, there are indications that ADEA enforcement has, from the beginning, been a relatively low priority for the Department of Labor, the federal agency charged with the responsibility for administering it. Some government insiders have estimated that the Department would have to assign several *thousand* more employees than actually assigned to ADEA enforcement activities in order for the law to be effectively enforced (Knowles, 1984). More fundamentally, the protection afforded older workers by ADEA is of the after-the-fact, "make-whole" variety, where the provisions of the act only come into play after an allegedly discriminatory action has taken place. This puts much of the burden for effective enforcement on older workers themselves, who must be able and willing to file and document claims that they suffered as a result of an employer's discriminatory behaviors or policies. In contrast, programs that take a more proactive, preventive approach to worker-related problems, such as the Occupational Safety and Health Act (OSHA) and affirmative action programs designed to protect the rights of women, minorities, the handicapped, and veterans, place most of the responsibility for program implementation on employers and government agencies. However, this approach does not, by itself, guarantee effective, meaningful enforcement, because any administration can conceivably understaff and otherwise undermine agency enforcement efforts (Knowles, 1984; Mintz, 1984). Additionally, this approach tends to promote the proliferation of costly, unproductive bureaucracies in both the public and private sectors.

In view of private industry's well-known and somewhat understandable aversion to such programs, it would appear that a two-pronged carrot-and-stick strategy might have the best chance of succeeding in the fight against discrimination against older workers. On the one hand, efforts to disseminate and document the good news about older workers' high levels of efficiency and adaptability need to be accelerated. At the same time, a failure on the part of private industry to assimilate and utilize factual information about older workers might eventually help bring about the institution of OSHA- and affirmative-action-style bureaucracies designed to protect the rights of aging workers. This could help make managers and personnel administrators more receptive to truths about older workers that they might otherwise be inclined to overlook.

RETIREMENT AND THE OLDER WORKER

According to one contemporary dictionary, the word *retire,* when used in a work-related context, means "to withdraw oneself from business, active service, or public life, especially because of advanced age" (Webster's New World Dictionary, 1980). Traditionally, this withdrawal has been conceptualized as relatively abrupt and categorical, taking place after an individual has been doing more or less the same job for the same organization, or at least labored in the same industry or profession, for many years. However, such a unitary, unqualified conception of the retirement process may be obsolete. Older employees increasingly wonder whether organizations will be able and willing to continue offering them full-time employment until retirement age. According to Honig and Hanoch (1985), "The retirement process is far more complex than the simple dichotomy between full-time employment and full retirement" (p. 21). For example, Morrison (1981) has described several approaches to providing older workers with ways of disengaging themselves more gradually from full-time, continuous employment, including reduced workweek schedules, extra vacation time, reduced hours, job transfer programs, payroll-transfer programs (where a former employee is rehired through a private employment service), consultantships, and other temporary or permanent part-time work for retired employees.

The Meaning of Retirement to the Worker

One's work is an intregal aspect of personal identity (Chestang, 1982). Work affects status, prestige, social contacts, financial independence, and family roles. In addition, it structures time and provides a sense of accomplishment and mastery (Perlman, 1968). Older workers look back on their careers and search for indications that they have made an impact on the world. Their careers are a source of pride and satisfaction (Chestang, 1982).

Conversely, retirement can also be a negative event in a person's life. Terkel (1974) has referred to retirement as "forced obsolescence." Retirement can mean the loss of all that work has provided for most of an individual's adult life. Abruptly, the person no longer is what he or she does for a living. The social aspect of the work environment is gone. Time is suddenly unstructured and unregulated. Family roles and responsibilities shift. Money may not be as abundant as before, and major life goals are severely changed or forgotten (Chestang, 1982).

Retirement does not have to be a grim, unrewarding experience. With adequate planning and preparation, retirement can be the ultimate reward for years of hard work.

Helping Older Workers Plan for Retirement: The Past and the Present

Traditionally, most organizations in both the public and private sectors have been reluctant to play an active role in helping their employees effectively prepare for retirement. Two decades ago, Mitchell (1968) noted that programs designed to help prepare older workers for retirement can have a significant beneficial impact. More recently, Atchley (1980) has called attention to a variety of problems likely to beset workers who are entering into or proceeding through the retirement process without adequate preparation or assistance. Zimmerer and Hawkins (1981) found that preretirement planning programs can be an effective way of helping workers manage the strains associated with approaching retirement, and it seems likely that such programs could help inoculate employees against at least some of the personal problems that afflict many retirees.

Unfortunately, preretirement programs continue to be relatively rare and, where they exist, limited in scope. Thus Levine (1982), in a nationwide survey of 63 organizations, reported that only 20 had preretirement programs that included all the organization's employees, while another six had such programs for portions of their workforces. Similarly, Rowen and Wilks (1986) found that fewer than half of the public and private organizations in one midwestern city had some type of preretirement program for at least some of their employees, with program content tending to be sharply circumscribed. In general, it appears that most of the preretirement programs that are presently in place are focused primarily or exclusively on providing workers with some form of financial assistance (O'Meara, 1977).

Helping Older Workers Plan for Retirement: The Future

Programs that are mainly devoted to providing retirees with such benefits as pensions, health insurance, access to company services, and the like should perhaps not be considered preretirement programs at all, but should rather be regarded as retirement programs. A genuine preretirement program would ideally begin as much as 15 years before an employee's anticipated retirement, because the critical phase for adjustment to retirement is *before* retirement begins (Charatan, 1984). The first phases of such a program might well be oriented toward financial issues, so as to provide sufficient time for employees' investments to mature. Most of the preretirement period should be devoted to providing workers with educational and personal counseling services designed to equip prospective retirees with the skills that they will need to negotiate the transition from employee to retiree as painlessly and as successfully as possible.

Designing a Comprehensive Preretirement Program

The philosophy that underlies preretirement planning programs is essentially preventive. Preventive approaches are typically characterized by a sequence of steps or stages in which basic information is conveyed to a target population, available alternatives for action are outlined and compared with one another, and possible interventive strategies for dealing with problems that might arise are indicated. In a comprehensive preretirement program, the following substantive areas should play an important role in the informational/educational phase of the program (Rowen & Wilks, 1986):

1. *Financial planning:* This should include items pertaining to investments, borrowing on equity, setting up a small business, second career opportunities, Social Security, and so forth.
2. *Legal planning:* Information about wills, estate planning, power of attorney, contracts, income tax, and guardianship should be covered.
3. *Consumerism:* This should include information about consumer credit, term insurance, and home improvement and maintenance contracts, in addition to cautioning workers about confidence ploys and scams that target the elderly.
4. *Housing:* Information about various types of housing, relocation, taxes, transportation, alternative living arrangements, and sources in the community for housing assistance should be provided.
5. *Health planning:* Health insurance, physiological changes associated with advancing age, and the appropriate use of prescription drugs can be addressed. In addition, physical fitness and nutritional needs should be stressed, because cultivation of good health habits can help minimize physiological deterioration (Ward, 1984).
6. *Sociopsychological planning:* The development and cultivation of hobbies and leisure activities should be encouraged well in advance of retirement age. New activities are crucial to fill the void left by the loss

of work, and trying to learn a brand new skill at an age when frustrations are less easily tolerated is more difficult (Sheehy, 1974; Ward, 1984). The range of opportunites for engaging in volunteer work and different types of community involvement should be covered. In addition, stress management and coping with the loss of loved ones need to be addressed.

7. *Psychology of retirement:* Preparation for the various stresses and adjustments that accompany retirement itself, such as depression, loneliness, and loss of identity, should be covered.

An effective preretirement planning program is not feasible unless managers at all levels in a organization's chain of command have a commitment to its successful implementation. No such program can succeed without the tangible, visible endorsement of individuals at the highest levels of the organizational hierarchy. In addition, middle-management personnel may be able to effectively sabotage or undermine a preretirement program that does not have their confidence or support.

Managers and program staff should, at the outset, do two things to ensure that the program will have and retain a sense of purpose and direction. In the first place, program parameters should be identified and made as clear and explicit as possible. The following Five Ws might be utilized as an organizing strategy:

1. WHO will be served by the program?
2. WHAT content is to be included?
3. WHY is this content important?
4. WHEN will various elements or phases of the program be scheduled?
5. WHERE in the overall structure of the program will various content areas be addressed?

Secondly, one staff member should be designated whose primary job is to work with the preretirement program. This person would ultimately be responsible for seeing to it that the program's various disparate elements and actors work together in an effective, well-integrated way. The type of preretirement planning program that we have described is a highly complex affair that requires the well-coordinated participation of a variety of individuals if it is to achieve its goals. Managers cannot be expected to give such an enterprise their wholehearted blessing and support unless they know that there is one person who is responsible for ensuring that the efforts of various program staff are complementary rather than redundant or contradictory.

Preretirement Planning Programs: Roles for Social Workers

Kurzman and Akabas (1981) have enumerated several roles that social workers in occupational/industrial settings may be called upon to assume. The roles that they have described include (1) consultant, (2) program developer, (3) service deliverer, and (4) trainer.

Acting in the role of consultant, a social worker may be asked to help an organization that is considering starting a preretirement program decide on a set of program goals that are both desirable and feasible. Similarly, an organization that already has a preretirement program may request the assistance of a social worker in evaluating the program's effectiveness.

Social workers may also have the opportunity to participate in the actual development and implementation of a preretirement program. Social workers are trained to approach clients in a holistic manner, seeing the person as a multileveled, multifaceted organism with biological, psychological, and social characteristics, needs, and problems. This type of multidimensional approach is implicit in any comprehensive preretirement program; therefore, a social worker may be ideally suited to serve in coordinative and integrative capacities, both during the planning stage of programs and when they are actually implemented. Also, those social workers who have had training and experience in working in occupational settings are likely to appreciate the importance of securing the support and assistance of managers and to have the skills necessary to garner that support.

Additionally, social workers' training provides them with knowledge both about human behavior in its biological, psychological, and social aspects, and about the range of community services and resources available to help meet the needs of both troubled and well-functioning retirees. Thus, in addition to perhaps serving as the director or coordinator of a preretirement program, a social worker is apt to be well suited to provide direct service to program participants in these content areas.

Finally, social workers can help train program staff, some of whom, though competent in their own areas of expertise, may be relatively unschooled in the art of imparting technical information to an older lay audience. Many of these individuals may be unfamiliar with the specific goals and methods of a particular preretirement program and so may need to be oriented accordingly.

CONCLUSION

For some time now, older workers have been comprising an ever-larger proportion of the nation's workforce, a trend expected to continue into the next century. In spite of a dramatic increase in labor-force participation among older women, overall fewer and fewer individuals over the age of 45 are working full time, with early retirement becoming less the exception and more the rule (Copperman & Keast, 1983; Robinson, 1983). However, this reduction in the number of oldest workers is rapidly being offset as the demographic bulge of the post-World War II baby-boom cohort becomes older. Thus, by the year 2000 60% of American workers are expected to be 35 years of age or older (Robinson, et al., 1985).

The net result will be an unprecedented number of older Americans, whether they are employed or retired. In either case, social workers have an important and unique contribution to make in this area. For those older men and women who enter or remain in the workforce, social workers can do much to help industry take full advantage of their talents and capabilities. As retirement approaches, social workers are particularly well equipped to perform a variety of roles as they try to help make the transition from worker to retiree as free of unnecessary stress as possible.

REFERENCES

Andrisani, P., & Miljus, R. (1977). Individual differences in preferences for intrinsic vs. extrinsic aspects of work. *Journal of Vocational Behavior, 11*, 14–30.

Atchley, R. (1980). *The social forces in later life: An introduction to social gerontology*. Belmont, CA: Wadsworth.

Bolles, R. (1985). *What color is your parachute?* Berkeley: Ten Speed Press.

Charatan, F. B. (1984). Some common psychiatric problems of aging employees. In S. F. Yolles, L. W. Krinsky, S. N. Kieffer, & P. A. Carone (Eds.), *The aging employee*. New York: Human Sciences Press.

Chestang, L. W. (1982). Work, personal change, and human development. In S. H. Akabas, & P. A. Kurzman (Eds.), *Work, workers and work organizations: A view from social work*. Englewood Cliffs, NJ: Prentice-Hall.

Chown, S. (1972). The effects of flexibility-rigidity and age on adaptability in job performance. *Industrial Gerontology, 13*, 105–121.

Cleveland, J., & Landy, F. (1981). Influence of rater and ratee age on two performance judgments. *Personnel Psychology, 34*, 11–30.

Cobb, S. (1974). Physiological changes in men whose jobs were abolished. *Journal of Psychosomatic Research, 18*, 245–258.

Copperman, L., & Keast, F. (1983). *Adjusting to an older work force*. New York: Van Nostrand Reinhold.

Coser, R. L. (1984). Old age, employment, and social network. In S. F. Yolles, L. W. Krinsky, S. N. Kieffer, & P. A. Carone (Eds.), *The aging employee: Vol. VII*. New York: Human Sciences Press.

Craft, J., Doctors, S., Shkop, Y., & Benecki, T. (1979). Simulated management perceptions, hiring decisions, and age. *Aging and Work, 2*, 95–102.

Deal, T., & Kennedy, A. (1982). *Corporate cultures*. Reading, PA: Addison-Wesley.

Dirken, J. (Ed.). (1972). *Functional age of industrial workers*. Groningen, Netherlands: Wolters-Noordhoff.

Dubin. S. (Ed.). (1972). *Professional obsolescence*. Lexington, KY: Heath.

Haberlandt, K. (1973). Learning, memory, and age. *Industrial Gerontology, 16,* 20–37.

Honig, M., & Hanoch, G. (1985). Partial retirement as a separate mode of retirement behavior. *Journal of Human Resources, 20,* 21–46.

Hunt, J., & Saul, P. (1975). Relationship of age, tenure and job satisfaction in males and females. *Academy of Management Journal, 18,* 690–702.

Knowles, D. (1984). Middle aged and older workers—An industry perspective. In S. Yolles, L. Krinsky, S. Kieffer, & P. Carone (Eds.), *The aging employee*. New York: Human Sciences Press.

Kurzman, P., & Akabas, S. (1981). Industrial social work as an arena for practice. *Social Work, 26,* 52–60.

Levine, H. (1982). Pre-retirement planning and other retirement issues. *Personnel, 58,* 4–11.

McAuley, W. (1977). Perceived age discrimination in hiring: Demographic and economic correlates. *Industrial Gerontology, 4,* 21–28.

McFarland, R. (1953). *Human factors in air transportation: Occupational health and safety*. New York: McGraw-Hill.

Meier, E., & Kerr, E. (1976). Capabilities of middle-aged and older workers. *Industrial Gerontology, 3,* 147–156.

Mercer, W. (1981). *Employer attitudes: Implications of an aging work force*. New York: William M. Mercer.

Mintz, B. (1984). *OSHA: History, law and policy*. Washington, DC: Bureau of National Affairs.

Mitchell, W. (1968). Lay observations on retirement. In F.M. Carp (Ed.), *Retirement*. New York: Behavioral Sciences.

Morin, W., & Yorks, L. (1982). *Outplacement techniques*. New York: AMACOM.

Morrison, M. (1981). Reappraising retirement and personnel policies. In N. McClusky, & E. Borgatta (Eds.). *Aging and retirement: Prospects, planning, and policy*. Beverly Hills: Sage.

Murchinsky, P. (1978). Age and job satisfaction: A conceptual reconsideration. *Aging and Work, 1,* 175–180.

Noble, C., Baker, B., & Jones, T. (1964). Age and sex parameters in psychomotor learning. *Perceptual and Motor Skills, 19,* 935–945.

O'Meara, J. (1977). Retirement: Reward or rejection? New York: *The Conference Board*.

Panek, P., Barrett, G., Alexander, R., & Sterns, H. (1979). Age and self-selected performance pace on a visual monitoring task. *Aging and Work, 2,* 183–191.

Perlman, H. H. (1968). *Persona*. Chicago: University of Chicago Press.

Price, R., Thompson, P., & Dalton, G. (1975, November). A longitudinal study of technological obsolescence. *Research Management,* 22–28.

Robinson, P. (1983). *Organizational strategies for older workers*. New York: Pergamon.

Robinson, P., Coberly, S., & Paul, C. (1985). Work and retirement. In R. Binstock, & E. Shanas (Eds.), *Handbook of aging and the social sciences* (2nd ed.). New York: Van Nostrand Reinhold.

Rosen, B. (1985). *Older employees: New roles*. Homewood, IL: Dow Jones Irwin.

Rosen, B., & Jerdee, T. (1976). The nature of job-related stereotypes. *Journal of Applied Psychology, 61,* 180–183.

Rowen, R., & Wilks, C. (1986). Pre-retirement planning, a quality of life issue for retirement. Unpublished paper presented at Southwestern Social Science Association Annual Meeting, San Antonio.

Sheehy, G. (1974). *Passages.* New York: Dutton.

Sheppard, H., & Rix, S. (1977). *The graying of working america: The coming crisis of retirement age policy.* New York: Free Press.

Smith, P., Kendall, L., & Hulin, C. (1969). *The measurement of satisfaction in work and retirement.* Chicago: Rand-McNally.

Stagner, R. (1985). Aging in industry. In J. Birren, & K. Schaie (Eds.), *Handbook of the psychology of aging* (2nd ed.). New York: Van Nostrand Reinhold.

Suzuki, H. (1976). Age, seniority and wages. *International Labour Review, 113,* 67–84.

Terkel, S. (1974). *Working.* New York: Pantheon.

Ward, M. (1984). A look at the aging employee—medical aspects. In S. F. Yolles, L. W. Krinsky, S. N. Kieffer, & P. A. Carone (Eds.), *The aging employee.* New York: Human Sciences Press.

Weaver, C. (1980). Job satisfaction in the United States in the 1970s. *Journal of Applied Psychology, 65,* 364–367.

Webster's new world dictionary of the american language (2nd college ed.). (1980). New York: Simon & Schuster.

Yolles, S. F., Krinsky, L. W., Kieffer, S. N., & Carone, P. A. (Eds.). (1984). *The aging employee.* New York: Human Sciences Press.

Zimmerer, T., & Hawkins, B. (1981, Spring). Developing an effective pre-retirement program. *Arkansas Business and Economic Review* 1–6.

14 Assisting in Affirmative Action and Equal Employment Opportunity

Ruta J. Wilk

Equal employment opportunity (EEO) and affirmative action (AA) are realities faced by hundreds of thousands of employers in this country. Social workers practicing in occupational settings, either in-house or as outside consultants, can provide a bridge between the demands of society and the needs of individual employees by assisting employers in meeting their affirmative action obligations. This area of social legislation has been turbulent, demanding, and confusing for almost every affected employer at one time or another. The issues have been broad-ranging and sometimes emotional—discrimination against persons on the basis of race, religion, sex, or national origin, with additional protected groups added later—and the outcomes beneficial to the entire social fabric. Yet these important social advances are in jeopardy today. This chapter will discuss the history, major issues, and future trends of these antidiscrimination laws, as well as the roles social workers can play in working with employers.

BACKGROUND OF EEO/AA

A discussion of the role of social workers in promoting equal employment opportunity and affirmative action must begin with the specification of terms, especially because these phrases are often used interchangeably and therefore incorrectly.

- *Equal employment opportunity* is the right of all persons to work and advance on the basis of merit, ability, and potential.
- *Affirmative action* is the process of ensuring/guaranteeing that right.

Affirmative action is aimed at ending barriers to equal employment opportunity. Organizations that seek to achieve equal employment opportunity will take two kinds of affirmative action steps: (1) removing discriminatory barriers and (2) actively recruiting underrepresented groups.

Over the last 20 years, the courts have refined the meaning of employment discrimination to include such matters as "only using limited recruiting sources such as those which serve primarily white, male applicants; underrepresentation of certain classes of employees in specific departments, positions, or levels of employment; differential compensation for the same level of work via pay rate or fringe benefit plans," and many other discriminatory practices (Cannon & Smith, 1982, p. 7).

Nondiscrimination requires the elimination of all existing discriminatory conditions. Affirmative action requires that an employer do more than just that; the employer must take additional positive steps to seek out, employ, and promote qualified members of formerly excluded groups. When employers do not take positive steps to carry out affirmative action, employment discrimination may result.

Major Legislation

Title VII of the Civil Rights Act

The foundation of all recent EEO/AA laws is Title VII of the Civil Rights Act of 1964, as amended by the Equal Employment Opportunity Act of 1972 (PL 88-352, July 2, 1964, 78 Stat, pp. 241–268). This landmark federal legislation emerged from the era of civil rights activism in the United States, when national sensitivity to discrimination and social injustice was particularly heightened. It is a statement of general social policy and does not address specifics such as requiring affirmative action procedures. It was enacted 1 year after another relevant piece of employment-related legislation, the Equal Pay Act of 1963.

Executive Order 11246

The concept of affirmative action came with the signing of Executive Order 11246 (as amended by 11375) by President Lyndon B. Johnson in 1964 (3 CFR, 1966–1970 Comp. pp. 684–686, 1971 ed). These orders prohibit discrimination in employment by federal contractors and subcontractors and set out the obligation to take affirmative action steps.

Additional Legislation

Title VII has been followed by at least 20 additional laws, orders, regulations, and guidelines since 1964, in addition to complementary state laws. These state antidiscrimination laws usually cover the few small local businesses that may fall outside of the broad Federal coverage. Because any state laws found to violate Title VII are superseded by federal laws, and because of the limitations of space, this chapter focuses on federal requirements only. (For a summary of federal laws, orders, and regulations pertaining to EEO/ AA see Cannon & Smith, 1982, Appendix A.) Examples of some of the additional federal laws include Sections 503 and 504 of the Rehabilitation Act of 1973, the Age Discrimination in Employment Act of 1967 as amended in 1978, the Vietnam Era Veterans Readjustment Assistance Act of 1974, and the Pregnancy Disability Amendment of Title VII of the Civil Rights Act of 1964.

Effects of Legislation

The impact of these laws on the makeup and atmosphere of the workplace has been significant. New workers have entered the workforce. Persons who before had little hope of acquiring gainful employment, maintaining it, or achieving advancement were given new possibilities. Every promotion of a woman or minority employee has meant a chance for dignity and self-esteem for that class of individuals; every person hired has meant less dependence upon public benefits. "Women, members of minority groups, and the disabled have brought new skills and new needs into the workplace, and they are making new demands on employers and trade unions" (Kurzman & Akabas, 1981, p. 52).

There is no question that the impact of these laws upon the administration of organizations has been significant as well. As Googins and Godfrey (1985, p. 398) state, "The demands of regulatory legislation in hiring practices encourage management to take a proactive, preventive stance in managing the human relations of their workplace." Employers and trade unions now must keep additional, very specific documentation, must follow new procedures in relating to their employees, and must be accountable to governmental agencies. New positions and departments have been established to deal specifically with compliance issues.

Noncompliance exposes employers and trade unions to potentially devastating litigation and damage awards. The most dramatic evidence of the effect of EEO/AA legislation is that thousands of lawsuits have been brought against both public and private organizations for discriminatory practices. Two major lawsuits, with which anyone working in EEO/AA matters should be familiar, are (1) *Griggs v. Duke Power Co.* (1971), which determined that an employer may be found guilty of violating Title VII even though there was no active or malicious intent to discriminate and (2) *Albemarle Paper Co. v. Moody* (1975), which affirmed that discrimination occurs by systematic hiring practices and also clarified the issue of back pay as a remedy. Both of these were precedent-setting decisions in interpreting Title VII. Because the actual implementation of Title VII was left up to court interpretations via case law, staying current regarding the latest court decisions is vital to those working in the EEO/AA arena.

BASIC FACTS FOR SOCIAL WORKERS

Unfortunately for social workers acting as consultants to employers, the amount of information needed to be effective in working with EEO/AA issues is staggering. It also changes frequently. What follows is some basic information that must be viewed as a brief overview of this field.

Title VII of the Civil Rights Act of 1964

Title VII of the Civil Rights Act prohibits discrimination in employment on the basis of race, color, religion, national origin, or sex. It covers job applicants, employers, or organizations with 15 or more employees whose business affects interstate commerce; it also covers educational institutions, state and local governments, both public and private employment agencies, labor unions with 15 or more employees, apprenticeships, and training programs. Under Title VII, it is the employer's *implicit* obligation to discover discriminatory practice and eliminate it. The employer is also implicitly obliged to "make whole" all persons who have been denied equal employment opportunity. "This may require promotion (when openings permit), back pay, special training programs, or other corrective actions" (Humanic Designs Division, 1975, p. 2).

The major exception allowed under Title VII is for compensation differentials that result from merit, incentive, or seniority systems, provided that they are not discriminatory. There also have been cases where courts have allowed, within very narrow definitions, exceptions for bona fide occupational qualifications such as sex, religion, national origin, or "compelling business necessity" (Fountain, 1977, p. 9). Title VII is still the basic anti-discrimination law and the most comprehensive one, and it is administered by the Equal Employment Opportunity Commission (EEOC).

The Equal Employment Opportunity Commission

The EEOC is the enforcement body for Title VII of the Civil Rights Act. The EEOC's Congressional mandate is to investigate charges of discriminatory practice and to prosecute, if necessary, violations of Title VII. It has authority over all the entities to which Title VII applies. Complaints to the EEOC can be filed by individuals, organizations, or members of the EEOC themselves. The time limit for filing a charge is 180 days from the time of the alleged incident. Once a charge has been filed, the EEOC begins an investigation. If this results in a finding of probable cause, conciliation efforts are initiated. If these fail, a court suit is filed by the EEOC, the U.S. Attorney General, or by the individual. For those cases not resulting in a probable cause finding, the complainant still has the option of filing a civil suit (Fountain, 1977).

Organizations not in compliance with the law have two avenues of resolution: voluntary conciliation agreements to prevent a court suit, or court-ordered involuntary action. The remedies required by the courts can be summarized into three major categories: (1) prohibiting future discrimination, (2) ordering accelerated hiring, training, or promotion of identifiable class members, and (3) providing back pay.

The Office of Federal Contract Compliance Programs

The OFCCP was created to enforce Executive Order 11246, as amended by 11375, which prohibits discrimination in employment by federal contractors and subcontractors. It in turn delegated enforcement duties to 13 major federal government agencies and bodies to act as compliance agencies for their relevant contractors and industries. Among these are, for example, the Department of Defense, NASA, the Department of Agriculture, and the Department of Health and Human Services.

The OFCCP has jurisdiction over all federal contractors receiving federal funds of over $10,000. However, current regulations require written affirmative action plans and compliance reviews only of those who have 50 or more employees. As of 1980, Executive Order 11246 covered almost 100,000 contractors and subcontractors who employed more than 30 million people and received government contracts totaling nearly $81 billion a year (OFCCP, Dept. of Labor, cited in duRivage, 1985).

In order to implement the concept of affirmative action, the OFCCP has over time issued a series of administrative orders, popularly referred to as the "Revised Orders," setting out precise and detailed guidelines for employers. Employers are primarily concerned with Revised Orders No. 4 and No. 14, which spell out the obligations of employers to analyze the employment process, identify deficiencies, and take corrective action (Humanic Designs Division, 1975).

The OFCCP attempts to achieve voluntary compliance before imposing sanctions. When sanctions do become necessary, they include (1) making public the names of noncomplying contractors or unions; (2) canceling contracts; (3) recommending lawsuits by the Justice Department or by the EEOC; and (4) debarring employers from receiving future government contracts unless a willingness to comply with the law is demonstrated.

The Obligations of Employers

The Employment Process

Under Title VII, the employment process includes activities such as recruitment, hiring, training, assigning, promoting, compensating, evaluating/appraising, and dismissing employees. Each of these phases of the employment process is subject to the scrutiny and requirements of EEO/AA laws and regulations and includes both negative and positive obligations.

For example, it is forbidden to carry out only word-of-mouth recruiting when the workforce of the employer is not racially and sexually mixed and when the resultant practice tends to exclude protected groups of applicants (Matthies, 1976), or recruiting at only predominantly white educational institutions when there is an existing racial imbalance in the workforce. It is against the law to have job requirements, such as a high school diploma, where such a requirement is not related to performance of the job and has the effect of screening out groups protected under Title VII. It is unlawful to indicate a preference by race, sex, or any of the other categories named in Title VII in a printed or published job recruitment notice (Leshin, 1976, pp. D-7, D-8). Separate seniority lists, different standards of compensation, and so forth are against the law when their effect discriminates by race, religion, sex, age, physical disability, or other protected class category.

Regarding positive action and initiatives, employers must, for example, make "reasonable accommodations" to adjust or adapt a job to the needs of a disabled individual. They must also actively seek to change attitudes of supervisors and of other employees. Clearly stated policies and procedures regarding affirmative action must be contained in company documents, posted at the worksite, included in company publicity, and the like. Any testing, either for initial hiring or for promotions, must be job-related, valid, and free of cultural bias.

Record Keeping

Employers are required to keep systematic and careful records. The following are examples of documentation that is required. Companies with over 50 employees who do business with the federal government must have a written affirmative action plan consisting of the following elements: a survey and analysis of their existing employment structure, descriptions and classifications of all jobs, and goals and timetables for any improvement that may be needed. This is a quasi-public document and is discoverable (that is, available to an employee filing suit against an employer) in any litigation.

When recruiting for job openings, records of all minority and female applicants and what actually happened to them must be kept. With regard to discrimination against the disabled, contractors with the federal government must maintain records for 1 year detailing any complaints that disabled persons register concerning their treatment and describing any actions taken in response to those complaints.

In addition to mandated record keeping, employers who wish to protect themselves from lawsuits have found it advisable to tighten up on routine internal administrative record keeping. For example, employers concerned about charges of discrimination regarding termination decisions have the responsibility to take the following steps:

1. Providing clear-cut documentation of unsatisfactory work records.
2. Keeping employees informed about the quality of their performance and giving them reasonable opportunities to improve.
3. Informing all employees about the contents of their own job descriptions and the various company rules and policies governing employee behavior.
4. Administering the same punishment to all employees who violate rules and applying it consistently, with this point being one of the most critical (Klotchman & Neider, 1983, p. 65).

Protected Classes

The original legislation (Title VII of the Civil Rights Act) identified five groups or protected classes: those discriminated against because of race, color, religion, sex, or national origin. As other disadvantaged groups gained in strength and militancy, they pressured for inclusion in the categories for special consideration. Thus, later laws covered groups such as older persons, Vietnam veterans, and the disabled. Issues regarding employment discrimination for four of these groups—racial minorities, women, older persons, and the disabled—will be discussed below.

Racial Minorities

Racial minorities are one of the classes protected under Title VII of the Civil Rights Act. Unlike exceptions that can be found in certain cases when being a male or being a young person is necessary for employment, there are no instances in which race can be a bona fide occupational qualification.

Addressing the issues of discrimination on the basis of race, the OFCC's Revised Order No. 4 states: "Minority groups are most likely to be underutilized in departments and jobs within departments that fall within the following Employer's Information Report (EEO-1) designations: officials and managers, professionals, technicians, sales workers, office and clerical, and craftsmen (skilled)" (Humanic Designs Division, 1975, p. 73).

In cases of racial discrimination in hiring, the applicant bears the initial burden of proving a prima facie case of racial discrimination by showing that:

1. The applicant belongs to a racial minority.
2. The applicant applied and was qualified for the job.
3. The applicant was rejected despite the applicant's qualifications.
4. The position remained open after this rejection and the employer continued to seek applications from persons with the applicant's qualifications.

If the complainant is able to establish a prima facie case, the burden then shifts to the employer to demonstrate a legitimate, nondiscriminatory reason why the applicant was rejected (Leshin, 1976, p. L-2). This system was set up in the case of *McDonnell-Douglas v. Green* (1973). This same system is now being used by the courts in age discrimination cases.

Women

Discrimination against women is quite similar to that against disabled people, especially as seen in assertions such as "Women have poorer attendance records than men"; "We would need to construct separate facilities"; "Our jobs require too much heavy lifting"; "Customers would not accept advice from female sales persons (or from a physically disabled person, or from a black)."

The guidelines on discrimination because of sex are issued by the EEOC as revisions to Title 29, Chapter XIV, Part 1604 of the Code of Federal Regulations, as amended March 31, 1972. These guidelines address nine fundamental issues: (1) sex as a bona fide occupational qualification, (2) separate lines of progression and seniority systems, (3) discrimination against married women, (4) job opportunities advertising, (5) employment agencies, (6) pre-employment inquiries as to sex, (7) relationship of Title VII to the Equal Pay Act, (8) fringe benefits, and (9) employment policies relating to pregnancy and childbirth. According to EEOC guidelines, pregnancy must be treated as any other temporary disability (29 CFR Sec. 1604.9). An employer may not discriminate in administering benefits such as medical insurance programs, income-continuance programs, the accruing of seniority and vacation credits while away from work, and in returning to work after pregnancy.

Addressing the issue of discrimination on the basis of sex, the OFCCP's Revised Order No. 4 states, "Women are likely to be underutilized in departments and jobs within departments as follows: officials and managers, professionals, technicians, sales workers (except over-the-counter sales in certain retail establishments), and craftsmen (skilled and semi-skilled)" (Humanic Designs Division, 1975, p. 73).

Older Persons

The term *older* includes not only the elderly but also persons in their 40s and 50s who find themselves viewed as too old by employers—too old to spend money on for additional training, too close to retirement to be given new assignments and duties, too likely to be filing health insurance claims, and too old to hire when applying for a job.

The rights of this protected class were addressed in the Age Discrimination in Employment Act of 1967, as amended in 1978 (the ADEA). This law applies to both public- and private-sector employers with more than 25 employees, employment agencies, and labor unions. The protected age groups under the act are persons 40 through 70 years of age. The ADEA is administered by the EEOC. As is usual in discrimination complaints, attempts at voluntary compliance and nonjudicial resolution are made first. If these fail, the EEOC or the aggrieved individual may seek court action. Under the law, individuals may file private suits, providing they fulfill prior procedural requirements. One example of such a requirement is that in states with age discrimination laws a complainant must first invoke available state remedies. Courts may grant judgments providing employment, reinstatement, promotion, and back wages. More unusual awards may be granted as well. A 1975 District Court decision ruled that a person who is discriminated against under the ADEA may recover damages for pain and suffering as well as for "out-of-pocket losses." An employee who had been forced to retire at age 60 was awarded $200,000 to compensate him for physical ailments that developed after his forced retirement and were found to be the result of the employer's illegal age discrimination (*Rogers et al. v. Exxon Research and Engineering Co.*, 1975) (Leshin, 1976, p. F-8).

Although there is an exemption to ADEA requirements when a specific age is a "bona fide occupational qualification" (for example, age ceilings for pilots in the interest of public safety, or age requirements for actors portraying youthful or elderly roles), this has been interpreted inconsistently and sometimes quite narrowly in the courts (Novit, 1979, p. 23).

Some of the most problematic areas relating to age discrimination in employment have been illegal advertising, refusals to hire, and illegal discharges (Leshin 1976, p. F-8). Section 4(3) of the Act prohibits the use of printed or published advertisements indicating any preference, limitation, specification, or discrimination based on age. Advertising for "recent college graduates" is prohibited; specifications such as "retired person" or "supplement your pension" may or may not be acceptable, depending upon the exact situation. With regard to hiring, preemployment inquiries requesting the applicant's age are not in themselves illegal. However, the employer must be able to justify that such a request is for permissible purposes and not because age will be used as a factor in decision-making.

Another area related to age discrimination is mandatory retirement. In the past, forced retirement policies were a means of moving out older workers.

As of January 1, 1979, an organization having 20 or more employees cannot make retirement mandatory before age 70, except in a few specified circumstances.

The Disabled

Section 503 of the Rehabilitation Act of 1973 is the legislation that opened doors for the disabled while at the same time creating obligations for employers. Section 503 requires that employers who have contracts of more than $2,500 with an agency of the federal government shall, under certain conditions, take action to employ applicants who are disabled. A conservative estimate by the U.S. Department of Labor in 1978 placed the number of disabled Americans able to work at 7.2 million (Katz & Martin, 1982, p. 37).

Employers have a legal responsibility to initiate affirmative action and to recruit, hire, and promote qualified disabled workers. Their responsibility also includes efforts to change the attitudes of managers, supervisors, and other employees toward disabled employees. They can, however, refuse to hire a physically disabled person when the person's disability prevents the performance of job duties or when performing such duties would endanger the health or safety of the employee or of others. Should any litigation result from such a decision, it is the burden of the employer to prove that issues of capability and safety were valid ones. The agency that sets policy, investigates complaints, and monitors compliance with Sec. 503 is the OFCCP.

THE ROLE OF THE SOCIAL WORKER

Social workers in occupational settings fulfill two types of roles. For troubled employees they may act as brokers, making referrals and linking them to community services, while for employers they act as consultants and technical experts in the area of human resources.

Example 1: A social worker at the Polaroid Corporation, working as one of three staff members on the affirmative action team, set up equal opportunity programs, concentrating on recruiting and assimilating minority people. Some of the tasks included laying the groundwork for the personnel managers' acceptance of changes, documenting shortfalls in affirmative action programs, teaching interviewing techniques to managers, and helping to create informal networks for minority employees already in the workforce ("Devising Ways," 1980).

Example 2: A nationally known survey research firm hired a social worker as Manager of Employee Relations and Organizational Development; one of her first assignments was to assist the firm in centralizing hiring practices in the personnel office in order to meet affirmative action mandates. The practice had been that of managers "hiring workers first and notifying the personnel office second" ("Breaking Through," 1982, p. 14). She presented herself as being able to screen applicants for managers, thereby saving them time. Gradually building up relationships with managers led to further acceptance of her role and services ("Breaking Through," 1982).

Example 3: Working as the corporate community-relations consultant for a major electronics firm, a social worker developed relationships with organizations external to the firm in order to influence the acquisition and retention of minority and female employees. In addition, as consultant to one of the plants, she was instrumental in resolving a problem that was impinging upon the firm's being able to retain minority employees: She helped link company representatives with the local transit authority to extend bus services so that minority employees would have transportation to their jobs ("Industry–Community Partnerships," 1982).

More and more nontraditional roles for social workers are evolving. "In many companies, the early contracts to provide clinical or single-issue services are broadening. Social workers now work in affirmative action, human resources management, and labor and community relations" (Googins & Godfrey, 1985, p. 399). Therefore, the sites in the organization where a social worker might work have expanded. The traditional home base of the occupational social worker is the EAP program. This has the advantage of familiarity (i.e., social workers have provided counseling, referrals, brokering, and the like since the profession began). However, the field of EEO/AA challenges social workers to create new images of social work and to apply their training to new issues.

Harold P. Hayes (1980) conceives of the EEO arena as:

> standing on a tripod, with the law as one leg, data-based negotiations as another, and fundamental principles of human resources dynamics as the third. The latter leg seems not to have developed as well as the other two—leaving the arena in a shaky if not more seriously unstable condition. As learning continues, growth in the human resources leg needs to be accelerated and communicated. (p. 5)

It is in the shaky area of fundamental principles of human resources dynamics that social work may make its greatest contribution to employers.

Providing Information

The complexity of antidiscrimination legislation has left employers wondering, "What must we do to conform to the law?"—especially because the employer always bears the burden of proof in cases under question. Before an employer can begin to fulfill EEO/AA obligations, the employer must be aware of what they are. Therefore, one of the basic services a social worker can provide is to inform and update employers regarding their legal obligations. In addition, the social worker may assist with the monitoring of goals and timetables, as well as being involved in helping to gauge the impact of company efforts.

Assisting with Compliance

In addition, the social worker may be called upon to help the employer comply with EEO/AA. The social worker may work with the company's EEO/AA director or may work independently. It has been said that affirmative action programs are shaped by their directors, that is, their directors' perceptions of the probability of legal difficulties, their commitment to the EEO program, and their knowledge of EEO requirements. Thus, one of the major ways that social workers can affect EEO is through a sensitivity to the perceptions and needs of the director or other person in that role. In addition to heightening the awareness of key personnel, social work service may be provided in two other ways: helping employers find and/or support minority employees and helping with the in-house training of managers and supervisors.

Finding and/or Supporting Minority Employees

Social work traditionally acts as a link between the individual and the environment. In the case of occupational social workers, they may serve as links between employers and the community. Their knowledge of community resources, relevant community groups, grass-roots community leaders, and the like enables them to provide such services as seeking out and helping to recruit needed employees as well as representing the firm to these community groups. For example, if an employer would like to hire a qualified disabled person to do computer work, the social worker's role would be to contact the local Vocational Rehabilitation agency or similar resource, act as a liaison with this agency, perhaps even prescreen potential applicants, and assist the employer with formulating the appropriate types of questions to ask during the employment interview.

Once an employer is committed to hiring minorities such as the disabled, the social worker may assist the employer in making whatever reasonable physical job accommodations may be required. Helping the employer and employee share in open communication about their respective needs and expectations can make the difference between a successful and unsuccessful minority hire.

Training and Consultation with Managers and Supervisors

Although the commitment of top-level management to the principles of EEO/AA is necessary, the day-to-day implementation of this commitment falls to mid-level managers and frontline supervisors. Such individuals often have a deciding voice in hiring, promotion, and other opportunities for upward mobility. In order to have genuine progress in affirmative action, these managers and supervisors need to feel the same pressure from the company as the company feels from the government. Decentralization of EEO efforts is crucial because the further that one gets from the central policy-making level, the more diluted the policy becomes.

The social worker can provide two types of formal training: (1) factual information about laws, obligations, and so forth, and (2) training in human relations, through regular and repeated in–service training sessions at the worksite for both supervisors and middle managers. These training sessions call upon the unique skills of social workers in understanding human behavior. For example, they can train company staff concerning behavior toward, and appropriate expectations of, disabled employees; they can conduct group sessions to raise the level of awareness of men toward the issues of women, or of all staff toward the concerns of older workers.

Being a Liaison with Minority Employees

Simply hiring minorities is not enough. An employer must pay continuing attention to the progress and concerns of nontraditional groups within the organization, whether they are women working in traditionally male trades, or developmentally disabled persons hired for janitorial/cleaning service work, or young black junior executives. An effective communication system set up by the social worker can help the employer know what is really going on. Because of the social worker's relationship skills, the role of liaison between employer and such employees is another way in which social workers can help employers fulfill their obligations. Working closely and supportively with minority employees will not only meet their individual human needs, but may also prevent problems to employers such as grievances and even lawsuits.

EEO IN THE 1980s

Having explored the development of equal employment opportunity and the role of occupational social workers in its implementation, one must now consider the future directions in this field. The future cannot be predicted with certainty; however, the record of the last 5 to 10 years suggests some erratic and alarming trends.

The 1980s have seen a change in the social climate of the country. There are two themes: the reality of a declining economy and the political shift to conservatism. Both of these have had negative effects on the implementation of, and even the concept of, equal employment opportunity.

The Declining Economy

EEO/AA is demanding enough in the best of economic times. In bad times, it becomes even less relevant to employers who have to bow to the pressures of economic necessity. In recent years, an increasing number of firms have faced threats to their sheer survival and other considerations have become luxuries. In a declining economy, factors such as plant closings, corporate relocation, and capital mobility in general have particularly adverse consequences for racial minorities. Minorities are "underrepresented in those job categories where employers are more likely to offer protection against dislocation in terms of job rights, relocation privileges, or job hunting assistance" (Roberts & Squires, 1984, p. 41). Thus the changes and accommodations necessary to ensure corporate survival have been made by employers, often at the expense of individual employees.

"Social and economic conditions at this time do not support active enforcement of compensatory minority preferences. Thus, affirmative action officers may find themselves facing increased controversy on their jobs" (Spaights et al., 1985, p. 43). This means that at a time when legal protections are the most needed, they are less available than before. And in firms facing economic pressures, social workers who press for EEO/AA compliance may have to use all of their relationship skills to serve both the interests of the employer and the interests of protected classes of employees.

The Changing Political Climate

The promise of Title VII and of the EEOC has not been realized and has suffered recent setbacks. The history of the EEOC shows a weak record of initiating civil suits in federal district courts and litigating against systemic patterns of discrimination. The total number of lawsuits per year brought by the EEOC itself (known as Section 707 lawsuits, as opposed to Section 706 suits brought by individuals) is as follows (Hill, 1983, p. 52): 1977—181; 1978—178; 1979—172; 1980—163; 1981—199; 1982—82; 1983—40.

The predominant efforts to root out job discrimination have been through lawsuits initiated by private parties, and the present administration has encouraged an "emphasis on affirmative action as it applies to individuals rather than groups" (Spaights et al., 1985, p. 44). This means that social workers helping with EEO/AA can expect less large-scale governmental challenging of employer practices; the challenges will come from frustrated and assertive individual employees or small groups of employees. The two major philosophical points emphasized by the Reagan administration in relation to EEO/AA are (1) that individuals, not groups, suffer discrimination and (2) such discrimination is the result of specific or intentional acts. The former point has resulted in the threatened loss of protection to *all* members of a class, with the protection extending only to "victims," that is, those individuals who can prove they have personally suffered discrimination. The latter point ignores systemic discrimination, which may be subtle, unintentional, and harmful to greater numbers of people.

There is a "current retreat by this administration from not only affirmative action but civil rights in general" (Pollard, 1984, p. 22). The mood of the country, reinforced by policies and orientations at the federal level in the 1980s, has been to pull back from vigorous enforcement efforts. The slogan "get the government off our backs" has affected employers not only in areas such as formal deregulation of previously regulated industries, but also in a lightening up of pressure from agencies such as the Occupational Safety and Health Administration (OSHA) and the EEOC. Budget reductions in the EEOC and OFCCP have resulted in reduced capability, low employee morale, and high personnel turnover (Hill, 1983). All of this means less attention to the behavior of employers.

The Reagan administration has also initiated the possibility of self-monitoring of affirmative action plans rather than the usual government review (duRivage, 1985, p. 364). The first agreement between the government and a major corporation establishing this self-monitoring was negotiated with AT&T in 1982 ("Affirmative Action," 1984). The removal of pressure from an outside body, of course, opens the possibility of decreased efforts in the EEO area by employers. "Organizations may take the current (federal) political climate as an indication of approval to revert to pre-affirmative action hiring and work practices. Backsliding of this nature will require greater attention being paid to the practices of such organizations" (Spaights et al., 1985, pp. 43–44). If these trends of the 1980s continue, the occupational social worker's concern with EEO/AA will become more needed and at the same time more tenuous.

REFERENCES

Affirmative Action: A storm over self-policing. (1984, May 21). *Business Week*, pp. 141–142.

Albemarle Paper Co. v. Moody, U.S. Sup. Ct. Nos. 74–389 & 74–428, (June 25, 1975).

Breaking through corporate walls. (1982, September). *Practice Digest, 5*(2), 12–14.

Cannon, S., & Smith, E. (Eds.). (1982). *Resources for affirmative action: An annotated directory of books, periodicals, films, training aids, and consultants on equal opportunity*. Garret Park, MD: Garret Park Press.

Civil Rights Act of 1964, PL 88-352, 78 Stat, pp. 241–268 (July 2, 1964).

Devising ways to implement affirmative action goals (1980, June). *Practice Digest, 3*(1), 26–28.

duRivage, V. (1985). The OFCCP under the Reagan administration: Affirmative action in retreat. *Labor Law Journal, 36*(6), 360–368.

Executive Order 11246, 3 CFR, 1966–1970 Comp. pp. 648–686, 1971 ed.

Fountain, E. M. (1977). Development of an equal employment opportunity knowledge-based criterion-referenced test for managers. Doctoral dissertation, Georgia State University, 1977. *Dissertation Abstracts International,* 78–4951.

Googins, B., & Godfrey, J. (1985). The evolution of occupational social work. *Social Work, 30*(5), 396–402.

Griggs v. Duke Power Co., 401 U.S. 424 (1971).

Hayes, H. P. (1980). *Realism in EEO*. New York: Wiley.

Hill, H. (1983). The Equal Employment Opportunity Commission: 20 years later. *Journal of Intergroup Relations, 11*(4), 45–72.

Humanic Designs Division of Information Science, Inc. (1975). *How to eliminate discriminatory practices: A guide to EEO compliance*. New York: AMACOM.

Industry–community partnerships. (1982, September). *Practice Digest, 5*(2), 22–23.

Katz, A., & Martin, K. (1982). *A handbook of services for the handicapped*. Westport, CT: Greenwood Press.

Klotchman, J., & Neider, L. (1983). EEO alert: Watch out for discrimination in discharge decisions. *Personnel, 60*(1), 60–66.

Kurzman, P., & Akabas, S. (1981). Industrial social work as an arena for practice. *Social Work, 26*(1), 52–60.

Leshin, G. (1976). *Equal employment opportunity and affirmative action in labor-management relations: A primer*. Los Angeles: University of California, Institute of Industrial Relations.

Matthies, M. (1976). The developing law on equal employment opportunity. *Journal of Contemporary Business, 5*(1), 29–46.

McDonnell-Douglas v. Green, No. 72-490, 5 FEP cases 965 (May 14, 1973).

Novit, M. (1979). The retirement amendments: Why the concern? *Business Horizons, 22*(1), 22–32.

Office of Federal Contract Compliance Programs. (1979). *Making equal employment opportunity and affirmative action work* (Department of Labor Publication No. 79-17037) Washington, DC: U.S. Government Printing Office.

Pollard, W. (1984). The role of organized labor in achieving equal opportunity. *Journal of Intergroup Relations, 12*(1), 19–22.

Roberts, C., & Squires, G. (1984). The twilight of affirmative action? Civil rights and labor at the crossroads. *Journal of Intergroup Relations, 12*(2), 37–44.

Rogers et al. v. Exxon Research & Engineering Co., U.S. District Court of New Jersey (Nov. 5, 1975).

Spaights, E., Dixon, H., & Nickolai, S. (1985). Affirmative action strategies used by organizations. *Journal of Intergroup Relations, 13*(1), 34–45.

15 AIDS in the Workplace

Wilbur A. Finch, Jr.
Kathleen O. Ell

Acquired immune deficiency syndrome (AIDS) was first identified by the Center for Disease Control (CDC) in June 1981 (Foege, 1983). Five homosexual men, hospitalized at the University of California Medical Center in Los Angeles, were suffering from diseases resulting from the fact that helper T-cells, needed to ward off infection and viruses, were dangerously depressed. Since this initial discovery, scientists have isolated the human immunodeficiency virus (HIV), the probable cause of AIDS, and clarity has been achieved as to how this virus is transmitted.

Although AIDS is a highly infectious disease, evidence indicates that it is *not very contagious*. Transmission occurs primarily through intimate sexual relations, by the use of unsterilized needles, or from infected mother to newborn infant. Earlier risks of transmission through blood transfusions have diminished with the use of an AIDS antibody test by blood banks and by heat-treating blood-clotting products, thereby killing the virus. Evidence is mounting that AIDS is not transmitted through casual social contact (Steinbrook, 1986a). Families and friends who have cared for patients have not developed antibodies to the virus through normal caretaking activities. Even more importantly, medical personnel practicing basic contagion control in encounters with blood and bodily fluids in caring for AIDS patients since 1981 have not demonstrated exposure to the virus (Steinbrook, 1986b). Based upon evidence of this kind, the CDC issued guidelines for the workplace recommending against the routine blood screening of employees and also against restricting the work activities of persons known to be ill with related diseases (Cimons, 1985a). Because AIDS cannot be transmitted through the preparation and serving of food, job screening is unnecessary even for persons in these more sensitive occupations.

Despite the clarity of these work guidelines and evidence of minimal risks, the response among businesses, industries, and government organizations to individual employees varies dramatically ("Four Concerns," 1985). At one extreme, employees with an AIDS diagnosis have faced immediate loss of work and the termination of critical job-related benefits. At an opposite extreme, employers have responded with care and compassion, often extending job benefits well beyond the worker's ability to meet work expectations—even when illness has prevented continued employment. Moreover, like the corporate community, local and state governments' responses to the growing numbers of AIDS-infected persons found within the workplace have been inconsistent. A number of California communities such as Los Angeles, San Francisco, West Hollywood, and Hayward have passed antidiscrimination ordinances to protect AIDS patients from the irrational response of individuals and organizations. For example, several state legislatures have banned the use of blood-screening tests as a basis for discriminatory hiring (Willis, 1985). Whether such actions will provide sufficient protection to AIDS victims has yet to be determined. On the other hand, despite lack of scientific findings to support them, proposals to test the blood of food handlers have been introduced in Miami, Houston, and Los Angeles (Press, 1985). Over the objections of public health officials, Miami has enacted the only ordinance to date requiring twice-yearly testing of such employees (Shipp, 1985).

Such a range of responses would suggest that administrative and political actions are currently based upon much more than scientific evidence. When knowledge is incomplete, personal preferences and value judgments are more likely to determine organizational and governmental response. In fact, the complexity of work-related issues is only now being recognized. How, and in what ways, might a more thoughtful organizational response be planned, knowing that an increased number of employees with an AIDS diagnosis will be found in the workplace? This question has special relevance for all social workers concerned with the plight of individuals and their families that accompanies AIDS. The question poses specific challenges for health care and occupational social workers.

The purpose of this chapter is threefold. First, the AIDS crisis will be reviewed, and those areas where knowledge continues to be incomplete will be identified. Second, the response of the corporate community to employees with an AIDS diagnosis will be examined, including the reasons for diversity of reactions to similar case situations. Third, specific work-related issues will be identified in the hope that as problems are anticipated a more planned and thoughtful future response will be possible. Finally, an agenda for social work intervention is proposed.

THE AIDS CRISIS

The Center for Disease Control's definition of AIDS requires both a defective immune system *as well as* a life-threatening condition such as Kaposi's sarcoma (a skin cancer commonly found among AIDS patients) or infection with *Pneumocystis carinii* (a virulent type of pneumonia). This definition, however, obscures the fact that a much broader spectrum of health-related problems currently exists as a result of the AIDS virus. Most persons infected by the HTLV-3 virus have not developed serious illnesses. Scientists estimate that as many as 2 million persons may be symptomless carriers of the virus (Adler, 1985). Current estimates that from 10% to 30% of such persons eventually will develop an AIDS condition may not prove accurate (May, 1985). On the one hand, some scientists argue that if infected persons can carry the virus for life, the chances of developing one or more of the symptoms associated with an AIDS infection may increase with time. Under such circumstances, destruction of the immune system may be only one of several consequences of infection. If this proves accurate, illness could occur increasingly even though there is an absence of a severely depressed immune system (Langone, 1985). In contrast, other research has followed homosexual and bisexual men infected with the virus over a 4-year period and has found that many have not developed AIDS-related symptoms (Lieberson, 1986). Current information about the longer term effect of HIV remains far from complete.

A second group of carriers experience mild immune system depression with symptoms such as tiredness, weight loss, fevers, and swollen lymph nodes. These persons probably represent the largest group of individuals who are seen in clinics and physicians' offices. Estimated at from 60,000 to 120,000 individuals, it is believed that from 10% to 20% of these persons, who have what has been termed AIDS-Related Complex (ARC), eventually may fully develop an acquired immune deficiency syndrome. A few persons in this category appear to improve. For the majority of such persons, however, the symptoms continue to persist. In some instances, the debilitating nature of associated illnesses has resulted in death without the individual ever meeting the requirements of the CDC's surveillance definition of AIDS.[1]

AIDS is the category that includes those individuals who experience the most serious manifestation of illnesses resulting from this newly identified virus. Patients with such a diagnosis are increasingly susceptible to a variety of infections and cancers. In its final stages, a catastrophic breakdown of the body's immune system leaves these victims vulnerable to a number of often fatal illnesses from which others would easily recover (Zonana, 1985). The variety of illnesses that AIDS patients experience commonly includes pneumonia and a variety of other respiratory ailments, painful and disfiguring cancers, fungal attacks on the brain resulting in dementia, a viral attack to retinas causing blindness, or an uncontrollable diarrhea caused by exotic

[1]For a more complete discussion of the clinical manifestations of AIDS, see R. Liebmann-Smith, *The Question of AIDS* (1985). New York: The New York Academy of Sciences, pp. 26–41.

parasites. In fact, people who are seriously ill with AIDS often will have more than one disease.

Because the immune deficiency is both persistent and progressive, the disease has been irreversible and eventually fatal for most persons. The majority of AIDS patients live an average of 18 months after diagnosis. The victims of AIDS differ markedly from persons suffering from many other illnesses. The special tragedy of AIDS is demonstrated by the youth of its victims (Kaplan, 1986). For example, homosexual and bisexual men represent approximately 66% of the known AIDS victims (a drop from 94% in 1981). AIDS victims more often are from 25 to 40 years of age, more often have a college education, and report an above average income. Recent data estimates 40% of current American cases are blacks and Hispanics, many of them heterosexual (Lieberson, 1986).

CORPORATE RESPONSES

Because of the limited number of AIDS cases identified during the early years of this epidemic, most corporations have yet to develop a thoughtful policy in relation to AIDS. Many companies indicate that they plan to continue the employment of AIDS patients and to handle these persons in the same way as they handle those with other castastrophic illnesses ("AIDS Costs," 1985). At the same time, the reluctance of some employers to share information about their handling of individual case situations suggests that uncertainty about an appropriate reponse continues to exist. Certainly, the dangers of overreaction are much greater when an increasing number of cases are not anticipated and planned for.

From the beginning, persons with AIDS have suffered discrimination in a variety of forms. Many have been evicted from their homes, refused medical and dental care, fired from their jobs, and after death have been refused burial services. Companies, such as Delta Airlines, have refused to transport or otherwise provide normal service to AIDS patients ("AIDS Costs," 1985). During the past year, more than 300 complaints of discrimination against gay men and lesbian women (many AIDS-related) were received by the New York City Commission on Human Rights (Shipp, 1985). Similarly, more than 40 cases have been settled through arbitration since August 1985, when the City of Los Angeles passed an ordinance banning discrimination against individuals suffering from AIDS-related illnesses (McGraw, 1985).[2] These early reactions have been attributed primarily to a pervasive societal fear of contracting AIDS (Christ & Weiner, 1985). The Federal Rehabilitation Act of 1973 and the laws of most states prohibit discrimination on the basis of

[2]In employment cases, settlements typically result in persons with AIDS relinquishing their jobs but receiving cash and future references while retaining medical benefits.

handicaps. To date, however, whether AIDS constitutes a handicap has not been adequately addressed judicially or administratively.

Discrimination in employment, however, has not been limited to persons suffering from AIDS. In some instances, individuals have been fired from their jobs for merely knowing a person infected with the AIDS virus. William Krause, an employee of the New Orleans Hilton Hotel, revealed to a fellow worker that a friend of his had AIDS ("AIDS Job," 1986). As a result, the hotel demanded medical documentation, and this verified that Mr. Krause did not have antibodies to the AIDS virus. However, when fellow employees appeared at work wearing gloves to avoid contamination, his "inability to function in the department under present circumstances" was given as the reason for dismissal. In Houston, Patrick de Battista, a public school teacher, agreed to pose for a photograph to be used in relation to an article about AIDS (Press, 1985).[3] Because a local television personality criticized the use of this picture, even though Mr. de Battista was not identified in the accompanying article, the school district removed him from the classroom. In Los Angeles, a gay chef who did not have AIDS was fired because of his employer's fear of this disease (McGraw, 1985).

A number of corporations have avoided development of a policy in relation to AIDS patients, preferring to handle situations on an individual case-by-case basis. Under such circumstances, however, it is not uncommon for legal action to result. For example, United Airlines placed a flight attendant with AIDS on unpaid leave—an action that has resulted in union arbitration proceedings ("AIDS Costs," 1985). Similarly, a suit has been filed by Bob Anthony against WNOL-TV in Louisiana. He was dismissed from his job as credit manager a month after he was diagnosed as having AIDS ("AIDS Job," 1986).

Citing uncertainties in the cautious way in which scientists communicate new knowledge, a small but growing number of firms are arguing that by removing AIDS carriers from certain positions, they are seeking to protect other workers from the possible spread of the virus. Thus, Enserch Corporation, parent firm of Dallas' Lone Star Gas Company, placed Terry Ulrey on an involuntary leave of absence followng an AIDS diagnosis ("Four Concerns," 1985).[4] California's Department of Fair Employment and Housing has brought legal action against Raytheon Company of Goleta, charging that it had discriminated against John Chadbourne when it would not allow him to return to work after his AIDS diagnosis. A Raytheon spokesperson responded: "We did not discriminate against John because he has AIDS. We

---

[3]He eventually was given another teaching assignment on January 8, 1986, after meetings between his attorney and Houston Independent School District Officials. "Ousted Gay Teacher Given New Teaching Post" (1986, February 5). *Update*, Issue 215, p. 3.

[4]In addition, this company has insisted that all food-service employees, as well as new job applicants, take blood tests for signs of infection.

did not introduce him to the workplace because he had a communicable disease" (Japenga, 1985).[5] Can an employer bar AIDS victims from the workplace because of the remote chance that the disease may spread through casual contact? This is the legal question that will be addressed in this first California court action involving employment discrimination.[6]

At the other end of the spectrum, many employers have sought to protect individual privacy, confidentiality, civil liberties, and welfare in policy considerations. Dawn Dedeaux, the owner of a small New Orleans publishing company, for example, allowed Rick Dahl, an assistant editor, to remain on his job and supported him until he died ("Four Concerns," 1985). Time, Inc., has argued that AIDS employees are fully entitled to ethical considerations as well as legal rights ("AIDS Cost," 1985). In the majority of such companies, AIDS has been treated like any other catastrophic illness. In San Francisco, a spokesperson for Wells Fargo stated the belief that it would be "immoral, if not illegal" to screen prospective employees or to try to change health coverage of persons who have contracted AIDS.

The most successful corporate policy (in terms of measured accomplishments) has involved a proactive stance in response to employees with AIDS. Many of these reported situations have occurred in the San Francisco Bay area and involve corporate-sponsored training programs for employees (McGraw, 1985). Certainly, some initial concerns about dealing with issues of sexuality and terminal illness in the workplace are to be expected. However, the dominant response of employees attending in-house seminars and workshops on AIDS has been positive. For example, employees in the offices of Crocker Bank demonstrated both a decreased fear of contracting the virus through social contacts and an increased knowledge as a result of AIDS seminars. A more supportive atmosphere for AIDS employees who returned after a period of sick leave occurred following Wells Fargo and Company workshops ("Four Concerns," 1985). Bell Telephone employees have been offered both in-house seminars as well as AIDS-related articles in an employee newspaper (McGraw, 1985). In cooperation with Levi Strauss and the San Francisco AIDS Foundation, Bell Telephone is working now on the development of films and booklets that will eventually be available to other companies and to the general public . The degree to which such efforts

[5]The complainant also filed a complaint with the U.S. Department of Labor's Office of Federal Contract Compliance Programs (OFCCP), alleging that Raytheon had violated Section 503 of the Rehabilitation Act of 1973. The OFCCP found that the complainant qualified as a handicapped individual. However, it found that Raytheon was "reasonable and legitimately concerned for the physical and mental health and welfare" of its employees. *Moving Forward*. (1986). Vol. 2(2), p. 6.

[6]Because AIDS has been defined as a disability, discrimination often is prohibited under related laws. A few states, such as New York, make it illegal to discriminate against anyone who is *perceived* to be disabled. Awareness of this fact may encourage some companies to offer other reasons for job termination. To date, most AIDS disputes between employers and workers have been privately settled to avoid adverse publicity.

have benefited individual employees by lessening their likelihood of contracting AIDS through sexual activity cannot be determined. However, their
success in eliciting a more concerned and beneficial response has been
clearly demonstrated.

The concentration of more proactive responses among corporations located in the San Francisco Bay area lends support to the argument that the
environment influences organizational response. A recent nationwide survey
found a higher proportion of Bay Area residents favoring laws to protect
homosexuals against employment discrimination, despite the increasing
number of AIDS cases being reported (Balzar, 1985a). Similarly, a majority
of residents in San Francisco, New York, and Los Angeles were sympathetic
toward the homosexual community and its concerns (Balzar, 1985b). As
previously noted, corporations in these latter two cities remain less willing to
discuss corporate policies and practices as these relate to employees with an
AIDS diagnosis. Nevertheless, social service agencies serving AIDS patients
(such as AIDS Project Los Angeles, the San Francisco AIDS Foundation,
and the Gay Men's Health Crisis in New York City) are receiving an
increasing number of requests from industry to conduct workshops for
employees (McGraw, 1985).

Special Problems

For hospital and other health care employers, AIDS poses special problems.
Health care workers have not been immune to the panic generated by
AIDS. Initially, many institutions have hastily developed protective policies
that are inconsistent with medically accepted recommendations for dealing
with AIDS. Public Health Service guidelines advise basic contagion pre-
cautions that are routinely practiced with other bloodborn infections and
guidelines previously set forth in the case of hepatitis B. Evidence strongly
suggests that the highest risk for transmission is a result of needle pricks or
cuts from sharp instruments contaminated with the blood of an infected
person. To date, very few health care workers have tested positively following such an incident. Therefore, risk is minimal.

Several potential problem areas require specific policy development and
intervention. In some cases the requirement that medical records be kept
confidential conflicts with employees' rights to know about health and safety
hazards in the workplace. At this time, information is generally shared on a
"need-to-know" basis with emphasis on preserving patient confidentiality.
Because the likelihood of transmission from worker to patient is highly
remote, there is no reason to routinely tell patients that a health care worker
has AIDS. Employee refusal to care for AIDS patients is responded to on the
basis of the reasonableness of the employee's rationale. Where recognized
guidelines are institutional policy, and when employee educational pro-

grams are provided, such on-the-job problems are significantly diminished. Recently there is growing recognition that family members of workers may also benefit from educational programs. The extent to which AIDS presents liability issues under Worker's Compensation and Unemployment Compensation will undoubtedly emerge and require judicial and administrative review.

Employee Health Care Benefits

With medical insurance premiums paid by employers accounting for 9.1% of pretax profits by 1983, the containment of health care costs has been a growing concern of business and industry (Shiver, 1985). Annual increases in medical costs slowed to 6.1% in 1984, from a high of 12.1% in 1981, primarily because of alternative health care plans adopted by employers. For example, a growing number of prepaid medical plans, such as health maintenance and preferred-provider organizations, are replacing fee-for-service arrangements, especially among companies that bear the full cost of employees' health insurance claims ("AIDS Costs," 1985). For this reason, the cost of providing medical care to an increasing number of AIDS patients will be a concern both for industry, which covers employees under a variety of group plans, and for government, which must meet the health costs of patients after they are no longer covered by work-related policies. In an early study of AIDS patients, for example, 38% had no insurance or had their insurance terminated when fired from their jobs following diagnosis (Christ & Weiner, 1985). Today, about one fourth of all AIDS patients in California are receiving medical treatment under the state-run Medi-Cal program (Jacobs, 1985).

AIDS is a very expensive illness. The cost of the first 10,000 AIDS-related deaths has been estimated at $6.3 billion (Eckholm, 1986). This represents approximately $1.4 billion in hospital and other direct costs as well as $5 billion in disability payments and lost productivity. While a nationwide average of $147,000 is spent for each AIDS patient, these costs have been considerably lower in San Francisco, where expenditures typically range from $25,000 to $32,000 (Cimons, 1985b). Higher costs in New York City have been attributed to the longer duration and intensity of required care, repeated illnesses requiring hospitalization, and the isolation of patients (Sullivan, 1985). Often, extended hospitalization has been necessary because less costly forms of outpatient and nursing care services have been refused or opposed by communities who fear the presence of AIDS patients.[7]

[7]New York City officials recognize, however, that a lack of hospice care, outpatient treatment, and home health services have contributed to this inflated price. "Helping AIDS Victims While Cutting Costs," (1986, January 2). *New York Times*, National Edition, p. 18.

In contrast, the city of San Francisco has invested considerable funds in its General Hospital AIDS program, as well as contracting with a wide range of voluntary and nonprofit organizations to provide comprehensive services. Such services include emergency and subsidized housing, food, personal care, free legal advice, and home health care services ("A Crisis," 1985). As a result, AIDS patients at San Francisco General Hospital have an average stay of 11.4 days, in contrast to 22 days in Los Angeles, 31 days in Philadelphia, and 50 days in New York City (Cimons, 1985b). Not surprisingly, San Francisco service arrangements are becoming a model for other cities, which increasingly recognize that a comprehensive plan of services can be cost effective.[8]

Corporate response to financing care for employees with AIDS has varied. Some corporations have contributed financially to voluntary agencies providing more individualized services to AIDS patients. San Francisco companies, such as Wells Fargo, plan to alter their health insurance coverage to allow for reimbursement of such alternative, less expensive out-of-hospital services without reducing or eliminating already existing benefits.[9]

As one means of controlling increasing costs, a few corporations are considering the possible use of the blood-screening test as part of pre-employment physical examinations. Current tests, however, have proven unreliable, with positive results occurring when there are no antibodies in the blood. In such situations, additional testing can be done to clarify whether or not a seropositive finding is correct. More importantly, this test to detect antibodies to HIV does not indicate either the current presence of the virus or whether the person will eventually develop AIDS (Shiltz, 1985). Awareness of such test limitations, however, have not prevented some insurance companies and the military from instituting such practices (Kristof, 1985). A danger with such practices is that increased screening could deny jobs to many capable employees.[10]

At the present time, 85% of the health insurance in the United States is underwritten on a group basis. Because of this, beneficiary selection is made upon criteria of employment, rather than state of health, avoiding issues of

[8]For example, Johns Hopkins Hospital opened up a special care unit in February, 1986, modeled on San Francisco General Hospital's program. "Special Care Units Limit AIDS Costs, Improve Patient Morale" (1986, January). *AIDS Alert*, pp. 20–21.
[9]Insurance coverage of in-home treatment rarely has been considered. However, as efforts to control health care costs increase, in-home care of AIDS patients becomes more attractive to hospitals and insurers. For-profit companies are beginning to offer nonacute care at home as a preferred alternative for many AIDS patients. R. Hanley, "A Caring Alternative for Many AIDS Patients," *The Los Angeles Times*, 1986, February 16, Part 4, pp. 1, 6.
[10]Defense Secretary Caspar Weinberger has rejected the idea of requiring families of servicemen and of Pentagon civilian employees to be tested. "Weinberger on AIDS Testing" (1986, January 31). *New York Times*, National Edition, p. 28.

adverse selection (Achtenberg, 1984).[11] One California employer, angry about the medical expenses of an employee's son with AIDS, was denied permission to change the company's insurance plan to exclude payments for sexually transmitted diseases by the California Insurance Department ("AIDS Costs," 1985). To date, exclusion of coverage of sexually transmitted diseases in general, or AIDS in particular, has rarely been attempted.

California and Wisconsin currently have laws that require informed consent before testing for HIV antibodies (Lacayo, 1985). In California, tested individuals may designate to whom test results will be released ("Following Strict," 1986). Similar legislation is now under consideration in New York, Massachusetts, Ohio, Texas, and Washington, DC, in part to prevent insurers, employers, and others from discriminating against AIDS patients. An increasing number of states are expected to pass legislation of this kind, even though they may not go as far as California law, which specifically prohibits the use of blood testing in determining insurability or suitability for employment. Regardless of whether specific legislation exists, facilities testing for HTLV-3 antibodies can be held liable when failing to adequately protect patient confidentiality.

The Life Insurance Controversy

Unlike health care benefits, which are primarily underwritten on a group basis through employment, life insurance is more commonly secured through individual policies. Insurance companies are increasingly fearful that, without prescreening, a growing number of life insurance claims will have an adverse effect upon the industry. More than 75 companies have adopted such screening policies in the last few months (Kristof, 1985).[12] Insurance companies currently can inquire about AIDS or related immune deficiencies on insurance applications. In addition, they can request a disease history from applicants (Keppel, 1985). They cannot, however, inquire about individual sexual preferences or practices.

Certainly, abnormal losses are a valid concern of any industry. Concomitantly, insurance companies carry an obligation to offer the protection of life insurance to those who seek it. Because the AIDS virus has affected a relatively large number of young people, however, actuarial tables normally used to set life insurance premiums are no longer valid. Therefore, one must

[11]Adverse selection occurs whenever insured persons are not selected by objective criteria but rather because of their potential for possible illness.

[12]In California, where state law forbids the use of AIDS antibody testing, Transamerica Occidental Life screens applicants using a T-cell test that detects general immune system problems rather than the presence of an AIDS virus.

assume that the life insurance applications of persons who test positive for AIDS antibodies will be rejected, at least until some basis for calculating higher premiums is established, increasing the likelihood of turning down an unnecessarily large group of persons.

Society currently requires equitable corporate behavior that does not exclude persons on the basis of sexual orientation or any other factors not derived from established underwriting principles. Therefore, the use of lifestyle screening represents the most controversial practice adopted by some life insurance companies, asking their agents to eliminate applicants who may be at risk of contracting the AIDS virus. Such practices require the identification of a variety of characteristics frequently associated with AIDS.[13] Such practices are evoking increasing criticism. The Chief of Policy Approvals for the California Department of Insurance indicates that agency objections could be expected if insurance companies seek information about a sexual preference (Keppel, 1985). A California senator believes that lifestyle screening raises serious ethical and legal issues in violation of the Unruh Civil Rights Act, which protects private citizens from discriminatory business practices.[14] Certainly, prejudicial stereotypes continue to influence the adoption of such business practices. For example, an executive of one insurance company recently suggested that applications from male fashion designers and hairdressers will receive particular scrutiny (Adler, 1985).

SOME KNOWLEDGE LIMITATIONS

A major reason for growing corporate concern about AIDS has been the increasing number of new cases identified each year. The number of such cases is currently doubling approximately every 14 months. At the same time, it is important to recognize that the rate of increase has been declining. For example, the rate of increase from 1980 to 1981 has been calculated at 449%. By June of 1985, this rate had declined to 50%. In October 1985 the Pentagon began screening all new recruits, barring from military service those who had a positive antibodies test. Analysis of the first approximately 35,000 tests yielded an incidence rate of 1.14 per 1,000. A higher rate of 2 or 3 per 1,000 cases had been expected ("Military Rejects," 1985). At least among homosexual men, there is some evidence that AIDS may be stabiliz-

---

[13]For example, persons in high risk would include single or divorced men between the ages of 20 and 49 who currently live in New York, San Francisco, Los Angeles, Houston, Miami, or Newark. They may have a history of sexually transmitted diseases or rectal problems and name an unrelated male as beneficiary. Similarly, anyone who has had a blood transfusion between the years of 1981 and 1983 may be similarly considered to be at risk of contracting AIDS.
[14]Letter from Art Agnos to Mr. Lewis Keller, August 23, 1985.

ing as a result of educational efforts.[15] At the same time, the risk of contract-ing the AIDS virus remains high for gay men, simply because of the large number of persons already carrying the virus. Moreover, increasing num-bers of cases are found among intravenous drug users and their sexual partners.

Such findings reflect the difficulty of projecting future expectations on the basis of current incidence rates. As human behavior changes, a very different profile of AIDS patients may emerge, calling for an altered corporate re-sponse.

IMPLICATIONS FOR SOCIAL WORK

Uncertainty about prognosis, lifestyle changes, and disease and treatment sequelae affect the quality of life of persons with AIDS and ARC and even those who evidence only exposure to the HTLV-3 virus. Each of these groups has special needs directly associated with response within the work-place. The extent to which corporate response enhances social resources available to employees and helps in mobilizing coping strategies un-doubtedly will influence patients' physical and psychological well-being. Evidence of such efforts already is well identified for cancer patients (Feld-man, 1982). The evidence reviewed suggests that social workers in health and occupationally related practice develop intervention strategies in several specific areas.

Personnel Practices

Social workers increasingly are asked to participate in policy formulation processes in hospitals and industry. As a result, social workers are in a strategic position to gather informed data from which such organizations can set policy to guide hiring and personnel practices. Training seminars and workshops further offer a forum in which information about AIDS as well as organizational policies regarding nondiscrimination at work can be reviewed and reinforced. In addition, social workers can help corporations exert

[15]In 1984, the incidence of AIDS among single men in San Francisco was higher than in any other American city. L. McKusick, J. Wiley, T. Coates, R. Stall, G. Saika, S. Morin, K. Charles, W. Horstman, and Marcus A. Conanat (1985, November–December). "Reporting Changes in the Sexual Behavior of Men at Risk for AIDS, San Francisco, 1982–84," *Public Health Reports*, Vol. 100(6), pp. 622–628. By December 1985, the County Health Department reported that the spread of AIDS in San Francisco had leveled off. "Spread of AIDS Levels Off in San Francisco" (1985, December 1). *The Los Angeles Times*, Part 1, p. 24. After four months of blood tests on people fearful of having been exposed to the AIDS virus, a Long Beach health center found only 31% had developed antibodies to the AIDS virus, about half the number expected. W. Nottingham. (1985, November 22). "31% of Gay Men Tested Show Evidence of AIDS," *The Los Angeles Times*, Part 2, p. 3.

influence on benefit providers, such as health- and life-insurance carriers, by providing requisite information about the care needs of employees with an AIDS diagnosis. Social workers in health care who serve on institutional ethics committees will undoubtedly be called on to address concerns associated with both patients and employees.

Educational Program Development

It would be remiss to assume that social workers are immune to fears surrounding AIDS. Therefore, a first agenda must address the task of educating the profession about this disease and its psychosocial sequelae. Moreover, because the majority of AIDS patients are members of all-too-often socially stigmatized groups, practitioners are advised to prepare themselves to provide care and services sensitive to unique issues facing these clients.

Social workers in voluntary AIDS programs and in health care have been in the forefront in developing and providing educational programs for both lay and professional audiences. Drawing on this growing professional knowledge base, social workers in hospitals and industry appear ideally situated to assume comparable leadership in educating employers and employees about AIDS. Accurate information is a powerful mechanism in reducing unwarranted responses. Equally important, employers and employees who understand the nature and impact of AIDS can provide a supportive environment needed by patients returning to work after initial diagnosis and following periods of illness. Skill in using educational formats to aid employees in social and emotional processing of the information and its implications provides a unique advantage to social workers carrying out this function.

Employee Assistance Counseling

Early evidence confirms empirically that persons infected with the HIV virus experience numerous problems in sociopsychological functioning, including problematic encounters with the health care system, personal networks, and work environments (Christ & Weiner, 1985). For those persons continuing to work, the EAP social worker may become the most accessible primary counselor, providing individual help or appropriate referral. First, however, EAP counselors must be perceived as sensitive to the concerns of these employees. For example, these persons often are worried that their personal lives can unduly affect their job. For this reason, assuring confidentiality is critical to any outreach effort. Visible information about AIDS as well as materials about the availability of gay-related services in the community are further ways of demonstrating EAP openness to the concerns of this population. In addition to providing comprehensive services to patients, families, and primary supporters, social workers in health care are strategically placed to counsel health care employees and their families when deemed appropriate.

Interagency Collaboration

Social work skill in collaborative activity is especially appropriate in achieving coordination among multiple systems. Social workers, therefore, are challenged to develop regular communication channels and collaborative services among various health and social service agencies that may be providing a range of services to persons with an AIDS or ARC diagnosis.

SUMMARY

This chapter has reviewed the response of government and industrial organizations to the growing number of employees with an acquired immune deficiency syndrome diagnosis. It has also considered employment issues as these relate to health care workers, employee health care benefits, and life insurance, as well as explored the possible limitations of current knowledge. Clearly, occupational social workers can respond to the AIDS crisis at a variety of organizational levels in order to enhance the social resources available to employees.

REFERENCES

Achtenberg, R. (Ed.). (1984). *Sexual orientation and the law* (pp. 4–45). New York: Clark Broadman.

Adler, J. (1985, September 23). The AIDS Conflict. *Newsweek*, 18, 20–24.

A crisis in public health. (1985, October). *Atlantic*, 256(4), 18, 20–24, 26, 28–31.

AIDS Costs: Employers and insurers have reasons to fear expensive epidemic. (1985, October 18). *The Wall Street Journal*, Western Edition, 1, 10.

AIDS job bias suits filed (1986, January 8). *Update*, No. 211, 3.

Balzar, J. (1985a, December 19). Tough new government action on AIDS backed. *The Los Angeles Times*, Part 1, 1, 30.

Balzar, J. (1985b, December 20). American views of gays: Disapproval, sympathy. *The Los Angeles Times*, Part 1, 1, 30.

Christ, G., & Weiner, L. (1985). Psychosocial issues in AIDS. In V. T. Devita (Ed.), *AIDS: Etiology, diagnosis, treatment, and prevention* (pp. 275–297). Philadelphia: Lippincott, pp. 275–297.

Cimons, M. (1985a, November 15). AIDS workplace guidelines win praise. *The Los Angeles Times,* Part 1, 6, 7.

Cimons, M. (1985b, September 16). Cost of AIDS near $6 billion—and climbing. *The Los Angeles Times,* Part 1, 1, 6, 7.

Eckholm, E. (1986, January 10). Economic impact of AIDS in U.S. is put at $6.3 billion in study. *New York Times,* National Edition, 11.

Feldman, F. (1982). Work and cancer health histories. In J. Cohen, J. W. Cullen, & L. R. Martin (Eds.), *Psychosocial aspects of cancer* (pp. 191–208). New York: Raven.

Foege, W. (1983). The national pattern of AIDS. In K. M. Cahill (Ed.), *The AIDS epidemic* (pp. 7–17). New York: St. Martin's Press.

Following Strict Informed Consent, Confidentiality Guidelines for Tests. (1986, January). *AIDS Alert,* 8–9.

Four concerns show a variety of ways to treat a valued employee with a terrible disease. (1985, October 18). *The Wall Street Journal,* Western Edition, 10.

Jacobs, P. (1985, December 21). 30,000 new AIDS cases expected in state by 1991. *The Los Angeles Times,* Part 1, 1, 36.

Japenga, A. (1985, November 29). Job discrimination suit is legacy of an AIDS victim. *The Los Angeles Times,* Part 4, 1, 22, 23.

Kaplan, J. (1986, February). A modern-day plague. *Natural History,* Vol. 1(2), 28, 31, 32, 33.

Keppel, B. (1985, October 11). Insurers try to screen out AIDS cases. *The Los Angeles Times,* Part 4, 1, 4.

Kristof, N. (1985, December 26). More insurers screen applicants for AIDS. *New York Times,* National Edition, 20–21.

Lacayo, R. (1985, October 21). Putting Them All to the Test. *Time,* 126(16), 61.

Langone, J. (1985, December). Report: AIDS. *Discovery,* 6(12), 29–33, 36.

Lieberson, J. (1986, January 16). The reality of AIDS. *The New York Review of Books,* 43–48.

May, L. (1985, November 2). Insurers citing high costs of health care, tell panel of need to screen for AIDS. *The Los Angeles Times,* Part 1, 3.

McGraw, C. (1985, Decmeber 31). AIDS in the workplace: New issues. *The Los Angeles Times,* Part 1, 1, 12.

Military rejects 66 potential recruits after tests for AIDS. (1985, November 26). *The Los Angeles Times,* Part 1, 12.

Press, A. (1985, November 18). AIDS and civil rights. *Newsweek,* 86, 89.

Shiltz, R. (1985, September 13). Insurers want to require AIDS test. *The San Francisco Chronicle,* 4.

Shipp, E. R. (1985, October 26). Concern over spread of AIDS spurring a spat of lawmaking nationwide. *New York Times,* National Edition.

Shiver, J. (1985, September 23). Companies shift to alternative health plans to cut costs. *The Los Angeles Times,* Part 4, 1, 6.

Steinbrook, R. (1986a, February 6). Study sees no risk to families of AIDS patients. *The Los Angeles Times,* Part 1, 1, 32.

Steinbrook, R. (1986b, January 20). AIDS fear—Hospitals seek to cope. *The Los Angeles Times,* Part 1, 1, 14, 15.

Sullivan, R. (1985, December 23). Bellevue tries to cope with disease it cannot cure. *The Los Angeles Times,* National Edition, 1, 11.

Willis, C. (1985, August 12). AIDS: A growing threat. *Time,* 40–45, 47.

Zonana, V. (1985, September 1). Drug giants give low priority to AIDS. *The Los Angeles Times,* Part 5, 1, 5.

IV Organizational Development

16 Developing Effective Organizations

Gary M. Gould
Seth Knoepler
Michael Lane Smith*

Organization development (OD) is a term that means different things to different people. Kuriloff defines OD as:

> A long-range process . . . directed toward improving the effectiveness of organizations. Effectiveness implies peformance showing acceptable profitability, innovative approaches, productive efficiency, fulfillment of public responsibility, concern for members as human beings, and a healthy psychological climate supporting human growth. (1972, p. 44)

Pfeiffer and Jones describe OD as a family of purposeful interventions that targets an organization in terms of its "effectiveness, its capacity to solve problems, its capacity to adapt, its capacity to do an effective job in creating a high quality of life for its employees" (1977, p. 178). As summarized in Weiner's (1982) excellent overview of organization development, Brown (1974) describes OD in terms of interventions directed toward the following:

1. Improving organizational health and effectiveness.
2. Improving organizational ability to identify and analyze internal and external problems, to make decisions, and to achieve effective action on these.
3. Achieving selected, specific ends of the organization.
4. Developing the capabilities and options of individuals so that they can better achieve their own ends.
5. Achieving greater congruity between the individual and organizational ends.

*Authors have contributed equally and are listed alphabetically.

6. Bringing about the attitudes and mechanisms essential to organization-al self-awareness and cooperation.
7. Improving the ability of organizations to cope with their environments, with change, and with internal forces of deterioration.
8. Developing congruity of purpose within the organization and among subunits of an organization where the subunits share a common stake in the outcome.

Most generally, organization development activities are appropriate when executives of an organization wish to use the findings of behavioral and social science to enhance organizational effectiveness or to improve the quality of work life for employees. These activities typically reflect OD practitioners' wishes to see the discoveries of contemporary social science applied to practical problems in ways that will result in the "greatest good for the greatest number."

This chapter focuses on organization development and the importance of occupational social workers mastering OD skills. Many of the skills and much of the knowledge base for OD practice are already a part of the professional repertoire of many practicing social workers, and bona fide professional competence for OD practice is either already established or within reach for thousands of social workers who may wish to explore this exciting arena of practice. What follows is a brief description of types and phases of OD practice. Areas of overlap between it and the conventional practice of social work are identified, as are the knowledge and skill areas important for effective organization development intervention.

THE OVERLAP BETWEEN ORGANIZATION DEVELOPMENT AND SOCIAL WORK

Social work and organization development share a number of important characteristics. For example, Burke (1971) argues that the primary value expressed through OD is that of the humane and nonexploitive treatment of people in organizations. Weiner argues that OD is "bedded in values almost identical with human services management" (1982, p. 367). Among these values are respect for and acceptance of the individual, the importance of participation, openness, and facilitating human growth.

Like social workers also, OD practitioners are involved in change efforts directed toward resolving problems (Weiner, 1982). In other words, both social workers and OD practitioners are professional change agents. Each works to resolve problems that occur within an array of actors and systems—for example, intragroup conflict, intergroup conflict, total system dysfunc-tion, individual system dysfunction, and so forth. Consequently, both the practice of social work and competence in OD intervention require that the practitioner:

1. Be familiar with the dynamics of change and be skillful in eliciting and managing change processes, especially those involving significant emotional or interpersonal content.
2. Be competent in working with others (i.e., clients) through various stages of problem solving, paying special attention to the difficult balance between client self-determination and adequate resolution of identified problems.
3. Be knowledgeable in working with various forms of client and target systems (i.e., individuals, groups, and larger systems).

As this brief list suggests, significant overlap exists between the knowledge, skills, and roles of OD practitioners and social workers. This overlap is further clarified by a brief explication of a term already used—*intervention*. With the substitution of *system* and *system members* for the terms *organizational* and *organization's employees*, Weiner's definition of an OD intervention would read as, "any activity, usually methodically planned in advance, that attempts to interrupt or halt [system] functioning for the purpose of changing the way the [system members] think or act" (1982, p. 373). Intervention deals with:

1. Social interaction between individuals.
2. Interaction between groups.
3. The procedures used for communicating, making decisions, planning action, and setting goals.
4. The strategies and policies guiding the system.
5. The norms or values of the system.
6. The attitudes of people toward work, the organization (i.e., the system), authority, and social values.
7. The distribution of effort and reward within the system (Weiner, 1982).

The overlap or parallels of OD intervention (so defined) with social work practice are unavoidable. With only minor modification, OD intervention is descriptive of the practice of social workers engaged in various forms of individually oriented change, family intervention, welfare administration, and a variety of community organization activities. Consider the following brief examination of social work practice and skill areas.

Social work is defined as "the professional activity of helping individuals, groups, or communities to enhance or restore their capacity for social functioning and to create societal conditions favorable to their goals" (NASW, 1973, p. 3). Two of the general goals that social workers seek to promote are (1) enhancing the problem-solving, coping, and developmental capacities of people and (2) promoting the effective and humane operation of systems that provide people with resources and services (NASW, 1982). This requires social workers to master the following knowledge and skill areas (areas also applicable to the practice of organization development):

1. Knowledge of casework and group work theory and techniques.
2. Knowledge of the theories and concepts of supervision.
3. Knowledge of the theories and concepts of social welfare administration.
4. Knowledge of social and environmental factors affecting clients to be served.
5. Knowledge of the theories and methods of psychosocial assessment and intervention.
6. Knowledge of the theory and behavior of organizational and social systems and of methods for encouraging change.
7. Knowledge of the theories of human growth and development and of family and social interaction.
8. Knowledge of small-group theory and behavioral dynamics.
9. Knowledge of the theories of group interaction and therapeutic intervention (NASW, 1982).

Certainly, there are a large number of knowledge and skill areas that are applicable to the practice of both social work and OD. The nature of their application to organization development can be better clarified as the various families of OD interventions are described.

THE HISTORY AND SCOPE OF ORGANIZATION DEVELOPMENT

As it has been practiced over the last quarter century or so, modern organization development has drawn much of its inspiration from four social science traditions, specifically:

1. The Hawthorne studies, conducted at the Western Electric Company's Hawthorne Works in Chicago during the 1920s and 1930s by researchers from the Harvard Business School, which used modern social science research techniques to discover some of the ways in which sociological and psychological factors affect workers' morale and productivity.

2. Industrial psychology, especially as it developed in large industrial and military organizations during the 1940s and 1950s, which showed how sophisticated self-report questionnaires can be used to measure the impact of

organizational interventions on the attitudes and behaviors of employees, especially managers.

3. The work of Floyd Mann, Rensis Likert, and others affiliated with the University of Michigan's Institute for Social Research during the 1940s and 1950s, in which it was shown that the way results of questionnaire surveys of employees' attitudes and beliefs are reported or "fed back" to them can affect whether and how such information influences their subsequent behavior.

4. The work during this same period of the social psychologist Kurt Lewin and his students and colleagues at MIT's Research Center for Group Dynamics, in which it was found that much insight into and enhancement of individual and group behavior can result if participants in training workshops let each other know how their actions have affected and been perceived by their fellow workshop participants. The findings of Lewin and his associates became the basis for the sensitivity training groups (or T-groups), which eventually came to represent one of the most popular techniques employed by OD consultants.

Organization development has drawn from these roots and others and continues to evolve as a loose family of skills, knowledge, and intervention strategies useful in altering organizational processes and the ways in which individuals relate to organizations.

The various strategies that OD consultants employ to affect the behavior and structure of client organizations or those who work for (or with) them can be categorized in a number of different ways. Harrison (1970), for example, finds it useful to classify interventive techniques according to the extent and intensity of the investment that a client must make in the interventive process. Argyris (1970) suggests categorizing interventions according to the degree to which the OD consultant and his or her client are able to make use of standard "off-the-shelf" interventive theories and techniques. For present purposes, however, a classification based on the sheer size and complexity of the OD client system is as well suited as any other categorization for helping to describe the range of activities that OD consultants have engaged in since the field began to acquire a distinctive identity in the late 1950s and early 1960s.

Individually Focused Interventions

OD interventions are mainly concerned with enhancing an organization's ability to adapt to and thrive in the environment in which it must operate. Salutary effects on the lives of the individuals who work for or with the organization are generally regarded as secondary to the main thrust of OD efforts, however much these may be regarded as desirable by either organization managers or the OD consultant. Nonetheless, there will be times in the professional lives of most, if not all, OD consultants when the best opportunity for accomplishing organizational change requires that OD consultants focus their attention on individual managers and others who play particularly important roles in the organization. Thus, for example, when the General Foods Corporation was planning to open a new food-processing plant during the 1960s, the company hired an OD consultant to help it design a procedure for selecting personnel who would function well in an organization that would be run according to highly participative managerial principles.

Similarly, OD practitioners may use a variety of techniques, including sensitivity training, Gestalt therapy, Transactional Analysis, Blake and Mouton's (1978) managerial grid, and the Travistock groups, based on some of the theories of Lewin (1948) and Wilfred Bion (1961), in efforts to help managers and others acquire insights into their own behavior and the skills that they need in order to function more effectively with their subordinates, superordinates, and colleagues. Originally, one assumption that lay behind such interventions was the belief that the best interests of the company lie in whatever is best for its employees. More recently, OD consultants have emphasized using only those training and development techniques designed to encourage cognitions and behaviors that are relatively compatible with the cultural and value orientations that prevail within the organization.

In general, social workers seem well equipped for individually focused OD intervention by virtue of the importance they attach to the concept and dynamics of social functioning and their mastery of counseling and consulting techniques. As Bartlett (1970) points out, the social functioning concept focuses attention on the interaction or transactions between the individual and the environment. It speaks to the behaviors necessary within a given social situation to satisfy both personal and system-wide needs. It is just this focus that lies at the heart of individually oriented OD interventions: What can the individual do to better satisfy organizational demands while simultaneously satisfying the fundamental OD values with respect to openness, individual dignity, participation, and the like? Traditionally, social workers have emphasized the needs of the individual in the social functioning equation (excepting, perhaps, institutionalized and powerless populations) whereas OD practitioners have given priority to the demands of the organization. The emphasis has been different, but many of the skills and much of the knowledge are easily transferable from social work practice to OD intervention and vice versa.

Group Interventions

OD consultants are frequently called upon to suggest and help implement changes in the processes by which work groups accomplish their assigned tasks or maintain a sense of cohesiveness among their members. Thus, an

OD consultant may help a group decide how to organize its activities, solve problems, make decisions, or delegate leadership responsibilities, considerations that are particularly relevant to accomplishing group tasks. Alternatively, consultants may help to facilitate communication among group members to enhance mutual trust, support, or tolerance of members' differences, thereby building group morale and otherwise encouraging the members to identify their own individual interests with those of the work group.

Team building is the name typically assigned to a variety of techniques OD consultants employ to try to effect such changes in work groups. Such techniques are most likely to be effective when organizational goal achievement requires sustained cooperation among employees who are highly dependent upon one another for accomplishing their own individual work tasks. Indeed, enhancing group members' awareness of the extent of their interdependence can play an important role in a team building intervention.

On the broadest level, OD team builders typically base their efforts on at least one of the general theories of group behavior and functioning that have enjoyed some measure of acceptance in the field. Some examples are Argyris' (1962, 1971) three-facet theory of interpersonal competence, which emphasizes the importance of emotional honesty, expressiveness, and willingness to trust one's colleagues and experiment with new or unusual ways of doing things; and Bion's (1961) ideas about the tendency of different "basic-assumption groups" to respond in characteristic ways to typically unconscious and unacknowledged anxieties about the future of the group and its members. A number of OD consultants have used McGregor's (1967) catalogue of the characteristics of effective managerial teams when deciding whether a particular team-building intervention might be appropriate or whether such an effort has been effective. McGregor's list includes mutual trust, support, and openness of communication among team members, a high degree of consensus about and commitment to team goals, readiness to acknowledge and manage differences among team members, the ability to decide when to delegate decision-making tasks to the team as a whole, the ability to put and keep together a team whose members collectively possess the skills that are required to accomplish team goals, and the presence of at least one leader who is able to supervise the team's attempts at achieving or acquiring the other desirable attributes on McGregor's list.

More concretely, team builders may concentrate on one or more of the following possible purposes of a team-building intervention:

1. Helping to establish team goals or priorities.
2. Clarifying the roles and responsibilities of various team members.
3. Analyzing or facilitating the procedures and processes by which the team seeks to achieve its goals. Some of these include establishing and maintaining group norms, habits, and processes of communication, and

the ways in which leadership and decision-making responsibilities are discharged.
4. Examining or facilitating relationships among individual team members.

Some OD consultants (e.g., Beckhard, 1972; Burke, 1982) try to approach the preceding list in a hierarchical fashion, on the theory that there is a tendency for problems in more basic areas (e.g., establishing team goals or priorities and clarifying team members' roles and responsibilities) to generate difficulties in other, more peripheral areas.

Team building is an exceptionally popular OD activity and, again, one that depends for its success on many of the practice areas already mastered by many social workers. The focus of team building is the small group, its composition, structure, and functioning. The knowledge and skills of social group work and family therapy are generally applicable to team building as well. In team building, the social worker acts as a "process consultant" to encourage (1) greater awareness of group structures, processes, values, and norms, (2) greater acceptance of group members for one another, and (3) greater harmony between group members and the demands made on the group for higher levels of organizational productivity.

Dealing with Conflicts between Groups

Individuals and groups that specialize in performing particular tasks are frequently more effective and efficient than generalists who "do a little bit of everything." Consequently, virtually all modern organizations are subdivided into semiautonomous groups, each of which is responsible for fulfilling some portion or aspect of the organization's goals. However, the very same narrowing of focus within departments or task groups that tends to give such functionally differentiated organizations an advantage over their less differentiated competitors can produce or exacerbate conflicts between organizational subgroups as each subgroup develops its own procedures, values, and norms in response to the exigencies of its tasks or the needs and personalities of its members. Indeed, some organizations have developed special units whose job is to minimize or resolve conflicts between various departments or divisions and otherwise help such units to better coordinate their efforts with each other and with the overarching goals of the parent organization.

Whether functioning as an in-house specialist in this area or in a time-limited consulting capacity, one of an OD practitioner's more important roles is likely to involve the creative resolution of conflicts between organizational subunits. For example, drawing on basic theoretical work by Sherif and Sherif (1953), Blake, Shepard, and Mouton (1964), and others, Burke

(1974, 1982) has proposed a seven-phase sequence for helping to overcome conflicts between two semiautonomous organizationl subgroups. The first two phases provide opportunities for group members to gain a better understanding of how the members of each group see both themselves and the members of the other group. Each group then generates a list of problems that seem to be rooted in differences between the groups. The groups then compare notes to discover areas of consensus, after which the two lists of problems are combined. The final phases are devoted to creating task forces comprised of members of both groups, each of which tries to find possible solutions to one of the common problems, to offering these proposed solutions to the entire combined group for criticism and advice, and to making plans for follow-up activities.

It is important to note that the purpose of OD intervention is not conflict resolution per se, but that of helping organizational leaders learn to manage conflict imaginatively and constructively (Weiner, 1982). The OD practitioner is concerned with helping clients learn from the conflict that has developed. Conflict itself is not necessarily bad—as social workers familiar with general systems theory recognize (Compton & Galaway, 1984, p. 121). Conflict can be the catalyst for vital changes.

Conventional social worker roles useful for this family of OD interventions include those of enabler, mediator, broker, expert, and consultant.

Large System Change

Perhaps the most difficult and ambitious OD interventions are those that attempt to induce relatively enduring, systemic changes in entire organizations. Some of the features that may be targets for such large system interventions include the organization's goals, the norms and values that guide the behavior of its employees, its structure, and its working procedures (Beckhard & Harris, 1977).

Large system OD interventions can be classified according to the degree to which they offer highly structured programs typically designed to push an organization toward a more participative style of management or a more humanistic overall work environment. For example, the survey–feedback method developed at the University of Michigan is often used to elicit more active involvement from organization managers at a variety of levels, while Blake and Mouton's managerial grid technique tries to instill in managers attitudes that combine a strong concern for production with an equally intense interest in helping employees whose active cooperation is essential to accomplishing the organization's goals. An example of a less highly structured type of large system intervention would be some form of open-systems planning, such as the one described by Beckhard and Harris (1977), which requires the OD consultant to assist an organization through a series of steps whereby organization managers determine the organization's "core mission," generate maps of the demands that the organization's environment is making on it and of the responses that it typically makes to those demands, try to predict any changes that can be anticipated in the organization's "demand system," define a "new, improved version" of the organization that will be better adapted to meeting current and future demands, and plan cost-effective activities that, it is hoped, will move the organization closer to this desired state.

ORGANIZATION DEVELOPMENT:
A FRAMEWORK FOR PRACTICE

Several writers have attempted to outline analytically the underlying processes that, in one form or another, play a critical role in almost any OD operation, regardless of the size or characteristics of the target organization. The following description of the phases of generic OD practice identifies a number of commonalities that underlie the family of organization development interventions.

Phase 1: Entry

After an initial contact is made by either the OD consultant or a prospective client, each party will try to assess the prospects for a collaborative effort between them. The client will typically be especially concerned with whether the OD consultant's professional training and experience have prepared him or her to effectively supervise the type of OD effort that is envisioned, whereas the OD consultant will try to determine whether the client possesses the motivation and other resources (including, especially, sufficient power within the organization) that are necessary if an intervention is to have a reasonably good chance of taking hold and lasting.

Phase 2: Contracting

Having decided to work together, the client and the OD consultant must agree, however tentatively, about what each party will have to do to give the OD effort a good chance of accomplishing its goals. Specifically, there must be general agreement concerning the amount of time that client and OD consultant should expect to contribute to the OD effort, the financial and other benefits each party can expect to reap from it, and the nature of the procedures and processes that will structure their interactions with one another (Weisbord, 1973).

Phase 3: Diagnosis

This part of the OD effort can be conceptualized as being comprised of separate activities devoted, first, to collecting information about organizational structures and processes, and then to analyzing the information according to a theoretical model that seems relevant to the current situation. In practice, however, it is usually difficult to make such a clear distinction between raw data, on the one hand, and analytical theory and technique, on the other, since some analytical models are quite specific about the type of data that must be gathered if the model is to be used effectively, and even a consultant's most tentative and unstructured attempts to discover an organization's weaknesses and strengths will be affected by the theoretical and conceptual frames of reference that the OD consultant typically employs.

Phase 4: Feedback

Here the OD consultant attempts to convey to appropriate people in the organization the results of the data collection and analysis activities that were undertaken during the previous phase. Burke (1982) has suggested three possible purposes for the feedback phase: (1) helping clients understand what the OD consultant has learned about the organization; (2) encouraging clients to feel that this information "belongs" to them, since they will have to develop and implement a program of organization change that is based on it; and (3) arousing and focusing clients' energies in such a way as to facilitate their being used to effectively plan and implement appropriate changes. The initial phases of an OD effort are apt to arouse feelings of hope, anxiety, fear, or defensiveness in clients; therefore, the OD consultant must carefully manage the information that is presented during the feedback phase, so that clients emerge from this phase with enhanced (or at least undiminished) confidence in the ability of consultant and client to collaborate effectively (Nadler, 1977).

Phase 5: Planning Change

After having had an opportunity to absorb the data that were presented during the feedback phase, the client must work together with the OD consultant to generate a list of possible ways of addressing the problems that have been discovered and then to decide how best to proceed in implementing them. During this phase it is critical that the OD consultant continue to facilitate the process, begun during the feedback phase, of making sure that the client, having accepted the validity and relevance of the diagnosis of organizational strengths and weaknesses that has emerged, realizes that it is the client, more than the OD consultant, who will have to live with the consequences of whatever interventions are attempted.

Phase 6: Intervention

These are the activities that, it is hoped, will result in the "double-loop learning," whereby an organization makes changes that make it unlikely that the same types of problems will recur (Argyris & Schon, 1978). Although only clients can make the final decision concerning which intervention(s) to attempt, the OD consultant's greater familiarity and experience with the latter can play an extremely important role with regard to advising clients about the range of possible interventions that might be appropriate under the circumstances, guiding clients through whatever interventions are selected, and helping clients to anticipate and respond effectively to unanticipated side effects.

Phase 7: Evaluation

It has been said that "the evaluation phase of OD practice can be compared to an annual physical examination—everyone agrees that it should be done, but no one . . . wants to go to the trouble and expense of making it happen" (Burke, 1982, p. 327). In fact, while a number of interested parties may believe that some evaluation of an OD effort is desirable, they are apt to have somewhat different and occasionally conflicting reasons for feeling that way. Consequently, the first question that must be addressed during this final phase of any OD effort concerns what purposes are to be served by evaluating all or part of the OD enterprise. Indeed, thinking much earlier in the OD process, during its initial phases, about the form that an evaluation will assume can help OD consultants and their clients clarify their understandings about what each party can reasonably expect to give to and get from it.

There is frequently much to be said for conducting an evaluation that is planned and implemented by someone who has had no prior role in the OD effort, because both the OD consultant and client(s) are likely to be too close to the situation to be entirely objective about the intervention's intended and unintended consequences. However, the advantages of having such a disinterested party conduct the evaluation must be balanced against its disadvantages. These include having an evaluation performed by someone who may not have knowledge of the OD effort's origin and evolution, or who may have priorities concerning the goals of the evaluation that compete with those of the OD consultant or client(s).

In a number of ways these phases of OD intervention parallel the problem-solving model employed by social workers. Compton and Galaway describe the social work problem-solving process as:

> The process by which worker and client decide (1) what the problem or question is that they wish to work on; (2) what the desired outcome of this work is; (3) how

to conceptualize what it is that results in the persistence of the problem in spite of the fact that the client wants something changed or altered; (4) what procedures should be undertaken to change the situation; (5) what specific actions are to be undertaken to implement the procedures; and (6) how the actions have worked out. (1984, p. 314)

This problem-solving approach unfolds through a series of phases similar to that outlined for the OD practitioner, and includes:

1. The contact phase (dealing with problem and goal identification and exploration).
2. The contract phase (dealing with problem assessment, formulation of a plan of action, and prognosis).
3. The action phase (involving carrying out the plan, termination of the relationship, and evaluation) (Compton & Galaway, 1984).

In both OD and social work practice the change agent must take care to permit the client to "own the problem," and, consequently, the agent engages the client in a consultive, dynamically interactive relationship. Both types of practice develop sequentially and are characterized by distinct phases, each with its own unique set of practitioner and client tasks and responsibilities. Both OD and social work require their practitioner to assume a host of roles, many of which are identical across the two fields of practice. Finally, and while not a dimension of the interventive models, both OD and social work call for much of the same knowledge of individual, small group, and organizational behavior and many of the same or similar skills in inducing, managing, and stabilizing change. A closer examination of even more personal attributes of OD practice further develops the compatibility of social work with organization development.

ROLES AND QUALITIES OF THE OD CONSULTANT

Beer (1980) has identified a number of characteristics deemed desirable for anyone who wishes to engage in organization development. Such an individual should:

1. Possess both a general familiarity with organizational administration and special expertise in the area of organizational diagnosis and intervention.
2. Be able to connect the client to needed resources and to identify and facilitate necessary linkages among various individuals and groups within the client organization.

3. Be neutral with regard to competition and conflicts among individuals and groups within the client organization.
4. Have the ability to inspire confidence in the OD consultant's ability to diagnose organizational problems and guide the organization toward their solution.
5. Be relatively comfortable operating in situations where the OD consultant role is marginal, sitting astride the boundary between two better-established and better-understood roles.

Similarly, Burke (1982) has identified the following 10 qualities as critical to an OD consultant's effectiveness:

1. The ability and willingness to take a flexible, "experimental" attitude toward applying general theories and specific techniques to actual consulting situations.
2. The ability or charisma necessary to persuade or influence others.
3. The willingness to confront difficult, emotionally loaded issues.
4. The ability to be (and to be perceived as) generally supportive of and nurturant toward others.
5. The ability and willingness to listen empathically to others, particularly in situations where the speaker is under a great deal of stress.
6. A high degree of awareness of the OD consultant's own feelings, intuitions, and the like.
7. The ability to conceptualize the complex and subtle relationships that can be found among organizational systems and subsystems, and the ability to articulate these in language that is accessible to the layperson.
8. The ability to detect sources of energy in clients and self and to channel it into productive uses.
9. Effectiveness in teaching or facilitating learning in others.
10. The ability to avoid taking oneself too seriously, and the ability to maintain a sense of humor, even under stressful or disappointing circumstances.

With but a few exceptions, Beer and Burke provide useful (although but partial) lists of the characteristics of effective social workers. It is difficult to avoid the conclusion that occupational social workers—given their knowledge and skills and located as they are with access to the human and procedural machinery of organizations—have available the opportunity to improve the quality of life for workers by becoming more active in organization development. Such efforts may involve risks (as commonly occurs whenever one moves out into new practice arenas), regardless of how well and versatile one's professional armamentarium may be. The fact remains, however, that employing organizations remain vital systems that continually impact workers' levels of social functioning. The occupational social worker who neglects to alter these systems neglects to do all that is professionally expected on behalf of present and future generations.

A CASE EXAMPLE: TEAM BUILDING IN A UNIVERSITY

The School of Fine Arts at a nationally prestigious university was potentially a fine place to work. Staff were personable, dedicated, and hard working, Faculty and students were creative, original, and stimulating. There was always something going on—an event or planning for an event—that promised some reward. The Dean in charge of the School was both an accomplished artist himself and an administrator of considerable talent, integrity, and honesty. Yet, despite these true assets, productivity within the Dean's Office was far from acceptable.

The Dean, his three administrative assistants, and the three secretaries were not blending into an effective work unit. Two of the secretaries refused to speak to each other except when absolutely necessary—one even going so far as to make faces at the other when the latter was distracted. One of the administrative assistants—new to the office—considered herself to be the informal assistant dean, potential confidante to him, and first in the staff pecking order. The second administrative assistant, about the same age as the first, had occupied various positions within the Dean's Office for over 10 years, rising through the limited ranks after having graduated from this very School. Quiet but thoroughly competent, she possessed a vast knowledge of personages, processes, and episodes important to the functioning of the School but felt deep resentment at the apparent attempt of the new arrival to displace her as the Dean's primary assistant. The third assistant was a generation younger than her colleagues, bright and ambitious. She had assumed the informal status of office manager over the two quarreling secretaries, a duty that increasingly took her attention away from her official responsibilities in overseeing all budgetary matters for the School. Finally, there was the third secretary, seen by all as the private secretary to the Dean. This woman avoided the animosities, jealousies, and intrigues of her office mates but maintained a posture of "I hear all; I know all." Far from working well together, members in this key group sometimes found it difficult just to be in the same room. Productivity was falling off, several major projects were floundering, and people were complaining of working without adequate cooperation or appreciation. At this point the Dean, agreeing with several of his assistants, asked for consultation with the University Counseling Service (an internal EAP).

The Counseling Service social worker had a short series of meetings with the administrative assistants and the Dean. The social worker and the Dean agreed that the former would initiate a round of survey feedback wherein he would talk with each member of the Dean's Office regarding his or her impressions of the work environment, co-workers, and his or her feelings about working in the office. Afterward, the social worker would condense these findings and provide them to the Dean in preparation for an office-wide discussion of work-related problems.

This was done. Two critically important developments resulted from the survey feedback activity. First, each staff member had a chance to talk honestly about his or her impressions, feelings, and hopes about work, and each saw the social worker's role as representing a real possibility for constructive changes in office roles and procedures. Secondly, staff members' comments made it clear that workers shared different conceptions about their individual roles and duties within the work group. Something far more profound than "a failure to communicate" (the Dean's belief) was wrong with this group: People privately disagreed over their conceptions of their responsibilities to each other and to the School.

Following a discussion over these matters, the Dean and the consulting social worker agreed to initiate a team-building effort within the group with the goal of reaching consensus on work roles and responsibilities. The team-building activities were structured around several off-site, half-day "retreats" and specific "homework assignments" during the interims. Assuming the roles of expert and process consultant, the social worker helped the Dean prepare for each session and participated in them, offering feedback to group members on communication style, decision-making patterns, and strategies of coping and ignoring characteristic of the group. The Dean encouraged each staff member to take some personal risks during these sessions and then modeled his request through some honest and sensitive disclosures that were important to the way he hoped to manage the School. Increasingly, process within the group during these sessions became more open and honest, with people willing to identify areas of importance to them and with group members offering to compromise or otherwise problem-solve on issues related to positions, responsibilities, and procedures.

Working through the group's "internal" consultant (the youngest administrative assistant), the social worker continued to provide feedback, ideas, and suggestions to the group over the next several months. The group successfully altered its ways of doing things, and group members continued to relate to one another in far more humane and productive ways throughout this period and beyond. Team building had made a difference—a difference that could be measured both in terms of increased work productivity and increased employee growth and satisfaction.

CONCLUSION

Social workers are playing a more important role in the field of organization development. Although OD's theoretical underpinnings come primarily from other disciplines, administrators in many organizations are coming to appreciate the extraordinarily close fit between the training and temperament of social workers and the knowledge and skills that form the basis for effective organization development practices. Companies that have in-house employee assistance programs or that contract for EAP services are ideally positioned to arrange to use social workers to help plan and implement OD efforts, and several social work schools that have industrial concentrations have been making special efforts to prepare their students for the types of challenges that OD activities are apt to pose. From its beginnings, organization development has been burdened by great expectations about its potential for helping individuals and organizations work together in an efficient, synergistic fashion (Burke, 1982). Social workers have a chance to ease this burden by helping OD realize more of this potential than ever before, while moving into a practice arena that offers unique opportunities to apply their professional knowledge and skills in new and exciting ways.

REFERENCES

Argyris, C. (1962). *Interpersonal competence and organizational effectiveness.* Homewood, IL: Dorsey.

Argyris, C. (1970). *Intervention theory and method.* Reading, MA: Addison-Wesley.

Argyris, C. (1971). *Management and organization development.* New York: McGraw-Hill.

Argyris, C., & Schon, D. (1978). *Organizational learning: A theory of action perspective.* Reading, MA: Addison-Wesley.

Bartlett, H. (1970). *The common base of social work practice.* New York: National Association of Social Workers.

Beckhard, R. (1972). Optimizing team-building efforts. *Journal of Contemporary Business, 1* (3).

Beckhard, R., & Harris, R. (1977). *Organizational transitions: Managing complex change.* Reading, MA: Addison-Wesley.

Beer, M. (1980). *Organization change and development.* Santa Monica, CA: Goodyear.

Bion, W. (1961). *Experience in groups.* New York: Basic Books.

Blake, R., & Mouton, J. (1978). *The new managerial grid.* Houston: Gulf.

Blake, R., Shepard, H., & Mouton, J. (1964). *Managing intergroup conflict in industry.* Houston: Gulf.

Brown, G. (1974.) A working definition and specification of organization development (OD): Framework for a discussion. Presented at the 1974 National Conference of the American Society for Public Administration, Chicago.

Burke, W. (1971). A comparison of management development and organization Development. *Journal of Applied Behavioral Science, 7*.

Burke, W. (1974). Managing conflict between groups. In J. Adams (Ed.), *New technologies in organization development: 2*. San Diego: University Associates.

Burke, W. (1982). *Organization development: Principles and practices*. Boston: Little, Brown.

Compton, B., & Galaway, B. (1984). *Social work processes* (3rd ed.). Homewood, IL: Dorsey.

Harrison, R. (1970). Choosing the depth of organizational intervention. *Journal of Applied Behavioral Science, 6*.

Kuriloff, A. (1972). *Organization development for survival*. New York: American Management Association.

Lewin, K. (1948). *Resolving social conflicts*. New York: Harper.

McGregor, D. (1967). *The professional manager*. New York: McGraw-Hill.

Nadler, D. (1977). *Feedback and organization development: Using data-based methods*. Reading, MA: Addison-Wesley.

National Association of Social Workers (NASW). (1973). *Standards for social service manpower*. Silver Spring, MD: Author.

National Association of Social Workers (NASW). (1982). *NASW Standards for the classification of social work practice, policy statement 4*. Silver Spring, MD: Author.

Pfeiffer, J., & Jones, J. (1977). *Organization development: Selected readings*. La Jolla, CA: University Associates.

Sherif, M., & Sherif, C. (1953). *Groups in harmony and tension*. New York: Harper & Row.

Weiner, M. (1982). *Human services management: Analysis and applications*. Homewood, IL: Dorsey.

Weisbord, M. (1973). The organization development contract. *OD Practitioner, 5*(2).

17 Influencing Management Policy

Vincent E. Faherty

The explosive growth of EAPs within the corporate environment during the past decade is richly documented throughout both the human service and business literature. This growth has not always been steady and uneventful. Indeed, the dialogue and interactions between the private sector manager and the professional helper are fraught with inherent conflicts over such essential elements as treatment goals, problem causality, client progress, and confidentiality. That such dialogues and interactions have continued to grow at an impressive pace in spite of some very real obstacles is a tribute to the strong commitment of both industry and the human service professions to view the workplace as an appropriate—even desirable—site to identify and treat an array of individual and social problems. A recent survey of more than 500 human resource executives published by the Conference Board documents vividly the business community's sensitivity to human needs and its willingness to be a contributing partner in a professional response to those needs (Troy, 1986). Among other results, this survey reported that:

- More than 80% of the companies offered counseling for a wide variety of problems (in addition to substance abuse) either directly or through referral procedures.
- 40% of the companies offered counseling services to former employees and their families.
- Almost 40% provided some form of child care assistance (usually information and referral and partial subsidy).
- Almost half of the companies offered fitness programs.
- Almost one third reported that they had changed the focus of their community-funding efforts so as to relate to crisis needs such as those for food, clothing, or shelter, and to emerging problems such as domestic violence.

An earlier version of this chapter was presented at the NASW Occupational Social Work Conference, Boston, May, 1985.

Viewing this development of employee assistance programming and its concurrent role for social workers, it appears opportune to recall Ozawa's seminal article (1980) in *Social Work* (see Chapter 1 of this volume). In this work, Ozawa posited a multilevel progression of increasing responsibility for occupational social workers as new opportunities are offered and new services provided. If it is true (as this author believes) that there exists an ever-expanding network of EAPs under varied structural configurations and, further, if one accepts Ozawa's premise of multilevel functioning within a corporate environment, then some adjustments to the educational experience of industrial social workers seem not only warranted but absolutely essential.

The purpose of this chapter is to show the need for a more comprehensively trained social worker who is comfortable with the language, the issues, and the perspective of the business community and who is able, therefore, not only to deliver direct social services but also to impact policy decisions made in executive planning sessions. Following a brief discussion of the kinds of expanded social services that could be delivered by a retrained human service professional, the chapter describes the competencies necessary to impact realistically on the business environment. This chapter concludes with a presentation and discussion of a case example in which a nontraditional role for an occupational social worker is highlighted.

EAP SERVICES: AN EXPANSIVE VIEW

Even a cursory review of the relevant literature reveals persuasively that the EAP movement has progressed far beyond the historical and traditional service delivery system that provided only direct counseling to the alcoholic employee. What follows here is a listing of specific areas of service delivery that can and should be within the province of EAP programming if social work professionals assume a truly expansive view of their role and their clients' needs (Burud, Aschbacker, & McCroskey, 1983; EAPs/Wellness Programs, 1984; Foegen, 1984; Johnson, 1984; Kastiel, 1984; Kepler et al., 1983; Masi, 1982; McClellan, 1985; Schumacher, 1985):

- Relocation assistance
- Child care
- Wellness and nutrition
- Family life education
- Basic literacy education
- Crisis hot line
- EEO/AA consultation
- Employee training, career development, and performance evaluation

- Supervision and motivation
- Labor relations
- Employee benefits
- Safety and health services
- Human resources audit
- Management and organizational development
- Corporate social responsibility and community relations

Professionally trained social workers can undoubtedly respond in an effective and efficient manner to *some* of these expanded services simply on the basis of their educational preparation and work experience. But other areas of service delivery, particularly those that require a technical knowledge of business functions, appear to require additional education and experience. With this increased knowledge base, the occupational social worker has the potential to exert a long-range and significant impact on corporate policies that affect individuals, families, the community, and the society at large. The next section presents a competencies model whose components can be used to train social workers to function competently in the workplace.

COMPETENCIES FOR POLICY/PROGRAM IMPACT

This author proposes that there are at least six business functions with which every industrial social worker should be familiar: marketing, finance, accounting and control, production and operations management, human resource management and organizational development, and strategic planning. A broad composite definition for each function is provided in an attempt to remove some of the possible misconceptions relative to these functions. A listing of specific competencies is also offered as a guide to social workers who accept that part of their role is to be appropriately assertive in affecting corporate policy changes. Finally, a brief mention is made of conventional social work knowledge/skill that is related to the business function competency being discussed. This latter point is an extremely important one. Graduate-level education in social work does serve as an excellent base upon which can be built some additional competencies more relevant to the private, corporate sector.

BUSINESS FUNCTION 1: MARKETING

Composite Definition:

Human activity to satisfy needs and wants through the exchange process . . . business activities designed to plan, price, promote, and distribute wanted goods and services to present and future customers . . . includes all the operations of a business that influence present and future demand for goods and services in the marketplace and activate the supply to meet the demand . . . relates to the satisfaction of either a felt or latent demand . . . marketing is not just a business function, it is a consolidation of the entire business. (Gist, 1974; Levitt, 1974; Lipson & Darling, 1974; Stanton, 1975)

Competencies Required:

- Ability to understand the concepts of "marketing mix" and "product life cycle."
- Ability to understand the purpose and utility of a marketing plan.
- Ability to recognize the essential differences between marketing and advertising/promotion.
- Ability to accept the central role that marketing plays in corporate operations.

Conventional Social Work Knowledge/Skills:

Human behavior and the social environment.

BUSINESS FUNCTION 2: FINANCE

Composite Definition:

Relates to the problems involved in the use and acquisition of funds . . . concerns what assets are needed and in what form (cash, property, equipment) and how required funds should be financed . . . involves financial planning, managing assets, and raising funds . . . finance is applied microeconomic theory . . . monitoring of financial consequences of past and current operations and raising funds to meet present and future needs. (Johnson, 1971; Jones & Dudley, 1978; Spiro, 1977)

Competencies Required:

- Ability to distinguish between capital budgeting, working capital management, and capital structure.
- Ability to understand the concepts of risk analysis, net present value, and internal rate of return.
- Ability to understand the variety of financing options available to a private corporation.

Conventional Social Work Knowledge/Skills:

General economics; quantitative methods; administration.

BUSINESS FUNCTION 3: ACCOUNTING AND CONTROL

Composite Definition:

Concerned with the accumulation, classification, and analysis of information that aids in the fulfillment of organizational objectives . . . provides information for the assessment of operating performance and the establishment of objectives . . . reports the nature and status of the capital invested (balance sheet) and measures changes in capital resulting from operating activities. (Backer & Jacobson, 1964; Gray & Johnson, 1973)

Competencies Required:

- Ability to understand an income statement, a balance sheet, a cash flow statement, and a proposed/actual budget statement.
- Ability to accept the orientation toward profit as neutral and valueless in essence.
- Ability to utilize cost/benefit analyses in program planning exercises.

Conventional Social Work Knowledge/Skills:

Research; quantitative methods; administration.

BUSINESS FUNCTION 4: PRODUCTION AND OPERATIONS MANAGEMENT

Composite Definition:

Concerns the relationship between input and output . . . relates to the process flow in any organization . . . utilizes the application of scientific methods to decision problems of business and other organizations . . . relates to complex system analysis and design of solutions for organizational problems . . . a highly structured decision-making process focused on the development of predictive models helpful in solving executive-type problems. (Gupta & Cozzolino, 1979; Hartley, 1975; Riggs & Inoue, 1975)

Competencies Required:

- Ability to understand and use various models of operations management (e.g., CPM, PERT, GANTT).
- Ability to conceptualize simulation theory and queuing theory and their applications in business contexts.
- Ability to accept the approaches of quality control and efficiency in production and service operations.

Conventional Social Work Knowledge/Skills:

Systems theory; research; quantitative methods; organizational theory.

BUSINESS FUNCTION 5: HUMAN RESOURCE MANAGEMENT AND ORGANIZATIONAL DEVELOPMENT

Composite Definition:

The successful management of people is one of the essential elements in the effective operation of any organization . . . relates to the selection and training of employees for the appropriate jobs, to their continuing motivation to exert maximum effort, to performance evaluation, and to just remuneration . . . human resource management values the employee group as an investment that can improve organizational effectiveness through satisfaction of personal needs . . . organizational development is a long-term effort to improve an organization's problem-solving and renewal activities . . . organizational development is a systems approach to the set of role relationships in organizations. (Carrell & Kuzmits, 1982; Chruden & Sherman, 1976; Mathis & Jacobson, 1976)

Competencies Required:

- Ability to understand the entire range of human resource and personnel functions.
- Ability to engage in human resource research projects.
- Ability to remain objective in labor–management relations and in problems of staff communication.
- Ability to propose plans for employee, management, and organizational development.

Conventional Social Work Knowledge/Skills:

Human behavior and the social environment; organizational theory; communication skills; assessing needs; planning; evaluation; direct services.

BUSINESS FUNCTION 6: STRATEGIC PLANNING

Composite Definition:

Identification of the central purpose of the organization and the specification of the means it intends to operationalize this purpose in society . . . the procedure under which the future implications of every decision are analyzed in advance of implementation . . . the essence of planning is to assist corporate managers to face both risk and uncertainty . . . deals with the selection of business strategies that allow management to achieve long-term objectives based on present, limited information. (Dessler, 1973; Hussey, 1979; Naylor, 1979, 1982)

Competencies Required:

- Ability to conceptualize the entire corporation from a systems perspective.
- Ability to understand a variety of planning models.
- Ability to be future-oriented.
- Ability to utilize quantitative and qualitative data to reduce uncertainty.

Conventional Social Work Knowledge/Skills:

Community organization; research; organizational theory; systems theory; administration.

DISCUSSION

The question that can arise in the reader's mind at this point is obvious: How and where does one learn to be competent in all of these functional areas? As stated above, a firm base of knowledge and skill has already been established through the MSW-level educational process. Certainly, if the student has decided on occupational social work as a career choice while in graduate school, then a joint MSW/MBA (if available) or elective coursework within a business school can provide these business-related competencies quite well. On a postgraduate basis, weekend "executive MBA programs" are also available in most urban areas for those social workers who seek the MBA degree as a credential. Barring these options, continuing education course offerings through a business school, a technical business institute, or the Small Business Administration can provide at least basic information. In addition, any one of several computer-based simulations, during which the participants function over an extended period of time as corporate managers, can be an excellent and creative method of learning these competencies. At a minimal level, the regular reading of major business-oriented journals (*Business Week, Forbes, The Wall Street Journal*, etc.) would at least make one familiar with relevant terms and issues.

The following case study of the Delta Corporation illustrates some of the intricacies of the business environment and in the process shows what an expanded role for occupational social work within that environment could be like. By intention, the critical policy decisions facing Delta in this case are not directly related to traditional EAP issues or services. The purpose of this case is to explore the role that the occupational social work staff *can* play in the complex decisions that must be made.

A CASE EXAMPLE: THE DELTA CORPORATION

The Delta Corporation, headquartered in Baltimore, Maryland, is a manufacturer of consumer and industrial electronic products. The company was
founded in 1920 by a German immigrant, Hans Dietrich. The present chief
executive officer (CEO), James Dietrich, is the grandson of Hans. James is a
Harvard-trained MBA who started working in the family business 15 years
ago as an industrial sales representative. He has been the CEO for the past 2
years and keeps an oil painting of his grandfather prominently displayed in
his office.

Production

The Delta Corporation manufactures 72 different consumer electronic products under contract with the major retail merchandizers like Penney,
Sears, K-Mart, and Wal-Mart. Delta is not a household name because its
products are resold under a variety of private label names used by Penney
and the other major retail chains. The products enjoy a good reputation
regarding their overall quality, performance, and price. Delta also produces
a variety of industrial products. These are highly sophisticated and are sold
directly to major contractors, like Boeing and McDonnell-Douglas, that are
involved in military, space, and high-technology projects.

Three manufacturing and distribution facilities are operated by Delta in
Baltimore, Philadelphia, and Detroit. All three plants were originally built
in the 1930s but only the Baltimore and Philadelphia facilities have been
modernized to current manufacturing standards. As result, the Detroit plant
has tended to be used for the manufacture of the less complex products and
as the warehouse for finished products of the other two plants.

Since 1974, Delta has also served as a major importer of a variety of
minerals and finished component parts from Brazil, Indonesia, South Korea,
and other third-world countries. The company utilizes approximately half of
these minerals and component parts for its own manufacturing operations.
The rest it sells on the open market to other major manufacturers.

Sales

Fortune magazine listed the Delta Corporation as one of the top 500 industrial corporations in 1984. During that year, Delta reported sales of $497
million, assets of $305 million, a net income after taxes of $18 million, and
shareholders' equity of $73 million. Sales have averaged an annual increase
of 6% for the past 10 years. Delta's resale of certain scarce minerals has been
particularly profitable in recent years. Industry analysts project escalating
profits in this area because the supply continues to decrease, demand

remains high, and the search for alternative sources for the minerals has proven unsuccessful.

Although foreign competitors have negatively affected Delta's sales to some degree during the past 4 years, James Dietrich is not overly worried because he believes that his company occupies a secure niche in the electronics market. In its consumer division, Delta is avoiding the cheap, low-priced end of the market where foreign competition is most severe and is also avoiding the expensive high-tech end of the market where manufacturing and advertising costs tend to be extremely high. Delta, instead, profits with its solid, good quality, middle-of-the-road consumer products. For its industrial division, Delta enjoys an excellent reputation among its large industrial customers because it has always delivered on time a product that was carefully inspected for quality. To a defense and space contractor, receiving a reliable electronic part on time is a critical variable in meeting production deadlines.

Human Resources

Delta employs 11,000 production, supervisory, and administrative staff in its three plants and corporate headquarters. There have been five attempts to unionize the production staff during the past 20 years. Each vote was heavily in favor of the company and against the union for reasons that have defied easy analysis. One of the reasons, undoubtedly, is the fact that there have never been any formal layoffs in the company's history. Although there have been periods of short work weeks and temporary pay reductions, no Delta employees have ever lost their jobs because of economic conditions. Thus, despite lower pay compared to unionized positions, Delta's employees seem to exhibit an allegiance to the company and a shared responsibility for continued growth.

Three years ago, Delta initiated a very extensive Employee Assistance Program, which offers individual counseling and referral for all employees and their immediate family members, as well as a professionally staffed 24-hour hot line for emergency situations. Six MSW-level social workers and one Ph.D. psychologist are employed directly by Delta for the EAP. The program coordinator, also a social worker, reports directly to the Director of Human Resources, who, in turn, is responsible to the Vice President for Employee Relations.

Present Situation

James Dietrich had just closed his office door and asked his secretary to hold all calls and interruptions. He needed to clear his mind and focus on two critical issues that were confronting his company at the present time. The issues seemed simple and uncomplicated when posed as questions to be answered:

1. Should we purchase two mining operations in Brazil and Indonesia?
2. Should we be doing anything differently to prepare for the company-wide vote on collective bargaining that will take place 6 months from now?

After an hour of scribbling cryptic notes on a yellow pad and long, detached glances out of the window of his penthouse office, James Dietrich sat back and reviewed the series of subquestions he had developed from these two general questions. Satisfied that this list could evoke both animated discussion and creative solutions, he directed his secretary to type and distribute it to his Vice Presidents and general counsel. Dietrich also invited this group to meet with him 1 week from today and to come prepared to answer these questions concretely and factually. Because the fate of Delta could depend on how these questions were decided strategically, the senior company officials and the general counsel were urged to seek the advice of all appropriate staff who reported to each of them. Table 17-1 contains a copy of this memo sent by James Dietrich.

TABLE 17-1 Memorandum

TO: Vice Presidents for Finance, Marketing, Corporate Relations and Planning, Employee Relations Skelling Group, International Operations Group, Knowles Group; and General Counsel
FROM: James Dietrich, CEO
RE: Strategy Meeting
DATE: January 14
    Please clear your calendars and plan to spend the entire morning of January 21 with me in an important strategy session. I would request that you come prepared to discuss concretely and factually the following questions:

(1)   If we acquire the Quito Mine in Brazil and the TDX Mining Corporation in Indonesia, what impact will that have on the general direction and present operations of Delta?
(2)   Is there a sufficient market to absorb the excess minerals we will be able to import? Can we increase our own production at home to utilize the additional minerals we will have available?
(3)   How will we finance the acquisitions? Issue bonds? Additional stock? Float a loan? Or generate and use cash reserves?
(4)   Perhaps we should consider again last year's proposal to close the Detroit plant and sell the assets as a means of financing this acquisition?
(5)   What would be the public reaction to Delta's closing a national domestic operation and expanding into two foreign countries?

(6)   Can our present Human Resources staff handle the closing of the Detroit operation and/or our thrust internationally?

(7)   How much do we know about the local labor force in Indonesia and Brazil? What about local customs and attitudes toward American ownership?

(8)   What is the time frame for net profits and what is the projected return on investment?

(9)   Should we postpone the foreign acquisition plan and, instead, modernize our Detroit plant facilities to increase our production capacity there?

(10) If we do pursue (9), then where should our marketing strategy change— toward the consumer or industrial markets?

(11) Within the general business community, is this a good time to expand or to hold down expenses and stay "liquid"?

(12) What about this latest threat from unionization? In the past the company did not engage in much active resistance: Should we follow that course or do things differently now?

(13) If we are forced to accept the union, what impact will that have on our costs and, therefore, our pricing structure?

(14) Do you believe there are any strategic connections between our expansion into mining and this threat from the union? If yes, where do we focus our planning resources: equally to both? Or should we put one of the two issues/decisions on "hold" for a while?

One final point: I would like you to discuss these matters with appropriate staff who are under your supervision in order to get as wide an opinion sample as feasible. Please be judicious in whom you share these details with, since we do not want to initiate any employee unrest or concern.

See you on the 21st. My secretary, Mrs. Donaldson, will follow up with further details and background materials.

CASE DISCUSSION

It does not appear to be unrealistic to assume that the program director of Delta's EAP would be asked for advice regarding these important questions affecting the company's near and long-term future. Indeed, there are some rather obvious issues that—depending on the strategy finally chosen— impact directly on the responsibilities and operations of the EAP social work staff. Undoubtedly, plant closings and international expansions will demand a concerted and coordinated effort on the part of the EAP staff as well as the entire Employee Relations Division. Speaking generally, if the social work staff were to act from a *preventive* mode of intervention, they would plan to have available a comprehensive range of counseling and referral services for the expected array of human problems that would surface as a result of the closing of the Detroit plant and the transfer of a cadre of managers and their families to foreign assignments. Even after the events took place, there would undoubtedly be a continuing need for the same type of counseling and referral services from a *rehabilitative* mode of intervention.

If these preventive and rehabilitative interventions were the *only* reactions the EAP staff could offer to the corporate planners, then invaluable opportunities for organizational development and for the enhancement of occupational social work services would have been forfeited. What would have been required in this case—and what is required in every occupational social work setting—is for the social work staff to be competent in, first of all, *understanding* the complex business issues under discussion; then *relating* them to each other as appropriate; and, finally, *proposing solutions* that are integrative and expansive rather than focused narrowly on only a limited range of operations. That process raises the social worker from the status of a mere functionary providing a professional service on the periphery of the company to the status of a professional manager who is informed and involved in the entire corporate enterprise. Stated otherwise: The EAP staff should know about the entire business, not simply the human resource component.

Given the focus of this chapter, we will not engage in a highly detailed discussion of what impact a more comprehensively trained EAP staff could have on corporate policy in the particular case of the Delta Corporation. Some general observations, however, are in order. Assuming for the purposes of this chapter that the EAP staff, in addition to their social work skills, had also attained *a beginning level of competence* in marketing, finance, accounting, operations management, human resource management, and strategic planning, then they could easily and confidently advance the following policy-related proposals:

- Complete a series of forecast scenarios concerning the range of possible reactions from the community to Delta's closing a plant in Detroit and expanding internationally.
- Analyze the cost in monetary and human terms of firing and retraining such a large number of people.
- Gather information on the various social institutions (e.g., family, economy, government, education, religion, social welfare) in Brazil and Indonesia in order to prevent relationship problems that might arise between native-born workers and foreign managers.
- Develop a projective systems analysis of three events occurring, first individually and then in conjunction with each other: The Detroit plant closes; the company transfers management staff to Brazil and Indonesia; the union wins a majority of votes.
- If any quantified methods of decision making are employed (e.g., decision trees, probability models), it will be essential to include the human

resource factors (outplacement, retraining, relocation, morale, health and welfare benefits, etc.) and organizational development factors (structure, role and responsibility, communication, etc.).

- Point out that there should be a *conscious* decision to either support or deviate from corporate history, culture, and values in the face of present realities and future opportunities.
- Base decisions about the company stance in regard to unionization more on facts and less on subjective emotions that tend to be rigidly pro- or anti-union.

The Delta Corporation case chronicles the activities of the in-house type of occupational social work practice. An obvious question can be posed: Can the social agency or the individual professional providing EAP services under a contractual agreement exert a similar influence upon corporate policy decision making? Generally speaking, this author believes that it is extremely difficult for nonemployees to be allowed such access and influence *unless an individual is hired as a consultant to management on a particular issue that needs a resolution*. Mainly because of the competitive marketplace, business enterprises are not in the habit of sharing proprietary information with most staff within the organization and certainly with only a very few (if any) outside the organization. This is an essential business ethic that social workers from the public and voluntary sectors should realize and respect with utmost care. But corporations do hire on an ad hoc basis individuals who possess technical expertise either because that expertise is not present within the corporation or because there is a need for a second opinion on some particularly complex issue. Limited access and carefully screened information typically are provided to such consultants so they can exert some level of influence over policy and program. Thus, the occupational social worker who is not an employee of the corporation but who is competent in the business functions described above can be heard in the corporate boardroom as an independent consultant. That new role—distinct from the role as EAP consultant—can be gained through assertive marketing and demonstration of one's nontraditional competencies within the business setting.

CONCLUSION

The purpose of this chapter is not to make social workers experts on marketing or finance or any other business function, but to broaden their perspective and increase their sensitivity to the entire continuum of corporate existence. This means being willing and able to absorb sets of unfamiliar data regarding, for example, production schedules and market forecasts, and then being willing and able to analyze long-term effects on the organization before judging short-term effects on a particular unit or program.

Perhaps a helpful analogy to this discussion can be drawn from the role fulfilled by a registered nurse in a residential child welfare agency. The nurse's medical role on a day-to-day basis is clearly defined and readily understood by most staff. This nurse has a different professional orientation than do the rest of the staff. Clearly, the nurse intervenes with children for different reasons and in different ways. That nurse can choose to remain in a circumscribed role as the medical specialist with a set of assigned duties or can choose to affect the entire child welfare organization as a technical expert. Before that nurse can exert any policy or program influence at all, however, the nurse must give evidence of a knowledge of all the issues that the social work staff are struggling with and, furthermore, that this knowledge is incorporated in some manner within the changes that are being proposed.

Several years ago the business community was stirred by Peters and Waterman's provocative work *In Search of Excellence* (1982). In this study, the authors tried to identify what corporate dynamics were operating when a company was functioning at an observably "excellent" level of performance. One of the dynamics discovered by Peters and Waterman is especially relevant to the central thrust of this chapter. *In Search of Excellence* posits as one of its findings that *people* in a corporate environment—customers as well as staff—are considered essential, and the excellent corporation nurtures them in a variety of ways. Social work as a profession is supposed to know something about people, something about organizational change, and something about making organizations responsive to the needs and wants of people. Social workers have the unique opportunity for sharing their knowledge, skills, and values with their colleagues throughout the private sector of society. All that is needed is a willingness on the social work side to learn some new competencies and on the corporate side to listen to some new perspectives. Then the search for excellence can be a mutual search with mutual rewards.

REFERENCES

Backer, M., & Jacobson, L. E. (1964). *Cost accounting: A managerial approach*. New York: McGraw-Hill.

Burud, S., Aschbacker, P., & McCroskey, J. (1984). *Employer-supported child care: Investing in human resources*. Boston: Auburn House.

Carrell, M. R., & Kuzmits, F. E. (1982). *Personnel: Management of human resources*. Columbus, OH: Merrill.

Chruden, H. J., & Sherman, A. W. (1976). *Personnel management* (5th ed.). Cincinnati, OH: Southwest.

Dessler, G. (1973). *Management Fundamentals: A framework* (2nd ed.). Reston, VA: Reston.

EAPs/Wellness programs: Separate but equal. (1984). *Employee Benefits Plan Review, 39,* 126–127.

Foegen, J. H. (1984) Let's develop employee assistance programs to teach reading and writing. *Personnel Journal, 63,* 50–56.

Gist, R. R. (1974). *Marketing and society.* Hinsdale, IL: Dryden.

Gray, J., & Johnson, K. S. (1973). *Accounting and management action.* New York: McGraw-Hill.

Gupta, S. K., & Cozzolino, J. M. (1979). *Fundamentals of operations research for management.* San Francisco: Holden-Day.

Hartley, R. V. (1975). *Operations research: A managerial emphasis.* Pacific Palisades, CA: Goodyear.

Hussey, D. E. (1979). *Introducing corporate planning (2nd ed.).* Oxford, England: Pergamon.

Johnson, A. (1984). Relocation: Getting more for the dollars you spend. *Personnel Administrator, 29,* 29–32+.

Johnson, R. W. (1971). *Financial Management* (4th ed.). Boston: Allyn & Bacon.

Jones, R. G., & Dudley, D. (1978). *Essentials of finance.* Englewood Cliffs, NJ: Prentice-Hall.

Kastiel, D. (1984). Work and family seminars help parents cope. *Business Insurance, 18,* 26–30.

Kepler, J., Keppler, P., Garther, O., & Garther, M (1983). *Americans abroad: A handbook for living and working abroad.* New York: Praeger.

Levitt, T. (1974). *Marketing for business growth.* New York: McGraw-Hill.

Lipson, H. A., & Darling, J. R. (1974). *Marketing fundamentals: Text and cases.* New York: Wiley.

Masi, D. A. (1982). *Human services in industry.* Lexington, MA: Lexington.

Mathis, R., & Jacobson, J. (1976). *Personnel: Contemporary perspective and applications.* St. Paul, MN: West.

McClellan, K. (1985). The changing nature of EAP practice. *Personnel Administrator, 30,* 29–30+.

Naylor, T. (1979). *Corporate planning models.* Reading, MA: Addison-Wesley.

Naylor, T. (ed.), (1982). *Corporate strategy.* New York: North-Holland.

Ozawa, M. (1980). Development of social services in industry: Why and how? *Social Work, 25,* 464–470.

Peters, T. J., & Waterman, R. H. (1982). *In search of excellence.* New York: Harper & Row.

Riggs, J. L., & Inoue, M.AS. (1975). *Introduction to operations research and management science.* New York: McGraw-Hill.

Schumacher, A. (1985). Employee assistance: How to help victims of domestic violence. *Personnel Journal, 64,* 102+.

Segal, S. (1984). The working parent dilemma. *Personnel Journal, 63,* 50–56.

Spiro, H. (1977). *Finance for the nonfinancial manager.* New York: Wiley.

Stanton, W. J. (1975). *Fundamentals of marketing* (4th ed.). New York: McGraw-Hill.

Troy, K. (1986). *Meeting human needs: Corporate programs and partnership.* New York: The Conference Board.

V The Role of Industry in the Community

18 Services to Customers: Customer Assistance Programs

E. Gregory de Silva

It is evident from the preceding chapters that social work in the workplace encompasses a wide range of professional activity while, at the same time, requiring much in the way of social work knowledge and skill. However, in this developing field of practice there appears to be an intensive preoccupation with developing and implementing services to employees through Employee Assistance Programs. This focus largely excludes other very important segments of the population with whom industry interacts. It has to be remembered that employees are only one segment of that population.

A broader definition of occupational social work envisions it as the application of social work knowledge and skill in responding to the personal, organizational, and community needs and problems of organizational employees, customers, and relevant publics in their interactions with organizations. A major component of this definition is its identification of three populations with whom organizations interface—employees, customers, and the local community. It is true that, often, a representative of one of these groups belongs to another group as well. However, the roles they play and the corresponding services they need differ by virtue of the unique role an individual plays as an employee, a customer, or a member of the general public or community.

The focus of this chapter is on one group that tends to be neglected by social workers—*customers*. Who are customers? The word *customer* poses a problem because it is closely related and very similar to the word *consumer*. The distinction between these two words appears to be a subtle one. Webster defines *customer* as "one that purchases some commodity or service systematically or frequently" (Webster, 1976, p. 559). A *consumer*, on the other hand, is defined as "one who consumes, one that utilizes economic goods" (Webster, 1976, p. 490). There appears to be an element of purchasing inherent in the use of the word *customer*, whereas there appears to be a predominance of the elements of utilization and consumption inherent in the word *consumer*. However, for our purposes here, we use both words interchangeably.

What needs to be acknowledged is that there is a large population of customers who are in need of services as a result of their interaction with industry. Consequently, a need for Customer Assistance Programs (CAPs) is fast emerging—a need comparatively unknown to and unheeded by social workers.

WHY SERVICES TO CUSTOMERS?

Customers are an important segment of the population. If there were no customers, for whom would employees in the world of work manufacture goods or provide services? Employees and customers depend on each other. Employees and customers are often the same human beings.

Each of us assumes a customer role with many businesses or organizations countless times in our lives. Just to name a few of these, we are customers of banks, utility companies, department stores, insurance companies, real estate companies, and funeral homes.

The customer–provider relationship is at times smooth and at other times problematic. For reasons of profit, public relations, and survival, it is essential for the provider to keep the customer satisfied. There is often the risk that the customer can take business elsewhere. However, at times, the customer does not have that option, for instance, when the utility service one uses is predetermined by the location of one's residence. Either way, the quality of the customer–provider relationship determines whether special services are needed.

Several industrial organizations have begun to respond to special needs of customers by developing a wide range of services unique to their businesses. They are not necessarily employing professional social workers, although several of the functions performed fall legitimately within the purview of social work. If social workers are to ensure that they are not excluded from these new developments, they need to learn of the emerging issues in the interactions of customers with industry. They also need to obtain the necessary educational preparation to work in this specialized field.

AN OVERVIEW OF EXISTING CUSTOMER ASSISTANCE PROGRAMS

Three major industries that provide services to customers illustrate the potential that customer assistance programs have for addressing human needs. An examination of each industry, individually, further documents the growth of CAPs and the need for their inclusion as legitimate sites for social work practice. These industries include utilities, banks, and funeral homes.

CAPs in Utility Companies

In recent years utility companies have been adopting new approaches in dealing with their customers. With the advent of the energy crisis, the escalating costs of energy, and new energy regulations, there has also been a corresponding increase in the number of consumers with delinquency problems. This has resulted in an increase in bad-debt write-offs for utility companies.

The response of some utility companies across the country to these issues has been significant. Operating under the principle of corporate social responsibility, several utility companies have established varying models of customer assistance programs. Space permits mention of only a few of the many utility companies that have adopted a human service approach in responding to the needs of their customers.

At the New York State Electric and Gas Corporation (NYSEG) in Binghamton, New York, a consumer affairs program was established in 1977 with the appointment of its first consumer representative. Since then seven more have been employed—all from outside the company. The major criterion for employment was a minimum of 5 years previous social work experience. The functions performed by these consumer representatives provide a model for service delivery and focus on crisis intervention, liaison with social agencies, consumer education, and employee training. Consumer representatives have also been responsible for developing several new programs in response to the expressed needs of consumers. Seniors Lending a Hand was one such program, established as a pilot project to demonstrate the feasibility of conducting a weatherization program for senior citizens and implemented with the assistance of other senior citizens (New York State Electric and Gas Company, 1984).

Pennsylvania Power and Light Company in Allentown, Pennsylvania, has had a special customer assistance program entitled CARES since October 1980. CARES is an acronym for the Customer Assistance and Referral Service. It began as a pilot project with a staff consisting of a coordinator and three representatives. The staff has increased since then with the addition of three more CARES representatives. The major functions performed by these representatives are customer-service-focused and include budget counseling and home visits. "This type of assistance has two immediate benefits. . . . It can help avoid termination of customers' electric service and obtain revenue to which the company is entitled" (Hatzai, 1984, p. 2).

In Milwaukee, Wisconsin, the Good Neighbor Energy Program was developed in the early 1980s by Wisconsin Electric Power Company and its subsidiary, Wisconsin Natural Gas Company. The primary purpose of this program "is to address customer needs in areas such as bill payment, conservation and energy information. . . . The Good Neighbor Energy Program is an umbrella program which presently emcompasses five special services" (Wisconsin Electric, 1984, pp. 7–8) for special groups such as the elderly and the handicapped. These programs operate under the supervision of an assistant vice president and director of consumer affairs. The direct services to consumers are provided by 20 full-time energy advisors.

The Community Representative division at the Northern States Power Company in St. Paul, Minnesota, was established in 1974. The fundamental mission of this division has been to assist all hardship customers in obtaining and retaining utility services by going beyond the normal credit and collection procedures. The customer representative "insures that the Customer Business Office is dealing fairly and efficiently with all the customers they handle . . . without compromising the trust placed on them by the customers or the company. Empathy, personalized humanistic attention and confidentiality are emphasized in all contacts with customers" (Northern States Power Company, 1983, p. 1). This program is administered by an Administrator and eight community representatives.

The Portland General Electric Company began its consumer Assistance Services Program in 1977 with services to the elderly. Since then, it has extended its services to the handicapped, the mentally ill, and low-income groups. These services are staffed by a manager and six consumer representatives.

Several other utility companies have developed a wide variety of programs with a major focus on assisting customers who are experiencing crises in paying their utility bills. The goal of these programs is avoiding a disconnection of utility service. Brief assessment and referral to community agencies are the approaches they use to deal with their customers' problems. Special services to the elderly are also a major characteristic of these programs. Some companies, for example Peoples Natural Gas Company (PNGCO) in Pittsburgh, have established consumer advisory boards to function as liaisons between the company and consumers. Other companies have sponsored hardship funds of one type or another to assist utility customers to pay their bills. Such funds are often administered by third-party social service organizations (for example, Project Helping Hand at Jersey Central Power and Light Company in New Jersey).

In developing CAPs, the major focus has to be on the relationship between the customer and the company. Services to be developed can have both preventive and remedial objectives. The provision of services can ensure the preservation and continuation of a good relationship. Consumer advisory boards and consumer education are examples of the preventive approach. Prolonged inability to pay utility bills and the interruption of utility services in particular can contribute to an adversarial relationship between the two parties. The introduction of a customer representative to function as an intermediary can assist in easing the conflict by providing specific services.

Key contributions that may be provided by a social worker in a utility company include:

1. Interviewing customers who are threatened with discontinuation for nonpayment of utility bills, assessing the source of difficulty, and assisting the customer in initiating the steps needed to regain financial stability.
2. Assisting customers with budget, financial, and personal counseling and referring to appropriate community agencies, if necessary.
3. Conducting follow-up activities to determine the status of customer referrals to social agencies.
4. Knowledge about energy legislation, federal and state programs, the internal resources of the company, and the external resources of the community.
5. Expertise on local community issues and ability to interpret the company's viewpoint on these issues.
6. Assessing the needs of consumers and keeping company management informed of these needs, recommending special programs when necessary.
7. Promoting a high level of sensitivity to an understanding of customer concerns and needs among company employees.
8. Developing and conducting training for customer service employees in the utility company.
9. Preparation to function as advocate for the customer.
10. Maintaining contact with special consumer groups, for example, senior citizens, through social agencies representing them, and developing meaningful working relationships with these agencies.

Although CAPs do vary from one utility company to another, the social service element in most of these programs cannot be ignored. What is regrettable is that, except for one company (NYSEG), the recognition of the need to employ social service personnel is minimal. In examining the nature and function of several utility companies that have established CAPs, it is apparent that preference is given to personnel who have worked in their traditional customer relations departments in staffing the CAPs. The emphasis in customer relations has been more fiscal, public-relations oriented, and focused on portraying a good public image for the company. The stress on customer benefit and interest is minimal. Hence, for staff appointments to CAPs, educational background and social work knowledge and experience have not been the major criteria for selection.

Most social workers who have explored employment in industry will agree that industry still has some negative and outdated notions of social work. Hence it is not surprising that in utility companies knowledge of business and customer relations experience receives more preference than the helping skills needed to function in CAPs.

The utility industry is expanding its programs of customer assistance in response to the pressure of current federal legislation on behalf of utility consumers. However, it is also evident that the utility industry does not see a role for social work in CAPs. Social workers who are interested in working in the utility arena need to be more aggressive in marketing their services. Social workers, equipped with specialized knowledge and skill, as discussed here, need to explore the need for CAPs in utility companies where such programs do not exist and need to lobby for their establishment. As CAPs expand and new positions are advertised, social workers need to be alert to their ability to function in these programs. Knowledge of federal regulations related to utilities and an understanding of rights of utility customers are major factors in negotiating for the establishment of and employment in CAPs. It is accurate to state that social workers have been just as ignorant of the potential scope of their services in the utility industry as utility companies have failed to recognize the relevance of social work to CAPs.

CAPs in Banks

Banks serve customers in a variety of ways. They may hold customers money in trust, make investments on their behalf, and give loans. Often the initial fiscal relationship develops into the bank's assumption of roles beyond that of taking care of customers' finances. An elderly trust customer's health may fail and she may be unable to continue to live at home. The bank, as her only surviving contact, may find itself in the role of having to explore alternative living arrangements for this client. Similarly, the sudden death of parents who had already set up a trust with a bank for their young children may place that bank in the role of guardian. Such a role may involve the bank in a host of activities that are far from fiscal. This type of nonfiscal activity is increasing and is daily becoming more evident in the interaction of banks with trust and loan customers, including home mortgage customers.

The role of social work in the trust department of a bank has been demonstrated at three banks in Pittsburgh from 1978 to 1980. Two of these three banks decided at the completion of this demonstration project to create positions of social service specialists and employed two master's-level social workers. Meanwhile, quite independently, a similar development had taken place in St. Louis, Missouri in March 1973, when a professionally trained social worker was employed by a bank there (Tyson, 1980). Since then, two more social workers have begun working for trust departments in banks in Portland, Oregon, and Boston, Massachusetts, thus making a total of five banks with social workers in their trust departments. It is noteworthy that all five social workers have master's degrees in social work.

The model of service delivery adopted by these CAPs is to employ a professional social worker as an on-site employee or off-site consultant to function as a resource person to trust officers as well as to develop and provide needed services to trust customers. According to one bank trust social worker:

> There are advantages to both options. Being on staff allows him or her to look at files, project costs, explain statements to clients and be part of the confidentiality that clients expect from a trust department. . . . The task of an outside consultant is simplified and limited to the task at hand for a particular client, i.e., an evaluation, periodic institutional or home visit, meeting with family, assessment of medical bills, a discharge from the hospital and so on. The consultant charges by the hour for service and has more freedom to pick and choose tasks. (Goldsmith, 1983, p. 23)

The need for a social worker in the trust department arises out of customer need. Although the vast majority of trust customers can handle their accounts routinely, there are many who have lost all their relatives and close friends or who have been declared senile or incompetent. People in this latter category need more help than the trust officers can customarily give.

> The problem presented by these groups of human beings, technically, are not the business of the bank and its trust officers. Their job is to administer the trust competently so that the beneficiary receives a satisfactory return on the investment involved and to pay the client's bills in cases where that is also the bank's obligation.
>
> But trust officers are human beings too. They know these problems exist. Yet, they lack the time, the expertise and the experience in dealing with elderly people to handle the problem satisfactorily. (Norris, 1974, p. 48)

In examining the roles and functions performed by these social workers, it is evident that these banks have attempted to make their services more personalized and customer-oriented and have embarked upon a program of creative social services in their trust departments. On the basis of their experience as well as our own experience in assisting banks in Pittsburgh to set up these programs, it is possible to identify a range of functions that a social worker in a trust department may perform. They include:

1. Assessing the social, psychological, and health status and needs of trust customers and referring them to community agencies, if necessary.

2. Providing short-term counseling, when so indicated, to trust customers.

3. Arranging for alternate living arrangements for trust customers when deteriorating health or a change in life circumstances warrants such a move.

4. Making home visits when necessary and monitoring the home health care provided to trust customers by contracting agencies and thereby ensuring the reasonable well-being and comfort of these customers.

5. Functioning as liaison between customers and their trust officers by interpreting (when requested) their accounts to customers to enable them to understand legal and financial matters as well as investments and expenditures made on their behalf by the bank.

6. Exploring alternative funding resources for trust customers whose funds have been exhausted or are diminishing.

7. Monitoring the care provided to trust customers in nursing homes, hospitals, and other retirement facilities to ensure that they receive the quality care for which they are paying and to which they are entitled.

8. Monitoring the adequacy of whatever services have been arranged for with referral agencies.

9. Being knowledgeable about public and private benefit programs, for example, Medicare and Medicaid, as well as resources in the community that are needed by trust customers.

10. Providing consultation to trust officers on concerns of the customers and their families as well as providing information about community resources.

11. Functioning as advocate for trust customers with their banks, families, and community agencies.

Social workers in trust departments serve varying groups of customers. While the greater majority are elderly customers, other groups served include the mentally retarded, the mentally disabled, wards of the court, and minors.

There are benefits to a bank when it uses the services of a social worker.

Not only does the provision for professional social services in business and finance assure quality control and add a human touch to people in need of personal attention, but the facts point to an important marketing advantage. Families of older people and the seniors themselves are very enthusiastic about having a social worker involved. Having an expert in geriatric care on a financial management team is a great comfort and convenience to all. (Goldsmith, 1981, p. 53)

Other benefits include "freeing trust administrators from their time consuming tasks of monitoring services for elderly clients and providing an edge in selling trust services to attorneys as well as overall promotion of good public relations" (Carcione, 1985, p. 3).

Besides serving trust customers, attempts have also been made to serve mortgage customers. In Pittsburgh, a social work intern placed in a savings and loan bank counseled customers who were experiencing difficulty keeping up with their home mortgage payments. Besides loss of jobs due to increasing unemployment in the area, it was discovered that other factors, notably marital conflict, were contributing to customer delinquency. There have been recent reports that services to mortgage customers are being developed elsewhere, too.

The Wall Street Journal recently reported the efforts of the mortgage insurance industry to stave off foreclosures by providing counseling to customers who were about to lose their homes.

> Because lenders and insurers increasingly agree that everybody loses when people lose their houses, many troubled homemakers are getting extra help to stave off foreclosures. The help comes in the form of free financial counseling, partial repayment loans and re-structured or re-finance loans. . . . The new aid programs are starting to pay off. (Lubin, 1986, p. 31)

While the counseling referred to here may not necessarily be provided by social workers, the potential for CAPs utilizing social workers is evident.

CAPs in Funeral Homes

In a yet-limited though somewhat surprising way, a similar development is taking place in the funeral industry. Here customers are being identified as a group needing specialized services from social workers. There was a time when "death was as natural as birth and funerals were never morbid or scary. But today, for many people dying, funerals and mourning can be frightening and unbearably painful" (Abel, 1984, p. 1). Because of changes in modern society, the directors of funeral homes are being called upon to provide more services than simply arranging for the funeral.

A few farsighted professionals have pioneered the development of social services in funeral homes. For example, two professional social workers in Portland, Oregon work as bereavement counselors for two funeral establishments, each of which owns several funeral homes. One of them assisted 225 families in a 9-month period. Her approach is to contact the families who have used the services of the funeral company, 2 to 4 weeks after the death, by either writing or phoning to see how the family is doing. An offer is made at this time to send educational materials on grief and bereavement as well as to offer information about related community resources. Where there is evidence of a high degree of stress, such as in loss of a parent, spouse, or child, the counselor makes a home visit. The purpose of the home visit is to give individuals and families an opportunity to express and explore their feelings of grief and assess the need for additional services.

Another bereavement counselor works for a funeral home in Tucson, Arizona. She prefers to wait a few months after the funeral to offer assistance. Her procedure is to send the bereaved a sympathy note and offer of help if there is need. Not every funeral home customer is in need of counseling. Counseling for those who do may involve just one or two sessions or may continue for months (Abel, 1984).

On the basis of the limited information available on the range of functions these bereavement counselors perform, the following activities are suggested for social workers in a funeral home:

1. Providing short-term counseling to individuals and families who have difficulty in coping with the death of a loved one, if and when they are receptive to such counseling.
2. Making home visits, if so indicated, to bereaved individuals and families for the purpose of providing emotional support and ensuring their comfort and adjustment to the loss.
3. Assisting with funeral and burial arrangements, if necessary.
4. Providing feedback to funeral directors regarding questions or concerns customers may have about the services provided by the funeral home.
5. Educating bereaved individuals and families about the normal grief process and the common feelings associated with it.
6. Developing and promoting death- and grief-education materials for the general public.
7. Providing bereaved individuals and families with educational materials on grief and bereavement related to their specific loss, such as death of a child, widowhood, or suicide.
8. Providing information about community resources in reference to financial problems, home care, and alternative living arrangements.
9. Providing informal education, support, and training to funeral home staff.
10. Engaging in public speaking to lay and professional groups to provide education on death and the grieving process.
11. Developing and coordinating support groups to meet the needs of special bereaved groups (e.g., widows, widowers, the elderly, and families of violent-death victims).

It is quite evident from the experiences of these bereavement counselors that a need exists for the inclusion of social services in the range of services provided by funeral directors. However, more work is indicated for social workers if more funeral directors in this country are to come to accept this need.

PRACTICE IN CUSTOMER ASSISTANCE PROGRAMS

While the untapped potential for customer service exists in a wide range of businesses, a good deal is already known about the actual activities of CAP workers in the industries and programs already described. A survey conducted by researchers at the University of Pittsburgh on individuals working in CAPs provides important information on the nature of their practice. The major objective of this study was to obtain information regarding the functions performed by these service providers, their knowledge and skill base, and their recommendations regarding the preparation desirable for new entrants into these industries.

Respondents rated consumer education as their most frequently performed function. In the utility industry, in particular, consumer education has implications for both the consumer and the utility company. Consumers need to be made aware of the variety of energy assistance programs available from federal, state, and local sources for payment of their utility bills as well as for energy conservation. Utility companies also need to educate their customers regarding their policies, procedures, and eligibility criteria pertaining to bill payments and unique programs for special population groups.

Assisting with bills was identified as the next most frequently performed function. Customers of trust departments, utility companies, and funeral homes are all clients who may need assistance in the payment of their bills. Trust customers, especially the elderly, while having financial resources, often need help in money management. Utility customers, on the other hand, may be delinquent in their payments due to lack of financial resources. They need assistance with their bills as well as help in exploring community resources and seeking company concessions, if any, in order to void disconnection of utility services. The funeral home customer may need this form of assistance on the death of a spouse or other significant family member, when the emotional crisis may paralyze the client from taking care of finances.

Short-term counseling ranked third in regard to frequency of use. Considering that the greater majority of CAP personnel participating in the study did not have a counseling background, it is significant that short-term counseling received this high a ranking. It may be that in the performance of their functions, CAP personnel are confronted with their clients' needs for some type of counseling. Irrespective of the ability to counsel on the part of CAP personnel, the counseling function is unavoidable due to the needs of customers.

Other functions performed by respondents were staff education, liaison, and referral. Less frequently performed functions were program development, budget counseling, interpreting regulations, and monitoring. However, these functions are indicative of the broad range of activities in a CAP. With the expansion of these programs and the employment of more personnel, it can be anticipated that these functions will receive more emphasis.

The study also attempted to explore the social work skills that CAP personnel are currently utilizing. These skills were broadly classified as interpersonal, administration, community–organization, and research skills.

The most frequently used interpersonal skills were communication and information giving. Considering that consumer education and assisting with bills had been already identified as the most frequently performed functions, the high ranking for these two skills seems logical. Communication and information giving are the more relevant skills for the performance of these two functions. Referral was rated as the next most frequently used skill. At the current level of functioning of CAPs, referral to other community resources is a major activity. Interviewing is another skill basic to all other functions performed in CAPs. Short-term counseling skills also received a high rating. Other skills frequently used by CAP personnel are monitoring, eligibility determination, and budget counseling. Less frequently used skills are long-term counseling and psychosocial assessment.

Administration skills most frequently used by CAP personnel are public relations, marketing, writing, public speaking, and policy development. It would appear that these skills would be more relevant in the development and implementation of CAPs through their initial stages. The important inference here is that individuals employed in CAPs need a wide range of administration skills in addition to clinical skills.

A variety of community–organization skills are also required to function adequately in CAPs. In the study the most frequently used community-organization skills cited included working with community groups and agencies, performing mediator functions, and advocating for customers. Program development and developing community resources are other community–organization skills frequently performed by CAP personnel. Whether the host setting is a bank, a utility company, or a funeral home, these skills emphasize the linkage activities between the host agency and the community that need to be performed on behalf of the CAP client.

Research skills identified by respondents as most frequently used and most relevant to the functioning of CAPs are surveying special customer groups and program evaluation. CAPs are currently emphasizing the needs of special populations such as the elderly; hence the importance of the ability to do surveys with a view to deriving information that can contribute to program development. Program evaluation is also an important and frequently used skill, since companies are constantly needing evidence that these new programs are cost effective. Program evaluation in CAPs ensures accountability to the company and provides clues as well for program modification.

CAP personnel depend upon both theoretical and practice knowledge to perform their functions. In theoretical knowledge, human behavior is rated as being the most helpful. Administration–organization theory and counseling theory are the next most helpful areas of knowledge. Legal information, business, and economics are other knowledge areas identified as being helpful.

Considering the essential component of relating to people inherent in CAP functions, knowledge of human behavior is basic and indispensable. Hence, the high ranking of its helpfulness is not surprising. Counseling also continues to receive recognition consistently in regard to function, skill, and theoretical knowledge.

In exploring the helpfulness of practice skill knowledge, communication skills received the highest ranking as an area of practice skill most helpful to CAP personnel. But communication theory received a much lower ranking as a helpful area of theoretical knowledge. Some speculation is possible to explain this discrepancy. Considering the educational background of the respondents, there may be a notion that communication skills are primarily derived from ongoing practice rather than from theory. Because the majority of respondents to the survey were nonprofessionals, there could have been some skepticism in regard to the need for theoretical knowledge to enrich and refine previous practice skills.

The discussion up to now has focused on what CAP personnel are really doing. A final question sought respondents' recommendations for additional areas of knowledge important to social workers planning to work in CAPs. In regard to classroom courses, business and economics received the highest ranking. Human behavior received the next highest ranking, followed by communication theory and counseling theory.

CAP personnel identified several areas of practice knowledge as important for social workers entering CAP positions. These areas include public relations, knowledge of community resources, teaching skills, legal knowledge related to the particular industry, and learning how to balance the production needs of the company with the human service needs of the customer. These are all very important experiences for the new learner and should be included in the field experience.

Counseling and communication skills received the high emphasis they had recieved earlier from CAP personnel. Prior work experience was identified as an important component in the preparation of social workers for CAPs. Prior work experience, in whatever capacity, is associated with exposure to the nature and demands of the workplace as well as with some acquaintance with the world of corporations and unions.

In regard to other observations and recommendations about requirements for working in CAPs, those currently working in these programs highlighted a variety of personal qualities and skills. Of high importance were the ability to relate to the fiscal needs of clients and the ability to be free of prejudice.

They also emphasized the abilty to be aware of how social work goals can contribute to business goals. Previous work experience in business and social agency settings was identified as yet another advantage.

Though most CAP personnel in the Pittsburgh survey were not formally trained to be helping professionals, they clearly were able to identify the knowledge and skill base their jobs require as well as the inherent professional components of those jobs. Knowledge of human behavior as well as counseling and communication skills consistently recieved high emphasis.

CUSTOMER ASSISTANCE AND
THE SOCIAL WORK CURRICULUM

Any social work curriculum to prepare students for work in CAPs needs to be developed in the context of the M.S.W. degree and within a special curriculum for practice in the workplace. Many schools of social work are currently developing industrial social work curricula. For students desiring practice in CAPs, additional courses in consumer behavior and customer relations are highly recommended and are available in schools of business. However, it is important to exercise caution in the selection of these courses. Business professionals define consumer behavior as "acts, processes, and social relationships exhibited by individuals, groups and organizations in the obtainment, use of and consequent experience with products, services and other resources" (Bagozzi & Zaltman, 1975). Often, marketing of products receives more emphasis than services in business school courses. Ideally, collaboration between faculty of schools of social work and business is needed to develop consumer-oriented courses that are more relevant to the service needs of customers. Such course content could be generic in that it would be applicable to customer service in a wide range of industries where CAPs are feasible.

Another area of course content relevant to CAPs is the knowledge of laws and regulatory practices relevant to different industries. Although our respondents gave a low ranking for this knowledge area, social workers without exposure to the federal, state, and local regulations pertaining, for example, to a utility company would have difficulty providing consumers with needed information or performing an advocacy role. Similar knowledge related to the banking and funeral industries is also compulsory for social workers working in those settings. For social workers planning to work in trust departments, a course on trusts and estates, available in most schools of law, is essential.

Most of the other course knowledge required by CAP social workers is already available in the regular M.S.W. curriculum or the special courses prescribed for industrial social work students. Depending on the particular setting (e.g., utility company, bank, or funeral home), students need to select courses appropriately. A course on death and dying is highly relevant for bereavement counselors. Likewise, a short-term treatment course is highly desirable for CAP social workers, just as it is for EAP social workers.

With regard to the field curriculum, securing field placements in companies that already have customer service programs and encouraging companies without CAPs to undertake such programs on a pilot-project basis, utilizing M.S.W. students, appear to be effective approaches. The practice skills currently being used and recommended by the Pittsburgh survey respondents merit highlighting. Overall, most of them are basically used by social workers. Performing these functions with a social work focus may enhance the quality as well as the effectiveness of practice. Communicating, counseling, and utilizing administration and organization skills that received high rankings are all within the ability of social work graduates. Our experience in placing students in both employee and customer service programs warrants the assumptions presented here. The business world, in spite of initial reluctance and caution, has been pleasantly surprised and impressed that social work interns can perform successfully in the workplace.

CONCLUSION

The review of the Pittsburgh survey findings as well as the growing scope and functions of customer assistance programs in the utility, banking, and funeral industries should provide a fair indication that there is yet another population group, besides employees, that merits the attention of social workers.

Identifying the needs of customers and of relevant industries as they relate to each other and developing CAPs to meet those needs are new opportunities and challenges to the social work profession. Lou Harris and Associates, in a recent survey, reported:

> The consumer movement in the United States is thriving and has vast potential for growth. The Consumer Federation of America indicated, in a recent study, that 45% of active consumer groups across the country with more than two million members have utility issues as their top advocacy priority. . . . In the present activist environment, many utilities have acted aggressively to determine consumer concerns. (American Gas Association, 1984, p. 1)

The other two industries mentioned in this chapter have similar consumer concerns.

Industrial social workers could be of service both to consumers and consumer-oriented industries in responding to these concerns. But unless social work recognizes customers as potential clients and aggressively offers its expertise to customer-oriented industries, social work may find itself overtaken by other disciplines. Educators and practitioners in occupational social work need to assume the responsibility to prevent that from happening.

REFERENCES

Abel, B. (1984, August 11). She's expert at helping the bereaved cope with pain of death in the family. *Tucson Citizen Magazine*, 1–2.

American Gas Association. (1984). *A summary of a survey on face-to-face consumer participation programs* (rptej091884). Arlington, VA: Consumer Affairs Committee.

Bagozzi, R., & Zaltman, G. (1975). *A structural analysis of the sociology of consumption*. Paper presented at the American Sociological Meetings, San Francisco, CA.

Carcione, S. G. (1985, February). A trust department social worker—The advantages. *Resources*, American Bank Marketing Association Newsletter, 3.

Goldsmith, S. A. (1983, August). Trust clients and the social worker: A holistic approach. *Trusts & Estates*, 41–42.

Goldsmith, S. A. (1981, October). A social worker gets the job done. *Trusts & Estates*, 52–53.

Hatzai, S. (1981, March). CARES program offers help when hardship causes customers' bill-paying problems. *PA Power and Light Reporter*, 9–11.

Lubin, J. S. (1986, February 18). Home mortgage holders get counseling. *The Wall Street Journal*, 31.

New York State Electric and Gas Company .(1984). *Consumer affairs annual report*. Binghamton, NY: Consumer Affairs Department.

Norris, A. (1974, February). Trained social worker assumes "care" burden from trust officers. *Mid Continent Banker*, 47–49.

Northern States Power Company. (1983). *Procedure manual for community representatives*. St. Paul, MN: Ruiz.

Tyson, D. O. (1980, October). Social workers in three trust departments look after confined beneficiaries. *American Banker*, 7–9.

Webster Third International Dictionary of the English Language. (1976). Springfield, MA: Merriam.

Wisconsin Electric Power Company. (1984). *To be of service*. Milwaukee, WI: Author.

19 Influencing Corporate Philanthropy

Eleanor L. Brilliant
Kimberlee A. Rice

In the past decade the amount of corporate philanthropy in the United States has more than doubled, rising from $1.174 billion in 1973 to an estimated $3.100 billion in 1983. This growth in contributed dollars was accompanied by the development within the corporate world of new centers of responsibility for the allocation of these resources and by the emergence of an increasingly identifiable group of corporate contribution professionals. Surprisingly, social workers have paid relatively little attention to the rise of this new group of professionals charged with responsibilities of great significance to our profession and to the potential for influencing the choices they make in fund allocations. Indeed, social welfare causes may continue to receive a decreasing share of charitable contributions unless we pay more attention to the corporate dollar, because competition for private funds is increasing in a climate of government cutbacks (Salamon, 1984).

The underlying thesis of this chapter is that social workers need to look carefully at the phenomenon of corporate support—both at the end product (the amounts that are distributed) as well as the process by which decisions are made. Despite the pronouncements of the Reagan administration about private-sector initiatives, there is considerable room for growth in the total amount of corporate contributions. Questions have also been raised about the manner in which corporate funds are allocated. These questions are surfacing widely, along with a renewed interest in the relationship between voluntarism and philanthropic activities. It therefore seems timely to remove the veil of mystery that surrounds the corporate contributions function.

This is a revised version of a paper first presented at the NASW Occupational Social Work Conference, Boston, May 31, 1985 under the title, "Social Work's New Constituency: Influencing Corporate Philanthropy." The authors wish to thank Aileen Hart and Alex Plinio for their helpful comments on the paper.

In our discussion we explore the institutional role of philanthropy and community relations within the corporation as well as the specific role of the corporate contributions staff. We consider the variety of different structures used for carrying out corporate philanthropic activities and the impact that organizational cultures have on philanthropic functions. Social workers' reluctance to be involved with corporate philanthropy will also be addressed directly. Finally, we argue that there are significant possibilities for influencing corporate decisions about community services and that social workers should pursue these possibilities in line with their commitment to occupational social work (National Association of Social Workers, 1984).

CORPORATE SOCIAL RESPONSIBILITY AND CORPORATE GIVING

Corporate philanthropic activity exists within the broad framework of corporate social responsibility and is also an aspect of the external relations of the corporation with all its publics or constituencies. Moreover, there is no one monolithic view of the philanthropic function, just as there is no universally accepted definition of the more general notion of corporate social responsibility.

In its broadest meaning, corporate social responsibility includes the social effects of all activities that a company undertakes, or the impact that any corporate activity has on quality of life in the community and society.[1] The impact of these activities is delineated in relation to the many constituencies with which a corporation interacts: consumers, stockholders, employees, governments, other businesses, and local community groups. Among the policies that fall under the corporate social responsibility rubric, therefore, are affirmative action, purchasing policies, human resource activities and workers' benefits, investments, corporate philanthropy, and consideration of economic externalities or environmental effects from company activities such as waste disposal. We do not deny the importance of this broader

[1]There is considerable controversy about this subject, ranging from the most restrictive view point expressed by Milton Friedman ("The Social Responsibility of Business Is to Increase Profits," *New York Times Magazine*, September 13, 1970) to those concerned with how business ought to measure its impact on the society, as discussed by David F. Linowes (*The Corporate Conscience*, New York: Hawthorne Books, 1974). The dilemmas of corporate philanthropy are discussed in Jules Backman (Ed.), *Social Responsibility and Accountability* (New York: New York University Press, 1975); Melvin Ashen, *Corporate Strategies for Social Performance* (New York: Macmillan, 1980); and Leonard Silk and David Vogel, *Ethics and Profits: The Crisis of Confidence in American Business* (New York: Simon & Schuster, 1976). Harsher critiques of the social and economic impact of corporate activities are found in Marshall Clinard and Peter C. Yaeger, *Corporate Crime* (New York: Free Press, 1980); and Robert Heilbroner, *The Limits of American Capitalism* (New York: Harper & Row, 1966).

definition of social responsibility. In this discussion, however, we are concerned with only one aspect of corporate social responsibility, and that is corporate contributions.

Secondly, the term *corporate contributions* specifically refers to gifts of cash or grants made by corporations to charitable organizations. But corporations may also provide other kinds of assistance to charitable causes. Contributions, or assistance in a broader sense, can be divided into several classes, including in-kind contributions, direct cash contributions, and indirect contributions. Again, our focus in this paper will be restricted. We are primarily concerned with the issue of direct cash contributions, or with the grant-making function of the corporate entity. Nevertheless, we note parenthetically that in the past few years corporate assistance has grown greatly in terms of in-kind contributions, loaned personnel, and technical assistance to community groups and human service organizations. Moreover, we recognize the significance of the time and support that many corporations give to organizations such as the United Way in holding their charitable drive for payroll deductions from employees.

Third, and finally, corporations, corporate leaders, and others concerned with corporate social responsibility and the contributions function express widely divergent ideas about their commitment to these activities. Contrast the following three statements by business leaders, representing different points of a continuum of views about the significance of corporate giving:

- "The social responsibility of business is to make profits" (business leader quoted in Silk & Vogel, 1976, p. 139).
- "A corporation is an integral part of our society and as such it should be a responsible and responsive member of society . . . the corporation should utilize its resources to respond to the challenge to improve our society in those areas where it can make a significant contribution" (chairman, major insurance company, quoted in Harris & Klepper, 1976, pp. 17–18).
- "Such IBM activities (contributions) are founded in our own self-interest. It has always made good sense for IBM to support worthwhile projects in the communities where our employees live and work" (letter to the employees of IBM from John R. Opel, President and Chief Executive Officer, January 1982, quoted in United Way of America, 1983, p. 52).

With such an apparent divergence of opinion among corporate leaders themselves, it should not be surprising that there is confusion in the minds of the general public about corporate philanthropy or that social workers should be concerned about their involvement in it.

QUESTIONS ABOUT CORPORATE PHILANTHROPY

Our profession's questions about corporate philanthropy seem to derive primarily from concern about differences between values dominant in the corporate world and those reflected in social welfare goals (Bakalinsky, 1980; Kurzman, 1983).[2] In earlier days, community chests and community funds (which have since become "United Ways") were by far the largest recipients of corporate philanthropy, particularly in the health and welfare field (Brilliant, 1985). The federated fund-raising field also provided the primary arena in which businessmen and social workers intermingled (Lubove, 1969). After the 1960s, however, social workers became more skeptical about this kind of close corporate involvement. Nonetheless, social workers today cannot avoid an interest in corporate philanthropy, or curiosity about the reasons corporations give support and how they decide to whom this support will go. Social workers' reluctance to confront these issues therefore probably reflects ambivalence about the power corporations represent, as well as an insecurity about our capacity to deal with this power. An important first step in developing such capacity is an understanding of the questions we have so that we may respond to them.

Motivations for Giving

We begin with the basic question of motivation. As the quotations above indicate, motivations for corporate philanthropy vary greatly with different individuals in different companies and positions in the corporate world. Some scholars have suggested that the differences are more apparent than real, and that corporate giving is always tied closely to profits (Burt, 1983). A slightly different view emerges from a study conducted by James Harris and Anne Klepper for the well-known business research organization, the Conference Board. Interviews for that study were conducted with over 400 chief executive officers (CEOs) of large corporations about their reasons for undertaking corporate contributions activities (Harris & Klepper, 1976). Harris and Klepper note that the enthusiasm and commitment of the top executive of a corporation are primary factors in relation to the size and quality of corporate giving programs. In addition, they reported the three most important factors affecting certain key activities of the corporate-giving program (United Funds, higher education, and the arts) to be (1) the practice of corporate citizenship, (2) the desire to protect the environment in which the

---

[2]Most recent social work literature on this subject discusses the values issue primarily in terms of direct service delivery (e.g., counseling) inside the corporate setting. Current literature referring to corporate philanthropy and social work is rare, and is generally focused on the corporate relationship with the United Way; see, for example, Eleanor L. Brilliant, "United Way at the Crossroads," in *The Social Welfare Forum, 1982–83*, (Washington, DC: National Conference of Social Welfare, 1985, pp. 250–262).

corporation functions, and (3) benefits to the employees. In the more inclusive arena of public-affairs activities, social responsibility/corporate citizenship and self-interest/long-range survival were by far the most frequent reasons given (respectively 63% and 40%). In regard to levels of corporate giving, however, this study and other comparable inquiries report very different factors to be at work. Harris and Klepper found that 52% of their respondents considered previous levels of giving to be a major factor in determining levels of giving, followed by more amorphous answers such as "no fixed figure—each contribution is decided separately" (44% of respondents), and the amount necessary to achieve philanthrophic goals (noted by 33% of respondents) (Harris & Klepper, 1976, p. 21). Apparently, most corporate leaders share a reluctance to be pinned down about dollar amounts of giving, and changes in dollar amounts will tend to be incremental.

A reading of the literature, personal experience, and in-depth interviews with CEOs leads us to conclude that the notion of enlightened self-interest expressed by IBM in the quotation above is a norm for many corporations that undertake fully developed philanthropic programs (Committee for Economic Development, 1971, pp. 26–29). Enlightened self-interest for corporations may indeed be analogous to enlightened self-interest in individual giving, because potential benefits to the community are considered to be congruent with benefits to the individual or corporation. We rule out pure altruism as the motivation for corporate giving, since corporate givers must be expected to act within the defined concept of corporate interest and corporate goals. The real issue then turns around the meaning of the word *enlightened*. To what extent is the corporation's notion of enlightened self-interest likely to be congruent with the interests of the community as a whole, with its employees, or with needy subgroups of the community? And in line with the theme of this chapter, to what extent can social workers hope to influence corporate decisions about giving in the community, and therefore to mold corporate giving in line with social work's definition of enlightenment?

The Effectiveness of Corporate Gifts

A closely related question concerns the effectiveness of corporate giving. This issue has two sides—it involves the overall amounts of corporate giving, and it concerns the way those dollars are distributed. In regard to the amounts of dollars given, one source has stated:

Business is a relatively untapped source of philanthropic income. Consider this: Of the total number of United States corporations (now about 2.1 million) only about 25 percent make cash contributions. And only about 6 percent contribute more than $500 a year . . . stated another way, less than 0.007 percent of all corporations give one-half of all contributions. (A. W. Clausen, President and Chief Executive of Bank America Corporation, quoted in Tuthil, 1980, p. 67)

The person who made that statement was not a social worker, but a leader of a major corporation who recognized that although corporate contributions have risen considerably in past years, they are far below what they could be. A 1981 study for the Council on Foundations noted that on the average the companies on the Fortune 1300 list made cash contributions of only about 1.1% of their total pretax income. The study found that smaller companies and intermediate companies were somewhat more generous, giving at 1.7% and 1.3% respectively (White & Bartolomeo, 1982, p. 103). Percentages should be interpreted in the context of the 1981 Tax Act, which allows corporations to give up to 10% of their pretax income to charities.[3]

In regard to corporate choices in allocations, social workers must recognize the competitiveness of the charitable marketplace. Although within the scope of this chapter we do not lay out a total plan for achieving more responsible corporate giving, we can certainly demonstrate why social workers should be concerned about the current directions of corporate charity. Table 19-1, based on Conference Board figures, clearly shows that even though the amount going to health and welfare causes has risen in absolute dollars since 1970, the relative percentage, or marketplace share, of the corporate contributions dollar going to health and welfare has declined in the past decade, from 42% in 1972 to 31% in 1982. During this period, contributions to culture and art rose from 4.1% (1972) to 11.4% (1982), and education rose from 36.9% to 40.7% of the total corporate philanthropic dollar.

These data suggest that corporations may respond to environmental influences more than they like to admit. Apparently, as a result of the turmoil of the 1960s, the amounts going to civic and community (urban) causes rose in the early 1970s and hovered at over 11% until the 1980s. In 1983, with renewed pressure from new and emerging groups in the community, the reported share of corporate giving to civic activities increased to 14.8% of the total (Klepper et al., 1984, p. 12). Although it is not entirely evident what activities are included in these various classifications, it does seem that some traditional health and welfare organizations are losing out in the competitive struggle for the corporate dollar while other newer causes are gaining. Corporate patterns of giving evidently do shift, even if slowly, and it is therefore important for social workers to play a part in influencing the direction of corporate giving, in congruence with social change goals.

Another basic question concerns the nature of corporate power and the

---

[3]The Economic Recovery Tax Act of 1981 increased the level of charitable deductions that corporations could take from their taxable income from 5% to 10% but because of other changes in the way taxable income is calculated, many experts believe that the percentage change only maintains the incentive for giving at the same level.

TABLE 19-1 Percentage of Corporate Contributions Given to Health and Welfare, Education, Culture and the Arts, and Civic and Other Activities, 1970–1982.

Year	Health & welfare*	Education	Culture & arts	Civic	Other
1970	38.6%	38.3%	5.3%	8.1%	7.4%
1971					
1972	42.0	36.9	4.1	9.1	6.6
1973					
1974	38.5	36.0	7.3	10.4	7.7
1975	41.2	36.2	7.5	10.3	4.6
1976	39.3	37.3	8.2	11.0	4.2
1977	38.3	37.0	9.0	11.5	4.2
1978	36.9	37.0	10.1	11.4	4.5
1979	35.0	37.7	9.9	11.6	5.8
1980	34.0	37.8	10.9	11.7	5.6
1981	33.6	36.7	11.9	11.7	6.1
1982	31.0	40.7	11.4	11.7	5.2

Source: *Annual Survey of Corporate Contributions, 1982 Edition,* pp. 30–31; and *1984 Edition,* pp. 32–33 (New York: The Conference Board). Used by permission.

*Includes federated campaigns.

question of whether corporations should give to charities at all. In this regard, a strongly ideological point of view is shared by individuals on both the left and right of the political spectrum. The classical statement of this view is expressed by the conservative economist Milton Friedman: "Few trends could so thoroughly undermine the very foundations of our free society as the acceptance by business of a social responsibility other than to make as much money for their stockholders as possible" (Friedman, 1962, p. 133). On the left, skeptics doubt that corporate giving is useful to anyone but the corporations and are concerned about the additional power it represents. This viewpoint, however, is harder to maintain currently, when so many human service organizations are clamoring for corporate support and when other sources of funds, particularly government grants, are being curtailed. Indeed, while corporate funding is helpful to popular organizations like the Metropolitan Opera or the Metropolitan Museum of Art, struggling community groups also are fighting for vital seed money from corporate sources. In the face of need, power becomes not an absolute argument but a relative argument, and community interest in the arts has to be compared with community interest in advocacy groups. Difficult choices for whoever makes them, but withdrawal of corporate support does not seem the appropriate answer.

Accountability

Finally, there remains the somewhat problematic issue of accountability in the corporate decision-making process regarding charitable giving. This issue is related both to the complex role of the corporate contribution function in the organization and to the procedures followed. Many corporations have attempted to deal with the ambiguities of the contributions function by establishing corporate foundations. In addition to becoming mechanisms for the handling of fluctuations in funds available for giving (for example, when profits decline or taxes change), such foundations are generally managed by full-time corporate contributions staff, and they tend to have fully publicized policies and procedures for grant making. Moreover, by law they are required to make different kinds of public disclosures from the corporations themselves: as 501(c)3 organizations, corporate foundations file annual reports with state charities-regulating bodies and file 990 PF tax forms, which provide more public detail about their grants than required with their direct-giving programs.

Companies concerned with establishing corporate giving programs in a more formal sense are increasingly utilizing corporate contributions staff. This staff participates in developing formal rules and procedures for grant making and priority setting for the use of corporate resources in the community. On the other hand, many corporations still treat corporate giving as if it were personal charity, building on the legal fiction of the corporation as a persona. Accountability in these cases is more questionable, and less may be known publicly about the corporation's philanthropic activities.

CORPORATE PHILANTHROPY: LOCUS OF DECISION MAKING

There is an enormous variety of specific models for decision making in corporate philanthropy. Therefore, we explore some of the major elements that must be considered in constructing any model of corporate philanthropy.

Structuring of Corporate Contributions

As already noted, there are two major structural arrangements for corporate giving that occur in both large and small companies: (1) direct corporate giving and (2) giving through corporate foundations. (Clifford Trusts are also used by mutual insurance companies, because of their special situation concerning use of investment income or "profits."[4]) From a corporation's

---

[4]A Clifford Trust is a device used by mutual insurance companies to set aside funds for corporate contributions. Since they cannot legally deduct their contributions from investment income, these companies utilize a percentage of assets to establish trusts with a 10-year life period, known as Clifford Trusts.

point of view there are both advantages and disadvantages to the establishment of a corporate foundation. Among the advantages generally cited is the
fact that separate foundations help to "cushion the company's giving in lean
profit years . . . they insulate top managers from many requests for support,"
and they can also "take advantage of a 2 percent tax rate on the earnings used
to make direct grants.[5] . . . Foundations (also) provide a formal way to focus
the company's giving program" (Plinio, 1982, pp. 38–41). Alex Plinio, President of Prudential Foundation, also cites the following disadvantages
attached to the foundation model: Gifts to company foundations cannot
revert to the company's control; reporting requirements for foundations
require extra work, including the handling for tax purposes of appreciated
property; and, additionally, "there is the normal tension in deciding which
grants appear to be so directly related to the company's interests that they
should not be made by the foundation." Apparently, then, a foundation is
presumed to have a broader scope and should be at least somewhat more
disinterested in its grant making than would be the case with corporate
contributions given directly by the company. Finally, corporate foundations
are used by both large and small corporations; but particularly where there
are larger contribution budgets, corporations may have both direct-giving
programs and foundations. In 1981 there were 701 corporate-sponsored
foundations reported in the *Foundation Directory*.[6]

Major Individuals Involved in Contributions Decision Making

A Yankelovich, Skelly, and White study in 1982 reinforced what most
observers of corporate philanthropy believe: "The CEO is most important in
corporate giving decisions, but other prominent corporate figures also play
key roles." Groups outside the corporation have a minor impact on these
decisions (White & Bartolomeo, 1982, p. 104). Whether a company foundation or a direct-giving program is used, corporate giving is highly influenced
by the commitment and public-mindedness of the CEO, or by whether the
CEO perceives corporate philanthropy to be in the interest of the corporation. Moreover, even when a foundation exists, the board of the foundation
will include corporate representatives, and the executive of the foundation
reports to corporate executives (generally, but not always, to the CEO). In
addition to the CEO, the Yankelovich study lists a number of other factors in
the corporate decision-making process, in the following order: corporate-
giving staff, top executives at headquarters, top executives in other locations
tied in importance with boards of directors, community members/soliciting

[5]As of 1986, this top rate was changed to 1%.
[6]For a discussion of foundations as a corporate giving mechanism in a sample of surveyed
companies, see Kathryn Troy, *The Corporate Contributions Function* (New York: The Conference Board, 1982, Report No. 820). In 30% of the sample of 435 companies, direct–giving
programs coexisted with corporate foundations.

organizations, shareholders, and employees. Note, however, that in bigger, intermediate, and smaller companies there are differences in the key actors who participate, and these differences affect the strategy for social work intervention.

In companies with direct corporate contributions programs, a committee, usually with the title of Public Affairs or Corporate Contributions, is general- ly responsible for overseeing the distribution of corporate gifts. Members of this committee typically represent the company's top executives or top management team, because corporate contributions are considered sensitive matters, related as they are to the company's external relationships with its constituencies. Where significant amounts of money are involved, these committees increasingly rely on staff work. In companies giving out sub- stantial grants, contributions staff are likely to be responsible for researching requests for grants and recommending appropriate levels of support to the committee.

Levels of Approval

Levels of approval vary greatly from corporation to corporation, and accord- ing to the total contributions budget. These levels typically include lower- level staff, middle managment, and top corporate executives. In 1980 the Prudential Foundation surveyed 40 major companies about the location of approval authority in their organizations (Plinio, 1982, p. 41). For grants of $1,000 or less, 45% of the companies allowed contributions staff to make the decision, with only 6% indicating that board approval was necessary, and 49% requiring various levels of approval beyond the staff level but below the board level. For grants between $5,000 and $10,000, 16% of the companies reported that staff approval only was required, while 32% said that grants of this magnitude go to the board. None of the companies reported giving the staff approval authority over grants exceeding $25,000, and 66% of the companies said that they required board approval above this amount. Staff members, however, were generally responsible for background research and for recommendations to board members. Not surprisingly, those contribu- tions officers who are closest to the CEO usually have more freedom to improve the professionalism of the philanthropic activity than do their counterparts at a lower level on the managerial scale.

Characteristics of Corporate Contributions Staff

In response to mail surveys by the Conference Board, 435 companies on the Fortune 1300 list provided profiles of 524 corporate contributions staff (Klepper, 1981; Troy, 1982). By the Conference Board's definition, only a few hundred major corporate contributions programs were in existence at that time. A contributions program by their definition probably has a full-time, appropriately titled professional staff member in charge, with a program that is distinguishable from unplanned or lower levels of giving. The staff person is likely to oversee a budget of more than $1 million, generally carries discretionary authority to approve grants, and is employed by a corporation with net annual sales of more than $1 billion. Corporate contributions officers are also likely to have responsibilities for other activities including community or civic affairs, support work for the activity of top corporate executives, volunteer programs, education activities, matching gifts programs, and United Way drives.

According to the Conference Board findings, the majority of contributions professionals have 4-year college degrees, with more than half having done some graduate and advanced degree work. More than 70% of the 524 contributions professionals were over 40 years old, with the largest group between 51 and 60 years old. Most had worked for their companies for 10 years or more; about half of the group had been with the company for more than 15 years. Most of the staff involved with contributions programs had business backgrounds. Only 6% came from outside the corporate world: 5 from government, 11 from academic institutions, and 9 from nonprofit organizations.

Among the full-time contribution professionals, men work with larger contributions budgets than do women. Approximately 35% of the men, but only 18% of the women, work with budgets of more than $5 million. Men have a higher level of education, and they are older as a group (in 1980 three quarters of the men were more than 40 years old). Men also earn considerably higher salaries. Finally, Klepper notes that more women are assuming these positions, a phenomenon she suggests bears further examination (Klepper, 1981, pp. 12–13). With older men retiring, contributions positions could become more available to newcomers to the corporation, but the scope may also change.

SOCIAL WORKER STRATEGIES FOR INFLUENCING CORPORATE PHILANTHROPY

Corporate philanthropy cannot replace public support for vital human needs or services to the disadvantaged, including welfare payments, Social Security, and basic provisions for the physically and mentally ill. Enlightened leaders in the corporate world and social workers alike recognize this (Orski, 1982, p. 68). But rightfully used, corporate dollars can provide support for new and emerging groups in the community, for projects in the public interest, and for the improvement of life in urban neighborhoods. For example, some corporations have "adopted" schools in disadvantaged neighborhoods; many businesses fund youth-related employment programs; and some corporations have been involved with day care for their employees (Kamerman & Kingston, 1982; Magid, 1983). Nevertheless, corporations have given far less than they are able to under the benefits of tax laws and have generally been conservative in their use of corporate gifts (Koch, 1981).

In short, working with corporations presents some dilemmas and challenges for social workers, while at the same time offering opportunities to influence corporate involvement for community "good." Social workers must seize the opportunity to help ensure corporate support for socially responsible community projects. Intervention in this arena can take place in a variety of ways, both from within the corporation and from the outside. The following list suggests some of the major avenues by which social workers can influence the direction of corporate philanthropy and help ensure constructive corporate participation in the community:

1. Social work schools can train people for jobs inside corporations and especially in corporate philanthropy. Given the relatively small numbers of positions available in this field, we are not suggesting that all schools do this—but certainly some should. This would not require drastic changes in most curricula. Program planning, research, evaluation, and community organization are already taught in most schools; social work students also learn about social service agencies and human service delivery systems. More work on budget analysis may be called for, as well as a broadening of the scope of program planning and evaluation techniques so that they can be applied to the arts and sciences as well as human services. Content on organizational development is also relevant for corporate positions (see Chapter 16 of this volume). In any case, since some social workers are already employed in corporate philanthropy, this idea is not radically new, but an extension of existing practice.

2. Social work schools could provide training programs for corporate philanthropy staff who already work in the field but who have gaps in their training. Certificates of advanced training in corporate philanthropy could be given; content could be tailored for short-term intensive courses, incorporating social work knowledge in such areas as community organization and priority-setting techniques. This program will be more difficult to develop than the entry of social workers directly into the corporation, because corporate personnel are not likely to consider themselves in need of social work training. Social work schools will, therefore, have to market their special expertise, and they will have to adapt their programs for the corporate setting.

3. Social workers can serve as consultants to corporate philanthropy programs. Many corporate philanthropists seem to be interested in creative approaches to program development in the community and in strategic

research about community needs. This would be a natural connection for social work schools and for individual consultation by social workers with expertise in these areas.

4. Social workers outside the corporate world can increase their communication and interactions with corporate personnel and local business leaders. Executives of many large human service organizations in the voluntary sector already do this. They get contributions from local corporations, and corporate personnel serve on their boards. Even smaller organizations, with more divergent or advocacy stances, should pursue this approach. An evident side benefit of this would be the education of corporate leaders about the variety of real human service needs in the community. Cultivation of corporate personnel is a slow process, but it may have important ramifications for the community welfare.

5. Social work schools need to place greater emphasis on placing students in corporate settings, specifically in corporate philanthropy departments. Where there are no MSWs in these departments, schools may have to provide off-site supervision.

CONCLUSION

Social workers need to interact more with their corporate neighbors in a variety of ways. Many social work professionals are already involved in providing services to employees inside the corporation, as direct-service agents dealing with the problems of individual workers and their families. Other social workers are interested in the human resources role, or in the position of personnel and benefits management.

In this chapter we have urged social workers to become involved with corporate philanthropy. They can do this by getting inside the corporation and assuming positions as corporate contributions personnel. Or they can do it from the outside, by building bridges to corporate contributions staff and corporate leadership. Either way, it takes a combination of professional skills and knowledge that social workers already have and can use more fully. But it may also mean moderating social workers' styles to accommodate corporate norms in manner and procedures. Our purpose has been to help social workers understand key aspects of the corporate contributions function—as a first step in an effective approach to influencing it.

REFERENCES

Ashen, M. (1980). *Corporate strategies for social performance*. New York: Macmillan.

Bakalinsky, R. (1980). People vs. profits: Social work in industry. *Social Work, 25*(6): 471–475.

Backman, J. (Ed.). (1975). *Social responsibility and accountability*. New York: New York University Press.

Brilliant, E. L. (1985). Corporate giving patterns to United Ways. In *Giving and Volunteering: New Frontiers of Knowledge*, Working Papers of the 1985 Spring Research Forum of the Independent Sector and the United Way Institute, March 15, 1985, New York, pp. 257–287.

Burt, R. S. (1983). Corporate philanthropy as a cooptive relation. *Social Forces, 62*(2): 419–449.

Clinard, M., & Yeager, P. C. (1980). *Corporate crime*. New York: Free Press.

Committee for Economic Development, Research and Social Policy Committee. (1971, June). *Social responsibilities of business corporations*. New York: Committee for Economic Development.

Foundation directory (8th ed.). (1981). New York: The Foundation Center.

Friedman, M. (1962). *Capitalism and freedom*. Chicago: University of Chicago Press.

Harris, J. F., & Klepper, A. (1976). *Corporate philanthropic public service activities*. New York: The Conference Board. (Report No. 688)

Heilbroner, R. (1966). *The limits of American capitalism*. New York: Harper & Row.

Kamerman, S. B., & Kingston, P. (1982). Employer responses to the family responsibilities of employees. In S. B. Kamerman & C. D. Hayes (Eds.). *Families that work: Children in a changing world*. Washington, DC: National Academy Press.

Klepper, A. (1981). *The corporate contributions professional*. New York: The Conference Board. (Research Bulletin No. 109)

Klepper, A. et al. (1984). *Corporate contributions outlook 1984*. New York: The Conference Board. (Research Bulletin No. 146)

Koch, F. (1981). *The new corporate philanthropy: How society & business can profit*. New York: Plenum.

Kurzman, P. A. (1983). Ethical issues in industrial social work practice. *Social Casework, 64*(2), 105–111.

Lahn, S. M. (undated). Corporate philanthropy: Issues in the current literature. New Haven: Institution for Social and Policy Studies, Program on Non-Profit Organizations. (Working Paper No. 29)

Lubove, R. (1969). *The professional altruist: The emergence of social work as a career 1880–1930*. New York: Atheneum.

Magid, R. Y. (1983). Child care initiatives for working parents: Why employers get involved. New York: American Mangement Association.

Orski, K. (1982). The corporate response to cuts in government spending. In *Corporate philanthropy: Philosophy, management, trends, future, background*. Washington, DC: Council on Foundations.

Plinio, A. J. (1982). The organization of a corporate philanthropy program. In *Corporate philanthropy: Philosophy, management, trends, future, background*. Washington, DC: Council on Foundations, pp. 38–41.

Policy statement on occupational social work. Adopted by the Delegate Assembly of the National Association of Social Workers, November 1981 and amended September 1984.

Salamon, L. M. (1984, July–August). Non-profits: The results are coming in. *Foundation News*, 16–23.

Silk, L., & Vogel, D. (1976). *Ethics and profits: The crisis of confidence in American business*. New York: Simon & Schuster.

Troy, K. (1982). *The corporate contributions function*. New York: The Conference Board (Report No. 820)

Tuthil, M. (1980). The growing impact of business giving. *Nation's Business, 68*(10), 67.

United Way of America (UWA). (1983). *Contributions programs: A sampler of policies and statements*. Alexandria, VA: Author.

White, A. H., & Bartolomeo, J. S. (1982). The attitudes and motivations of chief exectutive officers. In *Corporate philanthropy: Philosophy, management, trends, future, background* (pp. 102–111). Washington, DC: Council on Foundations.

20 Corporate Community Relations

Edmund M. Burke

Corporate community relations is part of a company's social responsibility mission. It can be defined as those programs and activities of a corporation that are designed to contribute to the improvement of a community's health, welfare, culture, community development, and other needs. The programs can include contributing money and in-kind services to community-based organizations; providing employee volunteers and loaned executives for community and government agencies; allowing leave programs for employees to work for a social service organization for up to a full year; sponsoring a partnership with a local school system; conducting a health fair; sponsoring an arts and cultural bazaar; tutoring poor and disadvantaged children; supporting and encouraging community problem-solving and planning activities; underwriting costs of rehabilitating low-income housing; and a great variety of other community activities.

Corporate community relations appears to be a peculiarly North American phenomenon. Although there are examples of business support for community chests and United Ways in the Far East, particularly in the Philippines and Japan, corporate community relations is a practice that flourishes primarily in America. In part, that may be due to the pragmatic way capitalism has developed in America. It may also be due to the attitude of Americans toward philanthropy and the voluntary support of organizations and institutions.

HISTORY OF CORPORATE COMMUNITY RELATIONS

Corporate community relations, some insist, has a long history in America. In some respects it has. Andrew Carnegie was largely responsible as a philanthropist for community libraries in America. Henry Ford developed programs to support the recreational and health needs of his employees (Drucker, 1984).

The modern concept of community relations, however, is a more recent phenomenon. The first book that touches on the subject, for example, was written in the mid-1950s. Written by Howard R. Bowen (1953), the book's major focus was on corporate social responsibility rather than on community relations. Corporate social responsibility, a much broader concept than corporate community relations, is the notion that a corporation in pursuing its policies must take into account the objectives and values of society (Burke, 1987).

Nonetheless, there is a background to what is now called corporate community relations. The development of corporate community relations occurred in phases with each phase reflecting the needs or pressures of the moment. In some instances the phase was short-lived—there was a burst of activity and then the activity waned. In others the phase was more long lasting, contributing to the expansion of activities in a successive phase.

Early Altruists

The first phase was the philanthropy of the early industrialists like Andrew Carnegie. Tied to the basic tenets of Protestantism, it was a personal form of community relations. It was seen as repaying the community for God's blessings. Highly paternalistic, this form of community relations lasted for many years. In fact, even today there are those who promote and encourage business involvement in community affairs on the basis of returning benefits to the community. A study sponsored by the Center for a Voluntary Society (Fenn, 1984) found that over 85% of top businessmen listed altruism as one reason for community involvement. One executive commented, "The businessman should return to the community that which he has gained in the form of services."

Federated Financing and Planning of Health and Welfare Services

The next phase in the history of corporate community relations was business's support of joint financing and planning of community health and welfare agencies—the forerunners of today's United Way organizations. The first joint financing of health and welfare agencies began in Denver in 1887. It was started by three clergymen—a priest, a minister, and a rabbi. The growth of federated fundraising, however, occurred much after 1887.

Up until the 1920s and 1930s the financial support of community health and welfare agencies was frequently in the hands of one or two wealthy philanthropists. As the demands for programs and services expanded, community organizations began to appeal to the general community for their financial support. Often the appeals were directed to business leaders. The multiplicity of campaigns led business leaders to seek a more efficient means of raising money for community agencies. The community chest proved to be the answer. (See Chapter 19 of this volume for a fuller development of corporate philanthropy.)

The community chest movement also gave rise to the development of community planning programs. The earliest forms of community planning, called councils of social agencies, were primarily social-agency-directed and controlled. Beginning in the 1950s and on into the 1960s, however, community planning agencies were restructured to encourage the participation of citizen leaders—a euphemism for business and labor leaders (Burke, 1965).

Recruiting business leaders for community planning activities was not easy—not as easy, of course, as recruiting them for fundraising jobs. Nonetheless, the community welfare councils in many cities provided opportunities for the involvement of business leaders in community planning (Burke, 1967).

More recently, the United Way has begun to reemphasize community planning. Separate community councils have been merged with United Ways in major cities (e.g., Boston, Worcester, Los Angeles). Moreover, the United Way of America has been encouraging local United Ways to expand their community planning, or what is now being called community problem-solving activities, and is encouraging them to involve community leaders in those efforts.

Heeding its own message, the United Way of America has recruited top corporate executives to engage in national planning projects. James D. Robinson, Chairman and Chief Executive Officer of American Express, for example, was chairman of the United Way of America Government Relations Committee when the United Way was asked by the federal government to assist in the distribution of emergency food and shelter funds. As chairman of the Committee, Robinson played a key planning and advocacy role.

Peter E. Haas, President and Chief Executive Officer of Levi Strauss, chaired the United Way of America's Special Study Committee on Community Problem Solving. This committee served to reemphasize and redirect United Way efforts, "in order to address unresolved community needs" (Haas, 1983, p. 9).

The influence of the United Way as a means for involving American business and labor leaders in social work issues has often been underestimated. Over the years, the United Way has served as the principal social work vehicle for the involvement of business and labor in community social programs. Moreover, a number of the executives of United Way organizations in major cities are graduate social workers, including the national President of the United Way of America, William Aramony. Through the involvement of business leaders and labor officials in the fundraising, budgeting, and planning activities of a United Way, business and labor leaders have become more educated and more sensitive about social agency programs and needs.

Urban Turbulence in the 1960s

The urban riots of the mid-1960s proved to be the stimulus for the next phase in the involvement of business in community affairs. The riots during the summers of 1965 through 1968 shocked and frightened America. It was a display of violent protest that most Americans believed could not happen.

The business community was especially shocked. The chairman of General Motors, it was said, looked out his office window on July 23, 1967 and saw the city of Detroit burning around him. It was a fearful sight, and it galvanized him and other business leaders into action. The presidents of General Motors, Ford, Chrysler, and Dayton Hudson formed the New Detroit Committee. General Motors, J. L. Dayton Corporation, and Ford each contributed $100,000 to rebuilding parts of downtown Detroit.

On August 24, 1967 the Urban Coalition was formed. A business-sponsored program, the Urban Coalition brought together mayors, trade union presidents, civil rights leaders, and corporate executives to begin working on urban problems. It was also an attempt to rally support from all segments of society to address the problems of the poor and to avoid the then-continuing deterioration of America's cities (Urban America, Inc., 1969).

Also in 1967, the Life Insurance Committee on Urban Problems was formed. It pledged $1 billion for investment from life insurance agencies in urban ghettos. The investment went primarily into rebuilding and rehabilitating housing.

The activity of business leaders in urban problems waned as the federal government began to invest heavily in urban programs. Although still in existence, the influence of the Urban Coalition is not as prominent as it once was. John Gardner, one-time president of the Urban Coalition, left in 1970 to form Common Cause. Subsequently the organization began experiencing difficulties in achieving consensus on its mission. Sol Linowitz, former United States Ambassador and former executive of Xerox, took over in 1972 (Shandler, 1972).

Affirmative Action

The next phase in the development of increasing community relations of corporations was prompted by the passage of the Equal Employment Opportunity (EEO) Act in 1972 and subsequent executive orders related to affirmative action in the workplace. To comply with these laws and regulations, corporations initiated programs to recruit and retain women and minorities. Very often this meant working with community-based organizations and schools in minority communities. One study of affirmative action in nine major companies—Digital Equipment Corporation, General Electric, GTE, Hewlett-Packard, Johnson & Johnson, Kodak, Kraft Foods, Procter & Gamble, and Xerox—found that all of the companies were active in the local communities (Gertsenfeld & Burke, 1985). All of the companies, moreover, made substantial contributions either in cash or in equipment to educational institutions and to community-based agencies.

The emphasis on affirmative action has prompted many corporations to work with local schools, particularly schools with high percentages of minority students. Companies donate money and equipment to schools and provide advice and assistance to guidance counselors. Companies also loan employees to universities and colleges for 1- or 2-year lectureships. The EEO officer in a company, moreover, often serves as a liaison between the company and community-based organizations (Hollander, 1975).

The Public's Approval of Business

Another event serving to stimulate the increase in community relations and which occurred simultaneously with the affirmative action activities was the loss of approval of business on the part of the American public. A survey conducted by the Yankelovich organization in 1971 reported that society's approval of business had declined from a high of 58% in 1969 to a low of 29% in 1970. The Yankelovich report stated also that 7 out of 10 adults supported the consumer protection movement, increased government regulation of business, and severe penalties if business failed to meet new pollution standards (Bernays, 1975)

Business leaders were highly sensitive to this report. The loss of status and approval could lead to increasing regulation of business. Business leaders consequently set out to improve their image. Articles in the form of advertisements extolling the free enterprise system appeared in major newspapers (Sethi, 1979). Contributions to philanthropy increased dramatically. Between 1970 and 1980 corporate contributions to philanthropy increased 34%, rising from $797 million to $1.2 billion. Between 1965 and 1970 corporate contributions had remained stable, increasing from $785 million to $797 million (Chemical Bank).

Reagan Initiatives

The next phase in the development of corporate community relations occurred in the 1980s. The reduction in federal aid to local communities initiated by the Reagan administration pressured community agencies to look for new sources of financial assistance. They turned to America's corporations, who suddenly found themselves besieged with requests for money, loaned staff, and equipment. And the pleas for help came not only from the traditional voluntary organizations, but also from state and local government agencies who also were faced with large-scale budget reductions.

In addition, President Reagan urged the corporate leaders to assume some of the costs of supporting community groups. In a 1981 speech to the National Alliance of Business, he challenged the business community to become involved in alleviating social problems. He also formed a 44-member task force headed by C. William Verity, Chairman of Armco, Inc., to stimulate the involvement of companies in solving community problems. He also asked corporations to double their philanthropic contributions (Verity, 1982).

Corporations did respond. Between 1979 and 1984 corporate contributions increased $1.3 billion. Significantly, contributions to philanthropy did not decline in 1980, a year in which there was an absolute decline in corporate profits. In the past, contributions to philanthropy have been affected by corporate profits (Chemical Bank, undated).

Equally significant have been the growth and diversity of corporate programs that have emerged in the 1980s. Corporations are supporting—either directly through the release of staff or through financial contributions—a wide variety of community programs, examples of which were given at the outset of the chapter. The following are addtional examples:

- Encouraging the public to serve as foster parents for hard-to-place children.
- Providing job training and employment for students of a school for the deaf.
- Allowing employees leaves of up to a year to work for a social service organization.
- Promoting literacy programs.
- Organizing and supporting neighborhood youth programs.
- Loaning executives to community agencies.
- Organizing and supporting a community food bank.
- Providing a social service information and referral program.
- Offering fingerprinting programs for children.
- Developing business–education partnerships.
- Engaging in community development programs.
- Rehabilitating housing for low-income citizens.
- Job training for the unemployed.
- Sponsoring shelter for the homeless.

INCREASING IMPORTANCE OF CORPORATE COMMUNITY RELATIONS

The Reagan initiatives have merely highlighted a development that had been persistently expanding over the 1970s. A Conference Board study conducted in the late 1970s reported that 9 out of 10 companies surveyed had been involved in some kind of voluntary effort to assist local communities (Witnner, 1981). The notion of public–private partnerships urged by President Reagan was supported by the Business Roundtable as early as 1978. Also, President Jimmy Carter had involved a number of major corporations in working with state human service administrators in improving their planning and management practices (Walter, 1980).

There are three reasons to explain the increasing importance of community relations in today's corporation. One is the changing attitude of American citizens, who believe that decisions affecting their communities cannot be made arbitrarily and without their participation. The second is the increasing role of government as a regulator of business and industry. And the third is the strategic management orientation of the modern corporation, which requires managers to recognize the impact of the external environment on corporate decision making.

Shifts in Attitudes

The attitude shift is one that has its origins in the citizen participation activities in the 1960s. The civil rights struggle and then later the anti-poverty activities in local communities proved that individuals when joined together can be a powerful force for change. Governmental agencies learned to be responsive to community groups in the 1960s.

In the 1970s and 1980s it was corporations who began to hear from community groups. The Codex Corporation, a susidiary of Motorola, for example, spent 7 years fighting with environmental groups to build its corporate headquarters on a 55-acre site adjacent to Route 128 outside of Boston. Although it did get permission to build, the environmental groups— all voluntary—did wring concessions out of the company on how the site could be developed.

In Cambridge, Massachusetts the Arthur D. Little Company, a world-renowned research organization, is fighting with community groups over its right to conduct germ-warfare research. In response to neighborhood organizations, a half dozen major corporations in Hartford, Connecticut have renovated apartment buildings for inner-city poor residents. The companies have also funded job-training programs for the unemployed in Hartford (Lueck, 1985). Activist organizations and community groups, consequently, have brought about a change in corporate management.

Government Regulations

The second significant change contributing to the increase in corporate community relations activities in the mid-1980s has been the increasing influence of government as a regulator. Certain industries, banks, and utilities face more governmental regulation than others, but all are in some ways affected. Peter Drucker (1972, p. 16) cautioned business leaders in the early 1970s that communities and government would be demanding accountability from big organizations. "Under any circumstances," he said, "we are moving in the direction of demanding that our institutions take responsibility beyond their own contribution. We will be demanding this not only of business enterprises but of all other institutions as well—the university, the hospital, the government agency, the school."

Regulation, consequently, has become a way of life for today's business. As Irving Shapiro (1979), former President of DuPont, explained, "At DuPont, for instance, we can expect government to continue to tell us whether we can build a plant at a chosen location. General Motors and Ford can expect the government to continue to help them design cars. All business people can expect government to continue to tell us what fuel to burn in the furnace, what sort of affirmative action we should take in hiring and promotion, and how many pounds, if not tons, of reports we shall submit.

"Without suggesting for a minute that the private sector ought to take all this lying down, I must admit that some of the government's involvement is desirable and another piece of it is probably inevitable, at least over the short term" (Shapiro, 1979, p. 49).

The modern corporation accepts the consequences of a regulatory environment. They are responding, however, by assigning professionals and managers to work with the regulators. They are also trying to forestall increasing regulations by engaging in activities that prevent the need for further regulations. Many of the activities are positive community programs that are beneficial both for local communities and businesses.

Strategic Planning

The third explanation for the increasing importance of community relations is the development of strategic planning in today's corporation. Strategic planning has had a profound influence on almost every aspect of management from marketing to production to human resources. It is to be expected, therefore, that its influence would spread to corporate social responsibility— particularly to the rapidly developing community relations function. One business text on strategic planning (Ansoff, 1984) points out that a firm's business strategy cannot be built solely on dollars-and-cents considerations any longer. The firm's strategy has to include political and social considerations along with commercial considerations.

There are two ways that strategic planning has influenced corporate social responsibility. For one thing, it has caused managers to become sensitive to society and the impact of society on the long-term future of the business. Company survival often depends upon the ability of managers to analyze and cope with an uncertain and turbulent environment. What happens in society and in local communities—sometimes to the embarrassment of managers—does have an impact on the firm.

Some firms consequently have begun to factor community analysis into their strategic plans. As Robert Coladzin (1981, p. 3), former Vice President of Champion International, commented, "A corporation's strategic plan that does not deal with [community] affairs is incomplete. Our thesis is simple, we believe that 'public affairs' is as susceptible to strategic planning as any other function of our business, that it can be just as useful, and that it should be annually included in the process."

A second lesson of strategic planning is that the successful positioning of a company requires intervention into the external environment for the purpose of bringing about change. Modifying attitudes toward the company and its products is one example. Influencing the development of governmental regulations is another example.

Consequently, business firms are intervening into community activities in order to influence and shape those activities for the best interests of the firm. Secondary education is a good illustration. Companies are involved in educational programs in order to assure themselves of an educated and technically competent workforce. Speaking before the American Federation of Teachers, John Creedon, President of the Metropolitan Life Insurance Company, said, "Business is beginning to act on the recognition that it wants well educated employees, customers, and voters." He also added, and this is the strategic perspective of corporate involvment, "It [business] must participate in formulating and advocating the public policy measures" (Maeroff, 1984, p. a19).

Health promotion is another illustration. Life insurance companies are promoting nonsmoking campaigns in the workplace. This reduces health care costs for society and can lead to increased profits for insurance companies.

The strategic planning and strategic management focus attached to community relations ensures that it will become an accepted function in the management of the business.

EMERGING TRENDS

There are three emerging trends in corporate community relations that may have consequences for social workers and social work.

Career Opportunities

One is the increase in the volume of community relations activities on the part of corporations. As pointed out earlier, community relations is a growth function in today's corporation. The function is expanding and becoming formalized (Staff, 1983). According to one study (Post, 1982), 85% of 400 companies surveyed by the Boston University School of Management rated community relations as a key function in public affairs.

More recently, The Conference Board (Staff, undated), reporting on a study by Madelyn Hochstein, Senior Vice President of Yankelovich, Skelly and White, indicated that the current social and political climate may be termed the "Era of New Maturity." Hochstein said, "Corporate leaders anticipate greater commitment to community and socially directed activities. They are also becoming more interested in affecting the public policy debate on such social issues as education and health care delivery— particularly where they perceive a lack of action on the part of public policymakers" (p. 3).

Professionalization of Function

The second trend is the expanding "professionalization" of community relations. Less than a dozen years ago the community relations function, if it existed at all, was restricted to overseeing contributions to the United Way and representing the corporation on local committees. This is rarely the case now. Increasingly, acccording to the Conference Board, the function is aimed toward "activism," (Staff, undated). Moreover, it is directed to a wide variety of community needs. The five top community issues of concern to corporations, according to the Conference Board, are:

1. Local economic development.
2. Primary and secondary education.
3. Health care and hospitals.
4. Unemployment and job training.
5. Arts and culture.

As evidence of the activist orientation, it is now not uncommon for corporations to conduct community needs assessments. The needs assessment has many purposes. One is to assist in determining how to allocate the company's contribution dollars. Another is to provide a focus for the company's volunteer programs. The needs assessment helps to identify those organizations in a community that need specialized assistance. Volunteers in a company are matched to an organizational need. And a third purpose is to assist in identifying emerging community issues and needs.

The community-activist focus has led some corporations to become directly involved in community planning projects. In Lynn, Massachusetts, for example, the General Electric Company was concerned with a report that suggested that the local school system was not in a position to prepare high school graduates for the technological needs of the 1990s. The General

Electric Company has a large presence in Lynn and a major stake in the local school system.

To address the issue, the company sponsored and worked with three graduate social work interns to develop a public/private partnership. The interns focused on preparing a process of developing community support for the partnership. They conducted a community analysis and identified key leaders and organizations in the local community and within the school system. Using primarily focus-group interviews, they conducted a survey of community leaders and groups.

Although the survey stage was used as a data-gathering activity, it was also used as a means to begin the process of community involvement in the school system. Community groups and leaders were involved through interviews and meetings in designing recommendations for the planning project. And the formal report was presented at a community meeting involving school teachers and administrators, political leaders, including the incoming mayor, people in business, parents, students, business leaders, and union officials.

The process brought about broadened community support for the school system and the development of a business and education partnership that had the endorsement and support of both the business community and the mayor's office. The General Electric Company realized that, without community and political support, any projects it would initiate would eventually flounder (Gross et al., 1985).

In effect, the interns working on behalf of the school system and General Electric were engaged in a traditional community organization and planning project—one that could come straight out of an early textbook on community organization (Ross, 1955).

Decentralization of the Community Relations Function

A third trend is the decentralization of the community relations function. Major corporations are insisting that line or plant managers begin to assume the responsibility for community relations. The line or plant manager is the personal presence of the company in the community. He or she, therefore, can best understand the community and its needs and is best able to respond to emerging community and social issues.

Corporations consequently are encouraging local managers to become involved in community organizations and groups. One reason is to improve the community's opinion of the company. The second is to learn more about a community and its organizations. The latter is an "issues-sensing" function. The participation becomes a way for the company to learn what the important issues in a community are and to prepare, if necessary, ways for the company to respond (Useem, 1985).

CONSEQUENCES FOR SOCIAL WORK

Corporate community relations, as it is now being practiced, is a new and emerging function in business. It is beginning to provide opportunities for social work and social workers. The directors of community relations programs at Time, Inc. and Borg Warner, for example, are professionally trained social workers.

For social workers it can provide employment and career opportunities. The skills and knowledge that are now needed for community relations personnel are precisely those skills and knowledge that have long been advocated and taught for community-organization-trained social workers (Lynde, 1959). Examples include:

1. The ability to locate and work with community leaders.
2. An understanding and working knowledge of social welfare, housing, community development, health, recreation, and other community organizations.
3. Knowledge of health and welfare needs.
4. The ability to conduct a community needs assessment.
5. The ability to analyze agency and organization budgets and requests for contributions.
6. The ability to recruit and involve volunteers both within and outside the corporation in community projects.
7. The ability to facilitate and to act as a catalyst for the involvement of company executives—line and staff—in community programs and projects.
8. Knowledge of the community organization process.

In effect, the community relations executive needs to be skillful in organizing and planning. She or he should be an enabler, assisting individuals and groups within the corporation to identify the community needs the corporation will be willing to support.

The primary role is that of an expert, as described by Ross (1955). The community relations executive should be able to provide data and advice on a number of community issues and problems. He or she should also serve as an expert in community analysis and diagnosis and the evaluation of community and corporate community programs. She or he should be knowledgeable as well about other corporate and community programs.

For social work, the growing community relations activities of corporations provides a unique opportunity to educate and influence the business community about social welfare needs and programs. As noted earlier, except for the United Way, social work has not worked closely with the business community. This has been a mistake. Business and organized labor can play an important educative and supportive role in developing social welfare programs. They are critical and essential elements in every community. To exclude them from participating in social welfare activities is undemocratic and shortsighted.

REFERENCES

Ansoff, H. I. (1984). *Implanting strategic management*. Englewood Cliffs, NJ: Prentice-Hall.

Bernays, E. L. (1975). Social responsibility of business. *Public Relations Review, 1*(3), 5–16.

Bowen, H. R. (1953). *Social responsiblities of the businessman*. New York: Harper & Brothers.

Burke, E. M. (1965). The road to planning: An organizational analysis. *Social Service Review, 39*(3), 261–270.

Burke, E. M. (1967). The search for authority in planning. *Social Service Review, 41*(3), 250–260.

Burke, E. M. (1987). Corporate social responsibility. In *Encyclopedia of social work*. New York: National Association of Social Workers.

Chemical Bank. (undated). *Giving and getting: A Chemical Bank study of charitable contributions through 1984*. New York: Author.

Coladzin, R. S. (1981). Redefining the role of the corporation in the community. Speech to Public Affairs Council, November 18, 1981.

Drucker, P. F. (1972). The concept of the corporation. *Business and Society Review*, (autumn) 12–17.

Drucker, P. F. (1984). Doing good to do well: The new opportunities for business enterprise. In H. Brooks, L. Liebman, & C. S. Schelling *Public-private partnerships: New opportunities for meeting social needs* (pp. 285–302). Cambridge, MA: Ballinger.

Fenn, D. H., Jr. (1984). Executives as community volunteers. In D. N. Dickson, (Ed.), *Business and its publics*. New York: Wiley.

Gerstenfeld, S. V., & Burke, E. (1985). Affirmative action in nine large companies: A field study. *Personnel, 62*(4), 54–60.

Gross, S., Kamali, S., & Pizzuto, A. (1985). *A plan for achieving business and community support for the Lynn school system*. Chestnut Hill, MA: The Center for Corporate Community Relations, Boston College Graduate School of Social Work.

Haas, P. E., Sr. (1983). *Report of special study committee on the role of United Way in community problem solving. September 14, 1983*. Alexandria, VA: United Way of America.

Hollander, J. (1975). A step-by-step guide to corporate affirmative action. *Business and Society Review* (Fall) (15), 67–73.

Lueck, T. J. (1985, November 25). Companies giving a hand to Hartford's poor. *New York Times*, pp. B1, B4.

Lynde, E. D. (1959). The role of the community organization practitioner. In E. B.

Harper & A. Dunham, *Community Organization in Action* (pp. 472–479). New York: Association Press.

Maeroff, G. I. (1984, August 23). Teachers listen to business chief. *New York Times*, p. A19.

Post, J. E. (1982). *Public affairs function*. Boston: Boston University School of Management.

Ross, M. G. (1955). *Community organization: Theory and principles*. New York: Harper & Row.

Sethi, S. P. (1979). Grassroots lobbying and the corporation. *Business and Society Review* (Spring) (29), 8–14.

Shapiro, I. (1979). The process. In D. N. Dickson, *Business and its public* (pp. 47–52). New York: Wiley.

Shandler, P. (1972). Whatever happened to the urban coalition? *Business and Society Review* (Summer) (2), 22–27.

Staff. (undated). Business in the community: Where vanguard companies are focusing. *The Conference Board Research Bulletin*. New York: The Conference Board.

Staff. (1983, January). More and more firms are formalizing community relations function. *Impact*. Washington, DC: The Public Affairs Council, pp. 1, 5.

Urban America, Inc. (1969). Urban coalition: Turning the country around. In A. Shank, *Political power and the urban crisis* (pp. 466–474). Boston: Holbrook Press.

Useem, M. (1985). The rise of the political manager. *Sloan Management Review*, 27(1), 15–26.

Verity, C. W., Jr. (1982). Preface and acknowledgements. In P. A. Berger, K. S. Moy, N. R. Pierce, & C. Steinback, *Investing in America: Initiatives for community and economic development*. Washington, DC: The President's Task Force on Private Sector Initiatives.

Walter, S. (1980). *Proceedings of the White House Conference on Strategic Planning*. Washington, DC: Council of State Planning Agencies.

Witner, L. (1981). Business and the cities: Programs and practices. *Information Bulletin, No. 87*. New York: The Conference Board.

VI Managing the Challenges of the Future

21 The Changing World of Work

Henry Morgan

For a large number of Americans, the world of work is in a state of siege because of very strong forces acting on businesses. These forces are creating change at an accelerated rate and creating stress for millions of people. Understanding the forces and developing coping strategies should be a major agenda for those concerned with providing support to people under stress, and not just for those concerned with the economy. There are four forces that will be discussed:

- The internationalization of business.
- Rapidly changing technology.
- The deregulation of many sectors of the economy.
- The current mania of mergers and acquisitions.

This chapter makes clear that any one of the four can produce formidable pressures on many people. The combination of all four operating at the same time is overwhelming. A description of their effects is developed. Some suggestions are proposed as a tentative agenda for educational and social service institutions to help people prepare for the necessary changes in today's business environment.

THE INTERNATIONALIZATION OF BUSINESS

Since World War II, there has been an extensive trend toward increased international competition. In the 1950s and 1960s, the United States was the primary leader and beneficiary of this trend, developing multinational companies and making heavy exports primarily to a product-starved Europe. Since 1970, however, there has been a major shift. The United States is becoming a net importer of manufactured goods, with the Far East, and Japan in particular, the major suppliers.

We have witnessed a rapid loss of manufacturing jobs to lower-labor-cost countries. Over 1.5 million manufacturing jobs have been lost since 1979. The major losses have been in textile and shoe manufacturing, the smokestack industries like steel and shipbuilding, automobile parts and assembly, and electronics.

In the past 5 years, another change has become apparent. Instead of nations importing and exporting from factories in their homeland, we now see the establishment of international companies with factories all over the world—worldwide suppliers to worldwide markets. Let me cite some examples and some of the impact on American workers, both blue and white collar.

The Ford Motor Company is the second largest manufacturer of cars and trucks in the United States. In Europe, particularly Great Britain and Germany, Ford is either the largest or second largest manufacturer by virtue of its production there. Ford is producing parts for its cars in more than 20 countries. These parts are assembled into finished cars and trucks all over the world. A Ford Escort assembled in Michigan for sale in the United States has over 50% of its labor content in overseas jobs. So-called American-made products are invariably internationally made.

We have seen American Motors Company taken over by the Renault company of France. We have seen Chrysler enter into joint-venture agreements with Mitsubishi of Japan, Volkswagen of Germany, Simca of Italy, and Samsung of Korea. We have seen General Motors build an assembly plant in California in partnership with Toyota of Japan. We have seen Honda, Volkswagen, Nissan, and Mazda build manufacturing facilities in the United States.

What once was the haven for the highest-paid union-protected jobs in America, the automotive industry, has been shattered into a worldwide network of manufacturing, assembly, sales, and service delivery systems, with a severe cut in the number of well-paid jobs for blue- and white-collar workers in the United States. The year 1986 brought the introduction of new low-cost economy cars from Yugoslavia and Korea.

The Cummins Engine Company, headquartered in Columbus, Indiana, has been the leading producer of high-quality diesel engines for trucks and tractors worldwide for over 50 years. Cummins has been one of the quality U.S. companies, from its products to its treatment of employees to its high sense of social responsibility. Cummins is now facing heavy competition from a Japanese manufacturer of diesel engines, Kumatzu, which is producing and selling in the United States equal, if not better-quality, engines at one third less cost. Cummins must meet this attack on its market by reducing its prices by one third while improving its quality. To do this, Cummins has announced that it will reduce its workforce worldwide by 35%

to 40%. The lost jobs will be manufacturing, support services, managers, engineers, and professionals.

Sanyo Electric Company of Osaka, Japan, has established two manufacturing plants in the United States. One in Arkansas was purchased from an American company and in the process saved American jobs. The other in San Diego was built new and created American jobs. In the recent slide of the American dollar against the Japanese yen, Sanyo management was busily shifting its product mix between its American factories and its Japanese counterparts. Changing values of currency, although viewed as benefiting American manufacturers, in reality merely contributes to a global chess game. Ford in Europe benefits from the strong dollar, Sanyo in the United States benefits from the weaker dollar. American jobs are created by the international network of international companies.

A different sector of the economy is equally a player in international markets. United States agriculture has become one of the major export sources for the United States economy. Here there are different sets of forces. While manufacturing is driven by the marketplace, agriculture is more likely to be driven by international politics. Sale of wheat and grain to the Soviet Union depends more on the temperature of the Cold War than it does on price and supply of food. Shipments of food internationally are determined from Washington as a weapon in power politics. The recent impact on the farm economy has been devastating.

Yet another area of international impact is the banking industry. The commercial banks in the money centers of the United States—New York, Chicago, and San Francisco—have been engaging in extensive foreign borrowing and lending to nations all over the world. There are more branches of Continental Bank of Illinois in Brussels than there are in Chicago. American banks are in competition with foreign banks who operate branches in the U.S.

American jobs in this industry are affected by international competition and are closely coupled to the success or failure of loans made to foreign businesses and governments. In fact, U.S. depositers are unwitting participants in this world financial game. An additional factor in world economics is the emergence of the United States as one of the debtor nations, with large inflows of foreign capital to finance its large governmental budget deficits.

The full impact of this internationalization on the world of work in the United States has not yet been felt fully. It is obvious, however, that changes are occurring—changes that increase competition for goods and services, changes that involve worldwide participants, and changes that affect the jobs of millions of Americans. These changes affect the nature of work, the rewards for work, the identity of the worker, and the long-term stability of employment.

CHANGING TECHNOLOGY

It is almost trite to say that technology is profoundly changing the way we live and work. In every facet of our lives, we have been affected by technological change. In health and medicine, in agriculture, in communications and transportation, and in education, things are different from what they were 10, 20, or 50 years ago, and the rate by which they become still more different is breathtaking.

Buoyed by their successes in the late 1800s and early 1900s, the railroad companies did not realize they were in the transportation industry and not just the business of moving people and goods over paths predetermined by the laying of track. While trains still move material, particularly low-cost bulk material like coal, the airlines now move people faster and farther. The railroads did not keep pace with the technological changes that created a partial obsolescence, resulting in the losses of many good jobs.

The appearance of jet engines and wide-body aircraft also has changed the nature of travel, of tourism, and of the hospitality industry. The state of Hawaii has lost its dependence on the agriculture crops of sugar and pineapples and is now heavily dependent upon the flow of tourists from East and West to spend time and money at resort hotels. Without the large jet plane, a technological creation, there would not be as many service jobs in the hospitality businesses. The Hawaiian economic base has shifted from agricultural work to hotel work. The new jobs are generally lower paid.

Technological change has direct and indirect impacts. Jobs are changed, jobs are lost, and jobs are created. Technology also impacts the nature of the international competition discussed above. Let us look at examples.

Polaroid, a household word, is a corporation merely 50 years old. Originally founded to capitalize on one concept, uses of polarizers to reduce glare, the company has gone through the transformation to a photographic company with a second technology 35 years ago, and is presently undergoing another transformation—to a highly diversified multiple-technology company. As it was originally conceived, the company was a community of high technical competence that subcontracted most of the manufacturing operations and lower skilled jobs to outside suppliers. With the introduction of the SX-70 line of products 15 years ago, manufacturing was brought into the company, creating manual assembly jobs in the Boston area and eliminating hand assembly jobs in Little Rock, Arkansas, and Chicago, Illinois, the bases of the subcontractors. New technology created new types of jobs for employees in one area of the country and eliminated jobs in another area.

An acquaintance of mine graduated from Boston University in 1956 to go to work in a business his grandfather started many years ago. This business had an established niche making a form of costume jewelry and had existed in that business for many years. In the 30 years since my friend has run the family business, he has had to change its very nature twice. Cheap foreign products eliminated the market of the original business. He transformed the company to take advantage of new plastics and a new market for molded plastic products. This new business lasted slightly more than 10 years, when new competition and new technologies required still another transformation. The continued survival of this company and of its jobs for employees has depended upon an ability to perceive new technological opportunities and the ability to adapt. Rapid adaptation to technological change has become a fact of life for management and worker.

The Samsung Corporation in Korea is one of the world's most successful conglomerates. Originally founded as a sugar-refining company, it is now a technological leader in shipbuilding, watchmaking, electronic manufacturing, and now automobile manufacturing in joint business with Chrysler. It will soon also be a producer of the most advanced microelectronic components. Samsung has succeeded through the adoption of and the development of the latest technologies. It did not see itself in the sugar business.

Technological change can be a threat to as well as an opportunity for the management of industry, and it can be a threat to as well as an opportunity for workers in industry. There is no future in being a modern Luddite. The critical differences between a threat and an opportunity are vision and adaptability. Technology is creating new opportunity; it has destroyed old opportunity. Technology has created new businesses, new procedures for conducting old businesses, and created new competitors.

Technological change is evident in the financial service industries. Look at what has happened to banking jobs through the adoption of large data processors. Individual transactions are processed electronically rather than by hand. Cash transactions are conducted more quickly, more conveniently, and more accurately through automatic tellers at some loss in personal relations. There are advantages and disadvantages in the loss, but the nature of banking is different.

Dramatic changes in work are evident in the health care industries. New pharmaceutical products have changed the nature of treatment, and other products have changed the nature of diagnosis. Further changes have been heralded through the development of biotechnology. Each of these changes produces changes in the jobs needed and in the nature of work. Old jobs change and new jobs are created. Here again, the pressures of change reward vision and adaptability and relentlessly punish the lack of those qualities.

EFFECTS OF DEREGULATION

The history of the regulation of American business and services reflects a desire to protect the consumer. A consequence of well-intentioned regulation has sometimes been the establishment and maintenance of protected turf. Regulation of the telephone industry, for example, preserved a huge monopoly for the Bell system. With this preservation was the entrenchment of a philosophy of serving customers but a less successful control of costs. Employees in protected industries enjoyed protected jobs in a noncompetitive environment. Similar protections have been enjoyed in the banking industry, the airlines industry, and in trucking. In each of these cases, competition was limited, service was the paramount objective, and job security was assured.

The past 10 years have seen massive attacks on regulated preserves. Among the most prominent has been the breakup of the Bell System. In August 1985, AT&T announced the elimination of 24,000 jobs. The bulk of these, 15,000, were administrative jobs. Restructuring of the telephone subsidiaries has caused other job losses. In addition, those employees who have been retained have had to undergo a massive attitude change to face and beat the new competitors. AT&T has also moved out of its old game preserve and entered new fields. Who would have thought that AT&T and IBM would now be in head-to-head competition in each others' park? IBM has moved into the field of data transmission, and AT&T has moved into data generation and storage. The new employee of AT&T must be adaptive and competitive. The very nature of work at the once-slumbering giant is changing. Technological change is also a factor, but the main source of pressure for change here is deregulation.

Another industry hit with widespread change is the airline industry. Deregulation of the airlines has resulted in increased competition from new, smaller regional lines that have taken over many of the shorter routes the large trunk carriers willingly give up. However, success in these unwanted routes has fed the new entrants, which in turn then enter the more lucrative longer-route market. The end result has been instability, job changes, gains and losses, and a loss of job security for many employees.

Other prominent changes caused by deregulation can be seen in the financial service industries. Competition in banking is no longer coming from other banks alone. Large brokerage firms such as Merrill Lynch are now essentially in the banking business. The same can be said of automotive companies that are offering consumer loans no longer restricted to the purchase of new cars. One such company, for example, is offering home mortgages. Another new banking source is the credit card issuer, who not only offers to finance purchases but now also offers cash advances, that is, loans.

Again we see the same result we have seen in increased internationalization and new technology. There are new competitors where they did not exist before. New competition puts pressures on existing employment patterns, eliminating some jobs, creating others, and greatly changing the nature of those that continue.

Each of these first three factors, internationalization, technological change, and deregulation, calls for the same response from industry. The response is to be more competitive, which in turn means to be more adaptive. Increased adaptiveness in turn calls for faster responses to change. Management, organizations, and in the final analysis individuals must be more quickly adaptive. Long-term security is lost. Dependence on reward for long-term loyalty must be forgone, and the ultimate security must now come from personal resourcefulness.

Some years ago there was a shake-out in the defense industry around Boston. Two of my friends, both highly trained plasma physicists, lost their jobs. Not only was the job lost in their company, there ceased to be a market for plasma physicists at all. One of them had wrapped up his whole identity in his training and his job. He was a plasma physicist; that is how he defined himself. Without a job as a plasma physicist, he lost his value to himself, his family, and the world. Unable to adapt or unable to see himself as other than a plasma physicist, he rapidly deteriorated. He lost his home and his family and was not able to recover his self-esteem.

The second friend, also a plasma physicist, did not limit his self-concept to his professional identity. Devoted to his home and to his family, he developed other interests. An ardent bicyclist, he started a business making racks to carry bicycles on the back of cars. While I am sure he is still a plasma physicist, he is not restricted in his self-concept to that role. He has allowed himself to be more than that. Just as Polaroid did not restrict itself to being a company that made polarizing devices to reduce glare, and just as the Samsung Corporation did not restrict itself to being a sugar refiner, he did not restrict himself to being a plasma physicist.

The same issues came up when many schoolteachers were laid off during the cutback in schools a few years ago. Some suffered great and permanent harm because they had identified themselves with one unchanging lifelong role. Others were able to find places in new careers, expanding their horizons and changing their self-concepts.

A visit to Gary, Indiana or South Chicago will reveal thousands of former employees of the steel industry who have their identities locked into their former jobs. Skilled steel workers have been unable to adjust to the facts of the permanent loss of their job and, with it, their identity. For some, similar jobs may exist in other states, necessitating a major uprooting of family to a new and strange community. In most cases, there is a strong resistance to give in, admit defeat, and move. For the vast majority, the choice is between unemployment or looking for a job in a nearby community that will not use the old skills. Psychological destruction of person and family hangs heavily over many heads.

The same situation exists in Michigan and Ohio with automobile workers. The dual impacts of foreign competition and automated manufacturing have permanently eliminated tens of thousands of jobs. The choice becomes one of three: move to another part of the country; remain unemployed; or take a job requiring new or lesser skills at lower pay. The loss of these skilled jobs, usually unionized, means a loss of high pay, family security, and the loss of the path to higher economic position in American life.

Farmers in Iowa are facing the same losses. The family farm has been a source of identity and security; with its loss come heavy stresses on individuals and families.

Lester Thurow (1980) and others have called attention to the increasing decline in the number of highly paid and skilled blue-collar jobs that have contributed to the swelling of the middle class. These jobs are being replaced by fewer but even higher paying technological jobs primarily available to the new, younger, and better educated employee entering the workforce; and by lower-paying, lesser-skilled service work available to both the younger, less skilled, and less educated new employee and the older displaced worker who has to step down in the world.

Even those who retain their jobs have to accept changes. Recent collective bargaining agreements in the automobile industry have focused on job security rather than on pay and benefit increases. One result of the emphasis on job security is that the more senior workers keep jobs at the expense of their younger, more recently hired colleagues. The president of a leading Japanese electronics company commented to me that it was his observation that American manufacturing workers were considerably older than their Asian counterparts. We had been discussing the lower productivity of American factories when his comment was made. Because more senior workers get higher pay, it is more expensive to produce in the United States, regardless of the relative productivity of young versus older workers.

A new practice accentuates this pay difference. Some companies have instituted a two-tier wage structure. Under this plan, older, more senior employees' wages are protected at existing rates, but new hires come in at a lower wage rate, a second tier. The consequences of first-class and second-class employees is rivalry, tension, and lowered morale.

EFFECTS OF MERGERS AND ACQUISITIONS

Many of the changes discussed above have had destructive impacts on semiskilled and skilled workers. The fourth major force at work today, a trend toward mergers and acquisitions, is having its devastating effect on middle and senior level managers and professionals.

In 1985 alone, there were over 35 merger transactions at $1 billion and over. A total of 3,001 mergers and acquisitions totalled a capital value of $179.6 billion, exceeding the 1984 record of 2,543 transactions worth $122.2 billion.

In most of these 5,544 deals, the financing to accomplish the transaction involved greatly increased corporate debt. The cost of carrying huge debt has to be met by operating efficiencies, which in turn have meant wholesale staff reductions. The current popular term is *downsizing*.

Let us look at one of the deals, the acquisition of the Gulf Oil Company by Chevron. This huge merger resulted in the elimination of the Gulf corporate headquarters in an imposing building in Pittsburgh. With the building went jobs, a loss whose meaning in human terms is clear. The loss of Gulf jobs in that city has had a "trickle-down" effect in the entire city. In addition, the campuslike research center outside of Pittsburgh has closed and the facilities sold. Thousands of scientific professionals and middle- and upper-level managers lost their jobs. Some, but very few, were offered positions with Chevron in California.

A similar impact was felt in Houston, Gulf's second headquarters. That once-thriving city has been dealt multiple blows by the loss of Gulf jobs and the general decline in the oil industry. Thus, highly trained and successful Gulf employees were not able to find other jobs in an ailing industry.

Downsizing is a general phenomenon in the largest companies in America. Like Cummins, every Fortune 500 company is planning to increase its sales with fewer employees. The major victims of downsizing are the middle managers aged 35 to 55. Most have been long-time loyal employees who are now asked to leave. Those at the upper end of the age bracket have been offered attractive packages of early retirement benefits. But what is the future for a 55-year-old manager with a retirement package?

The result of the last 2 years of merger mania is a dramatic loss of white-collar jobs with the largest corporations, the bastions of security. The pattern of employment is undergoing a major shift, with the results not fully understood by economists or sociologists. The pattern includes changes in managerial practices of the large corporations, with the permanent elimination of hundreds of thousands of staff and management jobs to reduce corporate "fat" and to streamline operations. This corporate dieting means reducing the number of employees, which translates to thousands of families under stress. In most cases, the middle managers have gone silently, without the press attention that comes with union layoffs.

In many cases, the families affected by these reductions are two-salaried families. Moving to another area for a new job for one member of the family means leaving behind the second job and looking for two new jobs in a new community. Consider the psychological stress on someone who has worked 20 years for one company suddenly having to go on the job market. A new industry has developed in the human resource field called outplacing (see Chapter 12 of this volume). Departing employees are given coaching and help in job seeking.

SUMMARY AND FUTURE DIRECTIONS

In today's world, social service professionals will meet many defeated individuals, many ruined families, and many others affected by the ripple effects. It may be helpful for the helping professions to know much more about the vast environmental changes in the world of work that defeat people who might have coped well in a different century.

There are clues, too, in the nature of the defeats, as to how to help. Today's workers and their families need to find identity apart from their work roles; they need to find it in their family roles, their avocations and interests, their sense of themselves in different work roles. People need practical help: how to find new jobs in new fields; how to relocate and make new friends; how to juggle dual careers when one is going well and one is not.

As I look at the combination of the four forces that have been presented here, I reach some conclusions that have implications for the educational establishment. I am reminded of a talk I heard by Malcolm Knowles over 15 years ago. He was talking about careers, how in the Middle Ages one career lasted many generations. The skills of being an artisan were passed on from generation to generation. On a recent trip to Japan, I met a young potter who was the eighth generation of his family to be in that trade. In America, there are very few who are carrying on the trade of their great-grandparents.

Dr. Knowles went on to say that for most of this century we trained for one career, one career that lasted a lifetime. We went to school to learn to be a doctor, or a lawyer, or we learned a craft of electrician or plumber. This was a lifetime career. As in the case of my two plasma physicists, the career also became an identity. We are our profession.

His third point was that in the present and in the future, one career will not last a lifetime, and most of us will have at least two if not more totally different careers in a lifetime. Each of the four forces is operating to produce this result. Each one is putting pressures that work against continued employment in one company and in one field.

Changing technology is the most obvious. Engineers and scientists go through extensive training, which is obsolete in 20 years unless they spend a great deal of time and energy staying current. The very tools of trades are changing, requiring skilled workers to retrain constantly. Each of the other forces are increasing competition, which in turn requires shorter and shorter response times to retain new product and service competitiveness. Shorter response times require flexible organizations and adaptive employees. Bureaucracy is the villain in today's world, and rigid bureaucratic practices spell defeat.

The total emerging picture that develops is one of a need for individuals who can adapt to change. We need individuals who can either teach themselves or who are psychologically secure enough to be able to change their roles completely without loss of self-concept. The survivor in this world will be the one who has learned to learn, the one who does not rely on skills and knowledge learned once, early in life.

Lawrence K. Frank foresaw this need in 1958:

> The great emphasis upon teaching subject matter . . . has ignored the importance, if not the necessity, of *unlearning* as essential. . . . So long as we lived in a relatively stable culture and a slowly changing social order, schools could operate as instruments for transmitting traditional lore, teaching the familiar academic skills and imparting the wisdom of the past. But today such a program is, I believe, productive of immeasurable confusion and social conflict, perpetuating the beliefs and assumptions, the obsolete ways of thinking that seriously handicap us or even blindly drive us to disaster while we accelerate our technological progress, utilizing completely different concepts and assumptions. . . . (p. 21)

Learning and work have to be parallel activities throughout life, so that individuals are not only keeping current in one career but are also learning a new career even before leaving the one they are in.

Can our schools prepare individuals for this lifetime of learning and unlearning? The best nursery schools and day care centers do it, a handful of colleges and a few of the graduate schools. The elementary and secondary schools do not seem to have these goals before them. The following quotation might well describe many of today's schools:

> Many are demanding a rigid program of strict academic instruction, beginning, some urge, in the kindergarten or nursery school, with increased pressure for achievement and progressive weeding out of those who cannot meet these requirements. Others are advocating a "crash" program in science and mathematics as essential to national defense. Few seem to realize how much of our teaching is devoted to anachronistic ideas and obsolete ways of thinking, a program of educating our students for a world that no longer exists. (p. 15)

Although an apt description of education reform in 1985, the above was also written by Lawrence Frank in 1958. Today's world needs a different approach in our schools, and all our educational services, toward the goals of vision and adaptability.

In closing, let me go back to the role of the social worker in this changing world of work. I have seen the important contribution that social workers have made in working within the industrial setting, helping employees to adapt to the pressure of the job. What I am seeing is the added stress of the change or elimination of many of those jobs. Individuals have to be helped to separate their self-concept from their work position. With the prospect of several career changes in a lifetime, individuals must be helped to adapt, to let go, and grasp a new identity in a new field. Social workers can help provide the support to the person while making the transition.

A new sense of self-identity is necessary, one that is apart from that given by the job. Individuals need to see that all is not lost if they can no longer make steel or no longer teach. I hope that the social workers can understand this need for job adaptability and can be helpful. Understanding the forces of change is an essential prerequisite to helping.

REFERENCES

Frank, L. K. (1959). *The school as agent for cultural renewal*. Burton Lecture, Graduate School of Education, Harvard University. Cambridge, MA: Harvard University Press.
Thurow, L. (1980). *The zero-sum society*. New York: Basic Books.

22 With a View to the Future

Michael Lane Smith

People seriously interested in social work in the workplace soon encounter its complexity and variety. From the early activities of the welfare secretaries of the past century, occupational social work has expanded spasmodically and unevenly to embrace an impressive array of problems and processes. Today, professional social workers provide consultation, intervention, and support with respect to the range of problems, target groups, and activities described in the preceding chapters of this book.

There is ample reason to believe that this ongoing maturation of occupational social work will continue into the coming decades. Indeed, we are likely to see the pace and intensity of change accelerate as more and more practitioners from a variety of human service professions and disciplines seek to carve out a presence or legitimacy in the workplace and as technological and broad social changes make their impact felt.

It would be nice to know what the future holds for social work in occupational settings. Obviously, any prediction can only be a guess. Consequently, this chapter is not intended as a blueprint for tomorrow. Rather, it describes a number of *emerging* issues that are sufficiently significant and complex to shape whatever it is that the future holds for industrial social work. For simplicity of discussion, they are organized around three broad categories: (1) the nature of work, work organizations, and the workforce; (2) professionalization and professional education; and (3) service delivery and intervention systems.

THE NATURE OF WORK, WORK ORGANIZATIONS, AND THE WORKFORCE

Work, workplaces, and the workforce are all changing. More and more, we have become an information processing society. More and more, service has replaced manufacture as an arena for economic activity. Computerized

343

technologies (from the robotics that transform assembly lines to the "end-of-train devices" that replace cabooses) have fundamentally altered the nature of work and the character of the workplace in many occupational sectors. For example, the explosive development of microcomputers and their increasing power and economy have made it possible for employees in a variety of businesses to telecommute to work. In fact, the workers remain at home or at satellite offices widely dispersed from their employing organizations. Rather than moving themselves back and forth by auto, train, or airplane, telecommuting workers send their electronic signals back and forth at the speed of light over ordinary telephone lines. For many of these workers, the notion of an office away from home—indeed, even the notion of a 9-to-5 workday—is something of the past. In addition, such changes in technology call for skills and demands different from those of the past, and they can fundamentally alter the social context of work as well.

Mergers, downsizing, and reorganization also change the social context of work. Mergers frequently necessitate the elimination of redundant organizational parts. Downsizing, an economic imperative rationalized through the "small is beautiful" argument (see Naisbitt, 1984), likewise involves the loss of jobs, job security, and (frequently) job benefits for many workers. Whatever the reason, reorganization has been touted as an attribute of many "excellent" companies (Peters & Waterman, 1982), and this practice is likely to become even more frequent in the years to come.

In addition to changes in the technologies and organization of work, the character of the American workforce is also changing. Federal, state, and private initiatives in equal employment opportunity and affirmative action practices have opened many work opportunities for women, racial minorities, and other people who have been victims of employment discrmination. As a result, greater numbers of these people are now (1) members of the workforce and (2) moving upward through organizational hierarchies.

Broad demographic forces are also changing the face of the typical American worker. Many of the people born during the post-World War II baby boom are now approaching 40 years of age. As always, they represent a significant bulge in the nation's population distribution. However, these maturing baby-boomers pose several important issues for the world of work. For one thing, their advancing age and raw numbers mean that the average age of the American worker increases each year. This alone is significant in terms of employment discrimination directed at older workers. Of equal importance for people accustomed to measuring self-worth through promotions and occupational advancement is the acute competition among this disproportionately large age cohort for the increasingly scarce upper management and executive positions available to them in the latter half of their work lives ("More Executives," November 14, 1986, p. 29). In short, employment discrimination, lack of advancement, and technological and social changes in the world of work threaten to assault an ever-larger number of people and threaten to challenge accustomed meanings they hold for their places in the work world.

PROFESSIONALIZATION AND PROFESSIONAL EDUCATION

The past decade has witnessed an explosion in the interest shown in occupational social work generally and in employee assistance programs especially. Employers and unions have recognized the importance of these programs to such an extent that over 8,000 EAPs now exist in the United States, including EAPs in 80% of the Fortune 500 companies (Maiden & Hardcastle, 1986, p. 63). No small part of this growth is attributable to human service providers themselves. Employee assistance work represents an attractive career field for social workers, psychologists, counselors (especially those certified in the chemical abuse field), and others (including in San Antonio, for example, some members of the clergy).

Given the disparate skills and conceptual orientations of this practitioner array, it is understandable that various groups have stepped forth to define minimum standards for practitioner skills, knowledge, and abilities. On the one hand, organizations like the Association of Labor/Management Administrators and Consultants on Alcoholism (ALMACA) and the American Association of Industrial Social Workers (AAISW) provide certification for employee assistance workers and (by implication) offer standards for such practice. On the other hand, many universities offer degree programs at the undergraduate or graduate levels for practice as either an industrial social worker or employee assistance counselor (Nida et al., 1987; Maiden & Hardcastle, 1986; Myers & Myers, 1986) and thereby implicitly assert minimum standards for professional competence in this arena. While there are some areas of agreement among these various bodies (for example, the importance of mastering fundamental counseling skills and the need for understanding the dynamics of substance abuse), the fact remains that major areas of disagreement continue to exist over the standards deemed necessary for professional-level practice in the workplace.

For social workers, several issues of major importance are implicated in this issue. For one, social work in the workplace is an arena far broader than just employee assistance. As described numerous times in preceding chapters, occupational social work embraces customer service and corporate community involvement activities as well as expansive organizational interventions—in addition to conventional employee assistance activities. Consequently, standards for employee assistance practitioners neglect a host of skills, knowledge, and abilities important for these other arenas of industrial social work.

With respect to "direct" social work practice in the workplace, the issue can be captured in the question, "Should social workers' practice in EAPs differ in any important respects from the practice of their non-social work colleagues?" In other words, is there any important difference in the knowledge, skills, or role of social workers staffing employee assistance programs when compared to EAP counselors who are not professionally trained social workers? If there are (or *should* be), then standards for social work practice in the workplace need to reflect such differences. If differences do not exist, then social work practitioners and educators need to admit one of two realities: either (1) that which is unique to social work is insignificant to employee assistance practice or (2) social workers have yet to develop the awareness or means whereby employees and work organizations can profit from the special contributions that social workers can potentially offer. Both these latter alternatives offer the social work profession critical challenges. Each is likely to drive the profession toward the goal of identifying the contributions most acceptably claimed as distinctive of social work practice in employee assistance, with consequent emphasis on the knowledge and skill building necessary for these contributions. It is doubtful that the profession can remain content with a perception that social workers simply duplicate the competencies of others.

While the very premises of these questions await more systematic study, it is clear that actors in the EAP field view various practitioner classes as offering different packages of strengths and weaknesses. When compared to psychologists, alcohol- and drug-abuse counselors, and others, social workers are commonly viewed as possessing competitive diagnostic and counseling skills and superior familiarity with community resources and organizational dynamics. Equally common, it seems, is the opinion that social workers need increased understanding and skills in the area of substance abuse (especially alcoholism)—knowledge that they have not acquired in their university-based training. This stereotype is reflected in the frequently whispered comment, "The ideal EAP counselor is an MSW with alcohol- and drug-abuse counseling certification."

A host of educational issues emerge from these points. For example, how extensive or comprehensive should occupationally focused social work education be? To what extent can (and should) social work educators prepare students for specialties within the broad industrial arena? What efforts should be made to educate undergraduate students to practice in the workplace, and what kinds of continua need to be developed to link undergraduate with graduate-level education in this area? What standards need to be developed to ensure high-quality internships for students interested in industrial social work (internships anchored to classroom curricula sensitive to practice in the workplace)? What nontraditional and continuing education opportunities can be created to assist interested social workers who have already earned their professional degrees? The challenges to social work educators are many, but excellent programs offered at several graduate schools of social work clearly show that they are manageable for at least some institutions and faculty.

SERVICE DELIVERY AND INTERVENTION SYSTEMS

It seems as though the decade of the 1980s will be known as the period when human service practitioners "discovered" the workplace. For a wide variety of reasons, employee assistance, drug screening, and wellness programs have all become popular options. In organizations offering combinations of these activities, policy linkages need very much to be developed. Equally important, the fundamental logic and purpose of each type of program need to be understood so that confusion between the purpose and procedures for EAPs and those of drug-screening programs, for example, is minimized. Confusion about programs is likely to create barriers to employee assistance program utilization.

Dispersion of the workforce of a company across a wide geographic area also creates barriers to program assessibility. This is especially true when employees lack convenient geographic access to their employing organization. Telecommuting workers, employees in small satellite offices, people whose jobs require regular and frequent long-distance travel, and individuals employed in rural industries all illustrate the problem of workers cut off from employee assistance services as these services are conventionally organized and delivered. One of the challenges facing occupational social workers, therefore, is that of designing service delivery systems that reach out to these underserved populations. One option that may offer some relief has been demonstrated by the nationwide contract through which employees of the Xerox Corporation are provided with EAP services by Family Service Association of America (FSAA) organizations. In short, the widely dispersed employees of a national organization are served under contract by another widely dispersed national organization. Continued innovation in such program design is necessary.

Equally necessary is continued development of organizational models for forms of occupational social work other than employee assistance. As EAPs evolve into the fourth stage described by Ozawa (1980), the logic of their structure and organizational location begins to break down. Many practitioners question whether employee assistance and broad-scale organizational intervention activities can appropriately be carried out under the same program umbrella. To date, little theory development for customer assistance, corporate community involvement, and social work organizational development activities has occurred. An important dimension that needs to be considered is that of the preferred organizational and policy structures that are appropriate to each of these forms of social work in the workplace. One need only look at how well developed employee assistance models are to realize the primitive state of our practice and theory in these other areas.

These observations can be rephrased in a more optimistic light: The future is figuratively bright with challenges and opportunities. Social workers are problem solvers and change agents. That's how we make our living. That's how we enjoy so much of our professional lives. None of the problems and issues identified in this chapter appears insurmountable, although many do require the best we can offer in the forms of imagination and mastery of our own profession. It should be obvious that the workplace is simply too rich in opportunities for professional reward and service to people for it to be abandoned. A task that lies before social workers is that of exploiting to the fullest the possibilities we have in order to serve humankind in the natural lifespace of work.

REFERENCES

Maiden, R. P., & Hardcastle, D. A. (1986). Social work education: Professionalizing EAPs. *EAP Digest, 7*(1), 63–66.

Myers, D. W., & Myers, P. S. (1986). Back to school: An EAP guide. *EAP Digest, 6*(5), 48–53.

Naisbitt, J. (1984). *Megatrends: Ten new directions transforming our lives*. New York: Warner.

Nida, S. A., Foley, K. S., Maze, B. L., & Braucht, G. S. (1987). Preparing undergraduates for careers in employee assistance. *EAP Digest, 7*(2), 57–61.

Ozawa, M. (1980). Development of social services in industry: Why and how? *Social Work, 25*, 464–470.

Peters, T. J., & Waterman, R. H., Jr. (1982). *In search of excellence*. New York: Harper & Row.

More executives finding changes in traditional corporate ladder. (1986, November 14). *Wall Street Journal*, p. 29.

Index

Index